A History of the Modern Chinese Army

A HISTORY

OF THE

MODERN CHINESE ARMY

XIAOBING LI

THE UNIVERSITY PRESS OF KENTUCKY

Publication of this volume was made possible in part by a grant from the National Endowment for the Humanities.

Editorial and Sales Offices: The University Press of Kentucky
663 South Limestone Street, Lexington, Kentucky 40508-4008
www.kentuckypress.com

11 10 09 08 07   5 4 3 2 1

Maps by Dick Gilbreath and Terry Hounshell

Library of Congress Cataloging-in-Publication Data

Li, Xiaobing, 1954-
  A history of the modern Chinese Army / Xiaobing Li.
      p. cm.
  Includes bibliographical references and index.
  ISBN 978-0-8131-2438-4 (hc : alk. paper) 1. China. Zhongguo ren min jie fang jun–History. 2. China–Armed Forces–History. 3. China–History, Military. I. Title.
  UA837.L484 2007
  355.00951–dc22   2007008984

This book is printed on acid-free recycled paper meeting the requirements of the American National Standard for Permanence in Paper for Printed Library Materials.

Manufactured in the United States of America.

Member of the Association of
American University Presses

For my parents,
Li Weiying and Zhang Xiaoyi

Contents

Illustrations

Maps

Photographs

Abbreviations

CCP	Chinese Communist Party
CMAG	Chinese Military Advisory Group
CMC	Central Military Commission
COSTIND	Commission on Science, Technology, and Industry for National Defense
CPVF	Chinese People's Volunteer Forces
CYL	Communist Youth League
DRV	Democratic Republic of Vietnam (North Vietnam)
ECC	East China Command
FFC	Fujian Front Command
GLD	General Logistics Department
GMD	Guomindang (Chinese Nationalist Party)
GPD	General Political Department
GSD	General Staff Department
HMA	Huangpu Military Academy
HPCC	Heilongjiang Production and Construction Corps
ICP	Indochinese Communist Party
LVT	landing vehicle, tracked
NBDA	Northeast Border Defense Army
NDU	National Defense University
NEA	Northern Expeditionary Army (GMD)
NKPA	North Korean People's Army
NLF	National Liberation Front (Viet Cong)
NPC	National People's Congress
NRA	National Revolutionary Army (GMD)
PAVN	People's Army of Vietnam
PLA	People's Liberation Army
PLAAF	PLA Air Force
PLAF	People's Liberation Armed Forces (Viet Cong)
PLAN	PLA Navy

POW	prisoner of war
PRC	People's Republic of China
RMA	revolution of military affairs
ROC	Republic of China (Taiwan)
ROK	Republic of Korea (South Korea)
ROV	Republic of Vietnam (South Vietnam)
SMAG	Soviet Military Advisory Group
UNF	United Nations forces
ZC	Zhejiang Command
ZFC	Zhejiang Front Command

Note on Transliteration

The pinyin romanization system is applied to Chinese names of persons, places, and terms. This transliteration is also used for the titles of Chinese publications. Persons' names are written in the Chinese way, with the surname first, like Mao Zedong. For some popular names of people and places, well-known spellings appear in parentheses after the first use of the pinyin, such as Jiang Jieshi (Chiang Kai-shek) and Guangzhou (Canton). The order is reversed for a few figures and places whose names are widely known, such as Sun Yat-sen (Sun Zhongshan), Tibet (Xizang), Yangtze (Chang) River, and Peking (Beijing) University.

Acknowledgments

Many people and institutes have contributed to this book and deserve recognition. First, I would like to thank Provost William J. Radke, Vice Provost Patricia A. LaGrow, Dean of the College of Liberal Arts Pamela Washington, Interim Dean of the Jackson College of Graduate Studies and Research John M. Garic, Assistant Vice President for Academic Affairs Daniel P. Donaldson, and Chair of the Department of History and Geography Kenny L. Brown at the University of Central Oklahoma. They have been very supportive of the project over the past several years. The faculty merit-credit program sponsored by the Office of Academic Affairs, on-campus mini grant sponsored by the Jackson College of Graduate Studies and Research, and Liberal Arts College research grant at UCO provided funding for my research and student assistants.

I wish to thank my Chinese colleagues and collaborators at the Chinese Academy of Social Sciences, China Society for Strategy and Management Research, China Foundation for International and Strategic Studies, National Defense University, Peking University, and provisional academies of social sciences in Fujian, Guangdong, Guangxi, Heilongjiang, Hubei, Jiangsu, Jilin, Liaoning, and Zhejiang. They made the many arrangements necessary for interviewing People's Liberation Army officers and retired generals in 1996–2004. I am grateful to Chen Zhiya, Li Danhui, Niu Jun, Shen Zhihua, Wang Baocun, Wang Fan, Yang Shaojun, Zhang Baijia, Zhang Pengfei, and Zhang Tiejiang for their help and advice on my research in China. Thanks also to the staff of the Mainland Affairs Council and the China Reunification Alliance in Taipei, Taiwan. They provided financial assistance and arranged many interviews during my trips to Taiwan in 1994–2002.

Special thanks to Stanley J. Adamiak and Kenny L. Brown, who proofread and critically reviewed most of the chapters. Chen Jian, Zhang Shuguang, and David Finkelstein read the entire manuscript and provided valuable comments and suggestions. You Ji, David Kaiser, Lyman Miller, Allan R. Millett, Charles Neimeyer, Richard Peters, Anthony Saich, Donald Sutton, Bin Yu, and Xiaoming Zhang made important comments on earlier versions of some chapters as conference papers. John Osburn reproduced all of the photos for the book. Candace Carollo provided secretarial assistance. Several graduate students at UCO contributed to the book, sometimes by reading parts of the manuscript and sometimes by working on the maps or bibliography. They are Lynn Brown, Wan-chun Chen, Phil High, Jason Hunter, Julie Bennett-Jones, and Hosok and Yukie O.

I also wish to thank the two anonymous readers for the University Press of Kentucky, who offered many suggestions and criticisms. At the University Press of Kentucky, Stephen M. Wrinn, executive director, and his staff patiently guided the production of the book. Any remaining errors of fact, language usage, and interpretation are my own.

During the research period over the past decade, my parents encouraged my interests in Chinese military affairs and helped me collect source materials in China. I dedicate this book to them. My wife, Tran, and our two children, Kevin and Christina, got used to my working weekends and holidays and shared with me the burden of overseas traveling. Their understanding and love have made this book possible.

Introduction

A SULTRY JULY IN BEIJING, the capital of China, did not slow down the summer programs at Tsinghua University (Qinghua University, China's MIT). The one-week symposium on arms control packed the facility with students, faculty members, and military experts.[1] Sun Lizhou, a graduate student from the College of International Relations, Peking University (Beijing University, China's Harvard), was one of the participants.[2] Sun was in his mid-twenties, tall, skinny, and wearing eyeglasses. His broad knowledge and sharp opinion impressed on me a sense that, upon graduation, he would make a fine social scientist. I was surprised to learn through other students that he later voluntarily joined the People's Liberation Army (PLA), China's armed forces, which include the army, navy, air force, and strategic missile force. I found it difficult to imagine Sun in uniform, carrying a gun. I have come to realize, however, that he is part of a new pattern.

The men and women in the PLA today differ from those who served in the Chinese Communist military of the past. Throughout the last half of the twentieth century, the armed forces of the Chinese Communist Party (CCP) consisted of rural conscripts and volunteers who generally had attained little education. Two of my uncles, for example, left their village and joined the PLA in the late 1940s. They were praised as "little intellectuals" (*xiao zhishi fenzi*) in their companies because they had finished their six-year elementary education.

1

Their fellow soldiers perceived a certain literary flair emanating from them. One of the uncles taught the other men how to read and write while stationed in Tibet during the Sino-Indian War of 1962. When I served in the armed forces for three years in the early 1970s, the completion of middle school (nine years) landed me a position in the Engineering Company of the Eleventh Regiment. With this above-average education, I became a machine operator at the Chinese-Russian border during the Sino-Soviet conflicts. By 1983, when I left for graduate study in America, only 4 percent of the 224 top Chinese generals had some college credit hours.[3] The PLA was a peasant army utterly lacking in education. Then, in the 1990s, tremendous changes began to take place in the Chinese military.

In 1995, the high command launched reforms to transform the PLA from a labor-intensive (*renli miji*) to a technology-intensive (*jishu miji*) army.[4] The current goal is to reshape the PLA with technology to win the next war under high-tech conditions. To meet the new demands, the Chinese government revised the Military Service Law in 1998, increasing the urban quota for conscription and emphasizing higher education. Previously, the PLA trained active officers strictly at military academies. A move to recruit and train future officers in colleges and universities followed shortly after the passage of the new law. In 2001, the PLA Air Force (PLAAF) began recruiting recent college graduates from fifty campuses, including Tsinghua and Peking universities, for pilot training.[5] In 2002, the PLA Reserve Officer Training and Selection program was established at more than two hundred colleges and universities across the country. The program began to enroll and recruit national defense students (*guofangsheng*). In 2003, the Reserve Officer Training and Selection office at Tsinghua University released a statement that noted that 329 national defense students enrolled in the program in the fall of that year, majoring in atomic physics, computer science, and electrical engineering.[6] The students would become commissioned officers upon graduation. Jiang Zemin, then chairman of the CCP Central Military Commission (CMC), said, "We should energetically push forward a Revolution of Military Affairs [RMA] with Chinese characteristics, so as to ensure that our armed forces keep up with the current rapid development of science, technology, and RMA."[7]

What are these Chinese characteristics, and how will they affect the country's military modernization? Who has shaped and changed these characteristics throughout the twentieth century? Why do Chinese youth want to join the Communist armed forces? Students of modern China and military history raise these questions when they face China's military buildup at the turn of the century. This book seeks to elucidate the origins of and changes to the Chinese military by examining the PLA's experiences from 1949 to 2002. Although it is a military history survey, it includes diachronic discussions to explore the reasons for change, constraints on the implementation of reforms, and the outcomes of those efforts. Through its detailed narrative, this book captures the essence of successive generations of Chinese servicemen and servicewomen while illuminating the themes and patterns of their development. The answers are pivotal in understanding the PLA and China today and in interpreting Chinese strategic concerns and other security issues in east Asia.

Changing Characteristics

The ongoing changes in the Chinese military and the inevitable implications for Asia-Pacific security have attracted great academic attention in the West, especially in the United States. Research on Chinese military history and modernization began to take off in the 1990s.[8] Recent insightful assessments by Ellis Joffe, David Shambaugh, and several other experts on the Chinese military offer objective surveys and comprehensive interpretations by analyzing PLA strategy, doctrine, command and control, structure of forces, and security concerns.[9] Other noted experts in the field, such as David Finkelstein, David Graff, Robin Higham, and Hans van de Ven, have edited essay collections or conference proceedings that address issues in PLA technology, budget and finance, defense industries, and operational histories.[10] The combined efforts of these scholars have laid solid groundwork for a better understanding of the Chinese military.

Much current research in the West engages in the academic debate on the "China threat," dominating attention and dividing scholars.[11] U.S. military historians are attempting to determine whether, and to what extent, China threatens America and security in the Pacific region in the twenty-first century.[12] The argument that China is a threat is based on the assumption that China's dramatic economic development will inevitably result in the "strengthening of its military power and its desire for expansion."[13] Proponents of this interpretation argue that no country that rose to power in modern world history did so in a peaceful manner, citing examples such as Great Britain in the eighteenth century, Germany toward the end of the nineteenth century, Japan during the first half of the twentieth century, and the Soviet Union after World War II. Conversely, they assert, any country that insists on the maintenance of peace will find it hard, if not impossible, to become a real power. Furthermore, they argue, the lack of political democratization in China and the distinct possibility of a war between the mainland and Taiwan make the future of China unpredictable and, therefore, extremely menacing. Others offer an entirely opposite view. Nevertheless, both sides of the argument pay attention to the links between military modernization and political democratization. Like the China threat debate, discussions about topics such as an impending collapse, Chinese exceptionalism, peaceful rising, China's replacing Russia, and China's replacing Japan center the issue of China's military modernization.

The research of some Western military historians is subject to major restraints, as they have very limited access to seemingly impregnable Communist sources. Their conclusions thus have to be drawn from publications in the West. Some Western researchers further have to depend on materials written in Western languages because of linguistic and cultural barriers. Some researchers still follow a cold war approach, using an ideological definition of the PLA as a party army or the party's tool, merely a political institution. Others employ an American-centered methodology, overemphasizing diplomatic efforts and international relations and viewing the PLA as an insignificant, passive spectator or lesser adjunct in world politics. A broader interpretation is needed to render an objective study of the Chinese military.

In China, scholars and historians are conducting their research on the Chinese military using a social historical approach.[14] Paying more attention to the links between the military and society, recent research by military historians in China focuses on the soldier's efforts to define his place within a socialist society. Moral issues, family values, individual concerns, a bureaucratic system, and educational factors are emphasized, for example, in recent academic discussions on the Korean War at the fiftieth anniversary of its armistice.[15] In these works, military culture is counterposed to an official culture that promotes bureaucrat-

China

ic control and civil-military integration. For political reasons, however, Chinese historians still have a long way to go before they can publish objective accounts of the history of the Chinese military in their home country.

This study looks into the relatively neglected inner life cycle of the Chinese armed forces, which has defined the PLA's characteristics and changed it in many different ways. The untold stories of the rank and file provide unique insights into those who have shaped the military and made unprecedented changes over the past fifty-three years. It puts individual soldiers and officers in the context of Chinese society, culture, and tradition and views them through their combat experiences, training and education, family lives, and social environments. As a relatively young army in Asia, the PLA acts according to its own consistent inner logic in its military affairs. An insider's view offers a better understanding of Chinese strategic issues and operational behaviors and identifies some general patterns among the generations that faced varied social conditions and made different choices according to their time. Some Western historians have overlooked the complex nature of the tremendous changes in PLA recruitment and personnel from one generation to the next. These patterns are studied in this work to illuminate previous PLA wars and predict the future of the PLA.

A Soldier's Story

Sun Lizhou told me he joined the army because he dreamed of being a career diplomat. Originating from Xinjiang Uygur, a remote northwestern autonomous region, Sun had neither experience in foreign service nor the necessary connections in Beijing. After receiving a bachelor's degree, he found there were no jobs available in the Ministry of Foreign Affairs. However, his search indicated that a master's degree from Peking University would qualify him for a position in the foreign affairs division of the PLA. After a two-year tour of duty as a foreign affairs officer, hopefully with overseas experience, he might be able to open the door to his desired diplomatic career in the government.[16]

Although it was still difficult for me to imagine Sun in the military, the service seemed necessary for his professional development. His plan, sound and reasonable, mirrors the plans of some of my American graduate students at the university where I have taught for the past fourteen years. "Educated youth can make a career out of military service": a fortune cookie for Sun! He appeared rational in thought and behavior for someone in a modern society in which individual self-interests are a reliable guide to behavior.[17] The public interest can best be served by individual self-improvement coupled with individual achievement within the workplace. A new personality with individualistic characteristics seems to permeate the Chinese military in the new century as a result of recent reforms.

By telling soldiers' stories, this work moves away from the conventional approach, in which Chinese soldiers are either in favor of the party policy or lost in the "human waves," invisible in the statistics.

It applies a social historical methodology to the Chinese military and intends to begin a different discussion while still reflecting established schools of Chinese military historiography. Included as well are the interfaces of political and military imperatives, the military as a professional caste system, and the transformation of civilians into soldiers. The primary objective is to move Chinese military studies toward the wider currents of social history while maintaining equitable scholarship.

Social factors such as demographic changes, marriage trends, wealth distribution, education, and retirement are as important as technological changes in the Chinese military. As a historical survey, this work interprets the major features of the principal existing social characteristics of the PLA as it was confronted by the superpowers in the Cold War and as it failed or succeeded in adapting to the modern military system in the twentieth century. As the central theme in the work, military modernization is examined as part of the social transition of China from a traditional society to a modern one. Such a transition requires a metamorphosis in the people and their day-to-day affairs. A structural overhaul can convert a weak, traditionally minded, agrarian society into a relatively new, active, and efficient society. The late-twentieth-century advancements, for example, that brought China to the brink of industrialization and urbanization created a new personality. The years between 1949 and 2002 saw a transition from a traditional China to an industrialized China. The period analyzed here is very important in terms of Chinese military reforms and modernization. These changes revolutionized the PLA and remade the soldier's life.

Many scholarly discussions of the PLA, both in China and in the West, present as revolutionary the transition from traditional imperial armies to the enlightened, technologically advanced Western armies that challenged the authority of Chinese political and social institutions. This book examines whether the old binary constructs of tradition versus modernity and China versus the West are adequate categories for historical and social analysis. Moreover, it questions whether historians have cast their nets broadly enough when attempting to comprehend changes the Chinese military underwent throughout the twentieth century.

Our question, then, is not the relationship of tradition to modernity, nor that of China to the West. Rather, it is how interactive the parameters of military changes were in foreign wars against Western powers, how flexible Chinese values were in the context of military modernization, and how expansive the Chinese military cultural repertoire was at certain historical moments that were crucial to building a "rich country and strong military."[18] The way the Chinese military both made remarkable changes and carried on longstanding traditions can be considered characteristic. The unique approach of employing past issues to overcome new challenges continues to serve the PLA into the twenty-first century.

A Note on Sources

Few areas in Chinese history pose more difficulties than military history because of the lack of readily available sources for Western researchers. The conclusions in this volume are supported by primary and secondary Chinese sources made available in recent years. Since the late 1980s, significant progress has been made in the study of Chinese military history. The flowering of the reform-and-opening era in China resulted in a more flexible political and academic environment than had been the case during the reign of Mao Zedong (Mao Tsetung; 1893–1976), leading to a relaxation of the extremely rigid criteria for releasing party and military documents. Consequently, some fresh and meaningful historical materials, including papers of former leaders, party and government documents, and local archives, are now available to historians. Certainly, the Chinese government still has a long way to go before free academic inquiry becomes reality, but the value of the opening of documentary materials for the study of military history cannot be underestimated.

The first collection of sources used in this book is official Chinese records, including party documents, government archives, and military materials. The documents of the high command and the CMC in the PLA Archives (Jiefangjun dang'anguan) under the General Staff Department (GSD) are still closed to scholars. It is important to note, however, that during most of the PLA's history, strategic and even tactical decisions were micromanaged by the CCP Central Committee. The primary sources include selected and reprinted party documents of the Central Committee, the CMC, and regional bureaus.[19] Among the valuable collections are the eighteen-volume *Zhonggong zhongyang wenjian xuanji, 1921–49* (Selected Documents of the CCP Central

Committee, 1921–49) and the twenty-volume *Jianguo yilai zhongyao wenxian xuanbian* (Selected Important Documents since the Founding of the State, 1949–66). Some People's Republic of China (PRC) governmental documents have also been released in recent years. In 2004 and 2006, the Ministry of Foreign Affairs declassified tens of thousands of diplomatic files from the early years. A large number of documents show China's involvement in wars in Korea, Vietnam, and India.[20] Some state documents can be seen at various provincial and regional archives, especially those from the period between 1949 and 1966. While in Harbin, Heilongjiang, and Shenyang, Liaoning, between 1996 and 2004, I had the chance to visit provincial archives and read some of the files with the help of the Center for Provincial Archives and Information in Harbin and the Provincial Academy of Social Sciences in Shenyang.

The second group of sources is the writings, papers, memoirs, and interviews of Chinese Communist as well as Nationalist leaders. With Mao as the undisputed leader in both theory and strategy throughout most of the PLA's history, the military leaders worked together and made most of the important decisions within the CMC. Their papers, fundamental for the study of the PLA, include military works, manuscripts, instructions, plans, and telegrams by Mao, Zhou Enlai (Chou En-lai; 1898–1976), Zhu De (Chu Teh; 1886–1976), Peng Dehuai (P'eng Te-huai; 1898–1974), Deng Xiaoping (Teng Hsiao-p'ing; 1904–97), Lin Biao (Lin Piao; 1908–71), and other top military leaders.[21] Among the most important sources are the thirteen-volume *Jianguo yilai Mao Zedong wengao, 1949–76* (Mao Zedong's Manuscripts since the Founding of the State, 1949–76), the four-volume *Jianguo yilai Liu Shaoqi wengao, 1949–52* (Liu Shaoqi's Manuscripts since the Founding of the State, 1949–52), and the three-volume *Selected Works of Deng Xiaoping.*[22]

In 1994, 1996, and 2002, I visited the Guomindang (GMD, or Kuo-min-tang, KMT; the Chinese Nationalist Party) Central Archives during my research trips to Taipei, Taiwan. I had the opportunity to interview the former secretary-general of the Republic of China's (ROC) Council of National Security, General Jiang Weiguo (Chiang Wei-kuo, 1916–97), who was both the son of Jiang Jieshi (Chiang Kai-shek, 1887–1975), president of the ROC 1927–75, and the adoptive brother of Jiang Jingguo (Chiang Ching-kuo, 1910–88), president of the ROC 1978–88. Among the other GMD military leaders I also interviewed in

Taiwan was Chief General Hao Bocun (Hau Pei-tsun, chief of the GMD General Staff 1981–89, ROC defense minister 1989–90, and prime minister 1990–93). Their personal accounts of the wars with the Communist forces are valuable in examining the PLA from the other side.

The third group used in my exploration of the topic is interviews, memoirs, and writings of Chinese generals and field commanders. From 1994 to 1996, my research focused on Chinese officers during the 1950s. I collected their memoirs and interviewed retired PLA generals in Beijing, Shanghai, Guangzhou, Wuhan, and Hangzhou.[23] The extensive details of their experiences made a remarkable contribution to this study by adding a new perspective on the subject. No matter how politically indoctrinated they might have become, the generals were culturally bound to cherish their memories of the past. More important, they had only recently begun to feel comfortable talking about their experiences and allowing their recollections to be recorded, written about, and even published.[24] The 1990s brought a considerable number of military and war memoirs to Chinese readers. Some are in the form of books, some appear as journal and magazine articles, and others are printed as reference studies for restricted circulation only.

Since 1996, my research trips have focused on a fourth category of sources: recollections and interviews of PLA soldiers and low- and mid-level officers in the Shenyang Regional Command, National Defense University (NDU), PLA Logistics Academy, and Chinese People's Armed Police Force Academy. They are an important source of information and opinion for concerned scholars and students of Chinese military history. The officers and soldiers offered special, personal insights into specific aspects of their experience, including chain of command, combat planning, operations, logistics, political control, field communication, and being a prisoner of war. More than two hundred interviews, from Heilongjiang in the north to Hainan in the south—more than fifteen provinces—offer direct testimony by the Chinese soldiers themselves.[25] Oral history is a vital source for historians who study Chinese military history, including the major events of the PLA. It has become more readily used not just to fill in factual gaps but also to serve as the main source for discovering both the theme and framework of this topic.

The last group of my research comprises secondary sources, both in Chinese and in English. The Chinese literature includes military publications, textbooks, and educational materials about the PLA's history. These sources add a viable perspective by reinterpreting a series of fundamental issues crucial to understanding the Chinese military. They cover many issues related to the Chinese military and therefore provide a useful research bibliography for students who are interested in the Chinese military and the history of modern China but who do not read Chinese.

This book covers the development of the principal existing military culture and the warfare experiences of the PLA over the past fifty-three years. It situates individual soldiers and officers in the context of the Communist revolution, Chinese tradition, and technological advancements while considering their motives, thoughts, and behavior with respect to their family background, education, recruitment, and training through combat. It does not intend, however, to provide a comprehensive history of the Chinese military in the twentieth century.

This work divides Chinese military development into the following phases. Chapter 1 provides a historical background of the Chinese military from the Qin (Ch'in) Dynasty in the second century B.C. to the early twentieth century, including the Qing (Ch'ing) Dynasty's new army, the 1911 Revolution, the Nationalist Northern Expedition, the founding of the CCP in 1921, and the first CCP-GMD coalition in the early 1920s. Chapter 2 covers the formative years of the CCP's military, from 1927 to 1949, by tracing the origins of the Red Army, its military revolution (1927–37), its WWII experience (1937–45), and the Chinese civil war (1946–49). Chapter 3 views the Korean War (1950–53) as jump-starting the modernization of the PLA, or the Chinese People's Volunteer Forces (CPVF), in Korea against UN and U.S. forces. Chapter 4 examines both the PLA reforms that occurred during the 1950s with aid from the Soviet Union and the first Taiwan Strait crisis (1954–55). Chapter 5 discusses China's strategic nuclear weapons research and development from 1955 to 1964 with an emphasis on bureaucratic control, intellectual roles, and the overseas students and experts who returned to China and built the bomb. Chapter 6 deals with the most controversial decade in PLA history, from 1964 to 1973, including the second Taiwan Strait crisis (1958), the Sino-Indian War (1962), and the major shakeup of the high command in Beijing. Chapter 7 covers China's involvement in Vietnam, including PLA operations in the French Indochina War from 1949 to 1954 and in the Vietnam War from 1965 to 1970. It also explains what happened to the PLA during the Great Proletarian Cultural Revolution of 1966–76 and the Sino-Soviet border conflicts in 1969–71. Chapter 8 is devoted to changes within the PLA during the reform-and-opening movement in the late 1970s and 1980s, beginning with the Four Modernizations of Deng Xiaoping (the second generation of Chinese military leadership) and ending with the Tiananmen Square events of 1989. Chapter 9 examines military reforms in the 1990s under the command of Jiang Zemin (the third generation), who launched missiles across the Taiwan Strait in 1997 and served as CMC chairman until 2004. It also discusses the recent transition from Jiang to Hu Jintao (the fourth generation). The conclusion provides an analytic wrap-up of the PLA experience and looks into some of the difficult problems of modernizing the military as well as other sectors of Chinese society.

A strong, effective military is imperative for a modern, democratic society. As the new leader at home, Hu Jintao applies his visions of "harmony and innovation" within the military and has tried to include the military in his "humanistic society."[26] Political support and the PLA's active participation in his new programs will certainly consolidate Hu's power and secure his presidency until 2012. Internationally, he has tried to convince the world in general and the United States in particular that China is not a threat but is rising peacefully. After his meeting with President George W. Bush at the White House in 2006, Hu reported that Washington had accepted him as a responsible stakeholder in the international community, where China is still trying to reposition itself as a fast-growing country and to adjust its relations with the world.

★ 1 ★

Peasants and Revolutions

CHINA IS ONE OF THE earliest civilizations in the world, with a recorded military history of five thousand years.[1] Because of China's unique geographic setting and demographic characteristics, its military tradition has emphasized mass mobilization of peasants, or farmer-soldiers, since the ancient age.[2] From the first unification of China in 221 B.C. to 1949, when the PRC was founded, roughly 85 percent of the Chinese population were farmers.[3] By 1969, farmers still composed 84.2 percent of China's workforce.[4] This chapter begins with an overview of the historical nature of peasants and examines why peasants served in the emperor's army and how they were organized into an effective force to protect ancient and imperial institutions.

The chapter traces the roots of peasant rebellions and radical revolutions in modern Chinese history as historical precursors of the Chinese Communist forces by elucidating the late Ming's uprisings (1641–44), the Taiping Rebellion (1850–64), and the Xinhai Revolution (1911). The 1911 republican revolution raises the question of why the revolution failed to gain the peasants' support in the struggle to end what would be the last dynasty of the two-thousand-year-old imperial system. The stories of Sun Yat-sen (Sun Zhongshan, 1866–1925) and Jiang Jieshi, who founded the GMD and the National Revolutionary

Army (NRA), show that the republican leaders depended on landowners and empowered them in the revolution, rather than the peasants, who would become the victims of the increasing warfare during the Warlord Period (1916–27) after the revolution.

This chapter follows the development of the Communist movement in China during the 1920s, including the establishment of the CCP in 1921 and the emergence of the most important Communist military leaders, such as Mao and Zhou—individuals who thought eclectically about social and military issues. As the first generation of Communist leaders, they had political and social concerns that were unprecedented among Chinese military leaders, inspired not only by a heightened awareness of ideas transmitted to China via Russia, France, and Japan but also by robust traditions dating back many centuries. Moreover, these leaders' visions and insights grew out of their active participation in the political and economic campaigns of the period, often as organizers and thinkers. The Chinese Communist military began during the CCP-GMD political coalition against the warlords in 1924–27, and eventually, in 1949, the Communist forces took over the country.

The Peasant and the Emperor's Army

Before 1949, the Chinese peasant lived in the village where his family had lived for generations and cultivated the soil, growing rice, wheat, or other grains. As a male farmer, he enjoyed his small-scale farming, marriage, family life, and village society. He was different from the medieval European serf and the Japanese farmer (*kenin*, "house man"). As John K. Fairbank and Merle Goldman point out, the Chinese peasant, "both in law and in fact, [was] free, if he had the means," to leave his village or to purchase more land.[5] He established a self-sustaining farm by owning a small piece of land. Jonathan D. Spence finds it difficult to distinguish the peasant from the landowner in China. "There were millions of peasant proprietors who owned a little more land than they needed for subsistence, and they might farm their own land with the help of some seasonal laborers. Others, owning a little less land than they needed for subsistence, might rent an extra fraction of an acre or hire themselves out as casual labor in the busy seasons."[6] Others further argue that rural China maintained the "ideal and legal structure of an open class pattern of social mobility" from imperialism to the

Republican Period, even though "mobility was highly constrained."[7] The dream of the Chinese peasant was to own more land and thereby to better provide for his family. His nightmare was losing his land and failing in his family responsibilities.

Traditionally, the Chinese emperor and his imperial system promised the peasant opportunities and protection. Therefore, the peasant sustained traditional ideas, ethical codes, and a mutual obligation between the emperor and himself to serve the empire. For more than two thousand years, the Chinese peasant was subordinate to the will of the emperor and tried to meet his duties. Even the Disney movie *Mulan* accurately depicts this obligation: the father, as the head of a peasant household, feels guilty and embarrassed about his daughter's participation in warfare not because of her gender but because of his inability to take his own place among the ranks to defend his country and protect his family.[8] Confucianism, an official ideology of classical China, justified an authoritarian family pattern as the basis for social order in political as well as domestic life.[9] The role of the emperor and his officials was merely that of the father writ large. A district magistrate who represented the emperor was called the father and mother of the people (*fumuguan*, "parent-official"). The philosophy of Confucius (551–479 B.C.) became classical because it provided ideas on how to overcome the disorders that all Chinese rulers had to face during the Spring and Autumn Period (770–476 B.C.) and the Warring States Period (475–221 B.C.), many years of ferocious warfare aimed at expansion and annexation among the seven states.

Continuing social disorder and endless warfare required solutions during these two periods. Many schools of philosophy and strategy flourished, creating a situation in which "a hundred schools contended." The best and most influential military work was *Bingfa* (The Art of War), a short book by Sun Zi (Sun Tzu).[10] His strategies dominate the thirteen chapters, and his goal, winning the battle, underlies the whole book. *The Art of War* is the first important work on strategy and theory in world military history. Michael Neiberg emphasizes that its "principles are still studied today the world over. Sun Tzu outlined many military doctrines that remain familiar to any soldier including surprise, mobility, flexibility, and deception. *The Art of War*, later revived by Mao in China, formed the basis of many guerrilla doctrines in the twentieth century."[11]

During the Warring States Period, the king of Qin embarked upon a dramatic conquest of the separate kingdoms. Having drafted a massive infantry army, he had an efficient military machine under strong commanders. Instead of using chariots, his army possessed cavalry, superior iron weapons, and crossbows, all relatively new developments.[12] His attacks on the other kingdoms, especially siege battles, were forceful and merciless. In 221 B.C., his effort was crowned with success when China was unified under Qin (Ch'in, from which China gets its Western name). The unification of China was followed by the establishment of a highly centralized regime, the Qin Dynasty (221–206 B.C.), the first of its kind in Chinese history. Ancient China was over, and imperial China had begun. Having concentrated all power in his own hands, Qin Shi Huang (who took the name Shi Huangdi, or first emperor; reigned 221–210 B.C.) proceeded to establish a huge bureaucracy. This monarchical, or imperial, system lasted for more than two thousand years without significant changes.

The emperor wanted to have a huge army to create a center of political gravity at his capital. A large number of peasants were drafted through a centralized taxation system. The entire imperial system was supported by two main social groups, taxpaying peasants and rich landowners. Qin terminated the city-state system and completed a transfer of landownership from dynastic families, relatives, and lords to private owners. The peasant paid onerous corvée and taxation. Regular taxes alone constituted two-thirds of his harvest. He was also required to spend a month every year fulfilling military duties and completing work on local roads, canals, palaces, and imperial tombs. If he failed to pay taxes, he had to extend his service in the army. The total number of peasants Qin Shi Huang recruited to build the Efang Palace and the precursor to the Great Wall and to serve as soldiers for the defense of the frontier exceeded two million.[13]

The Great Wall served two purposes for the empire. It was built for defense against the northern "barbarians," including the nomadic Xiongnu, Turks, Khitan, Mongols, Xianbei, Nüzhen, and Manchus. Internally, it walled in the Chinese society and created a political centripetal force toward the emperor. The construction of the Great Wall began in the western desert and ended at the eastern coast, stretching for two thousand miles. Qin Shi Huang had no difficulty in mobilizing manpower: China's population reached fifty-four million by the end of

Qin (at which time the population of the Roman Empire was no more than forty-six million).[14]

In Qin's draft system, all male peasants were required to register at the age of twenty-one. Many of them served for two years between the ages of twenty-three and fifty-six. The imperial bureaucracy carried out recruitment at different levels.[15] Reporting late for military duty was a capital offense. Through Qin Shi Huang's sponsoring of legalism, he influenced the whole future Chinese conception of law as a hierarchy in its function of establishing a general scale of worthiness and unworthiness, merit and demerit.

After Qin, the Han Dynasty (206 B.C.–A.D. 220) continued the conscription system through its provincial (*jun*) and county (*xian*) recruiting offices. Having witnessed the power of peasants during the period of peasant war and learned a lesson from the quick collapse of the Qin regime, the rulers of Han paid particular attention to the promotion of agriculture.[16] They carried out a policy of "less corvée and light taxation" to "enable the nation to recuperate and build up its strength."[17] Needless to say, a policy of this kind was most beneficial to economic and military development. The Han emperors began to conquer the territory outside the Great Wall. In 111 B.C., Wudi (the martial emperor; reigned 140–87 B.C.) destroyed and annexed the semi-sinicized state of Nan Yue and started a thousand years of Chinese rule over what is now northern Vietnam. He conquered Korea in 108 B.C., and a Chinese command remained at P'yŏngyang until 313 A.D.[18] Chinese soldiers began to wear lamellar armor, with overlapping leather or metal plates sewn onto a cloth. Light and flexible, the armor provided better protection during the frequent offensive campaigns.

The emperor needed a large expeditionary army for China's new central position in Asia. Successful military expeditions and territorial expansion had convinced the Han emperors and the people that their civilization was superior. The Han Dynasty became the first glorious dynasty in Chinese history, and the Chinese people began to call themselves the Han people (Hanzu; Han nationals, 90 percent of the current population). The Han emperors believed that China (Zhongguo) was the "central kingdom," "superior to any other people and nation 'under the heaven' and that it thus occupies a 'central' position in the known universe."[19] This perception, combined with a moral cosmology, elevated the Chinese emperor to the position of the son of heaven, who possessed supreme power and followed heavenly missions — the mandate of heaven. It justified Wudi's military invasions that incorporated the "barbarian" people into the Chinese civilization through a continuous process of acculturation. Han emperors' success forced many later rulers to compare their reigns with the glorious age of antiquity in terms of territory and geopolitics.

To secure China's central position in Asia, Han emperors maintained a large army of more than one million men. The conscription system, however, did not meet the extraordinary demands of frequent wars, even though the emperors had extended the age range of service to between twenty and sixty-five. The later Han emperors began to include criminals and paid recruits in the army. These measures failed to stop the decline of the dynasty. Its efforts to create an Asian powerhouse drained its resources and provided no significant economic return.

Chinese historians describe their past as a series of "dynastic cycles" because successive dynasties repeated this story.[20] After the collapse of the Han Dynasty, China had two long periods of division and civil wars (the Three Kingdoms Period, 220–80, and the Northern and Southern Dynasties, 317–582). During the Sui Dynasty (581–618), although the emperors reunified the country, they squandered an enormous amount of manpower and financial resources in building palaces for their own comfort and vanity. They attempted to reconquer Korea three times, and several million peasants were drafted as soldiers and laborers for the military expeditions. As a result, the peasants were exhausted and the Sui treasury was nearly empty. The burdens on the peasants had become unbearable. They began new uprisings, which dealt severe blows to the Sui regime. While the flame of peasant uprisings was burning across the country, local landlords were allowed to recruit troops of their own and occupy various parts of China. They safeguarded and then extended their power and influence. In 617, the aristocrat Li Yuan and his son Li Shimin started a revolt and quickly occupied Chang'an, the Sui capital. The following year, the Sui emperor was assassinated by one of his bodyguards, and his death marked the end of the Sui Dynasty. Li assumed the imperial title at Chang'an and called his new regime the Tang Dynasty (618–907), which became one of the most glorious dynasties and made China central to Asian affairs once again.

Tang emperors needed a self-sustaining army to prevent military spending from bankrupting the dynasty. To secure manpower and economic resources for military needs, Tang rulers carried on the *fubing* system, a peasant-soldier reserve system established by the Northern Wei Dynasty (386–535; established in north China by Turks), as the main source for new recruitments. There were 634 *junfu* (command headquarters) across the country. Each selected soldiers from among the local peasants who had received land through the land equalization system (*juntianzhi*). In 624, to increase the source of tax revenue, the Tang ruler adopted this land system and a tripartite tax system. Under the new system, a peasant above the age of eighteen received a small piece of land, of which one-fifth could be sold or left to his children. The other four-fifths must be returned to the government upon his retirement or death. The new land policy slowed the concentration of land in the hands of big landlords and redistributed it among the peasants.[21] The men in the fubing system were peasants in peacetime and reported to the local headquarters to serve in wartime. Locally, the two-tier system of provinces and counties prevailed except in border and strategic areas, which were administered by garrison commands. The chief executive of each command was responsible for military as well as civil affairs as a military governor-general.[22] The local power of military governors-general increased throughout the Tang Dynasty.

To stop the decentralization, after Tang, the Song Dynasty (960–1279) divided the fubing into the central or urban army (*panbing*) and the local or village militia (*xiangbing*).[23] The first Song emperor, Zhao Kuangyin (Chao K'uang-yin; reigned 960–76), former commander of the imperial guards, took several measures to prevent the reemergence of separatist local regimes so as to concentrate all power in the central government. The central government took over the authority hitherto belonging to the military governors-general, and only civil officials could be appointed heads of military and administrative affairs at the local level. This civil-military relationship became another part of the Chinese military tradition. Robin Higham and David A. Graff point out that, during the Song Dynasty, "civil bureaucrats and military officers were often rivals for influence at court, and the civil officials attempted to assert their dominance over the military sphere in various ways and generally had the upper hand. Civil officials with no practical military training or experience of command at the lower levels were sometimes sent out to direct military campaigns."[24] Neiberg considers the domination of the civilian bureaucracy in military affairs as one of the reasons that the Song Army had one of the worst military records of any Chinese dynasty.[25] In 1279, the Mongols destroyed the Chinese army and ended the Song Dynasty.

Peasant Rebellions

In imperial China, Chinese military culture emphasized the man as a social and political being, highlighting his duty within an agrarian society, according to Confucianism, Buddhism, and Daoism.[26] This was in sharp contrast to the emphasis that Indian and Mediterranean civilizations placed on the holy war and the man as God's soldier. The peasant soldier's experience and military culture, which developed from the ancient and medieval ages, stands out among the factors that differentiate the military traditions of the West and south Asia.[27]

The Mongols, who had the most powerful medieval military system, based their forces on cavalry that had speed and mobility that made them formidable.[28] Their men had been well trained since childhood in the mounted archer mode of fighting that had been dominant in central and western Asia for decades. Coming from the steppes, these skilled horsemen and hunters possessed tremendous stamina and speed. The Mongol rulers founded the Yuan Dynasty (1271–1368) in China and controlled Xinjiang (Sinkiang) in the northwest and Tibet (Xizang) in the southwest for the first time in Chinese history.

The Yuan emperor had an aggressive and victorious army. During the Yuan Dynasty, the Mongol rulers forcibly took over large amounts of land from Chinese peasants and distributed it among garrison troops and temples. In addition, taxes, in terms of produce as well as labor, were extremely heavy. The Mongol rulers also appropriated peasants' horses for military purposes. Many Chinese peasants in the north, after losing their land, became serfs to Mongols.[29] The Yuan rulers divided all the people into four classes. The highest class belonged to the Mongols, followed in order by the Semu people (including the Xia people and the Uygurs in the northwest and those who had migrated to China from central Asia), the Han people, and the southerners. The purpose of this division was to prevent people of different nationalities from forming a united front against the Mongols. Still, the cruel oppression precipitated resistance on the part of all peoples. In 1351, the Red Turban Army rose in Yingzhou, Anhui, and peasants in many other places favorably responded. One of the peasant forces captured Dadu (Beijing), the capital city of the Yuan, overthrew the Mongol regime, and established the Ming Dynasty in 1368.[30]

On many occasions throughout Chinese history, peasants became desperate and rose up against their rulers. In China, family has traditionally been an important determinant for peasants not only in marital but also in political, economic, and social affairs. Peasants rebelled when their duties and taxes became unbearable and their families faced an intolerable plight. Chinese anthropologist Fei Xiaotong (Fei Hsiao Tung) explains that "the traditional ideology in China suppresses individualism in favor of familism. The meaning, or value, of the individual's existence is defined by its being a link in the chain of social continuity which is concretely conceived in terms of descent."[31] In traditional Chinese society, the affluent extended family stressed the Confucian ethics of filial piety and the father-son relationship.[32] The dependence of each family member on this bounded group maintained a joint and corporate system that managed its own developmental cycle. Under this Confucian system, ancestor worship, economic cooperation, and property protection, all of which assured the welfare of a peasant family, could be performed only by the male members.[33] When the males, especially the senior males, in the family failed to perform their duties, they often sought changes in the society by attacking the system.

The impoverishment of the family led to a collapse of the kinship and then the village system. The kinship in China was patrilineal, the family headship passing in the male line from father to eldest son. Thus the men stayed in the family while the women married into other family households, in neither case following the life pattern that Western individuals take as a matter of course. The kinship and village systems are best understood in relationship to other social institutions: the organization of production, land tenure, religion, social stratification, political organization—in other words, the total production and reproduction of society.[34] Bureaucratic officials without much knowledge about farming usually did not intervene in affairs below the county level.[35] When the village system collapsed, the peasant became desperate, since he alone was now responsible for his family's survival. Rural crisis led to peasant rebellion, which positioned the peasant at center stage for social change and political reform.

In Chinese history, large-scale peasant rebellions frequently led to the total collapse of a dynasty, as happened to the Ming Dynasty (1368–1644). Toward the end of the dynasty, government corruption increased as court officials competed with one another for more power and privileges.[36] The emperors maintained two million central, provincial border troops, as well as village militias.[37] As the government became more bureaucratic and chaotic, land grabbing and wealth concentration became more intensive. Chinese historian Dai Yi explains that the poor peasant families who faced this kind of exploitation and oppression were totally helpless when natural disasters struck. During the last seventy years of the Ming, flood, drought, pestilence, and famine occurred repeatedly; fertile fields deteriorated into wilderness, and starvation was reported everywhere.[38] Forced to choose between family members' deaths and armed rebellion, the peasant masses did not hesitate.

In 1627, northern Shaanxi (Shensi) experienced a severe drought, and not one kernel of grain was harvested. Yet the government continued to pressure peasants for tax payments. As thousands of peasants died of hunger, those who survived raised the standard of revolt.[39] From Shaanxi and Gansu (Kansu) emerged such peasant leaders as Li Zicheng (Li Tzu-ch'eng) and Zhang Xianzhong (Chang Hsien-chung) and others who commanded dozens of insurgent armies jointly. Not only the Han but also the Mongolians and the Hui (Muslim) peasants participated in this rebellion. In 1635, the rebel leaders, commanding seventy-two battalions of troops, held a conference in Xingyang, Henan. Li raised the slogan "equal landownership and zero taxation," which reflected the poor peasants' pressing needs.[40] The demand for the change of China's landownership to a better system was unprecedented. Wherever they went, Li and his men were welcomed by the masses. The insurgents quickly grew to hundreds of thousands.

In 1644, Li's troops moved toward Beijing, meeting little resistance. In just over a month, they reached the capital, where the Ming troops, who used firearms and were supposed to defend the city, surrendered one after another. The Ming emperor lost his army. Having no place to go, Chongzhen (Ch'ung-chen; reigned 1627–44), the last Ming emperor, hanged himself at Coal Hill behind the Forbidden City. The grand army led by Li entered Beijing, and the Ming Dynasty came to an end.[41] In June, however, Manchu troops crossed the Great Wall from the north, defeated the peasant army, and established the Qing Dynasty (1644–1911). The failure of the late Ming uprisings demonstrates the fate of the typical Chinese peasant rebellion army entrapped in ancient ways as a nonideological and apolitical movement. Its leadership was unable to provide a new vision for the future of the peasants, a new system beyond the imperial one, and a strong, disciplined army for the country.

Another large-scale peasant revolt that is frequently cited by Chinese military historians is the Taiping Rebellion (1850–64). During the Qing Dynasty, capitalism and industrialization rose dramatically in the West. Many countries expanded their empires by encroaching upon Chinese territory. The Manchu rulers' closed-door policy made China more and more passive on the whole. In the nineteenth century, Manchu emperors commanded a diversified army of more than one million men, including the Manchu banner forces, regional armies, and local militias. In 1851, China's population reached 432 million, one-third of the world total.[42] The Qing Army improved its firearms technology somewhat and established a small naval force. Yet, in the first Opium War (1839–42), Great Britain defeated the Qing Army and partially opened China's market. Hans van de Ven suggests that "the Qing was ill-prepared to deal with Britain's naval challenge not because it was a backward country or a Confucian society with little regard for the military, but because it had faced different sorts of military challenges and followed a different path of military development than Britain."[43] The great Qing empire was gradually losing the central position and powerful status established by the Han Dynasty and increased by its early emperors, such as Kangxi (K'ang-hsi; reigned 1661–1722) and Qianlong (Ch'ien-lung; reigned 1735–96).

After the first Opium War, the suffering of the Chinese peasants intensified.[44] In 1851, the numerous streams of peasant resistance merged to form a gigantic torrent, the Taiping Rebellion, led by Hong Xiuquan (Hung Hsiu-ch'üan). A native of Huaxian, Guangdong (Kwangtung), he was born to a peasant family. Around the time of the first Opium War, Hong personally witnessed the cruelty of the British soldiers, the corruption and decadence of the Qing government, and the poverty and misery of the Chinese peasants.[45] Gradually, he cultivated the thought of revolt. In 1843, he, adapting some Christian ideas, organized a secret society, Bai shangdi hui (Society of God Worshippers). While propagating the new faith among the poverty-stricken peasants, he wrote such pamphlets as *Yuandao jiushige* (Doctrines on Salvation), proposing that "all people belong to one family and should share and enjoy . . . universal peace."[46] It was the first time in Chinese history that the leadership of a peasant uprising had adopted Western ideology to mobilize the Chinese masses.

On January 11, 1851, Hong formally raised the standard of revolt in the village of Jintian, Guiping County, Guangxi (Kwangsi). He called his regime the Taiping Tianguo (Heavenly Kingdom of Great Peace) and his army the Taipingjun (Army of Great Peace).[47] In September, the well-disciplined Taipingjun attacked and captured Yong'an (Mengshan) and introduced a new political and military system. The first stage of the new regime materialized. In April 1852, the peasant army broke through the encirclement at Yong'an, passed through Guangxi and Hunan, and attacked Hubei (Hupeh). In January 1853, it captured Wuchang, then the capital of Hubei, and enlarged its ranks to five hundred thousand men.[48] In February, it left Wuchang and moved eastward along the Yangtze (Chang) River. In March, the Taipingjun attacked and captured Nanjing (Nan-ching). Nanjing was renamed Tianjing (Heavenly Capital) and made the capital of the new regime. Then the Taiping Tianguo published *Tianchao tianmu zhidu* (Land System of the Heavenly Kingdom), which contained the idea that "all land under Heaven must be tilled by all the people under Heaven." Land was to be distributed according to household membership. A measure of this kind reflected the peasants' demand to stop land concentration, but it also reflected the utopian ideal of equality among small producers.[49]

Beginning in 1853, the Taipingjun of nearly one million launched northern and western expeditions to protect Tianjing and enlarge the regime's territory. In 1856, the army defeated two Qing forces sent to take over the insurgents' capital by controlling the northern and southern approaches to Tianjing.[50] This was the time when, militarily, the Taiping regime reached its highest point.

In 1856–58, however, struggle developed openly among the Taiping leaders. Wei Changhui, one of Hong Xiuquan's five kings and an ambitious man, killed the outstanding military leader Yang Xiuqing (Yang Hsiu-ch'ing) and more than twenty thousand of his followers.

Supported by both military and civil officials in Tianjing, Hong execut-ed Wei.[51] But another leader, Shi Dakai, mistrusted by Hong, left the capital with more than one hundred thousand men and fought alone. In 1863, his army was surrounded by the Qing Army on the bank of the Dadu River in Sichuan (Szechuan) and was completely wiped out.[52] The fortune of the Taiping Tianguo deteriorated quickly as a result of these internal struggles. The Qing Army seized the opportunity and counterattacked; it recovered many places in the middle and lower val-leys of the Yangtze River and reinstalled its north and south camps.[53] Once again, the Qing Army surrounded Tianjing. The military fortune of the kingdom degenerated from offensive victory to resistance. The cruelest and most bitter enemy of the Taiping regime proved to be Zeng Guofan (Tseng Kuo-fan), head of the Hunan Army.[54] In 1860, the Hunan Army surrounded Anqing, which was a shield for Tianjing; in September 1861, Anqing fell. The Hunan Army moved eastward along the Yangtze River and pressed hard on Tianjing. In June 1864, Hong died of illness. On July 19, Tianjing fell into the hands of the Qing Army.[55]

The Taiping Rebellion resulted in the deaths of at least twenty-five million people, the most destructive civil war in Chinese history. Chinese military historians argue that the Taiping leaders failed to pro-vide a new system for their rebellion, even though their ideas and scale reached a greater level than all the previous peasant rebellions.[56] The failure of the Taiping Rebellion also proves that the leadership was unable to overcome its self-destructive power struggle and to receive any support from "modern" Western countries. Nevertheless, Mao Ze-dong, cofounder of the Chinese Communist armed forces, said that he learned many lessons from both the success and failure of this and oth-er peasant rebellions. He concluded, "The scale of peasant uprisings and peasant wars in Chinese history has no parallel anywhere else. The class struggles of the peasants, the peasant uprisings and peasant wars constituted the real motive force of historical development in Chinese society."[57] He believed that "the poor peasants in China, together with the farm laborers, . . . are the broad peasant masses with no land or insufficient land, the semi-proletariat of the countryside, the biggest motive force of the Chinese revolution, the natural and most reliable ally of the proletariat and [the] main contingent of China's revolution-ary forces."[58] Ignoring Soviet advice and his opponents' criticism, Mao moved into the countryside and began to mobilize peasants in 1927. It was his peasant army that took over China and made him a national leader after twenty-two years of military revolution.

A Revolution without Peasants

In the late nineteenth century, the frequent peasant rebellions, foreign invasions, and domestic as well as overseas anti-Manchu movements undermined the Qing Dynasty's power. In 1895 China lost the First Sino-Japanese War, thereby losing its central position in Asia. The turn of the century marked major changes in Qing's military organization, institution, and technology. To survive, the Qing Dynasty established a new army, Zhiqiangjun (Self-Strengthening Army), in Hubei. The army of thirteen battalions was organized according to European patterns and trained by a team of thirty-five German officers.[59] Zhang Zhidong (Chang Chih-tung), the Qing official who founded the Zhiqiangjun, also opened a new military academy in Nanjing in 1896. As part of his reform efforts, he brought in Western military technology and weaponry. Zhang described his reform as "Zhongxue weiti, xixue weiyong" (Chinese learning for the fundamental principles, Western learning for the practical application). When he was appointed by the Qing court as governor-general of Hubei and Hunan, Zhang established an additional military academy in Wuchang, Hubei.[60] In 1897, another Qing official, Yuan Shikai (Yuan Shih-k'ai), also established an army, the New Army, in Hebei (Hopeh). He hired German instructors and purchased modern firearms from Germany and other European countries. By 1906, Yuan's consisted of five infantry divisions, totaling fifty thousand troops, near Beijing. Yuan created five officer training schools and military academies in Baoding and Tianjin, Hebei.[61] Soon Yuan became the father of the warlords in China. Nevertheless, military education and formal training were promoted by both European instructors and new technology. By the turn of the century, China's New Army was a far more effective force.[62]

Unfortunately, the New Army could not save the empire because the Manchu rulers refused to carry the reform beyond weaponry and instruction and into the organization of the military institution. Li Hongzhang, Qing's prime minister, once said that "Chinese civil and military systems are much superior in every aspect to these of the Westerners; only our firearms are far inferior to theirs."[63] The Manchu grandees' refusal of further reform and brutal suppression of the reformers also alienated the regular soldiers of the New Army and undermined their loyalty to the emperor himself.[64] Moreover, the early recruits were soon disillusioned by the government's corruption, mismanagement, and, worst of all, its failure against European, American, and Japanese forces during the Boxer Rebellion (1900).[65] During the first decade of the twentieth century, the Qing Dynasty's political order and economic system crumbled under Western invasions and increasing dissatisfaction, rapidly eroding Manchu authority in Beijing. John K. Fairbank, Edwin O. Reischauer, and Albert M. Craig point out that "students the government trained abroad, new armies it trained at home, merchants it encouraged in domestic enterprise, political assemblies it convoked in the provinces, all sooner or later turned against the dynasty. . . . For modernization now meant Chinese nationalism, which implied the end of Manchu rule."[66] Meanwhile, foreign concessions in treaty ports and foreign nations gave shelter to Chinese rebels. The anti-Manchu movement founded its revolutionary center overseas. Sun Yat-sen, one of the anti-Manchu leaders, made Japan his revolutionary base.

In 1905, Sun, the founding father of republican China, organized the Tongmenghui (T'ung-meng hui; United League) in Japan. Among the one thousand early members of the party were liberal students, Christian merchants, and patriotic young officers trained in Japan.[67] Sun and his secret society spread their revolutionary ideas and organization from Japan to the world by establishing offices in San Francisco, Honolulu, Brussels, and Singapore, and in seventeen of the twenty-four provinces of China. Thousands and thousands of Chinese, including many New Army officers, joined the Tongmenghui by participating in multiple anti-Manchu activities and accepting Sun's Sanmin zhuyi (Three Principles of the People): nationalism (both anti-Manchu and anti-imperialism), democracy (a constitution with people's rights), and "people's livelihood" (a classic term for social equality). These three principles "summed up much of the ferment of the age."[68]

On October 10, 1911, amid an anti-Qing plot in Wuchang, some New Army officers revolted. (October 10, or "Double Tens," would become National Day for the ROC.) The success of the Wuchang uprising led many officers to join the revolution. In the next two months, fifteen provinces proclaimed their independence from the Qing empire.

The rebellious provinces and Tongmenghui joined forces and set up a provisional government at Nanjing, which elected Sun president and inaugurated him on January 1, 1912, at Nanjing.[69] This great breakthrough in Chinese history ended two thousand years of monarchy and built the first republic in Asian history.

The Qing court's hopes rested with Marshal Yuan Shikai, commander of the New Army. In an attempt to avoid civil war, Sun and other revolutionaries negotiated with Yuan and offered him the presidency of the new republic. On February 12, 1912, Yuan forced the last emperor, only six years old at the time, to step down, thus ending the Qing Dynasty.[70] Then Sun resigned as president. On February 14, the provisional government elected Yuan the first president of the ROC. Yuan, however, tried to establish his own dictatorship against the revolutionaries. In August 1912, to fight against Yuan, Sun reorganized the Tongmenghui into a political party, Guomindang, to mobilize the masses. The power struggle between Yuan and the GMD-controlled parliament and cabinet continued, including mass rallies, assassination, and a military coup. After Yuan's death in 1916, the central government collapsed completely.

Sun Yat-sen in uniform. (Courtesy of the History Museum of the GMD Party, Taipei, Taiwan.)

Sun and the other revolutionary leaders never had control of any armed force. After Yuan's death, the country entered the Warlord Period (1916–27). Five or six major warlord armies divided the country and waged wars against each other. Hoping to seize control of the whole country, warlord armies competed for human resources by drafting young peasants. An estimated 500,000 men served in the warlord armies in 1916. The total increased to 1 million by 1918 and about 1.5 million by 1924.[71] Edward A. McCord points out that "the emergence of warlordism, a condition under which military commanders exercise autonomous political power by virtue of their personal control of military force, made the early Republican period (1912–27) a dark chapter in Chinese history."[72] The 1911 Revolution failed to turn China into a truly independent and democratic country. Nevertheless, it totally destroyed the Qing's central control, radicalized the masses, and showed angry peasants the power of revolution.

Republican revolutionaries did not, however, attempt to enlist the peasants in their struggle; rather, they tried to win over secret societies and the New Army. As the 1911 Revolution lacked social content, Sun's movement, composed largely of students and intellectuals, secret societies, and Chinese abroad, gave momentum to the cause. The revolt was almost totally urban. Initially, where the peasants reacted to the insurrection at all, they reacted positively. They saw opportunities to redress some of the wrongs suffered under the Qing regime, such as taxation and land concentration. But it soon became clear that the rebellion served the rich landlords rather than the poor peasants. The local landowners and gentry class greatly increased their power. Not only did they take over such duties as tax collection through self-government bureaus, but they also gained greater influence over the local magistrates.[73] Under such circumstances, the peasants' positive response quickly turned negative.[74]

The revolutionary leaders lacked an agrarian program that truly reflected the interests of peasants. Sun, who had been born into a peasant family, did sympathize with peasant concerns. Fearing the growing inequalities between rich and poor, Sun formulated as a clear goal in his revolutionary principles *minsheng* (people's livelihood), stating that equal rights to land should be guaranteed. Nevertheless, once the new regime was established, it did not heed the peasants' cry for land. The GMD had neither the ability nor the will to deal with these issues.[75] In short, on the one hand, the 1911 Revolution was elite, scarcely touching China's villages, except to demand more taxes. On the other hand, land reform was one of Sun's revolutionary ideas; however, he failed to implement any changes to win over the peasantry. Without a far-reaching land reform program, no revolution could succeed in an agrarian society such as China's. Thus the 1911 Revolution failed because of the lack of mass participation, even though Sun had created his political center, including his new ideology, a new political party, a republican state system, and international supports.

Mao and the Early Experience of the CCP

In the early twentieth century, the ideas of Marxism and Leninism seemed as effective as liberal democratic and republican ideas in inspiring outright revolution in China. Communist movements became an alternative solution to problems facing angry peasants and the urban poor, a large proportion of the Chinese population.

Mao Zedong should not have been one of the protesting peasants. Born in the village of Shaoshan, Hunan, on December 26, 1893, he grew up in a better-off peasant family.[76] His father, Mao Rensheng, moved up from a landless peasant to an independent farmer who owned two and a half acres of land by serving in the regional army for six or seven years and saving money.[77] His hard work and frugality put his son, Runzhi (later changed to Zedong), the first of four children, through private school. Mao Zedong's childhood and early education developed from this "plough culture."[78] Taught by Confucian teachers in the village, Mao enjoyed studying classic literature and ancient philosophy. Philip Short concludes, "Mao drew from Confucianism three key ideas which were to prove fundamental to the whole of his later thought." The three key ideas were, first, the need for every human being and every society to "have a moral compass"; second, the "primacy of right-thinking," or "virtue" in Confucianism; and, third, "the importance of self-cultivation."[79]

At age nine, Mao became disillusioned when his father took land that belonged to Mao's uncle, who had financial trouble and needed help. In addition, whenever young Mao questioned or complained about working in the rice paddy, his father humiliated him, often in front of the villagers. His father was supposed to make Mao, the oldest son, central to the family, instead of blocking him from the family center. Mao began to protest his father's authority in the family. At fourteen, he rebelled when his parents arranged a marriage for him.[80] As traditional Chinese ideas failed to solve the problems around him, Mao began to read new publications and accept radical ideas from the Hundred Days of Reform (Bairi weixin, or Wuxu bianfa) of 1898. After he returned to school in 1909, he wanted a "liberal mind and strong body." He respected reformers and rebels who fought against the Qing government. When a rice riot occurred in Changsha, the capital of Hunan, Mao considered the riot leaders, who were beheaded after their failure, to be heroes.[81] Mao once analyzed his character thus: "There is a tiger quality in me; that is my main quality. I also have a monkey quality, but that is secondary." Deng Rong describes Mao's tiger quality as imperial and tyrannical and his monkey quality as "pugnacious, rebellious. . . . The blend of those qualities in Mao Zedong gave him a dual personality. He was both a ruler and a rebel who used his role as a rebel to attain a new imperial realm."[82]

At eighteen, Mao heard the news of the rebellion in Wuchang. On October 24, 1911, the revolutionaries launched an armed rebellion in Changsha. Mao joined the revolutionary army in the city and served six months in the Left Company, First Battalion, Fiftieth Regiment, Twenty-fifth Brigade. During his military training, Mao read Western liberal works by Montesquieu, Thomas Carlyle, and John Stuart Mill.[83] He changed from a Confucian reformer to a radical liberalist. Disappointed by the inconclusive revolution, Mao left the New Army in 1912 and enrolled in the Changsha First Normal School. During the Warlord Period, Changsha was a hot spot in the battles between the northern and southern warlords. The city suffered frequent attacks, looting, and destruction. Following his belief in arming and training the population, Mao organized students at the normal school to collect weapons from warlord army deserters. In 1917, he established "student volunteer guards" and was elected guard captain to protect the campus from marauding warlord troops.[84]

After his graduation in 1918, Mao took a job at Peking University as a library assistant under the head librarian, Li Dazhao (Li Ta-chao), who would be one of the founding members of the CCP. The New Cultural movement in the 1910s and the May 4 movement of 1919 both took place in Beijing. In the capital city, Mao became inspired by Karl Marx and the Communist revolution in Russia.[85] The Russian Revolution of 1917 provided a model for the Chinese revolution to follow. On July 25, 1919, the Soviet government announced the abolition of all unequal treaties with China. The termination of all former czarist privileges in China portrayed new Soviet Russia as a better nation than the old, imperialist Western powers that had been dismembering China. As a radical liberalist, Mao was drawn to Marxism-Leninism and the Russian experience. He became a Marxist-Leninist revolutionary.

As Soviet ideology and the Bolshevik revolution were popularized, the time arrived for the founding of the CCP. In January 1920,

Li visited Chen Duxiu (Ch'en Tu-hsiu), professor and dean of letters at Peking University, to talk about the possibility of setting up a Communist group. In April and May, Gregory Voitinsky, a representative of the Vladivostok branch of the Bolsheviks' Far Eastern Bureau, visited Li in Beijing and Chen in Shanghai and discussed the establishment of Communist organizations in China.[86] In August, Chen founded China's first Communist group in Shanghai, and Li the first in Beijing. Meanwhile, Dong Biwu (Tung Bi-wu) in Wuhan and others in Guangzhou, Japan, and France formed their own Communist groups. In November, the first issue of the party's journal, *Gongchandangren* (the Communist), was published. China expert Tony Saich emphasizes that, "however 'sinified' Marxism-Leninism may have later become under Mao Zedong, it must be remembered that it was introduced into China by a generation of intellectuals who were profoundly disenchanted with their intellectual heritage and who sought China's salvation in a foreign ideology."[87]

Mao returned to Changsha in 1920 as head of a primary school. When his attempts to organize mass education were suppressed, he turned to politics, helping to found a Chinese Communist group in Hunan. The old system and traditional society made him a stranger in his own hometown. Warlords and landlords in Hunan made him a thinker and a political leader. Mao would become one of the founders of the Chinese Communist armed forces, founder of Communist China, and the most important Chinese Communist leader in the twentieth century. Deng Rong concludes, "Mao Zedong was a Marxist, with deep roots in China's traditional culture. He was thoroughly familiar with the nation's classical treatises; he knew China's history from her earliest civilization. The exciting events and striking figures of the past several thousand years were sharply incised in his mind. The benevolence and tyrannies of emperors and ministers, the romanticism and pride of literary creations, the rebelliousness of bravos against convention, and the special wisdom, philosophy and thought patterns with which China's history and culture are so imbued all permeated his very essence."[88]

In July 1921, the CCP was founded. The First CCP National Congress convened in Shanghai that month. Thirteen delegates, including Mao and representing about fifty Communist Party members across the country, attended. Most of the delegates and early CCP members were intellectuals. Soviet advisor Hendricus Sneevliet (alias Maring), the first official representative from the Executive Committee of the Communist International Congress (Comintern) in Moscow, instructed the CCP to focus its effort on the labor movement. The congress passed the CCP's first constitution and set up its prime goals to organize the working class and "promote a social revolution through the use of the strike weapon."[89] Chen Duxiu was elected secretary-general of the CCP Central Committee, which had its headquarters in Shanghai. Although military organization was not on the agenda at the first congress, the CCP began to prepare for revolution. In the winter of 1921, the CCP Russian branch sent Xiao Jinguang (Hsiao Ch'in-kuang) and four others to the Soviet Academy of the Red Army to study military training, doctrine, and ideology. This was the beginning of the military training of Chinese Communists in the Soviet Union.[90]

The CCP's mobilization of the working class went nowhere in the urban areas. As the warlords increased their control of the cities, their wartime headquarters—the urban union organizations—were in the hands of gangsters like the powerful Qinghong bang (Green and Red gangs) in Shanghai. The CCP did not have skilled personnel to organize manufacturing workers. The working class, however, composed only a very small percentage of China's labor force. In 1927, of the total population of 300 million, only 1.5 million were factory workers, and another 1.75 million were other industrial workers (miners, seamen, railway workers).[91] The party membership grew slowly.[92]

In July 1922, the Second CCP National Congress convened in Shanghai, with twelve delegates representing only 195 party members. This congress created the Central Executive Committee as the party's leading body and reelected Chen as the committee chairman. The congress's major task was to formulate the party's program for the Chinese Communist revolution. The party's basic goal, to launch an anti-imperialist and anti-feudalist revolution, still fell short of a military revolution and organization of peasantry.[93]

In December 1921, Maring had secretly met Sun Yat-sen in Guilin (Kuei-lin), Guangxi. Sun wanted to establish a modern armed force under his and GMD command. Whereas most Western powers rejected or ignored his idea, the Soviet Union was willing to help him. The Soviets requested that the GMD allow the Communist Party members to join the GMD as individuals, so that the CCP would maintain its political and ideological independence. In exchange, the Soviet government would help Sun and the GMD with their military establishment and officer training. Sun was interested since he was preparing a northern expedition to Guangzhou, the capital of Guangdong, to unify the ROC. At the Second CCP National Congress in 1922, Maring suggested that the party cooperate with Sun and his GMD. Chen opposed the idea, but when the Comintern approved Maring's proposal and the CCP applied for membership in the Comintern in late August, Chen had to accept that the CCP would enter the GMD and operate as a "bloc within" it. In September, the first group of CCP members, including Mao, joined the GMD (while retaining their CCP membership).[94]

In August 1922, Sun met Adolph Joffe, a top Soviet diplomat, who arranged financial aid and military training for the GMD. On January 26, 1923, Joffe and Sun issued a joint manifesto to pledge Soviet support for China.[95] In April, the CCP headquarters moved from Shanghai to Guangzhou. In June, the Third CCP National Congress met in Guangzhou. Thirty delegates, who represented approximately 420 party members, showed admiration for Sun's dauntless spirit and sent Li Dazhao and others to provide him with direct aid. The congress also encouraged more CCP members to join the GMD as individuals. Chen was again elected chairman of the CCP Central Executive Committee, and Mao was elected secretary. From now on, Mao would be one of the leading members of the CCP. And now, for the first time, among the resolutions passed by the party congress was a resolution regarding the peasantry.[96] In November, the GMD Central Committee passed a resolution establishing the Chinese Nationalist Party Army Officer Academy. Meanwhile, the Soviet envoys suggested establishing a capable party to unite the workers and peasants. Sun welcomed the assistance of the CCP and the Soviets and started to reorganize his GMD.[97] Maring returned to Moscow in August 1923, and Mikhail Borodin arrived in Guangzhou on October 6 as the permanent delegate of Soviet Russia.

The Coalition and CCP Officers

In January 1924, Sun Yat-sen convened in Guangzhou the First GMD National Congress. The party congress enacted a new constitution and agreed that Communists could join the GMD as individuals. CCP leaders, including Li, Mao, and Qu Qiubai (Ch'u Ch'iu-pai), participated in the GMD leadership as elected members or alternate members of the GMD Central Executive Committee. The congress adopted the three cardinal policies of "allying with Russia, allying with the Communist Party, and assisting the peasants and workers."[98] Sun adapted the Three Principles of the People to these three policies. The First GMD National Congress marked the formal beginning of the united front of the Nationalist (GMD) and Communist parties. The CCP supported Sun's political center at Guangzhou. The coalition government received both political and military advisors from the Soviet Union. After the congress, Borodin and the Soviet military advisors suggested to Sun that a military academy and a revolutionary armed force be established.[99]

On June 16, 1924, the Huangpu (Whampoa) Military Academy (HMA, China's West Point) was founded with the assistance of the Soviet Union, with Jiang Jieshi as the commandant.[100] Borodin was

Jiang Jieshi as HMA superintendent. (Courtesy of the History Museum of the GMD Party, Taipei, Taiwan.)

appointed as advisor to the GMD Revolutionary Committee. Sun believed the GMD "should use the students of this academy as a foundation for a revolutionary army."[101] Thereafter, Sun and Jiang began to build a military center in Guangzhou with sources including GMD and CCP members, college students, and warlord officers and soldiers who had revolted. From the beginning, the HMA's curriculum emphasized political training and ideological education to develop an officer corps loyal to the GMD. Obviously, Jiang intended to establish a party army. He also adopted a dual commanding system, or commander–political commissar system, from the Soviet Red Army.

The HMA faced three competing models: Japanese, German, and Soviet. Before the 1911 Revolution, Japan was the center for the Chinese nationalist movement. The modernization of the Japanese military between 1868 and 1912 attracted many Chinese officers, like Jiang, who studied in a military academy in Japan in 1908–10. After World War I, however, Japan's attempt to obtain German- and Russian-controlled territories in east and northeast China threatened China's sovereignty and independence. Nationwide anti-Japanese movements arose in the 1910s and 1920s, making the adoption of the Japanese military system impossible.

As we have seen, Qing armies were trained by German officers and adopted the German military system. After the 1911 Revolution, many German instructors stayed in China, training warlord troops and helping them to get new arms from European countries. The German instructors favored a large infantry army with a well-educated officer corps. The better-trained units could be used as cadres or instructors to train other units in order to prepare a large army for war in a short period of time. The German instructors also paid special attention to artillery firepower, telegraphic communication, and railway transportation. After Germany lost World War I in 1918, official exchanges ended, and its military influence declined. Nevertheless, Jiang and his army maintained some of the German doctrine through the 1930s. By 1937, the Nationalist Army had ten German-trained infantry divisions.[102]

The Soviet Union offered not only military training but also financial aid and political consultation. Therefore, the Soviet system was accepted in 1924 at HMA as the model for the Nationalist Army. The Russian model emphasized political control. China's acceptance of Soviet financial aid left the academy no choice but to accept Soviet

Red Army advisors and their military curriculum. Sun sent Jiang and a military delegation to Moscow in 1924 to study the Soviet military system; four months later, Jiang became the first superintendent of the HMA. In 1925, more than one thousand Russian military advisors, including Borodin and General V. K. Blücher (who would be one of the first five Soviet marshals) trained GMD-CCP officer corps in China.[103] The Russian advisors worked closely with both the GMD and the CCP at the HMA.

The CCP sent Zhou Enlai to serve as the director of the academy's political department and Ye Jianying (Yeh Chien-ying) and Nie Rongzhen (Nieh Jung-chen) as instructors. Many Communist Party members and Communist Youth League (CYL) members enrolled in the academy as cadets.

Zhou was born in Huai'an, Jiangsu (Kiangsu), on March 5, 1898. His uncle, who adopted him when Zhou was six months old, died soon after. His stepmother, who sent him through private school to study traditional literature and Confucianism, died when Zhou was only ten. He then had to move to another uncle's house in northeast China. In 1911, he studied in a secondary school in the city of Fengtian (present-day Shenyang, Liaoning), reading some of the republican publications and accepting their revolutionary ideas. During his study at Nankai High School (a Western-style school in Tianjin) in 1913–17, Zhou became more critical of warlord government policy and participated in many student movements. He studied Marxism and Leninism and learned about the Russian Revolution during his education in Japan in 1918–19. A year later, Zhou joined the European study program and went to France. He formed Communist groups in France as a student activist in 1920–21 and became a Communist leader among the overseas students in 1922–24 in Europe. On his return in November 1924, Zhou was appointed director of the political department of the HMA. Diplomatic and modest, he instinctively maintained cooperation between the GMD and CCP within the academy. The CCP continued to control the HMA political department in 1924–26. By June 1926, about 160 faculty and staff at the HMA were CCP members.[104]

Zhou's experience at the HMA certainly contributed to his successful organization of the Nanchang Uprising (1927), which established the Communist armed forces. With his organizational skills, Zhou was elected to the CCP Political Bureau (Politburo) in 1928 and became secretary-general in charge of military affairs of the Central Bureau in 1931. When Mao Zedong emerged as the top leader, Zhou became his chief supporter and closest colleague. Together they led the Red Army in the historic Long March, developed Communist forces through WWII, defeated the Nationalist Army in the Chinese civil war, and ultimately founded the PRC.[105]

Though its ideological and political agendas differed from those of the GMD, the CCP successfully implemented its policies and trained Communist officers at the HMA from 1924 to 1927. CCP cadets studied the Russian military curriculum alongside GMD cadets. They thought their friendship would last forever. By 1927, ten thousand cadets, many of whom would become the leading commanders of Jiang's military, had graduated in six classes from the academy. About three thousand were members of the CCP.[106] One of the reasons for the increasing CCP membership at the HMA was that the Soviet instructors promoted Communism in their curriculum and encouraged cadets to join the Communist Party. The Russian instructors apparently also favored the Communist students. Some of the students who were sent to the Soviet Union for further military training became CCP members before their return.[107]

The Soviet Union provided one hundred thousand rubles to the HMA. On October 7, 1924, the first Russian ship arrived in Guangzhou with weapons for the HMA and the GMD. The Chinese Communists thus started their military affairs inside the Nationalist military system, a Soviet Red Army system—a force based on the Communist Party membership. In December 1924, the CCP District Committee of Guangdong established the Armored Company for the Governor-General, the first Chinese Communist company. The team consisted of 120 soldiers and officers, most of whom were CCP members, some members of HMA's first graduating class. In November 1925, the district committee expanded the company into a regiment under the command of Ye Ting (Yeh T'ing), who had recently finished his military training in the Soviet Union. In 1926, it was reorganized as the Independent Regiment of the Fourth Army, totaling 2,100 men. This was the first regiment of the Communist armed forces.[108]

On January 11–22, 1925, the Fourth CCP National Congress met at Shanghai. Twenty representatives attended the meeting, representing 994 party members. The congress established the Central Bureau of the Central Executive Committee and elected Chen secretary-general of the bureau. Although many HMA officers had joined the Communist Party, its membership was developing slowly among the working class in the cities. Nevertheless, the CCP adopted its second resolution on the peasant movement at this congress. The resolution emphasized that "the crucial difference between Leninists and all the opportunistic Mensheviks" was that "the latter neglect the 'slumbering' peasants, whom they consider incapable of becoming a crucial element in the revolution." Without mobilizing the peasants, the CCP "cannot hope that the Chinese revolution will succeed or take the leading position in the nationalist movement."[109]

In fact, the CCP membership expanded rapidly after 1926, when the GMD-CCP Northern Expedition, a war against the warlords, began. Military revolution has frequently been a key factor in the Chinese Communist movement. The CCP's membership increased from 994 in 1925 to 57,900 in 1927, and many new members served in the GMD military. On July 1, 1925, three and a half months after Sun died in Beijing, the Nationalist government (Guomin zhengfu) formally came into existence in Guangzhou under the leadership of Jiang Jieshi. In July, Wang Jingwei (Wang Ching-wei) was elected chair, and Borodin senior advisor. On August 26, Jiang reorganized all the military units under the Nationalist government into the National Revolutionary Army (Guomin geming jun) with Jiang as its commander in chief.

Finally, Jiang and the GMD had their own armed force. At that time, the NRA had five armies (the student soldiers of the HMA became the First Army). Each army had three divisions, and each division had three regiments, including nine infantry battalions, totaling 5,500 men. GMD party representatives, or political commissars, and political departments were established at army, divisional, and regimental levels, following the Soviet model. Some CCP members were appointed as party representatives, responsible for political work in the various units.[110] The CCP controlled the Fourth Army's Independent Regiment, 2,100 men, under the command of Ye Ting. Ye and many other officers were CCP members.

On July 1, 1926, Commander General Jiang Jieshi issued a declaration on the Northern Expedition and so launched the punitive expedition against the northern warlords, including Wu Peifu and Sun

Chuanfang, two of the five major warlords. Jiang temporarily renamed the NRA the Northern Expeditionary Army (NEA), which had eight infantry armies, approximately one hundred thousand men. On July 9, the NEA left Guangzhou on three separate routes. The main battle-fields of Jiang's Northern Expedition were Hunan and Hubei. They quickly took Changsha and Yuezhou and destroyed Wu's main forces in Hunan. In September and October, Jiang captured the triple city of Wuhan, the capital of Hubei. Then the NEA troops moving along the other two routes occupied Nanchang, Anqing, and Nanjing. Thus, in less than six months, the NEA overthrew the two most powerful warlords. The others either surrendered or joined Jiang's forces, which in 1927 increased to forty armies—seven hundred thousand men. The Nationalist territory expanded from the southwestern coast to the Yangtze valley along the eastern coast, covering half of China. In mid-December, the Nationalist government and the Central Executive Committee moved from Guangzhou to Wuhan, in central China.[111] Edward L. Dreyer notes that "in 1926–27 the Northern Expedition was sustained by an idealism and nationalism that temporarily united [the] Chinese across a broad spectrum of political beliefs, and fiscal probity played an important supporting role in the KMT's success."[112]

As part of this victorious Northern Expedition, the CCP experienced an unprecedented membership increase. During the fighting, Ye Ting's Independent Regiment's combat success led to its expansion into six regiments in 1927; it became the NEA's Twenty-fourth and Twenty-fifth divisions, totaling ten thousand men. Among the troops were a large number of CCP members, who became the main force of the rebellion of the Nationalist Army later that year. At the Fifth CCP National Congress in April–May 1927, eighty representatives attended the meeting, representing 57,900 members. The congress established a new central committee with the Politburo as its standing executive body. Even though the congress criticized Chen Duxiu's softness toward the GMD's rightist attacks on the CCP, it elected him as the secretary-general of the Politburo. The meeting concluded that the Communist Party should support the friendly left wing (*zuopai*) and fight against the hostile right wing (*youpai*) inside the GMD. According to the Central Committee's survey, about 8.5 percent of the CCP, or about five thousand party members, served in the NEA. Many of them worked in the political departments at army and divisional levels.

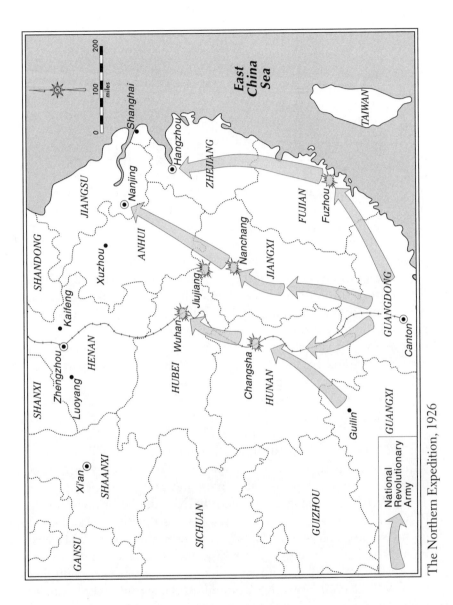

The Northern Expedition, 1926

The Soviet system seemed to work well, since the NEA had defeated the warlords' troops all along the Yangtze River and occupied several major cities, including Shanghai. These Chinese industrial and financial centers soon became centers of the power struggle between the GMD's right and left wings.[113]

The victories of the Northern Expedition sped up the development of the peasant movement by collapsing provincial and local governments. Hunan became the center of the peasant movements in the late 1920s. (Mao and some other Communist military leaders came from Hunan.) Peasant rebellions against tax collection there gained momentum and spread throughout Hubei, Jiangxi, Fujian, Zhejiang, Henan, and other provinces. In early 1927, membership in peasant associations exceeded ten million. The GMD had failed to mobilize peasant support in the 1911 Revolution, and it failed again in 1926–27, when the GMD leaders and army were preoccupied with taking over cities during the Northern Expedition. Thus the CCP filled the political vacuum in the rural areas and mobilized peasant communities by providing Communist leadership and revolutionary programs such as land reform. In late February 1927, at a special meeting in Beijing, the CCP Central Executive Committee decided that the party must strengthen its work among the peasantry during the Northern Expedition. In Hunan, Mao began to arm peasants and organize "peasant self-defense teams" in many villages across that province.[114] He reported in March that, "in a very short time, in China's central, southern and northern provinces, several hundred million peasants will rise like a tornado or tempest, a force so extraordinarily swift and violent that no power, however great, will be able to suppress it."[115]

In April 1927, Jiang established the national government of the ROC under GMD control in Nanjing, starting the Republican Period, or the Nanjing Decade, of 1927–37. However, the Communist movement's rapid growth across the country and its increasing influence in the GMD worried the right wing and conservatives, who controlled the GMD Central Executive Committee. They wanted to terminate the GMD-CCP coalition and put more pressure on Jiang, who did not intend to challenge the right wing, see a party split, or share national power with the CCP.

To contain the increasing Soviet influence and left-wing activities in the GMD and the Nationalist Army, and to secure his military victory and national leadership, on April 12, Jiang and the right-wing government in Shanghai began to purge CCP members. The Soviet Embassy compound in Beijing was raided. Li Dazhao and other CCP leaders were arrested, and Li was later executed. On May 21, GMD troops suppressed CCP-led mass organizations in Changsha; thousands were killed on that day in what is known as the Horse Day incident (Mari shibian). The GMD government made Communist activities capital crimes with charges like conspiracy, illegal rallies, and antigovernment plots.

Chinese historians refer to the events of April 12, 1927, as the beginning of the Chinese white terror (baise kongbu). Many CCP members were jailed or killed; others fled the country. Some left the CCP and joined the GMD.[116] In June, the right-wing-controlled troops attacked Wuhan, where there was strong sympathy for the left-wing movement. By July 15, the Wuhan government decided to follow Jiang and "separate the CCP," purging Communist members, disarming workers, and jailing Soviet advisors. Wang Jingwei, head of the GMD Wuhan government, said, "Better [to] kill one thousand non-Communists by mistake than allow a single true Communist to slip through the net."[117] Thereafter, Jiang and Wang joined forces. In June, Wang dismissed Borodin and all 140 Soviet military and political advisors from their posts in the Nationalist government. Thus the first political coalition between the GMD and CCP ended, and the urban-centered Communist movement failed. The CCP's membership declined rapidly, from sixty thousand in April to ten thousand in October.[118] Peter Zarrow points out that although "CCP histories have tended to make a scapegoat of Chen Duxiu . . . Stalin himself deserves most of the blame for exacerbating the Communists' problems just as fatal events began unfolding."[119] Joseph Stalin restrained all major CCP critiques of and challenges to the united front until too late. "The CCP was already decimated; Russian policy was in ruins."[120]

The CCP leaders learned a bloody lesson: the Communist movement in China needed its own armed forces. The revolution called for a violent movement against violent "counterrevolutionary forces."[121] In its last communication with the party before its evacuation from Shanghai, the Central Committee emphasized that "one of the most important tasks" for the party was to "create a new revolutionary army . . . of workers and peasants."[122] To save the Communist movement in

China, the CCP decided to correct its own mistakes and stage armed uprisings against Jiang's Nationalist government. The CCP believed its first revolutionary war had ended in failure because of the predominance of Chen's rightist opportunist line in the leading body of the CCP at the later stage of the war.[123] The failure taught the party that without a revolutionary army, there would be no revolution.

★ 2 ★

The Formative Years

THE CHINESE COMMUNIST PARTY organized its independent armed force following the white terror of 1927, the worst period in party history. The military became absolutely necessary for the CCP's survival. The party and the army established an interdependent relationship before WWII to create a center in rural areas for revolutionary authorities. The party mobilized peasants, trained officers, and received instructions and aid from the Soviet Union. The army protected the Communist base areas and eventually seized state power for the party by defeating the Nationalist Army on the mainland. Mao described this relationship on August 7, 1927: "Political power grows out of the barrel of a gun."[1] This was the beginning of the CCP's second revolution (*dierci geming zhanzheng*), the revolutionary war for land (*tudi geming zhanzheng*). In late 1927, Mao led his small troop into a remote, mountainous area and became the "king of the mountain mobs" (*shandawang*) by grouping with the local bandits. When Zhu De joined forces with Mao at the Jinggang (Chingkang) Mountains in 1928, they reorganized their troops into the Red Army and created a military base for the Communist revolution. Of their ten thousand men, 82 percent were peasants.[2] In 1931, Mao made his base region a government center for all CCP Soviets when he was elected chairman of the Executive Committee of the Chinese Soviet Republic. Mao's strategy and tactics became the basis for the Communist military revolution. By 1936, the Red Army maintained a contingency of approximately forty-five thousand troops.[3]

The Communist forces experienced significant development through the second CCP-GMD coalition during WWII. The Red Army became the Eighth Route Army and the New Fourth Army in 1937. Zhu became the commander of the Eighth Route Army. By the end of WWII, when the CCP and GMD ended their cooperation and resumed civil war in 1946, the Communist military forces had grown to 1 million regular troops, augmented by 2 million militia.[4] In 1948, the CCP renamed its armed forces the People's Liberation Army of China. In 1949, when the PLA defeated Jiang Jieshi's Nationalist Army in the civil war and gained control of mainland China except Tibet, it totaled 5.5 million regular troops.[5] Mao became president of the People's Republic of China in 1949, with Zhu as the commander in chief of the PLA.

This chapter examines the Red Army's origins, recruitment and organization, strategic doctrine, and operational tactics from 1927 to 1949. It explains why Communist ideologies, Soviet support, and a rural-centered military revolution attracted many poor peasants who had no hope of owning land under the ROC government. The stories of Marshal Zhu, Zhang Guotao (Chang Kuo-t'ao), Minister Ma Zhaoxiang, General Li Zhen, Jiang Shangqing, and Wan Qing show the characteristics of the first generation of Chinese Communist military officers. Leaving an old system that held little hope for their future, they became fearless revolutionaries and forged a peasant army under CCP leadership in 1927–34. Although tensions and even military coups surfaced from time to time, like the Zhang Guotao incident during the Long March of 1934–35, the party retained control of the army—an army that was different from the warlord and GMD armies it defeated. The chapter also outlines the Red Army's organizational changes and campaign experience in the Second Sino-Japanese War in 1937–45 and the civil war in 1946–49.

King of the Mountain Mobs

The leadership of the CCP learned that the Communist movement in China needed its own armed forces when the first CCP-GMD coalition ended in April 1927. The CCP Central Committee began its efforts to create a new revolutionary army of workers and peasants. But after Jiang's Nationalist government had announced that the CCP was illegal, antigovernment, and a capital crime, most of the party members had either been killed or left the CCP.[6] The Central Committee had hope in the CCP members of the Nationalist Army who had survived the white terror. In mid-July 1927, the Central Committee held an emergency meeting to terminate the leadership of Chen Duxiu and set up a five-member standing committee to save the party. To save the CCP-controlled troops in the Nationalist Army, the committee planned an uprising within the Nationalist Twentieth Army in Nanchang, the capital of Jiangxi (Kiangsi).[7]

On August 1, 1927, Zhou Enlai, then secretary of the CCP Field Committee, along with He Long (Ho Lung), Ye Ting, Zhu De, and Liu Bocheng, organized the CCP members in the Twentieth Army to revolt against the GMD. After a fierce battle, the insurgents eliminated more than ten thousand GMD garrison troops.[8] Several days later, He Long resumed his position as commander of the Second Group Army and reorganized other troops into the first Chinese Communist armed force, totaling twenty-three thousand men. Most of the insurgent GMD officers joined the CCP.[9] Although the Nanchang Uprising (Nanchang qiyi) failed to defend the city and establish an urban base, it marked the beginning of armed revolution independently led by the CCP and represented the Communist revolutionary army's first shot against the GMD and Jiang's government. August 1 is celebrated as the birthday of the Chinese armed forces.

To save the CCP's only army, Zhu and He moved it southward from Jiangxi in late August and attempted to return to Guangdong, a former revolutionary base. The GMD troops in Guangdong, however, advanced north and stopped the rebels' southern movement with a strong defense. Zhu and He lost half of their troops by October and were unable to launch another southern offensive. Many of the rebels surrendered, deserted, or returned to the GMD forces.[10] Out of the twenty-three thousand men and officers at the Nanchang Uprising, only two thousand survivors moved into Hunan under the command of Zhu as the Twenty-eighth Regiment. In April 1928, they joined Mao's forces.[11]

Zhu De was desperate as a career soldier. He was born into a poor peasant family in Yilong, Sichuan, on December 1, 1886. Landless, his father worked as a field hand for a landlord in the village. Five of the family's thirteen children died of starvation or illness during childhood. Zhu's uncle adopted him when Zhu was two years old. At five, he began to help his uncle on the farm and around the house. His uncle borrowed money and sent him to school in a nearby town from 1892 to 1904. At nineteen, he passed Qing's county and regional examinations and enrolled in the regional school, where some of the teachers had recently returned from studying in Japan. Zhu De learned Japanese and studied the Meiji Restoration and reform ideas from 1906 to 1908. After his graduation, he returned to Yilong for financial reasons and taught physical education at an elementary school for one year. But he was frustrated by the social problems in his isolated hometown under the Qing regime. He was soon attracted to the Infantry Academy of Yunnan. The newly established academy "was under the direction of a modern education and where students were also taught modern subjects." He joined the Tongmenghui in November 1909.[12]

In August 1911, Zhu graduated and served in the New Army as a squad leader in the Left Company, Second Battalion, Seventy-fourth Regiment, Thirty-seventh Brigade, Nineteenth Division.[13] When the 1911 Revolution took place in October, Zhu obtained the rank of second lieutenant, then captain in December, and major in 1912.[14] After the 1911 Revolution, he served as a company, battalion, regiment, and brigade commander in the warlord army of Yunnan.[15] He studied *The Art of War* so thoroughly that he could recite the entire book, and he used it in strategic decision making and battle planning during the Warlord Period. In 1916–22, Zhu was "a brilliant military tactician who was known as the Chinese Napoleon."[16] But soon he became a victim of warlord politics and military plots, which forced him to resign from his post and leave Yunnan.

Since his military career was over in warlord China, in September 1922, Zhu De went to Europe for further military study and joined the CCP in Berlin in November. He was arrested twice in 1925 in Germany for participating in pubic rallies sponsored by the German Communist Party. The German police did not return his passport after he was released from jail; thus he had to leave Germany for China by way of the Soviet Union. While in Moscow, Zhu enrolled in a short training program for international Communist leaders. From July 1925 to May 1926, he studied Soviet military history, operational tactics, automatic weapons, and guerrilla warfare at the Oriental University of the Communism and Labor Movement in Moscow. On his return to China in 1926, Zhu served as metropolitan police chief of Nanchang and also opened a GMD army academy, where he joined Zhou and others and led the armed revolt of the Nationalist Army in August 1927.[17] That fall, Zhu's units lost most of their men during urban battles. The Communist military rebellions failed in the cities. In early 1928, Zhu and the remnants of the Nanchang rebellion troops fled to the countryside. He then joined Mao in the mountains.

After the Nanchang Uprising in August 1927, Mao led the peasants' Autumn Harvest Uprising (Qiushou qiyi) in Hunan and Jiangxi. According to the Central Committee's plan, Mao was appointed as the secretary of the South Hunan Special Committee.[18] At the provincial party committee meeting, however, Mao insisted on postponing the rebellion because the Central Committee's plan did not rely on regular troops, a necessity for success. Mao argued that the peasants had no interest in such a large-scale rebellion unless the party was willing to center the movement in their areas, where a victory would benefit them.[19] The provincial committee agreed with Mao and changed the plan. They moved the armed workers, CCP-controlled troops, and security units from the cities to the countryside to support the peasants' rebellion. In accordance with the new strategy, the focus of the Communist military efforts shifted from urban uprisings to rural rebellion in Hunan and Jiangxi. Mao seemed more concerned about the peasants' mobilization and benefits for his region, south Hunan, than about the revolutionary movement in the provincial capital and other cities.[20]

In late August, Mao organized the First Division of the Chinese Revolutionary Army of Workers and Peasants (Zhongguo gongnong hongjun) with three regiments and five thousand men. Following the Central Committee's orders, on September 11, the division launched the Autumn Harvest Uprising along the Hunan-Jiangxi border. Soon the GMD and local self-defense troops organized by the landlords, who were the target of the peasants' rebellion, counterattacked. On September 29, the badly damaged First Division reorganized into a single regiment with one thousand men at Sanwan, Jiangxi.[21] The CCP then experienced a leadership crisis, and most of its instructions led to disaster. With weak leadership, local CCP leaders in many cases made their own decisions during this difficult period.

Next came a crucial as well as controversial moment in the history of CCP military revolution. Party historians in China have always described Mao as a military genius who planned to establish a military base in a remote, mountainous area to save the Chinese Revolutionary Army of Workers and Peasants after the Autumn Harvest Uprising. After the initial failure, however, the command and Mao led the regiment southward to join Zhu De's and He Long's troops in Guangdong. In early October, when Mao's troops reached the Jinggang Mountains, the bad news arrived that Zhu had fled Guangdong. The command panicked because all the CCP revolts had failed. The leading commanders abandoned their troops, and some men followed.

Mao led the remnants, about eight hundred men, into the Luoxiao (Lohsiao) Mountains. As Mao said, "We have traversed the whole range, and a comparison of its different sections shows that the middle section, with Ningkang as its centre, is the most suitable for our armed independent regime."[22] He joined the bandits in the mountains, meeting their leaders and giving them one hundred rifles on October 6 and another seventy on October 27. Mao became sworn brothers with two bandit leaders by drinking blood wine and marrying one of their sisters. He was soon known as shandawang. Mao said later that he was "bishang liangshan" (forced to go up to the mountain).[23] At that point, many CCP leaders did not believe Mao could survive, since there were no resources to support the troops and no people interested in the revolution in the mountains. Some considered Mao's move "up to the mountain" as defecting from the CCP and becoming one of the bandits. In November 1927, the Central Committee terminated Mao's alternate Standing Committee membership in the Politburo at an emergency meeting chaired by the Soviet advisors in Shanghai.[24]

Mao, however, survived and established a military base for the Communist revolution of 1928–34. Under Mao's command, the surviving Chinese Revolutionary Army of Workers and Peasants regiment established the Jinggangshan base along the Jiangxi-Hunan border. Zhu and his troops joined Mao in the mountains on April 24, 1928. On May 4, they established the Fourth Army, about five thousand men organized into six regiments, for which they had but two thousand rifles. Zhu was the commander and Mao the political commissar. Soon other Communist troops joined them at Jinggangshan, which became the cradle of the CCP's military revolution.[25]

Zhu De, commander of the Fourth Army. (Reproduced by permission of the People's Press, Beijing, China.)

The Fourth Army recognized the peasantry's importance to its revolution. To form a Communist revolutionary army, it created a voluntary system based upon the "Junshi gongzuo de zhishi" (Guideline for Military Tasks) issued by the army in April 1928. All the new recruits should be volunteers "in order to prevent any risk of professionalizing the Red Army." The army should not pay any man or officer for his service, though it would "provide [for] all needs with some pocket cash" for its men.[26] Obviously, Zhu and Mao tried to create an egalitarian society within their army, very different from the warlord and GMD armies.

To attract peasant volunteers, the Fourth Army initiated land reform in the mountainous area in 1928–30. The army usually sent an officer with a couple of men to a village to help the poor peasants by reducing their rents and taxes. In many cases, the officer took land from the rich landlords and redistributed it among the poor and landless peasants in small allotments. William Wei considers the Red Army officer "a veritable Chinese Robin Hood who robbed from the rich to give to the poor."[27] The land revolution movement became attractive to the peasants in this mountainous area, one of the poorest areas in the country. The officer also helped the peasants organize a peasant association, a new government, and a self-defense militia with some weapons and basic training to protect their new land. Then the officer moved on to another village. When all the villages in one area completed their land revolutions, the army took over that area and established a Soviet-style government (run by a CCP committee and enforced by the Red Army). A base area, or so-called red region (*hongqu*) or Soviet region (*suqu*), was founded. The army received material and human resources from its base areas and in turn provided protection for the local Soviet-style governments to continue their land reform movement. By the summer of 1930, the Communist governments and the Fourth Army had secured their base areas in Jiangxi-Hunan, including nine counties with a total population of two million.

During this formative period, Mao and Zhu also laid some groundwork for the Communist army. They set up three tasks for the Fourth Army: fighting, raising money for the revolutionary cause (later changed to production), and work of the masses. The Three Main Rules of Discipline and the Eight Points for Attention were formulated for the peasant army at this time.[28] Social equality was regulated within the army: "Officers do not beat the men; officers and men receive equal treatment; soldiers are free to hold meetings and to speak out; trivial formalities have been done away with; and the accounts are open for all to inspect."[29] The men seemed to enjoy this social equality. One captain wrote to his wife, "I march and fight battles almost every day without money, no new cloth, and no good food. But I am happy since we are brothers sharing the same goal and same spirit."[30] Mao believed that "apart from the role played by the Party, the reason why the Red Army carried on in spite of such poor material conditions and such frequent engagements is its practice of democracy."[31]

To win battles during these formative years, Zhu and Mao developed guerrilla tactics. Prior to the Jinggangshan period, most of the commanders followed examples from the Russian Revolution and Jiang's Northern Expedition. They realized, however, that the Russian experience of city-centered operations did not work for the Chinese Communist military revolution and that they had to look for new strategies.[32] Since the Fourth Army operated in remote, mountainous areas, away from the GMD military, which occupied the major cities, a guerrilla warfare strategy worked. During the defense of the Jinggang-shan region in 1928, Zhu and Mao perfected their guerrilla tactics, which they summarized as follows: "The enemy advances, we retreat; the enemy camps, we harass; the enemy tires, we attack; the enemy retreats, we pursue."[33] In late 1927, Zhu and Mao also established a munitions factory in Lianhua County. By 1930, it had more than eight hundred workers and produced 120,000 bullets and 30,000–50,000 mortar shells monthly.[34]

Following the Jinggangshan model, other surviving units established their military bases in the rural and border regions of Hunan, Fujian, Jiangsu, and Anhui.[35] And, finally, the Central Committee accepted Mao's "up to the mountain" approach after its last urban uprising failed in Guangzhou in December 1927.[36] On May 25, 1928, the CCP Central Committee issued CC 51, "Junshi gongzhuo dagang" (Military Task Guideline), the first systematic outline for CCP military organization, institution, and operation.[37] The document instructed the army to recruit "the active and brave members" of the peasant uprisings into the regulars.[38] In this document, the Central Committee officially incorporated all the Chinese Revolutionary Army of Workers and Peasants units into the Red Army. Praising Zhu and Mao's Fourth Army's guerrilla tactics and its experience in using land reform to win over the peasants, the Central Committee ordered other armies to follow its example. Clearly, Zhu and Mao had created a military center at Jinggangshan for the Communist revolution.

The Party's Army and the Long March

During the formative period at the Jinggangshan base, Mao also established the principle of the party's absolute leadership over the army. The army had used the GMD military tradition of the *dangjun* (party army) since Sun Yat-sen and Jiang Jieshi's HMA. Nonetheless, Mao now established party representation in the Red Army all the way down to the company level. (Jiang had GMD party representatives only at the army and divisional levels.) In 1929, the CCP representatives in the Red Army were renamed political commissars (*zhengwei*). In 1931, the company political commissars were renamed political instructors (*zhengzhi zhidaoyuan*). Mao pointed out, "Experience has proved that the system of Party representatives must not be abolished. The Party representative is particularly important at company level, since Party branches are organized on a company basis. He has to see that the soldiers' committee carries out political training, to guide the work of the mass movement, and to serve concurrently as the secretary of the Party branch. Facts have shown that the better the company Party representative, the sounder the company, and that the company commander can hardly play this important political role."[39] CCP membership in the Red Army increased from 24 percent in 1927 to 57 percent in 1929. In May 1929, for instance, there were 1,324 CCP members in the Fourth Army. Among these were 626 peasants, 311 workers, 192 students, and 100 merchants or small business owners.[40] The political indoctrination within the Red Army permitted the CCP to form an army different from warlord and GMD armies. Mao also emphasized the party leadership by stating that the party must control the gun, and the gun must never control the party.[41] With these military developments in the remote mountainous areas, the Communist movement survived the white terror and urban disasters of 1927 and made a turnaround in the countryside in 1928.

In June and July 1928, with the help of the Soviet Union, the Sixth CCP National Congress was held in Moscow. There were 142 representatives in attendance at the meeting, representing one hundred thirty thousand CCP members in China. Moscow began to change its negative position toward Mao's rural guerrilla warfare, although Stalin still considered it a supplementary method to the urban-centered revolution in China. Xiang Zhongfa (Hsiang Chung-fa) was elected chairman of the Politburo of the Central Committee, and Zhou Enlai was elected as one of its seven members. Even though he was absent from the meeting, Mao was also elected a member of the CCP Central Committee. Among the meeting resolutions was the Resolution on the Peasant Question, which requested that the party form a united front with as many of the peasantry as possible. Tony Saich points out that the party "was already becoming a predominantly peasant party. A breakdown of the party membership of 130,194 presented to the Congress showed that 76.6 percent were peasant, and only 10.9 percent workers." But the peasantry was "severely underrepresented among the eighty-four official delegates to the Congress. Workers accounted for 51 percent, intellectuals for 45 percent, and peasants for only 7 percent."[42]

The party congressional resolution also emphasized the importance of guerrilla warfare conducted by the peasantry.[43] The shift in policy direction at the sixth congress resulted in a steady growth of the Red Army and the Soviet areas. From 1928 to 1930, the Red Army engaged in many battles against the GMD and warlord armies and successfully defended its military bases, forming ten armies, about seventy thousand men, plus thirty thousand in local self-defense militias. Moscow increased its annual aid to the Jiangxi Central Soviet Region to 600,000 yuan (approximately $120,000). The weaponry and tactics improved.[44] The Red Army experienced a new period of rural-centered development in more than twenty base regions across the country.

In May 1930, the Central Committee secretly held a national representative meeting of the Red Army at which it renamed the Red Army the Chinese Red Army of Workers and Peasants. The Shanghai meeting was a turning point in the Red Army's development, transforming scattered guerrilla operations into a more organized, central operation.[45] All the regular and guerrilla troops were reorganized into one system that contained three basic levels: The first was village self-defense teams, which consisted of peasant militias and served during attacks. They usually received little training and few weapons and served primarily in the defense of their native villages. This structure mobilized peasants and village support for the Red Army at the grassroots level. The second level was local Red Army units, full-time regulars under district command. They operated and received their supplies locally. The third was the main strength of the Red Army under the command of the Central Military Commission (Zhongyang junwei) of the Central Committee.[46] The CMC issued "Zhongguo gongnong hongjun bianzhi cao'an" (The Formation of the Chinese Red Army of the Workers and Peasants) that summer, reorganizing its main strength into army corps, which were later changed to front armies, by three-three formation. It had three front armies, the First, Second, and Fourth, in the 1930s. Each front army group had three armies, each army had three divisions, each division had three regiments, and so forth.

After May 1930, Stalin began to praise Mao's rural guerrilla warfare during his conversations with Chinese visitors in Moscow. Soviet support brought Mao back to the party center in the fall of 1930, when he resumed his alternate Standing Committee membership in the Politburo. On November 11, 1931, a Soviet-style central government was established in the Jiangxi region, or the Central Soviet Region (Zhongyang suqu), which had several million people and several dozen counties. Having been elected chairman of the Executive Committee of the Chinese Soviet Republic, Mao created a government center for Chinese Communist authority across the country—the first in CCP history. In 1932, the party center moved from Shanghai to the Central Soviet Region with its Central Committee, party administration, and Russian advisors. Apparently, Mao's military success had made him central to the Chinese Communist revolution.

In his provisional central government of the Chinese Soviet Republic (Zhonghua suweiai gongheguo linshi zhongyang zhengfu), Mao formed the Central Revolutionary Military Committee as the high command of the Red Army.[47] It contained staff and political affairs departments. By the end of 1931, the Red Army totaled 150,000 members and had expanded its areas of operation. About 25 percent of the rank and file were CCP members. More than 4,000 young rural women joined the Red Army during this period, serving in a wide range of combat and noncombat military roles.[48] In May 1933, the staff department was changed to the general headquarters of the Red Army, including six bureaus: operations, intelligence, communication, training, recruitment, and organization.[49] By January 1934, the Red Army had thirty-two munitions factories manufacturing rifles, hand grenades, machine guns, and mortars in the Central Soviet Region. The Guantian Ordnance Factory alone employed more than one thousand workers.[50]

The rapid growth of the Communist troops and expansion of their controlled regions alarmed the Nationalist government. Jiang and the high command of the Nationalist Army centralized their provincial campaigns into a coordinated suppression to round up the Red Army. From 1930 to 1934, Jiang's central government organized five major offensive campaigns against the Communist-controlled areas and the Red Army bases in the border areas of Hunan, Jiangxi, Fujian, Hubei, Jiangsu, and Shanxi.[51] Both Mao and Zhu were on the most wanted list. General Jiang Weiguo recalled that his father employed the best troops of the GMD army and ordered them to "uproot" the Red Army by separating it from its base areas.[52] Jiang Weiguo believed that President Jiang's suppression campaigns were successful. The president's German advisors approved his strategy.[53]

During four countersuppression campaigns, Red Army troops developed their operation principles, focusing on "luring the enemy deep" into their territory and using mobile warfare to annihilate enemy troops.[54] In the summer of 1933, Jiang concentrated one million GMD troops to launch his fifth suppression campaign against the Red Army. In September, five hundred thousand GMD troops attacked the central region. By January 1934, CCP power struggles had caused Mao to lose his positions in the government. He lost his military authority to the Soviet advisors, including Li De (Otto Braun), a German Communist and military expert trained in Moscow for three years and sent to China as Comintern military advisor to the CCP.[55] The temporary Central Committee, under the leadership of Wang Ming and Li De, employed an "all-out offensive" and "two fists fighting back" in its fifth countersuppression campaign.[56] The Red Army failed, and Jiang's troops marched into the central region using his blockhouse strategy. Then the Central Committee organized a positional defense by "defending every point" and "using bunkers against the enemy bunkers." The total defense failed to stop the offensives. In October, the Red Army gave up its central region campaign and retreated westward. Thereafter, the CCP and the Red Army lost contact with the Soviet Union. The Red Army in other provinces abandoned all of its bases and Soviet areas across the country, except two in northwest China. The survivors of the Red Army began the Long March toward northwest China on October 10, 1934.[57]

The Long March (Changzheng) was an attempt to save the Red Army by moving its main strength away from the GMD-controlled central region and to develop a new strategic initiative in a remote region. The First Front Army (Diyi fangmianjun or Hongyi fangmianjun), however, suffered heavy casualties during its western movement as it provided protection for the Central Committee and party administration, which traveled all the way with the army. The army shrank from eighty thousand to thirty thousand men in late 1934.[58] In January 1935, at a meeting in Zunyi, Guizhou, the Central Committee criticized Wang Ming's leftist opportunism in military command and operations. Mao emerged as one of the top CCP leaders and became a member of the Standing Committee of the Politburo at this meeting. Thereafter, the CCP departed from Moscow's total control. After the Zunyi meeting, the CCP appointed Mao, Zhou, and Wang Jiaxiang (Wang Chia-hsiang) as the Red Army high command in charge of its organization and operation. Mao's promotion prepared him to be the undisputed leader at the top of the CCP party and military structure.

The new high command broke through the GMD siege of the Jiangxi Soviet base and moved the Red Army to the northwest to receive Russian aid directly and "to resist Japanese invasion."[59] The Central Committee worked out a new strategy and set up a central base in the northwest. From January to May 1935, Mao commanded the First Front Army as it broke the GMD's encirclement and escaped the pursuing forces. In June, the First Front Army further shrank from thirty thousand to ten thousand men before meeting the Fourth Front Army (Disi fangmianjun or Hongsi fangmianjun) in Sichuan. Zhu told Zhang Guotao, commander of the Fourth Front Army, which totaled eighty thousand men, that the First had lost all its artillery pieces and machine guns during the retreats. Each man had no more than five bullets.[60] In June, Mao and Zhang reorganized the two armies by appointing the First Front Army's commanders and officers to the Fourth Front Army and transferring to the First some troops and weapons from the better-equipped Fourth.[61]

However, the top leaders held divergent views about the Red Army's future. Zhang Guotao, then commissar-general of the Red Army, believed that the Red Army had a better chance to survive in Sichuan, one of China's "rice bowls," than in Shaanxi, one of the poorest provinces. Mao, on the other hand, insisted on the northward march to Shaanxi. At a top meeting, a majority supported Mao's plan. In August, the two armies continued their northward Long March in two columns, the First Front Army taking the western route and the Fourth an eastern route. In September 1935, however, Zhang and his troops moved southward. The Red Army faced a serious political crisis. Chinese military historians have criticized Zhang's attempts to "separat[e] the party and separat[e] the army."[62] According to recently available materials, however, on September 10, 1935, it was Mao who split with Zhang. Mao led the First, Third, and Central columns, about eleven thousand men, along with the Central Committee, north without informing the other armies. Mao believed that someone was plotting against him and the Central Committee. Zhang had no choice but to move the rest of the troops, eighty thousand men, southward to return to his base in Sichuan. On October 5, Zhang held a meeting in Zhumudiao, Sichuan, at which he dismissed Mao, Zhou, Zhang Wentian (Chang Wen-t'ien), and Buo Gu (Po Ku) from the party and founded a new Central Committee under his own leadership. The CCP now had two Central Committees. Some troops of the Fourth Front Army followed the First and continued their northward march. In 1936, Zhang agreed to give up his Central Committee.[63]

The First and Fourth front armies finished the rest of their journey and finally arrived in northern Shaanxi in October 1935. Over the course of those thirteen months, they had traveled through eleven provinces and covered about 8,000 miles, crossing perpetually snow-capped mountains and trackless grasslands, sustaining many hardships, and engaging in more than five hundred battles with the National-

The Long March, 1934–35

ist Army and local warlords' armies. Some soldiers had deserted their posts. Ma Zhaoxiang and Li Zhen were among the young soldiers who made it through.

Born to a poor peasant family in 1918, Ma Zhaoxiang joined the Red Army at Jinggangshan, Jiangxi, in 1934, when he was only sixteen. His village had a poor harvest that fall, and many young peasants left home in October to find seasonal labor in surrounding towns. Following two of his older brothers, Ma left his parents. Before they reached a town, however, they were recruited by GMD troops. Not only could a GMD soldier make more money than a day laborer, but the officer offered them free housing, hot meals, and uniforms. The officer also told the new recruits that they could keep the goods captured from the red regions during their campaign. After three weeks of training, their company was sent to the front. During Ma's first battle, his company collapsed. He and his brothers were captured by the Red Army. Most of the prisoners then joined the Red Army, since the CCP officers promised them that the Red Army was going to take over their hometown and then the country. Ma still remembered what the officer said: "From now on, you are fighting for yourself, for your own family, and for the poor peasants. Your parents and your village will be so proud of you."[64]

The Red Army, however, never made it to Ma's hometown. Instead, it retreated from Jiangxi in 1934. In November, Ma began the Long March. Although he was young, he served in the security troops for the First Front Army's commanding officers. His unit did not engage in formal battles and always had food. His two brothers, who served in the combat teams, lost their lives. When he was asked why he stayed in the Red Army through the Long March, Ma's answer was simple: "Nowhere to go." The GMD had a tough policy against not only the Red Army soldiers but also their families. Ma explained, "My family could have got killed if I had returned home." Ma made it through the Long March, joined the CCP, and got to know some important leaders, like Hu Yaobang, who would later become the party chairman.[65] Ma himself would later become the vice minister of China's Education Ministry. Most Long March soldiers and officers (Changzheng ganbu), having become the most valuable and trusted men in the Chinese revolution, later served in high-ranking positions in the army, party, and government. (Ma named his son Changzheng in honor of his survival of the Long March.[66])

Of the 3,000 women who participated in the Long March, only 149 survived. About 2,500 young women from rural Sichuan served in the Fourth Front Army under the command of Zhang Guotao, in such units as the Women's Independence Brigade, which was a logistics unit, and the Women's Engineer Battalion, which carried the hard currency of the Red Army. Thirty-two of the women soldiers in the First Front Army who survived the Long March were wives of the key leaders of the Red Army.[67] Twenty women served in the Second and Sixth Red Army corps, and Li Zhen was one of them. A native of Liuyang, Hunan, Li was born in 1908 into a poor peasant family with five other daughters. At six, she was taken as a child bride into another family, where she endured resentment and insults. In 1926, when the peasant uprisings became widespread in Liuyang, she rushed out of her home, had her plait cut, and joined the women's association. She became a CCP member in 1927. After the failure of the revolution, Li and her comrades hid themselves deep in the mountains until the Autumn Harvest Uprising. She joined the Red Army in 1928 and served as director of the political department of the Sixth Army and deputy chief of the organizational department of the Second Army Corps. She married a Red Army officer before the Long March began.[68]

Li Zhen, the first woman general. (Reproduced by permission of the People's Press, Beijing, China.)

During the Long March, Li and her husband climbed over snowy mountains, walked across wild grasslands, and finally reached north Shaanxi. Li recalled that many female soldiers and officers died of starvation and disease. Malaria frequently claimed women's lives when they delivered their babies. Li lost her young son during the Long March. She said that her life was given to her by her comrades. "After you see so many comrades die, you don't want to give up your own life easily. You feel like they're living in you. You want to go on."[69] After the Long March, Li served in the Second Sino-Japanese War, the Chinese civil war, and the Korean War. She was promoted to lieutenant general in 1955, becoming the first female general in the PLA's history.[70] The Long March experience in 1934–35 served her well through her military career.

On October 19, 1935, Mao, the CCP Central Committee, and the First Front Army arrived at Wuqizhen, a CCP-controlled area in the Shaanxi-Gansu (Shaan-Gan) region. In November, Mao combined the First Front Army with the Fifteenth Front Army, formerly the Shaan-Gan Red Army, with Peng Dehuai as the commander and Mao himself as its political commissar.[71] In November, the Red Army defeated a GMD offensive and consolidated a new base along the Shaan-Gan border. Then it launched an eastern expedition, expanding its northwestern base and increasing troop strength to nearly ten thousand men.[72] In July 1936, Moscow located the CCP Central Committee in Shaanxi and resumed telegraph communication with the committee, which it had lost in October 1934. In late August, Mao sent telegrams to Moscow formally requesting military and economic aid.[73]

In November 1935, the Red Army's Second and Sixth front armies followed the First Front Army's trail and began their northward Long March. Along the way, they merged into the Second Front Army, with He Long as its commander and Ren Mishi as its political commissar. Zhang and the Fourth Front Army joined the Second Front Army on the Long March. On October 10, 1936, the Second and Fourth front armies met the First Front Army in Huining, Gansu, and completed the strategic movement of the Red Army from the southeast to the northwest.[74] They made up the main strength of the Chinese Communist armed forces, totaling sixty thousand troops. Other units left behind in the south and southeast continued their guerrilla warfare throughout 1937 for their own survival. Maurice Meisner comments that the Long March was "the prelude to what proved to be the victorious period of the Chinese Communist Revolution, and in that sense it was an event filled with momentous political and psychological implications. Politically, it was the time when Mao Tse-tung achieved effective control of the Chinese Communist Party, a position of influence and authority."[75]

After the Long March, Mao saw an opportunity to solve the problems between his and Zhang's troops. In late October 1936, the Comintern requested that the Chinese Red Army open up a western route from Yan'an to the Chinese-Russian border through Xinjiang to receive Soviet aid. In response to Mao's requests, Stalin promised one thousand tons of Soviet military aid.[76] On October 25, Mao ordered Zhang and his thirty-five thousand men to cross the Yellow (Huang) River and establish a new base west of the river. During their crossing, the GMD army cut off Zhang's forces in the middle. Even though nearly twenty-two thousand men had crossed the river, they faced strong defenses in the west.[77] By early 1937, the GMD army had eliminated all the western expedition armies in the western deserts, with the exception of 494 troops under the command of Wang Shusheng, Li De, and Li Xiannian, who fled more than 1,800 miles west and reached Xinjiang to meet the Soviet representatives. The one thousand tons of Soviet aid never crossed the Chinese-Russian border, but Moscow wired the CCP Central Committee $150,000 through a U.S. bank in November and another $50,000 in December. In January 1937, Stalin provided another Soviet financial aid package worth $800,000.[78]

Mao blamed the western expedition's failure on Zhang's rightist opportunism.[79] Zhang was criticized inside the party for defeatist speculation about the revolution, making many mistakes, and committing "grave crimes." In April 1938, he left the Shaan-Gan region, traveled to Xi'an, and then joined the GMD in Wuhan. He was subsequently expelled from the CCP, later left China, and died in Canada in 1979.[80]

The Second Sino-Japanese War

The CCP-GMD war in south China in 1931–34 had a negative impact on China's security and sovereignty. On September 18, 1931, the Japanese Kwantung Army in northeast China seized Shenyang. The incident was the beginning of Japan's aggression in four provinces in

northeast China. In the mid-1930s, Japan showed its intention of pen-
etrating south of the Great Wall and invading central and east China,
which posed a direct menace to Jiang Jieshi's rule. The national government that Jiang and the GMD had established at Nanjing in 1928
was faced with three problems of overpowering magnitude in the early
1930s. First, Jiang had actually brought only five provinces under his
control; the remainder were still governed by local warlords. Second,
Jiang was confronted with an internal Communist rebellion and the
Red Army, at first in the central provinces and later, after their Long
March, in the remote northwestern region. Mao had set up a Soviet-
style government in Yan'an, Shaanxi. Third, Jiang's government was
faced with Japanese aggression. In dealing with these problems, Jiang
gave priority to the suppression of the Communist rebellion. In December 1936, he made a trip to Xi'an to visit the GMD forces that
formed the front line of his anti-Communist campaign.

In Xi'an, however, the Northeastern Army, commanded by Gener-
al Zhang Xueliang (Chang Hsüeh-liang), and the Seventeenth Route
Army, commanded by General Yang Hucheng, had agreed to the anti-
Japanese united front proposed by the CCP before Jiang's visit. When
Jiang arrived on December 4, they demanded that Jiang unite with the
CCP to resist Japan. Jiang refused and became still more active in his
suppression of the CCP. On December 12, Zhang and Yang ordered
their troops to arrest Jiang at Xi'an. Mao wanted to eliminate Jiang, but
Moscow opposed it, insisting that the CCP and GMD form a united
front.[81] After several days, Jiang was forced to accept the terms of unity
with the CCP and resistance against Japan. On December 25, he was
released. These events are known as the Xi'an incident (Xi'an shibian).
Two days later, on his way back to Nanjing, Jiang issued a public statement at Luoyang, Henan, promising to form a united front with the
CCP.

On July 7, 1937, the Japanese Imperial Army attacked the GMD
troops at the Marco Polo Bridge (Lugouqiao), southwest of Beijing.
This event, known as the Marco Polo Bridge incident or Lugouqiao
incident, marked the beginning of the Second Sino-Japanese War. On
August 13, Japanese troops attacked Shanghai and threatened Nanjing.
The GMD government came to an agreement with the CCP on joint
resistance.

As part of this agreement, the main force of the Red Army, then located in the northwest and numbering forty-six thousand men, became the Eighth Route Army (Balujun) of the Nationalist Army in August 1937, with Zhu as commander, Peng Dehuai as deputy commander, and Ye Jianying as chief of staff. Commanding three divisions—the 115th, 120th, and 129th—they followed the Yellow River eastward until they reached north China. Most of their units moved into the mountainous areas. As Mao had in the Jinggang Mountains, they conducted a guerrilla campaign in the mountains behind the Japanese lines. In the south, the Red Army guerrilla troops were reorganized into the New Fourth Army (Xinsijun) of the Nationalist Army, commanded by Ye Ting and totaling 10,300 men, including four field columns (divisions). Each field column had two to four regiments.[82]

In order to command its own troops, in August 1937, the CCP Central Committee established a Central Military Commission (CMC), which included general staff, general political tasks, logistics, and medic departments. The General Staff Department had operation, intelligence, and communication bureaus to command the seven divisions of the Eighth Route and New Fourth armies. In September 1937, the 115th Division of the Eighth Route Army killed three thousand Japanese troops at Pingxingguan, Shanxi, in the first CCP victory.[83] In September, the GMD publicly declared its cooperation with the CCP and recognized the legal status of the CCP, formally bringing into existence the anti-Japanese united front.[84] Moscow firmly supported the CCP-GMD coalition throughout the war. Although Stalin continued to send financial aid to the CCP, he began to support Jiang's Nationalist Army as well. Mao often complained about how little he received compared with the hundreds of millions of dollars Jiang had received from Moscow.

Since August 1937, the Japanese had occupied Beijing and Tianjin. In November, Japan concentrated 220,000 troops and began an offensive campaign against Nanjing and Shanghai. Jiang and the GMD high command deployed nearly 700,000 troops to defend the Nanjing-Shanghai region. On November 7, the Japanese Tenth Army successfully landed at Hangzhou Bay. In December, it seized Nanjing. After the Japanese troops entered the capital city, they killed 90,000 prisoners of war (POWs) and 260,000 civilians.[85] By March 1938, almost all of north China had fallen into the enemy's hands. In October, Guangzhou and Wuhan also fell. The GMD government was forced to move its capital from Nanjing to Chongqing, Sichuan. Jiang's troops were suffering heavy casualties. From July 1937 to November 1938, Jiang lost 1 million GMD troops while eliminating 250,730 Japanese soldiers. The Nationalist Army withdrew to China's southwest and northwest to conserve some of its troops when Jiang moved the seat of his government to Chongqing.[86] By 1941, the GMD had lost the coastal and other port cities that once had been its bases of power.[87]

After Jiang lost some of his best troops, Mao's successful guerrillas recruited a large number of peasants into his forces. The units of the Eighth Route Army marched to the enemy-occupied territories, where they carried out guerrilla operations and established military and political bases.[88] The Eighth Route Army increased from 46,000 men in 1937 to 220,000 men in 1939 and 500,000 men in 1940. It established bases in the border regions of Shanxi, Chahar, and Hebei; of Shanxi, Hebei, Shandong, and Henan; and of Shanxi and Suiyuan, as well as in the central section of Shandong. In south China, the New Fourth Army established bases in southern Jiangsu and north of the Yangtze River. Farther to the south, the Dongjiang and Qiongya bases were established in Guangdong and Hainan. At each of the bases, the CCP established a government, reduced the peasants' rents and interest, returned land to poor peasants, and armed the masses. In February 1940, the CMC ordered both the Eighth Route and New Fourth armies to recruit 300,000 more soldiers within that year. In November 1941, just before Japan's surprise attack on Pearl Harbor, the CMC issued "Guanyu kangri zhanzheng genjudi junshi jianshe de shishi" (Instructions on Military Buildup in the Base Areas), urging all the Communist troops to mobilize masses and enlist more new recruits.[89] The troops sent recruiting officers and "propaganda teams" to rural areas.

Jiang Shangqing, father of Jiang Zemin, the future PRC president and CCP chairman, was one of the team members in Jiangsu. Born in 1910, Jiang Shangqing joined the CYL in 1927 and the CCP in 1929. He married Wang Zhelan, who gave birth to Jiang Zemin in August 1926. During WWII, Jiang Shangqing left his teaching position and, with his wife, participated in a CCP culture and propaganda team in Liuan, Jiangsu. The team was divided into three groups, each with a few dozen members. They sang patriotic songs in the streets, performed heroic plays and operas in schools and theaters, and traveled to villages to explain CCP policy to peasants. Jiang Shufeng, Shangqing's younger brother, recalled in interviews that they also visited local troops and published anti-Japanese newsletters and weekly journals. During these years, many peasants as well as urban residents joined the CCP troops. In Jiangsu, the CCP troops numbered 90,000 in 1940 and increased to 270,000 in 1945. On July 29, 1940, Jiang Shangqing and one of his teammates were killed by a landlord's armed guards on their way to a village. After Shangqing's death, Shufeng helped Wang Zhelan raise Jiang Zemin.[90]

In order to establish a grassroots united front behind Japanese lines, the CCP modified its land reform policy, supporting small landlords and wealthy peasants and cooperating with Jiang's troops in guerrilla warfare, in a more nationalistic than Communistic policy. Saich argues that, "contrary to conventional wisdom, in the period after 1937 the rural elite were more readily attracted to the CCP program of resistance than was the local peasantry. Indeed, the threat posed by the Japanese forces bonded the CCP and the local elite together in an uneasy marriage of convenience."[91] In the base area of northern Shaanxi, the CCP established the government of the Shaanxi-Gansu-Ningxia border region, which became the general rear area of all the anti-Japanese bases. Yan'an, the CCP headquarters, became the command center for the Chinese Communist revolution, and it drew thousands of patriotic youths and urban intellectuals. In January 1937, the CCP reorganized the Military and Politics University of the Chinese People's Anti-Japanese War (Kangda) at Yan'an with Lin Biao as president and Liu Bocheng as vice president. Mao and other leaders visited the university frequently and gave lectures to the officer-students. By 1939, the university had ten branch campuses all over the base regions. In May 1941, the Eighth Route Army founded a military engineering academy.[92] Many young students left the Japanese-occupied cities and moved into the CCP-controlled base areas.

Wan Qing was one of the college students who joined the CCP armed forces during the Second Sino-Japanese War. Born in 1924 in Fengxin County, Jiangxi, Wan Qing majored in foreign language in college. As a freshman, he became an activist in the student anti–Japanese aggression movement and joined the CCP in 1942. He left college in 1943 and joined the CCP's New Fourth Army. With his Russian language training, he served as a translator at the Fifth Division headquarters of the New Fourth Army. Wan recalled that many college students joined the CCP rather than the GMD because the CCP developed its underground network in schools in Japanese-occupied cities. The CCP's underground mobilization and recruitment made it possible for many interested students to participate in the ongoing war against Japan.[93] Some artists, writers, and actors also joined the CCP movement through its underground network. Mao's wife, Jiang Qing, was one of the actors who traveled all the way from Shanghai to Yan'an during the war.[94]

In May 1938, Mao wrote a treatise titled "Lun chijiuzhan" (On Protracted War), which analyzed the basic characteristics of both sides of the Second Sino-Japanese War.[95] He pointed out that China could not win a quick victory but would surely be victorious after a long period of struggle. He stressed that China's resistance would pass through the three stages of protracted war: strategic defense, strategic stalemate, and strategic counteroffensive. He emphasized the paramount importance of a people's war. He said that "the army and the people are the foundation of victory" and "the richest source of power to wage war lies in the masses of the people."[96] Mao instructed the high command to organize extensive peasant militias through the network of the CCP, now a mass party. Party control and political education were also emphasized in mobilizing the peasants. Transforming illiterate peasants into capable soldiers became part of the Chinese military tradition. Indeed, military tradition is one of the areas where Chinese creativity was most evident in the twentieth century. Nonetheless, Mao still highly praised *The Art of War* and asserted that it contained scientific truths. He cited Sun Zi in his military writing: "Know the enemy and know yourself, and you can fight a hundred battles with no danger of defeat."[97]

In 1941–42, the Japanese command concentrated 64 percent of its troops in China to launch "mopping-up" operations against the CCP bases behind its line. Its policy was known as the three alls: kill all, burn all, and loot all. The Japanese wanted to stop the guerrillas in their rear area of operations by eliminating their human and economic resources. To overcome the shortage of food and supplies, Chinese officers and soldiers devoted themselves to increased production. Many of them—even leaders such as Mao, Zhou, and Zhu—participated in the opening up of wilderness areas for crop cultivation, the raising of hogs, and the making of cloth. After much hard work, many army units and offices attained total or partial self-sufficiency. The bases'

Mao Zedong at Yan'an.
(Courtesy of Xinhua News
Agency, Beijing, China.)

most difficult logistical problems were resolved by 1943, after which these areas continued to expand.[98] Mao observed, "Today we can say with confidence that in the struggles of the past seventeen years the Chinese Communist Party has forged not only a firm Marxist political line but also a firm Marxist military line. We have been able to apply Marxism in solving not only political but also military problems; we have trained not only a large core of cadres capable of running the Party and the state, but also a large core of cadres capable of running the army."[99]

In the wake of the Allied Forces' campaign against fascism and militarism across the globe, Jiang and his GMD government undertook "unprecedented activism" in international diplomacy with the Allied Forces. The new vigor of nationalism revealed a profound change taking place in China. External factors seemed to be behind this change, as Liu Xiaoyuan states, partly from "China's own tenacious resistance against Japan and partly from Washington's promotion."[100] But internal factors also played a role: Chinese warlords saw clearly the need for a fully centralized government to protect their local interests, and Jiang was willing to establish a united front that included all political parties. What Jiang and his government attempted in Cairo and Moscow was to improve the GMD government's international status to strengthen the Nationalist leadership at home. Having internationalized its status through its participation in WWII and formed an alliance with the United States against Japan, the GMD might have been able to nationalize China by the end of the war. Compared with U.S. foreign policy, the GMD's wartime diplomacy had a much narrower agenda, which "indicated both the pragmatism of Chongqing's diplomacy and its tenacious pursuit to regain China's regional influence."[101]

In the meantime, in 1944, the liberated areas under the CCP's control launched partial counteroffensives and won important victories against Japan. By the spring of 1945, the nation had nineteen liberated areas with a total population of 95 million.[102] The Seventh CCP National Congress convened in Yan'an on April 23, 1945, to prepare both for a final victory over Japan and for the decisive victory of the Chinese revolution. Attending the congress were 752 delegates and alternates representing 1.21 million party members across the country. The congress adopted an integral program to "boldly mobilize the masses, defeat the Japanese aggressors, and build a new China."[103] After the congress, the army continued to intensify the counteroffensive until it recovered large territories. By the fall of 1945, the CCP's regular army had grown to 1.27 million men, supported by militias numbering another 2.68 million.[104] The Eighth Route Army increased from three divisions in August 1937 to more than forty divisions in August 1945; the New Fourth Army increased from four divisions in 1937 to seven divisions in 1945.[105] On August 8, the Soviet Union declared war on Japan, and the Soviet Red Army attacked the Japanese in China's northeastern provinces. On August 14, Japan surrendered unconditionally; on September 2, it signed the instrument of surrender. The Chinese people, after eight years of bitter struggle, had finally won the Second Sino-Japanese War. The price in Chinese lives for resisting Japanese aggression was very high. The total number of deaths among the GMD forces was 2.4 million; among the Communist forces, 600,000. The civilian death toll was estimated at more than 10 million.[106]

Transforming the Army to Defeat Jiang

After Japan suddenly surrendered in August 1945, President Jiang Jieshi found himself far away from the country's economic and population centers and facing an unprecedented challenge from Mao. The GMD telegraphed the CCP that it was willing to negotiate to settle their differences and pursue domestic peace after WWII. At the same time, however, it prepared for a possible conflict with the CCP's armed forces. The GMD had a total of 4.3 million troops, including 2 million regulars.[107] Its forces were better equipped than the CCP forces, since they had received most of the weapons and equipment from the surrendering Japanese troops in China and continued to receive U.S. military aid. The GMD forces controlled three-quarters of the country, with three-quarters of the population, more than 300 million people. They occupied all of the large cities and controlled most of the railroads, highways, seaports, and transportation hubs.[108]

In August 1945, Jiang invited Mao to peace talks in Chongqing. Mao accepted the invitation and headed a delegation that included Zhou and Wang Ruofei. On August 28, U.S. ambassador Patrick Hurley personally escorted Mao from Yan'an to Chongqing for the negotiations. (In 1944, to prevent a collapse of the CCP-GMD coalition, Hurley had visited Yan'an, Mao's wartime capital, to propose a joint postwar government in China.[109]) The Chongqing talks lasted forty-three days, but agreement was never reached on the basic issues of the national government and army. Nevertheless, on October 10, both sides signed a document that recognized that "civil war must be avoided at all costs, and an independent, free, prosperous, and strong new China be created."[110] However, since the sides had different political agendas, the negotiations failed, and the two parties resumed their military conflicts in north China.

When the Chongqing agreement was publicized, hundreds of thousands of CCP troops moved from central to northeast China. From September to November 1946, GMD troops moved northward along the four major railroad lines—the Jin-pu, Ping-han, Tong-pu, and Ping-sui lines—and tried to advance into the CCP's liberated regions. They faced strong resistance in Shandong, Shanxi, and Hebei. The CCP adopted a policy of "giving them tit for tat and fighting for every inch of land."[111] After Hurley resigned in November, U.S. president

Harry Truman dispatched General George Marshall, former army chief of staff, as his envoy to China for further mediation. Both parties agreed to a brief cease-fire negotiated by Marshall on January 10, 1946. Though Jiang and Mao signed the cease-fire agreement, they made no political compromise and refused to cooperate with each other. Mao believed that America had intervened in the Chinese civil war on the anti-Communist side by providing Jiang with military equipment and financial aid. Full-scale civil war broke out in the summer of 1946, and Marshall announced the failure of his mission in January 1947. During this short "period of great uncertainty," involving many domestic problems, the CCP expanded its strength and influence in China.[112]

In August 1945, the CMC issued its decision on troop formations, dividing its troops into field and local units. That fall, to be prepared for a civil war, the CCP began to reorganize all of its troops, including the Eighth Route and New Fourth armies. It organized its best fighting troops into twenty-seven field columns (armies) and six field brigades as strategic forces, totaling about 610,000 men.[113] The reorganization of the Eighth Route Army and the New Fourth Army significantly changed the PLA's structure, transforming it from a guerrilla force to an army capable of large-scale mobile operations. The field armies as strategic units were directly under the CMC, the high command. Each field column had three divisions, and each division, no more than 7,000 men, had three regiments. The rest of the troops were reorganized into local units under the command of military districts.[114] The CCP militias, formerly self-defense units, which served at the village level, also played an important role throughout the civil war. The field armies supplied the local troops with surplus captured weapons and trained them based on their recent combat experience. The local troops provided the field divisions with needed replenishments and received new recruits from the village militias. Local units sent many noncommissioned officers to combat units for training to improve their combat effectiveness.[115]

To win the civil war, the CCP Central Committee in August 1945 ordered the Communist forces "to recruit several hundred thousand soldiers within the next three months."[116] The Chinese Communist and Nationalist armed forces began a full-scale war for supremacy in 1946. The focus of their struggle was in the northeast, where China's heavy industry, coal, oil, and chemistry sources lay, established by the

Japanese in 1931–45. Japan's surrender, along with the Soviet Red Army's withdrawal, created a power vacuum in that strategic region and invited GMD-CCP competition over its cities, industrial and commercial centers, and key points of transportation. Jiang sent a large number of his best troops to the northeast in early 1946.[117]

Chinese military historians divide the civil war into three phases. The first phase began on June 26, 1946, when Jiang launched an all-out offensive campaign against Mao's liberated regions (*jiefangqu*) with a major attack in central China and other offensive campaigns from south to north. He believed that, if he could squeeze the CCP forces out of their bases in three to six months, he could win the war. With U.S. aid and support, Jiang had superiority in both manpower and weaponry. The PLA totaled 1.68 million troops by the beginning of 1947.[118] But it was in fact an army equipped with "millet plus rifles." It controlled the countryside, with a population of about 100 million, while the GMD held the cities, with a larger proportion of the population.

The PLA's initial strategy was to maintain and concentrate a superior force to destroy the GMD's effective strength. Holding or seizing cities and other places was not its main objective. Then, in 1946, it adopted a new strategy: "offense in the north; defense in the south."[119] In 1947, the Central Committee transferred 110,000 troops with 20,000 party cadres to the northeast, for the first time in its history, to transform its military from regional to national. The northeast thereafter became its strategic base, a move that secured communication and transportation between the Soviet Union and the CCP. Soon after, the PLA offensive campaign started in the north and swept into the south. Throughout 1946, the PLA maintained most of its troops and stayed in its liberated areas during Jiang's all-out offensive campaign. The PLA and CCP managed to maintain their control of one-quarter of the country. Odd Arne Westad points out that the CCP's mobilization of the Chinese masses was achieved by its manipulation of local politics. Moreover, the party cadres were able to make their own decisions and practice their skills without "undue interference."[120]

Politically, the CCP strove to form a united front among all the people to oppose both U.S. imperialism and Jiang. Spiraling inflation, government corruption, and factional struggles within the GMD made elimination of the Communist forces impossible. Exploiting wide-

spread complaints and desires for peace after WWII, the CCP organized a second front against Jiang in major cities through student-led
antigovernment and antiwar movements to isolate the GMD politically. In 1947, students in more than sixty cities demonstrated in favor of
the patriotic and democratic movement and against hunger, civil war,
and persecution. In twenty-nine cities, including Shanghai and Tianjin, 3.2 million workers staged strikes and demonstrations. Jiang's all-
out offensive campaigns did not reach his goal. As Westad concludes,
the CCP's progressive reform movements, skillful propaganda, and
promise of a "new China" responded to a wide range of the complaints
against Jiang's government. Thus Mao mobilized the Chinese masses,
especially the peasants, by exploiting Jiang's weaknesses and mistakes
and expanding his revolution across the country.[121]

The peasant movement spread to seventeen provinces, and 1 million peasants participated in armed uprisings against the GMD government. In May 1946, the CCP stated that the policy of rent and interest
reduction, which had been carried out during WWII, would change to
a policy of confiscating land from the landlord class and redistributing
it among the peasants. In September 1947, the outline of the agrarian
reform was made public. It would replace the old land rental system
with one that incorporated the concept of "land to the tillers."[122] As a
result of the land reform, more than 96 million peasants in the liberated areas supported the PLA or joined the army themselves. From July
1946 to June 1948, the PLA enlisted 1.6 million peasants, new landowners, into their troops. The peasants' enthusiasm would bring about
the CCP's early victory in the civil war.[123]

In the war's second phase, from March 1947 to August 1948, Jiang
changed from broad assaults to attacks on key targets. Jiang concentrated his forces on two points: the CCP-controlled areas in Shandong
and those in Shaanxi, where the CCP Central Committee and its high
command had been since 1935. Jiang failed again. When the GMD
offensive slowed down, a CCP strategic offensive began. The main bat-
tlefields had by this time moved to the GMD-controlled areas. For example, Deng Xiaoping led 120,000 PLA troops across the Yellow River,
breaking through Jiang's line and bringing the GMD offensive to an
end in central China.[124] In October 1947, the PLA issued a manifesto
that called upon the people to "overthrow Jiang Jieshi and liberate all
China." It put forward this political program: "United workers, peasants,

soldiers, intellectuals and businessmen, all oppressed classes, all people's organizations, democratic parties, minority nationalities, overseas Chinese and other patriots; form a national united front; overthrow the dictatorial Chiang Kai-shek government; and establish a democratic coalition government."[125] In December, through its economic policy, the party again promised the peasants that the CCP would confiscate land from the landlords and redistribute it among the peasants. The policy received wide support from the peasants. Some Western historians attribute Mao's victories during the early years of the civil war to the CCP's popularity, political propaganda, and land reforms that gained peasants' support, but recent Chinese research highlights the importance of the CCP's efforts in its military reorganization, strategic changes, and weaponry improvements.[126]

According to the PLA's records, the number of automatic weapons and artillery pieces increased significantly during the first two phases of the civil war. It had 2,678 automatic rifles in June 1946, 7,946 in June 1947, and 58,995 in June 1948; 16,295 light machine guns in 1946, 25,078 in 1947, and 46,007 in 1948; and 476 60mm guns in 1946, 1,918 in 1947, and 3,570 in 1948. The total number of artillery pieces increased from 2,108 in June 1946 to 4,542 in June 1947 and to 9,555 in June 1948.[127] In addition, the PLA regular forces increased from 1 million men in June 1946 to 1.95 million in June 1947 and to 2.8 million in June 1948. Even though the PLA suffered 800,000 casualties between 1946 and 1948, the CCP was able to mobilize 1.1 million peasants in the liberated areas, send 450,000 wounded soldiers back to their units, and recruit 800,000 prisoners of the Nationalist Army into the PLA.[128]

The third phase of the civil war, from August 1948 to October 1949, was a PLA offensive from rural areas against GMD defenses in urban areas, including three of the most important PLA campaigns in the war: the Liao-Shen campaign (northeast China), Ping-Jin campaign (Beijing-Tianjin region), and Huai-Hai campaign (east China). The three campaigns lasted altogether 142 days, during which 1.54 million GMD troops were killed, wounded, or captured. In terms of scale—that is, the number of enemy troops destroyed—the three campaigns were unprecedented in Chinese military history. As a result of these campaigns, all of the northeast, most of the north, and the central areas north of the Yangtze River were liberated. Nearly all of Jiang Jieshi's best troops were wiped out.[129]

In November 1948, the CMC decided to reorganize its troops by changing the field column into a field army. The high command called all of the troops the Chinese People's Liberation Army. In January 1949, the CMC established four field armies: the First (Diyi yezhanjun) in northwest China, the Second (Dier yezhanjun) in central China, the Third (Disan yezhanjun) in east China, and the Fourth (Disi yezhanjun) in northeast China. Each field army had two to four army groups, and each army group had two to four armies. In the spring of 1949, the four field armies had a total of seventeen army groups, including fifty-eight infantry armies, numbering four million men.[130]

In March 1949, the CCP held the second plenary session of its Seventh Central Committee at Xibaipo, Hebei. The session determined the basic policies regarding the speedy attainment of a nationwide victory and the construction of a new China after the victory. After the meeting, the CCP Central Committee and the PLA headquarters moved to Beijing. On January 1, 1949, Jiang Jieshi asked for cease-fire talks. On January 14, Mao refused Jiang's request and made public his viewpoint on the current situation.[131] Jiang retired from the presidency on January 21, and Vice President Li Zongren (Li Tsung-jen) came to the forefront. The peace talks between the GMD and CCP began on April 1 and ended on April 20 when the sides failed to reach an agreement.[132] The PLA ordered 1 million troops to cross the Yangtze River on April 21. Two days later, Nanjing, the capital of the ROC, fell, and Jiang moved the seat of his government, along with 1 million troops and government officials, to Taiwan. The PLA pressed on in its drive into northwest, southwest, and central China. By September, it occupied most of the country, except for Tibet, Taiwan, and various offshore islands. The GMD lost 7 million troops and control of mainland China to the Communists in the civil war. The PLA suffered a total of 260,000 killed and 1.04 million wounded.[133]

Some historians in the West assert that the CCP's victory over the GMD was politically inevitable, considering the conflicts between the two parties, influences of American involvement, intellectuals' critiques, students' movements, and land reforms. Some, however, have questioned the emphasis on particular scenes or relations. Joseph W. Esherick, for example, observes that early works on the civil war and land reforms contain only partial analyses and rosy descriptions. He criticizes studies of the Chinese revolution that explain it in terms of polar structures such as "China and the West, state and society, urban-rural or class contradictions."[134] Suzanne Pepper stresses that, although the CCP's land reform succeeded in gaining support to match the GMD, people's attitudes were neither totally advantageous nor totally disadvantageous to either party during the war. Nevertheless, the CCP was a minority party and was not accused of being responsible for the war, whereas the GMD, already powerful, could not escape that blame.[135] Although it is conceivable that the draconian rule of the Japanese caused the Chinese people to turn against the Chinese state, it appears more likely that it was the failure of state-building during the GMD's control of the mainland that cost the Chinese state its legitimacy. The GMD had a chance to promote major changes short of revolution; its failure to do so accounts for the rise of Communism in mainland China. Edward L. Dreyer explains the outcome of the civil war in conventional military historical terms: "The Nationalists sent their best formations into a series of traps in Manchuria and North China, lost them, and afterwards never had a chance. Mao's revolution was a consequence, rather than a cause, of the communist victory on the mainland."[136]

Although a variety of factors could be, and indeed are, cited as vital to successful state-building, the importance of the civil-military relationship cannot be overstated. When the PRC was founded, the army, rather than the party, was the major vehicle of state expansion in rural areas, reflecting the immediate goal of liberation and security rather than rehabilitation of society and the economy. When, in 1949–50, the civil administration proved ineffectual as an instrument for nation-building and policy implementation, the country tended toward militarization of politics and administration. The central and local governments came to be largely controlled by the military, and resources were allocated according to military priorities.

On October 1, 1949, Mao declared the birth of the PRC. During their twenty-two years of military struggle on the road to power, the CCP and the PLA had acquired the experience, vision, and self-confidence to create a new Communist state in the world. Mao declared the "lean-to-one-side" policy, according to which the new republic would favor the Soviet Union and join the socialist and Communist camp in the post-WWII world. Mao visited Moscow and, in February 1950, signed the Sino-Soviet Treaty of Friendship, Alliance, and Mutual Assistance with Joseph Stalin.[137] The agreement between Beijing and Moscow was the cornerstone of the Communist international alliance system in the 1950s. China began to move to the center stage of the Cold War between the Soviet Union and the United States and their camps. The news of the Communist takeover of China swept through the United States like wildfire. Politicians, the media, and the public criticized the Truman administration for giving too little support to Jiang's government and therefore "losing" China. As David M. Finkelstein points out, even though Truman did not recognize the new Communist China, neither did he give full support to Jiang's government in Taiwan—until the PRC intervened in Korea in 1950.[138] In 1950, Secretary of State Dean Acheson published a one-thousand-page explanation of U.S. China policy in 1946–49, arguing that the situation of China's civil war was out of America's control.

★ 3 ★

Transformation
in Korea

THE FIRST GENERATION of Chinese Communist military leaders became the founders of the PRC after twenty-two years of military struggle. Having moved to center stage and gained control of the nation, they were characterized as Communist idealists and radical revolutionaries against an "old" world order, the post-WWII international system. Their alliance with the Soviet Union and North Korea pulled China into a war in Korea that changed the Chinese forces forever. China's intervention in the Korean War (1950–53) was a by-product of the Cold War between two superpowers, the Soviet Union and the United States. The combat experience the Chinese armed forces gained against United Nations and U.S. forces bolstered PLA modernization in accordance with the Russian military model.[1]

On October 25, 1950, the Chinese government announced that it would send the Chinese People's Volunteer Forces (Zhongguo renmin zhiyuanjun) to Korea "kangmei yuanchao, baojia weiguo" (to resist America, aid Korea, defend the country, and safeguard the home).[2] In fact, the CPVF troops had already crossed the Yalu River and entered North Korea on October 19. The Korean War then essentially became a conflict between China and the United States. China surprised the world when its troops launched a massive offensive south of the Yalu in early November. General Douglas MacArthur, supreme commander of the UN forces (UNF), reported to Washington that they faced "an entirely new war" in Korea.[3] Although it still confronted more than one million GMD remnants in Taiwan and southwestern China after the civil war, Beijing decided to fight the U.S. armed forces as well in a new international war, the Kangmei yuanchao zhanzheng (War to Resist America and Aid Korea). With its foot soldiers and obsolete weaponry, the CPVF seemed no match for the U.S. forces that formed 90 percent of the UNF and had vastly superior air, naval, and ground firepower.[4]

By July 27, 1953, when the Korean armistice agreement was signed, China had sent nearly 3 million men to Korea (out of 6.1 million PLA troops). Mao Zedong, CCP and CMC chairman, judged China's intervention a victory because it saved North Korea's Communist regime, prevented U.S. invasion of China, gained more Russian military and economic aid, and established the PRC's new world status.[5] Marshal Peng Dehuai, commander and political commissar of the CPVF, stated that the Korean War began the transformation of the Chinese military into a modern force.[6]

This chapter examines Beijing's decision to enter the Korean War, its mobilization and organization, and its tactical changes for the CPVF to execute new plans on the front. It focuses on Mao's decision making; Peng's major operational planning, which changed as the CPVF adjusted to changing conditions and continually reassessed its own commanding performance; and Soviet military aid, especially air power. The personal accounts of Generals Hong Xuezhi and Wang Hai show that changes in strategic thinking and tactical planning often occurred in the crucible of combat or after suffering casualties, but before a humiliating defeat. The stories of Captains Zhou Baoshan, Wang Xuedong, and Zheng Yanman detail the Chinese combat experiences of individual officers and soldiers. China's participation in the Korean War obviously began its military modernization. The lessons learned between 1950 and 1953 had an impact on subsequent development, including China's decision to make its own atomic bombs. Even if forgotten in America, the war in Korea is by no means forgotten in China.

Going to War against America

After the founding of the PRC in October 1949, the new Chinese government enthusiastically supported North Korea's bid for national reunification by force. By late 1949, the PLA began sharing military intelligence with the North Korean People's Army (NKPA). On January 7, 1950, the two countries signed an agreement to establish additional telegraph and telephone lines. Later that month, Kim Il Sung, North Korea's leader, sent a delegation to Beijing requesting repatriation of all Chinese soldiers of Korean origin to North Korea. During WWII and the Chinese civil war, many young Koreans had joined the Chinese Communist forces. In 1950, there were some twenty-eight thousand Korean soldiers in the PLA's 156th, 164th, and 166th divisions. The CMC and Kim Kwang Hyop, head of the North Korean delegation, agreed that one-half of the Korean soldiers would be transferred from the PLA to the NKPA.[7] Kim Kwang Hyop then asked Marshal Nie Rongzhen, acting chief of the PLA General Staff, to arm and equip these soldiers before their transfer. After receiving approval from the CMC, Nie and his staff transferred fourteen thousand Koreans with their weapons and equipment to North Korea.[8] These soldiers played an important role in Kim Il Sung's initial invasion of South Korea.[9]

On June 25, 1950, the NKPA launched a surprise attack on South Korea, beginning the Korean War. The Truman administration immediately responded by sending in armed forces under a UN resolution, adopted on July 7, that called for all possible means to aid the Republic of Korea (ROK; South Korea). That same day, at Mao's suggestion, the CMC established the Northeast Border Defense Army (NBDA; Dongbei bianfangjun) to forestall any emergency situation that might arise along the Chinese-Korean border.[10] On July 10, the CMC named Senior General Su Yu the NBDA commander and political commissar and Senior General Xiao Jinguang its deputy commander.[11] The PLA transferred four infantry armies and three artillery divisions, some 255,000 troops, to the NBDA command. The high command also increased its military intelligence capabilities by sending observers into North Korea. Colonel Chai Chengwen, an expert on American military forces and a trusted member of the PLA's intelligence directorate, arrived in P'yŏngyang with more than one hundred Chinese officers who were stationed in eight places in the North Korean capital.[12] On July 29, Zhou Enlai, vice chairman of the CMC and premier of the PRC, wrote to the North Korean ambassador to Beijing requesting additional telephone lines between the two countries to facilitate wartime communication.[13] Chai briefed Zhou on a regular basis.

On August 4, after the UNF had halted North Korea's invasion, Mao called a Politburo meeting to discuss preparations for possible involvement in the conflict. The next day, Mao ordered the NBDA "to get ready for fighting in early September."[14] At a mid-August meeting, most of the NBDA commanders said they believed the best time for the Chinese to take action would be after the UNF crossed the 38th parallel but before they had "established a foothold" in North Korea.[15] On September 6, the CMC transferred the Fiftieth Army from Hubei to the NBDA in northeast China. It also redeployed the Ninth Army Group, including three infantry armies, along the Long-hai Railway and transferred the Nineteenth Army Group, including three armies, from the west to the north. In the meantime, the CMC established new special units, including four air force regiments, three tank brigades, and eighteen antiaircraft artillery regiments.[16]

On September 15, General MacArthur successfully landed UN troops in Inch'ŏn, rapidly changing the military situation in Korea. Informed by periodic reports from his agents in P'yŏngyang, Mao watched these developments with growing dismay. Despite Chinese warnings of the UNF's landings at Inch'ŏn, Kim's army did not respond soon enough to prevent Seoul's being retaken in late September. Nor could Kim halt the collapse and retreat of the NKPA across the 38th parallel. Kim rushed his military representative to Beijing to ask for additional military aid. Among other things, he requested two hundred pieces of advanced artillery sighting devices, which Zhou immediately approved.[17]

On October 1, the UNF crossed the 38th parallel into North Korea to liberate the country from the Communist regime. After asking the Soviet Union for help, Kim proposed to Stalin that China also send troops to Korea. Stalin telegraphed Mao on October 1 and suggested that China "should send at once at least five to six divisions . . . so that our Korean comrades will have an opportunity to organize a defense of the area north of the 38th parallel under the screen of your troops." These Chinese soldiers could be "considered as volunteers" and remain under the Chinese command.[18]

Chinese leaders now faced the possibility of sending their troops to Korea. When the Politburo met on October 2, 1950, members expressed divergent views. As Mao's most influential and important advisors, they also held positions on the CMC. Most expressed deep

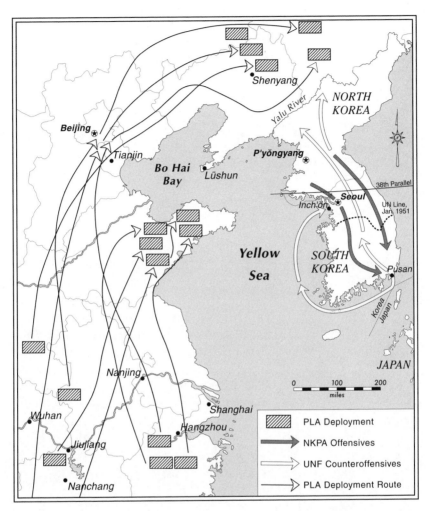

PLA Deployment, June–October 1950

reservations about any military intervention in the Korean War. Gao Gang, vice president of the PRC, chairman of the CCP Northeast Bureau, and commander of the Northeast Military Region, opposed the idea. Gao argued that the CCP had just won the civil war and the newly founded republic could not afford a major war against the United States. Nie Rongzhen agreed with Gao: "It would be better not to fight this war as long as it was not absolutely necessary."[19] Others at the meeting also worried about the poorly equipped PLA's ability to stop the superior U.S. forces in Korea. The military leaders knew that, even though they had won the civil war, the PLA was merely a revolutionized peasant army, not yet a professional, modern force. Marshal Lin Biao, vice chairman of the CMC, feared that China's ground forces would suffer very heavy losses and thought that the PLA should instead "strengthen the border defense" and "assist the North Koreans in fighting a guerrilla war." Lin surprised all the other military leaders, including Mao himself, when he declined Mao's request to command all Chinese forces in Korea.[20]

Mao, however, believed that the Sino-Soviet relationship left China no alternative to military intervention. The Soviet Union, he thought, might intend to isolate the new China from the socialist and Communist camp. Mao also worried about Stalin's distrust of the CCP.[21] Moreover, he wanted to prevent the Soviet Union from taking advantage of the Sino-Soviet treaty by sending Soviet troops to northeast China.[22]

Since the Politburo did not reach any decision on military intervention on October 2, Mao called an expanded meeting (*kuodahui*) of the Politburo on October 4 to break the opposition he faced. To have more political supporters outside Beijing, Mao sent an airplane to Xi'an to pick up Marshal Peng Dehuai. Peng arrived at about 1600 hours on October 4. Most of the expanded meeting participants focused on the disadvantages for China of sending troops to Korea. Mao, who was not happy about the "reasonable and logical" discussions of the majority, said, "When we, however, are standing on the side, just watching other people who are undergoing a national crisis, we feel terrible inside, no matter what we may pretend."[23] Peng expressed no opinions during the afternoon discussions.

With all these issues to consider, Peng could not sleep that night. As one of the PLA's most dedicated generals, he had worked closely with Mao since the Long March. Born into a poor peasant family, Peng lost his mother when he was eight and was begging for food on the street for his two younger brothers a year later. At seventeen, he enlisted in the Hunan Army and attended the Hunan Military Academy. He served as a GMD officer and became a brigade commander before defecting. In 1928, Peng joined the CCP, and then commanded the Fifth Army of the Chinese Red Army. His revolutionary fervor and mil-

Mao Zedong and Peng Dehuai in Beijing in 1951. (Reproduced by permission of World Knowledge Press, Beijing, China.)

itary aggressiveness gained Mao's attention and favor by 1930. Peng's army led the vanguard of the 1934–35 Long March. During the Second Sino-Japanese War, he served as deputy commander of the Eighth Route Army, acting secretary-general of the CCP North Bureau, and vice chairman and chief of General Staff of the Central Revolutionary Military Committee. During the civil war, he commanded the Eighteenth Army Group, the Northwestern Field Army, and the First Field Army. He became deputy commander of the PLA in 1949.[24] With Zhu De, he was one of the PRC's most experienced marshals.

Now, at the age of fifty-one, Peng faced the toughest decision in his military and political career. He could not enjoy the soft bed in the Beijing hotel. But after moving to the floor, he still could not sleep. Mao's words reverberated through his mind. Peng understood why Mao needed him here. In the early morning hours of October 5, Mao sent Deng Xiaoping, secretary-general of the CCP Central Secretariat, to the hotel to invite Peng to discuss matters with Mao at the Zhongnanhai compound. When the Politburo continued its discussion that afternoon, Peng expressed strong support for Mao's idea, arguing that "sending the troops to aid Korea is necessary. . . . If the American military places itself along the Yalu River and in Taiwan, it could find an excuse anytime it wants to launch an invasion."[25] Many participants at the meeting were impressed by Peng's firm stand.[26] His support convinced the majority to send troops to aid North Korea and resist American aggression.

On October 8, Mao issued orders reorganizing the NBDA into the CPVF and appointing Peng its commander in chief and political commissar.[27] According to Mao's order, the CPVF included four infantry armies and three artillery divisions, nearly 260,000 men. Despite its name change, the CPVF was simply the same Chinese troops assigned to the Korean border. The CPVF command was actually the PLA's front command. By using the term "volunteers" in the army's name, as Stalin suggested, Mao hoped to convince the world that the CPVF was organized by Chinese volunteers, not the Chinese government itself, and thereby avoid open war with the United States and the sixteen other nations that had contributed to the UNF in Korea. Peng once joked about the "volunteers" at the CPVF headquarters on the Korean front. "The volunteers, indeed," said the commander of the CPVF. "I am not a volunteer. . . . It is my chief who sent me here."[28]

Mobilizing an Uncertain Society

At 1730 hours on October 19, 1950, the first wave of CPVF troops, who had removed all Chinese army insignias from their uniforms, secretly crossed the Yalu River and entered North Korea, beginning Chinese participation in the Korean War. The first wave consisted of six armies, including eighteen infantry divisions, three artillery divisions, and 7,000 support troops—in all, about 300,000 men. All of these troops were in Korea by early November.[29] By late November, Chinese forces in Korea totaled thirty-three divisions, nearly 450,000 men. This was only the beginning of Chinese involvement. This rapid and unexpected deployment took place without being discovered by American generals. The Chinese high command believed its forces' superior numbers would offset their inferior equipment and technology and be a decisive factor in their victory.[30]

The PLA had no difficulty sending a large infantry force to Korea in late 1950. In May 1950, the PLA had a total of 5.5 million troops, including 5.4 million in the infantry, 38,000 in the navy, and 57,000 in the air force. The PLA planned postwar demobilization to ease the heavy financial burden on the new republic. On June 30, the CMC and State Council jointly issued the Resolution on the Task of Demobilization, which planned to retire 1 million troops in 1950. The Central Committee of Demobilization opened up more than one thousand veteran administration offices across the country in July to arrange for civil war veterans' retirement. By mid-October, just before China dispatched the CPVF to Korea, the PLA had been reduced to 4.6 million troops.[31] However, planned operations in Korea soon suspended demobilization. Many of the recently opened offices simply changed their signs from Veteran Administration Office to New Recruitment Office, using the same staff at the same location.[32]

Some officers recall the mobilization for the Korean War as a much easier task than the demobilization after the civil war.[33] Chinese historians have argued that the military victory in 1949 and the new order of society earned the PLA support for its Korean War mobilization in 1950.[34] Their writings show that this victorious sentiment and revolutionary enthusiasm produced more peasant volunteers than the recruitment officials could handle. In some places, officials had to send thousands of would-be soldiers home.[35] Why did millions of young peasants volunteer to go to Korea to fight against America? Several economic and political factors played important roles in their motivation. A uniform meant economic security and new opportunity under the Communist regime. After the civil war, many rural youths had nothing left to lose and everything to gain by joining the CPVF or PLA.

The eight-year Second Sino-Japanese War (1937–45) had deeply wounded China economically. Then, during the three years of civil war (1946–49), the Chinese paid another extremely high price. In rural areas, much of the best farming land lay fallow for more than a decade. Retreating GMD troops destroyed many crops, warehouses, bridges, and roads to prevent their capture by PLA troops at the end of the civil war. It would take the PRC's economy years to overcome the severe blows dealt by the two wars. Moreover, in 1949, most of the southern provinces suffered serious floods that produced seven million victims of starvation and disease. The CCP Provincial Committee of Hunan, for example, declared the entire province in an "emergency situation" on March 5, 1950, since 25 percent of its residents had no food.[36] And village life in Guangdong was "without hope."[37] In 1950,

Villagers send their sons to the PLA. (Reproduced by permission of the PLA Press, Beijing, China.)

land reform and redistribution had not yet been initiated for poor peasants in the countryside. More than fifty million peasants in north China were suffering and starving from an early drought.[38] Many peasant families were willing to send their boys to the CPVF or PLA, where they would be fed and clothed.

In urban areas, the economic situation was even worse. Economic depression and social disorder followed the Communist takeover. Many towns and cities—including Shanghai and Tianjin, the country's manufacturing and financial centers—were in ruins. GMD bombers continued to raid these large coastal cities throughout 1949–50. Shanghai struggled with nearly six hundred thousand unemployed, including war refugees and former GMD soldiers. More than 70 percent of Shanghai's factories were either shut down or inoperative. In 1950, China had a 13 percent unemployment rate, with forty million unemployed.[39] Xi'an had more than one hundred thousand unemployed, seventy thousand refugees, and forty thousand GMD deserters. The city had no water, food, shelter, or electricity. The Metropolitan Military Administration of Xi'an registered and enlisted many of the city's unemployed, refugees, homeless, and former GMD soldiers into the CPVF or PLA after a simple physical and political screening.[40]

Serving in the Communist forces thus became economically practical in both rural and urban areas after the civil war. The PLA was the only social institution that had the resources and opportunity to rebuild, especially in cities. The army played a major role in establishing a new order in the urban areas. The PLA established military administrations as a postwar urban control and management system in all cities from 1948 to 1953 after Chen Yun, deputy secretary of the CCP Northeast Bureau, brought his successful experience to the army. In November 1948, the Fourth Field Army had occupied Shenyang, the largest city in northeast China. Chen sent four thousand officers to the city to take over its legislative, executive, and judicial systems while he served as mayor. His troops replaced city law enforcement and security forces; took over the banks, utility companies, city transportation, communication, and school districts; and controlled the city's food, fuel, and other supplies.[41] Within a few months, order had been reestablished. Residents in Shenyang returned to their normal lives under the Communist military authorities.

In response to Shenyang's success, on November 15, 1948, the CCP Central Committee issued its "Zhonggong zhongyang guanyu junshi guanzhi wenti de zhishi" (Instruction on Military Administration) to the PLA. It ordered the military to administer all cities with one hundred thousand or more residents.[42] The CCP was largely interested in establishing credibility by providing an efficient governmental system through the PLA after years of foreign aggression and a bloody civil war. Many leading PLA commanders became city mayors, including Marshal Ye Jianying in Beijing, Marshal Chen Yi (Ch'en I) in Shanghai, General Huang Kechen (Huang Ke-cheng) in Tianjin, Marshal Liu Bocheng in Nanjing, Marshal He Long in Xi'an, and Generals Zhang Jiren and Chen Xilian in Chongqing.[43] A uniform meant revolutionary authority and political security.

There were also political reasons for the new recruits' motivation. With its rapid takeover of the country in 1949, the CCP launched nationwide political campaigns to identify supporters and opponents of the new regime. Most Chinese people, including urban residents, were willing to accept that the CCP had won the civil war and were ready to cooperate with the new government. Joining the Communist forces seemed the best way to survive the revolution and earn a new identity with the CCP. PLA officers and soldiers were protected from the political movements and class struggles of the 1950s. By serving in the military, they gained access to political security, individual reputation, and family recognition within the new Communist society.[44]

By 1950, the new regime realized the necessity of stamping out any resistance. The officers, new to the cities, were apparently insecure in this new social environment. The Municipal Military Administration of Chongqing, for example, had to enforce martial law from January to May 1950 because of endless riots, serious looting, and an organized insurgency in that city. During these months, the city's military administration employed some radical policies, such as dissolving the GMD and other political organizations, outlawing all religious groups, and confiscating properties of the "bureaucratic capitalists" (the formerly GMD government–owned properties, *guiliao zichan*). The city's military authorities next permanently removed the "bad elements" from the city by jailing 7,400 former GMD officials and soldiers and executing 361 of them. The city's military administration then disarmed the population.[45] The suppression worked well: the military administration regained control of the city in the summer of 1950.

Mao, the president of the new republic, justified and supported this suppression, stating that the GMD had left behind many bandits, spies, and officers who were conducting guerrilla warfare and sabotage and spreading rumors against the new government. In his report to the third plenary session of the CCP Seventh Central Committee on June 6, 1950, Mao recommended Chongqing's suppression efforts, though with some leniency.[46] With the outbreak of the Korean War, the efforts escalated into a nationwide movement—the campaign to suppress counterrevolutionaries (*zhenfan yundong*). The criteria of punishable crimes and sentences became clearer and noticeably harsher against former GMD officers and soldiers.[47]

Serving in the Communist forces could establish a revolutionary identity as well as much-needed political security. Many former GMD officers and soldiers joined the PLA or CPVF to escape the movement that was jailing or executing many former GMD officers. Those who had already joined the PLA, a large number of so-called liberated soldiers (*jiefang zhanshi*), were described as new men who wanted to stay in the PLA to establish new careers as revolutionaries. To survive under the new regime, they had no choice. When the PLA took over Beijing in January 1949, for example, 200,000 GMD troops surrendered. Between February and April, more than 150,000 of them were inducted into the PLA.[48]

After a large number of GMD troops joined the PLA, the high command faced a new task: to motivate these troops in the Korean War. The NBDA (later CPVF) headquarters prepared the troops in three ways before they entered Korea.

First, the NBDA/CPVF units received political education. Since mid-August, the leaders had been working on the "psychological condition of the soldiers who were preparing for the war."[49] After two-month political education courses, according to Lieutenant General Du Ping, director of the NBDA/CPVF political department, approximately 50 percent of the soldiers were ready "with a positive attitude toward participating in the Korean War." Most were civil war veterans and CCP members. Some even "submitted written statements asking to fight the American troops and help the Korean people" before the CCP Politburo decided to participate in the war. About 30 percent of the NBDA/CPVF troops were what Du called "intermediate elements," who would fight as ordered but did not care whether there was a war or not. The last 20 percent of the soldiers were "in an unsettled state of mind." They were afraid of fighting the U.S. troops; they named the Yalu bridge the "gate of hell," complained that "to resist America and aid Korea is like poking our nose into other people's business," and argued that it would only "draw fire against ourselves."[50]

Most troops in the 116th Division of the Thirty-ninth Army were liberated soldiers. Captain Zhou Baoshan explained that they had served in the GMD army and fought against the PLA during the civil war. After losing a battle, as we have seen, many GMD soldiers surrendered and became POWs of the PLA. Zhou's regiment took in a large number of the former GMD soldiers during the last phase of the civil war. According to Zhou, "These 'liberated soldiers' knew very little about the PLA or Communism, and wondered why they had to fight for a foreign country."[51] Captain Zhou, born to a peasant family in 1922 in the north, joined the PLA and became a CCP member in 1948. At twenty-eight, he was promoted to captain in the 347th Regiment, 116th Division, which fought all the way from the north to the south during the civil war. He and his men were happy when the division was transferred back to the northeast, near their hometown. They thought they would retire soon and go back to their homes to farm newly received land and to marry. Then came the Korean War. To motivate the men during their political education, regimental officers highlighted family protection as an aspect of homeland security. Zhou told his men that if they did not stop the Americans in Korea, they would later have to fight them in their hometowns in China. He explained, "To assist Korea is the same as defending our homeland."[52] Zhou related to his men facts about America's invasions of China and its recent occupation of Taiwan, concluding that the Chinese were victims of American imperialism. This argument made sense to the men, who believed that they had long been the victims of war and foreign invasion. Another part of the prewar political education campaign was to build up the men's confidence by portraying the American imperialists as a paper tiger (zhilaohu). Zhou and his men believed that the American troops were fighting an unjust war and suffering from low morale. Their forces were stretched thin and dependent upon lengthy supply lines. The Chinese knew that, although their weapons were not advanced, as Zhou said, "we enjoyed a numerical advantage."[53]

The second part of the NBDA's war preparation was combat training. Zhou recalled that, in September, Major General Wang Yang, the new commander of the 116th Division, organized an intensive training program with two phases. The first phase focused on small-group combat tactics, including small arms, antitank weapons, demolition, and antiaircraft training. The second phase focused on operational tactics, which were new to Zhou and his men. Zhou recalled that his battalion participated in a group attack exercise on a small hill with two other battalions. They felt crowded when hundreds of soldiers charged the same point at once. The division also brought in WWII veterans, who had fought alongside the American troops in Burma and recalled the American soldiers' training and characteristics. On October 15, in accordance with Mao's October 8 order, Zhou's division became part of the CPVF. A rocket artillery battalion and an antitank battalion were added to the division. The 116th Division also established a headquarters security battalion, an antiaircraft artillery battalion, and a medical battalion. After two months of preparations, on the evening of October 21, Zhou and his unit crossed the Yalu River. The first Koreans Zhou saw were the security troops of the NKPA, stationed on the Korean side of the Yalu bridge. They lined up and cheered in broken Chinese, "Welcome the Chinese People's Volunteer Forces coming to Korea to fight!"[54] The Chinese were impressed by the NKPA's Soviet-made automatic rifles and brand-new heavy machine guns. The CPVF troops had a mix of bolt-action Japanese rifles from WWII and old American rifles captured from the GMD army in the civil war.

The third preparation effort was the establishment of a logistics system to supply the Chinese forces in the war. During the civil war, the PLA had successfully employed the local command to supply its troops on the front lines. On July 26, the CMC ordered the Northeast Military Region to establish a new logistics headquarters to supply the NBDA. The northeast logistics headquarters began operating in early August through its weaponry and ammunition, financial, transportation, medical, housing, and personnel departments. On August 31, the northeast logistics headquarters was expanded into three headquarters totaling 7,800 officers and staff. By the end of September, they supplied the NBDA with 1,600 tons of ammunition, 10,000 barrels of gasoline, 1,054 trucks, and 995 artillery pieces, and stored 20 million bullets, 840,000 artillery shells, and 300,000 hand grenades. The NBDA standardized its army weaponry system for better and faster supply. Beginning in mid-August, the NBDA's Thirty-eighth Army began to replace all of its rifles and guns with Japanese-made weapons, while the Fortieth Army used mostly American-made weapons. The logistics headquarters also supplied 16,000 tons of grain, 400 tons of cooking oil, 920 tons of dry and canned food, 340,000 winter coats, and 360,000 pairs of winter boots to the CPVF troops.[55]

By late November 1950, China had dispatched to Korea thirty-three divisions totaling 450,000 soldiers. By the middle of April 1951, the Chinese forces in Korea had increased to 950,000 men, including 770,000 combat troops organized into forty-two infantry divisions, eight artillery divisions, four antiaircraft artillery divisions, and four tank regiments. Chinese support troops consisted of six supply services headquarters, four railroad engineering divisions, eleven engineering regiments, and one security division, totaling 180,000 men. During the Korean War, the Chinese army lacked the air force, tanks, and heavy artillery necessary for a successful campaign against the more powerful and mechanized UN troops. Still, Chinese commanders and soldiers believed that their "fighting spirit" would lead them to victory. Prevailing over, or at least not losing to, a technologically superior foe would be a matter of considerable pride to the Chinese army.[56]

Mobile Warfare

The sudden engagement of a million-man force in a war against the UNF put overwhelming pressure on the Chinese officer corps. Army group commanders and officers rose to the challenges of increased responsibility and unexpected problems. Six army groups (in the order in which they entered Korea, the Thirteenth, Ninth, Third, Nineteenth, Twentieth, and Twenty-third) were engaged in the war, commanding twenty-five armies—seventy-nine infantry divisions. The army command structure often favored personal relationships and political orthodoxy at the expense of ability and performance. The CPVF had not adopted the command and control doctrine to meet the requirements of modern war. In July 1950, when the NBDA was established, its Thirty-eighth, Thirty-ninth, and Fortieth armies were under the command of the Thirteenth Army Group. The high command wanted to send its best officers to Korea. General Deng Hua was appointed the new commander of the Thirteenth Army Group, which would go to Korea; General Huang Yongsheng, who had been commander of the Thirteenth Army Group, took Deng's place as the commander of the Fifteenth Army Group, which would stay in Guangzhou.[57] Upon acceptance of his new position, Deng sent the high command his request that the two army groups switch headquarters. On July 15, the CMC approved Deng's request. Ten days later, the new Thirteenth Army Group headquarters—Deng's staff—moved to northeast China with him.[58] Confusion and complaints arose from officer transfers, personnel replacement, headquarters relocation, and job changes throughout the summer. On the evening of October 19, the Thirteenth Army Group headquarters moved into Korea.[59]

Marshal Peng Dehuai had no staff when he was appointed CPVF commander and political commissar on October 8. During his ten-day stay in Beijing, he worked at the General Staff headquarters and summoned a dozen of his secretaries from the Northwest Military Region headquarters in Xi'an. At about 1430 hours on October 19, Peng left Andong with General Pak Il-u, North Korea's minister of the interior. At the other side of the Yalu bridge, Peng was received by Prime Minister Pak, who accompanied Peng to meet with Kim between October 19 and 22.[60]

On October 23, Peng arrived at the Thirteenth Army Group headquarters at Taeyudong. Two days later, he announced the CMC order that the Thirteenth Army Group headquarters was to become the CPVF general headquarters under his command, with Deng Hua as the CPVF's first deputy commander and vice political commissar, General Hong Xuezhi as the second deputy commander, General Han Xianchu as the third deputy commander, Major General Xie Fang as the chief of staff, and Du Ping as the director of the political department.[61] To work closely with the NKPA, Peng also appointed General Pak Il-u as the vice commissar of the CPVF. Pak was one of Kim's three most trusted generals in the NKPA. He had worked in China during WWII and spoke fluent Chinese.

The overnight upgrading of the group army headquarters to a general headquarters was an effort to engage the Chinese troops as soon as possible, but it led to some command and control problems between the general headquarters and army groups in the field. Peng's secretaries were in charge of planning, operations, intelligence, logistics, and security offices in the general headquarters. The former directors of the officers in the Thirteenth Army Group became associate or assistant directors to Peng's secretaries in the general headquarters.[62]

The CPVF's first battle in Korea was an unplanned engagement. From October 25 to November 5, the CPVF's armies had head-on engagements with the ROK's First, Sixth, and Eighth divisions and with the First Cavalry Division of the U.S. Army. During the first campaign, the CPVF used some of the same combat tactics it had perfected during the civil war. Among these was the achievement of numerical superiority and surprise to negate the usually superior enemy firepower. By maneuvering at night and resting during the day, Peng deployed his first wave of 300,000 Chinese troops south of the Yalu and remained undetected for two weeks in October.[63] In the first campaign, the CPVF headquarters concentrated 120,000 to 150,000 men in the area north of the Ch'ŏngch'ŏn River against 50,000 UN troops. Peng believed that the first campaign was a victory for the CPVF despite its 10,000 casualties.[64] The commander in chief recalled that the CPVF troops "eliminated six or seven 'puppet' battalions and a small unit of the American army"[65] and forced the UNF to retreat to the Ch'ŏngch'ŏn River and

Tŏkch'ŏn region.[66] Shuguang Zhang points out that the first campaign convinced the Chinese commanders that "they had accomplished a great deal: the troops had settled in North Korea and experienced their first combat."[67]

After the first encounter with the Americans, many in the CPVF command believed that the UN and U.S. forces' overreliance on technology might be their disadvantage.[68] The Chinese troops quickly gained battlefield experience, helped immensely by a nucleus of career officers and civil war veterans. For the first time since the Inch'ŏn landing, the North Koreans' situation was stabilized; the CPVF had provided valuable breathing space by pushing the front line south of the Ch'ŏngch'ŏn River.[69] Geography favored the Chinese. The mountains and forests camouflaged their movements and diluted UN air attacks. The narrow peninsula made it possible to fortify and defend a relatively short front.

Beginning November 11, the Ninth Army Group, the second wave of the CPVF, crossed the Yalu and moved east undetected. On November 27, its 150,000 troops launched a surprise attack on the U.S. First Marine Division at the Chosin Reservoir. Three days earlier, the CPVF had launched the second offensive campaign to counter MacArthur's "home by Christmas" offensive. Before his second campaign, Peng had 230,000 men on the western front against 130,000 UN troops, and 150,000 men on the eastern front against 90,000 UN troops.[70]

The Ninth Army Group, however, was ill prepared for combat. Its troops, from southeastern China, had assumed Taiwan in the south, not Korea in the north, would be their next target. Dressed in light canvas shoes and quilted cotton uniforms, they were not prepared for the bitterly cold Korean winter. Captain Wang Xuedong complained that the troops' supplies were insufficient. He and his superior officers had had no idea how cold the weather would be in North Korea. He recalled, "We came from southeast China, where the average annual temperature is about 72 degrees Fahrenheit. When we left our homes in early November, the temperature was about 60 degrees. Two weeks later, when we entered Korea, the temperature had dropped to below zero."[71] Many men became ill and could not keep up with the Fifty-eighth Division, Twentieth Army, Ninth Army Group, which had marched 120 miles in seven days, through mountains and forests in

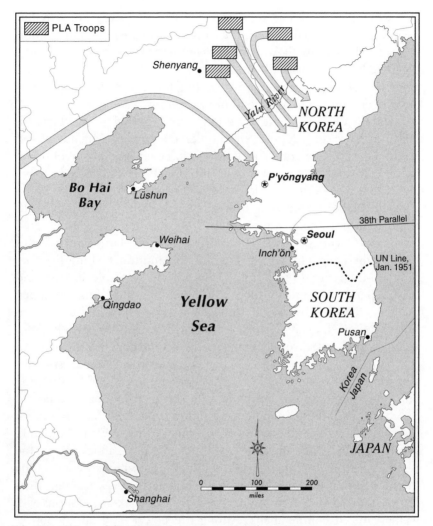

The First Wave of the CPVF into Korea, October 1950

cold weather. During its first week in Korea, his division lost seven hundred men to severe frostbite.[72]

The planners of the CPVF headquarters were not aware of the Ninth Army Group's problems. On November 25, Peng ordered General Song Shilun, commander of the Ninth, to launch his attack in the east, when the CPVF began its second all-out offensive campaign, but Song asked for a two-day delay, since his armies were not yet in position to attack. His Twentieth Army had arrived at the Chosin Reservoir area; the Twenty-seventh was still on its way; and the Twenty-sixth remained along the Chinese-Korean border, waiting for promised Russian weapons and equipment to replace its old weaponry.[73]

The CPVF headquarters had to accept the delay of its attack. Finally, on November 27, the Ninth ordered an attack, which centered on the Chosin Reservoir. The attacking force consisted of eight infantry divisions, including the Fifty-eighth. Captain Wang Xuedong believed that some of the tactics were very successful during the initial attack. First, they achieved a surprise, since his army's entry into North Korea and movement to the eastern front had remained undetected for ten days. Second, they separated the U.S. First Marine and Seventh Infantry divisions into five parts by the next morning. Third, the one-hundred-thousand-strong Ninth Army Group was able to surround these separated American troops.[74] Even though the Chinese trapped the First Marine Division at Hahwaok-ri (Hagaru-ri) and cut it into three sections, they could not destroy each section completely. After being divided and surrounded, the marines immediately formed defensive perimeters at three places. They also constructed a makeshift airstrip for receiving ammunition and winter equipment and for shipping out their wounded. On November 29, the marines counterattacked to break the Chinese encirclement and to unite their scattered units. Captain Wang remembered his engagement with the First Marine Division: "On the 29th our regiment launched a night attack against the marines. Our regiment recovered some of the positions we lost to the marines during the day, but we were unable to break through their lines before dawn. Next morning, the marines retook the positions with well-organized counterattacks, strong fire power, and air support."[75] The battle at Chosin swayed back and forth, but the fighting was always intense. During the three days of fighting, Wang's regiment suffered very heavy casualties. His troops ran out of ammunition and received less than half of their daily ration of food. The temperature dropped to twenty degrees below zero.

On November 30, the Ninth Army Group headquarters changed its plan. Instead of attacking the First Marine and Seventh divisions at the same time, it decided to concentrate its attack on the Seventh

The CPVF engage the UNF in the Korean War. (Reproduced by permission of the Liaoning People's Press, Shenyang, Liaoning, China.)

Division at Sinhung-ri (Chinhung-ri). On November 30, the Ninth Army Group employed its two infantry divisions and all its artillery pieces to attack the Thirty-second Regiment of the Seventh Division. On December 1, the attacking troops successfully eliminated the Thirty-second Regiment—the only time in the Korean War that the CPVF would destroy an entire U.S. regiment. On the same day, the marines broke through the Chinese encirclement and began their retreat to the south. Though unable to stop them, Captain Wang and his men were ordered to pursue the marines and slow their retreat until the Twenty-sixth Army, which was still more than fifty miles away, had a chance to catch up and eliminate the First Marine Division.[76] It never did. On December 12, having broken the Chinese roadblocks and fought through some attacks on its way south, the First Marine Division met the U.S. Third Infantry Division at Hamhŭng. The Ninth Army Group could not eliminate the First Marine Division. During its battle at the Chosin Reservoir, the Ninth Army Group had lost forty thousand men in three weeks of fighting, liquidating three divisions.[77] Some casualties were weather related. Having lost half of its troops, the badly depleted army group was recalled to China on December 17. China continued to funnel as many troops into Korea as its transportation and supply system could handle.

On the whole, the second offensive campaign was a major victory for the CPVF. American air power had forced the Chinese to take to the hills, mostly on foot, carrying much of what they required. But the Chinese forces had tremendous physical endurance, even though they suffered more than eighty thousand casualties.[78] They attacked from the surrounding hills, often establishing roadblocks, which not only forced the American troops back but also threatened to cut them off. The First Marine Division's retreat has become part of marine lore, but it was a retreat, not a victory. The fierce fighting, combined with the bitter cold, made Chosin one of the worst battles of the Korean War for the Americans.[79] Amazingly, even in these conditions, the Chinese troops found ways of moving artillery to their front-line positions high in the mountains of Korea. In nine days, the CPVF pushed the battle line back to the 38th parallel and recaptured P'yŏngyang, North Korea's capital. The second offensive campaign "represented the peak of CPVF performance in the Korean War."[80] Mao's conviction that any battle could be conducted using the principles of guerrilla warfare dominated Chinese military doctrine during the early offensive campaigns, from the fall of 1950 to the early spring of 1951.[81] Large-scale guerrilla tactics like encirclement proved very effective in the first two offensive campaigns. Chinese morale was high, and Chinese support for the war was at its strongest during this period.

On December 31, the CPVF, though still poorly provisioned (home-supplied food met only a quarter of the minimum needs of the CPVF), launched its third offensive campaign, across the 38th parallel against the entrenched UNF, an operation very different from earlier practices. In a matter of eight days, the CPVF crossed the 38th parallel, moved into South Korea, recaptured Seoul, South Korea's capital, and pushed the UNF down to the 37th parallel.[82] During this third offensive campaign, however, the CPVF faced mounting problems beyond shortages of food and ammunition. CPVF units were exhausted after days of constant movement and fighting. Troops became extremely fatigued, and reinforcements were delayed. The CPVF and NKPA lost 8,500 men during the third offensive campaign.[83] By this time, the U.S. and UN forces had established overwhelming firepower superiority on the ground and in the air and were inflicting heavy casualties and serious damage on the CPVF troops and their transportation and communication lines. The CPVF needed a more cautious strategy after the third offensive campaign.

Stalin and Kim Il Sung continually pressured the CPVF to launch the next offensive operation immediately to drive the UNF out of Korea with all possible speed. Mao also cabled Peng at the end of January and urged a preparation of the CPVF's fourth offensive campaign to drive the UNF farther south. The CPVF command was under tremendous pressure for a quick victory from the political leaders of all three Communist countries (China, the Soviet Union, and North Korea). But the gap between this political goal and strategic reality became wider at the end of each campaign.[84] As the CPVF struck farther south in the fourth campaign, the tactics that had been successful began to lose effectiveness. The UNF had recovered from their early surprise, and on January 25, 1951, they launched a counterattack to retake Seoul. From January 25 to April 21, the CPVF suffered fifty-three thousand casualties.[85] In the spring of 1951, the PLA sent more reinforcements to Korea. During the fourth campaign, the two sides engaged in a series of back-and-forth mobile battles. China had to keep sending reinforcements to offset losses and meet the new demands of the rapidly expanding military operations and the unexpected manpower needs.[86] Only ground forces were sent, since the CPVF air force had not yet been formally committed to the war.[87]

In the spring of 1951, considerable disagreement arose among CPVF officers regarding the fifth campaign. Most of the top commanders disagreed with Peng's idea (imposed upon him by Mao, Kim, and Stalin) of striking south. They preferred an "in-house" operation, engaging the UNF after luring them into the northern areas occupied by the CPVF. Despite these arguments, Peng was determined to launch his fifth campaign and regain the initiative. The fifth offensive campaign in April and May 1951 would be the largest CPVF operation in Korea. The Chinese and North Koreans deployed some 700,000 troops against 340,000 UNF troops, resulting in more than forty days of combat. No provision for air cover had been made, and the CPVF had to cope with an inadequate, heterogeneous collection of weapons as well as an overburdened and chaotic command structure. The campaign failed, and the CPVF suffered the loss of 85,000 men. The CPVF 180th Division was completely eliminated, totaling 7,644 troops, including 59 officers at division, regiment, and battalion levels.[88] Additionally, 17,000 POWs were taken by the UNF. More important, the front line was pushed farther north. It was only after this campaign that Mao concluded that the goal of driving the UNF out of Korea was unattainable. Peng later admitted that the fifth campaign in the Korean War was one of only four mistakes he made during his entire military career.[89]

Trench Warfare and Underground Tunnels

After the setback of its fifth campaign, the CPVF made some important tactical and strategic changes to limit casualties and negate the UNF's firepower. The CPVF headquarters adopted a different fighting system that focused on more cautious defensive strategies and tactics. By the summer of 1951, the nature of the war had changed. It evolved from a mobile war to a stalemate, a war of the trenches. At the outset, the CPVF had based its operations on the traditional approach of annihilating enemy units—entire divisions or regiments. But gradually, Chinese commanders realized that this practice proved difficult in Korea, where they faced a more formidable enemy on a limited battleground. It was difficult for either side to overpower its opponent completely, in contrast to the situation in both WWII and the Chinese civil war. In fact, the failure of the fifth campaign led Chinese leaders to change their goal from driving the UNF out of Korea to merely defending China's security and ending the war through negotiations. Chinese commanders thus shifted their focus from eliminating enemy units in mobile warfare to securing lines in positional warfare.

By the summer of 1951, the CPVF was no longer expected to recapture Seoul and drive into South Korea. Although the armies could achieve temporary successes in limited sectors, they came at a high cost. The Soviets were ready for peace talks that would secure North Korea's regime and strengthen the Soviet Union's position in Asia. On June 23, the Soviet ambassador to the UN, Jacob Malik, called for discussions leading to a cease-fire and an armistice. In Beijing, the CCP Central Committee discussed the Soviet proposal and the next step in Korea. Chinese leaders believed that they had already achieved their political goal of driving the enemy out of northern Korea. The halt at the 38th parallel, in fact, was a return to the prewar status quo that was acceptable to the parties in the war. Most committee members therefore considered it proper for the Chinese forces to stop at the 38th parallel but continue to fight while negotiating a settlement. Presided over by Mao on July 2, the CMC committed to this "dual strategy" for the rest of the war.[90] The Chinese also convinced the North Koreans to accept this new strategy through their visits and communications in the summer of 1951.[91] When the *Renmin ribao* (People's Daily) endorsed the Soviet proposal, it appeared that the key players in all the warring powers except South Korea were ready to negotiate.[92]

On July 10, the truce negotiations began at Kaesŏng, a neutral city between the lines. The UN delegation, however, soon discovered that the Chinese–North Korean delegation was more interested in using the event for propaganda purposes. During the early weeks of the meetings, the major source of disagreement was the demarcation line. In August, the negotiations were suspended. On October 25, the talks resumed in P'anmunjŏm, a village about midway between the two lines. From late 1951 to 1952, it was POW issues that deadlocked the truce negotiations. The UN delegation proposed a voluntary repatriation of POWs, while the Chinese–North Korean delegation insisted on the return of all their prisoners. The UN delegation believed that the Communists held more POWs (an estimated 65,000 captured) than the number they presented at the negotiating table (11,559).[93]

In the meantime, the fighting continued. In the fall of 1951, the CPVF began an active defense. It constructed underground tunnels to achieve a favorable negotiating position in any future settlement and to strengthen its defensive capacity. The underground great wall, as it became known, was built along the front line.[94] The Chinese commanders emphasized gaining and retaining the operational initiative in battles (including preemption) as an optimum strategy. Their trench defense and their tunnel system were tested by the sudden onset of the UN's Kŭmhwa offensive in mid-October 1952. The U.S. Seventh Division and the ROK Second Division began intensive shelling of the Chinese Fifteenth Army's positions in the Osong Mountain region on October 14 and occupied hills 597.9 and 537.7, two small geographic features known together as Triangle Hill. By October 16, the UN attack had forced the Chinese troops off the ridge and into their tunnels.

CPVF soldiers fight in their tunnels. (Reproduced by permission of the Liaoning People's Press, Shenyang, Liaoning, China.)

The 134th Regiment, Forty-fifth Division of the CPVF Fifteenth Army was part of the defensive force on the hills. Captain Zheng Yanman's company joined the tunnel defenses as reinforcements on October 18. When his company went underground, Zheng faced major tactical problems. The network suffered severe damage from the attacks, and the three tunnels were cut off from each other. Bodies, shells, and garbage were everywhere, and the soldiers suffered from shortage of supplies, food, and, more important, water. Captain Zheng recalled that there were about one hundred soldiers inside the tunnels, the remnants of six different companies. About fifty of the men were wounded and had received no medical assistance. In one of the shelter holes, Zheng found more than twenty corpses. "Neither did anybody care about safety," the captain recalled, "and there were seven accidental rifle and two grenade discharges in the tunnels during the first morning after we moved in. I was really mad when I learned that several of my men were wounded by these accidental discharges."[95]

Captain Zheng began to organize the tunnel defense by fighting a pattern of see-saw actions. During the day, the UN troops forced the

Chinese troops into the tunnels; at night, his men counterattacked and recovered their surface positions, only to lose them again in the daytime. The battle of Triangle Hill turned into one of the bloodiest of the war. During the night of October 29, the Eighth Company pulled out of the tunnels and moved down the hill. Zheng could not believe that only six men were able to walk down the hill with him. "When we moved up the hill just twelve days ago, I remembered, two hundred young men were running and jumping, full of energy and dreams. Now there were only six of them." At the 134th Regiment headquarters, Zheng learned that his regiment had lost most of its leaders, including 65 percent of its captains, 89 percent of its lieutenants, and 100 percent of its sergeants. The Forty-fifth Division lost 5,200 soldiers on the two hills. The Fifteenth Army suffered a total of 11,400 casualties from late October to early November, when the battle of Triangle Hill finally came to an end.[96]

By December 1952, the Chinese forces in Korea had reached a record high of 1.45 million men, including fifty-nine infantry divisions, ten artillery divisions, five antiaircraft divisions, and seven tank regiments. CPVF numbers remained stable until the armistice agreement was signed in July 1953. Mao committed nearly one-quarter of China's military strength to North Korea's defense.[97]

Reshaping the Chinese Forces

From the conclusion of the fifth campaign until the end of the war, the CPVF adopted more cautious and realistic strategies, including maintaining a relatively stable front line; increasing CPVF air force, artillery, and tank units; and beefing up logistical support. Indeed, the CPVF increasingly became a mirror image of its American counterpart in its prosecution of the war. The Korean War thus began China's military modernization and professionalization in terms of command, organization, technology, and training. In this respect, the United States turned out to be a "useful adversary" in the Korean War.[98] For instance, Chinese forces began to learn to execute joint operations. The first such effort took place in the last phase of the war, on November 30, 1951, when the Chinese forces launched an amphibious attack, supported by aircrafts, onto Dahoo Island, off North Korea's coast. Though the CPVF lost five of nine bombers during the joint attack, the landing succeeded.[99]

The Chinese army had previously fought in wars against the Japanese and Nationalist armies, but it knew little about American, British, Canadian, and other technologically equipped Western forces. Korea became a combat laboratory that offered Chinese officers and soldiers essential combat training. Starting in the fall of 1952, the PLA began to rotate Chinese troops into Korea to give them modern warfare experience fighting American forces as well as to relieve the CPVF troops already in Korea. As the result of this process, more Chinese troops were sent to Korea, including five Chinese air force divisions operating under the CPVF command. In all, about 73 percent of the Chinese infantry troops were rotated into Korea (25 of 34 armies, or 79 of 109 infantry divisions). More than 52 percent of the Chinese air force divisions, 55 percent of the tank units, 67 percent of the artillery divisions, and 100 percent of the railroad engineering divisions were sent to Korea.[100]

By the end of the war, the CPVF emphasized the role of technology and firepower and respected its technologically superior opponents. To narrow the technology gap, China purchased weapons and equipment from the Soviet Union to arm sixty infantry divisions in 1951–54.[101] Thereafter, Chinese weaponry was standardized. The Soviets also shared technology for the production of rifles, machine guns, and artillery pieces. Additionally, Chinese and North Korean armies received foreign aid from Eastern European countries, including Poland, Romania, and Czechoslovakia.[102] Romania provided forty-one railcars of war materials for the North Korean and Chinese troops in April 1951, including two railcars of hospital equipment and ten railcars of medicine for a one-hundred-bed hospital. Romania also sent twenty-two medical persons to China that month.[103]

The CPVF improved its logistics and transportation by establishing its own logistics department in Korea. On May 19, 1951, the CMC issued its "Guanyu jiaqiang zhiyuanjun houfang qinwu gongzuo de jueding" (Decision on Strengthening the Volunteer Forces' Logistics Tasks) and ordered that "the Logistics Department of the CPVF should be established immediately. It will command and manage all the Chinese logistics units and facilities within Korea (including the railroads, highways, and military transportation). The CPVF Logistics Department is under the direct command·of the CPVF leading commanders."[104] General Hong Xuezhi became the head of the new department.

Logistic units repair a road in Korea. (Reproduced by permission of the Liaoning People's Press, Shenyang, Liaoning, China.)

Having joined the CCP and the Red Army in 1929, Hong served as the commander of the Heilongjiang Provincial Military District and of the Forty-third Army of the Fourth Field Army during the Chinese civil war. After the founding of the PRC, he became the deputy commander and chief of staff of first the Fifteenth Army Group and then the Thirteenth Army Group. When the Chinese troops entered Korea, he became the deputy commander of the CPVF.[105]

As the head of the CPVF logistics department, General Hong set up a configuration system that fit the needs of the CPVF's new positional warfare doctrine. The new system aimed at directly supplying front locations rather than specific army units.[106] Before May 1951, the PLA system had first delivered food and munitions from the northeast logistics headquarters in China to each CPVF army headquarters. The army next distributed the supplies to its divisions, each division delivered them to its regiments, and so on. Supplies therefore always lagged behind operations.[107] During the first two campaigns, the CPVF met only 25 percent of the food needs of its front-line troops. In the third campaign, front-line troops received 30 to 40 percent of their minimum needs. These inadequate supplies seriously constrained CPVF operations. Hong's new logistics system established area supply depots along the front lines to supply all the troops stationed within that area. The troops moved in and out, but the area supply depot remained; it could be used by both Chinese and North Korean troops.[108] The new system improved CPVF logistics capacity at the regiment and battalion levels and increased front-line troops' combat effectiveness. As in many cases, the Chinese military's performance here reflected a learning curve, but it ultimately achieved its battlefield objectives.[109]

In the fall of 1951, the CPVF began to commit its air force to the war. The Fourth Division was the first air force division to be deployed on the front under the CPVF command, from January to September 1951.[110] The Second, Third, Eighth, and Tenth divisions joined the Fourth after October, and seven more air force divisions participated in the war through 1953, including sixty thousand pilots, ground personnel, and security troops. These air force divisions kept their bases in China proper while their Soviet-trained pilots flew into Korea to carry out their missions. Soviet air force officers also coordinated Chinese and North Korean air cooperation. By the end of 1953, the PLA had three thousand fighters and bombers, making China's air force the third largest in the world.[111]

General Wang Hai served as the wing (battalion) commander of the Third Division. Born in 1926 to a Christian family in the village of Fuyin (Gospel), Shandong, Wang Hai became a Christian when he was six. He participated in the village's underground anti-Japanese movement led by the CCP in 1944 and became a CCP member in 1945. Wang enrolled in the Mudanjiang Aviation School in Heilongjiang in June 1946 and studied aviation mechanics under Japanese air force engineers who had not returned to Japan after the war. In 1947, Wang, with fifteen other student pilots, began to learn flying. They had several out-of-date Japanese aircraft and a dozen Japanese veteran instructors. Their training facilities were tremendously improved in

1949.[112] In January, the CMC decided to establish the PLA Air Force (PLAAF). In July, the CMC delegation went to Moscow and signed a deal with the Soviet Union, which agreed to sell 434 military aircraft to the PLA and send 878 aviation experts to China to help establish the PLAAF. In October, the CMC announced the founding of seven aviation schools, including the upgrading of Wang's training school in Heilongjiang. On November 11, 1949, the PLA proclaimed the establishment of the Chinese people's air force.[113]

The development of the Chinese air force sped up after the Korean War broke out. Its first division, the Air Force Fourth Division, was formed in Nanjing in June 1950. The Air Force Third Division was formed in Shenyang in October, and the Air Force Second Division in Shanghai in November. Each division had three or four regiments; each regiment had four wing commands (*dadui*); and each wing command had eight to ten fighters.[114] Wang became the commander of the First Wing, Ninth Regiment, Air Force Third Division in December 1950. On October 20, 1951, the Third Division, including Wang's MiG-15 jet fighters, moved into the front airport along the Yalu. On October 22, they began to engage the American F-80, F-84, and F-86 fighters in North Korea. Before it pulled out of the front on January 14, 1952, the Third Division engaged in twenty-one air-to-air battles and conducted 2,318 sorties.[115] The division's second tour, from May 1, 1952, to January 26, 1953, saw a record thirty-one battles and 1,147 takeoffs. During the two tours, the Third Division had forty-four fighters shot down and nineteen damaged. The division lost eighteen pilots, including one regiment commander and six wing commanders. Wang was shot down once in 1953, but he was rescued by peasants after his parachute landed in China.[116]

We know now that the Soviet air force participated in the Korean War. At Stalin's suggestion, General Belov of the Soviet air force arrived in northeast China in August 1950 with one Soviet air force division. Twelve more Soviet air force divisions arrived in China under Belov's command within the next three months. Their mission was to protect the Yalu bridges, power plants, railroads, and airports fifty miles south of the China–North Korea border. The Russian pilots who flew into Korea, however, had to take off from China. They wore Chinese uniforms and swore never to tell of their Korean War service. The Russian pilots were not allowed to communicate in the air in Russian and, most important, could not be captured as POWs. All Russian airplanes were repainted with Chinese or North Korean marks. On November 1, 1950, seven days after the Chinese engaged the UNF, Russian fighters began patrolling Korean airspace. On that first day, six Yak-9 fighters engaged American fighters and bombers over the Anzhou area; the Russians claimed to have shot down two B-29 bombers and one Mustang fighter and lost two Russian Yak-9s.[117] General Belov reported to Stalin that his pilots shot down twenty-three U.S. airplanes in the first half of November. Stalin, impressed, sent 120 newly designed MiG-15 jet fighters to the Korean War.

In January 1951, as we have seen, the first three Chinese offensive campaigns had pushed the front southward to the 37th parallel. Peng requested an extension of Soviet air coverage to the south to protect CPVF transportation and communication lines. Stalin agreed immediately and ordered Belov to transfer two more Russian fighter divisions, the 151st and 324th divisions of the Sixty-fourth Air Force Army, into North Korea. On March 15, Stalin telegraphed Mao, informing him that two more fighter divisions would be transferred from China to North Korea.[118] By August, the Sixty-fourth Air Force Army had deployed 190 MiG-15s and two antiaircraft artillery divisions to North Korea. Still, Russian airplanes could not fly over UN-controlled areas, be engaged over the front, or fly south of the 39th parallel. The CPVF command complained about these restrictions. The Russian fighters could not support the Chinese ground operations. Russian bombers, which were needed most, did not participate in the war. In addition, Chinese forces suffered casualties and lost two airplanes because of friendly fire from the Russian fighters. But Stalin had his own considerations: the Soviet Union did not want a war with the United States in Korea or anywhere else in east Asia. The Soviet Union did what it could for the Koreans. From November 1950 to July 1953, twelve Soviet air force divisions engaged in the air war, including 72,000 Russian pilots, technicians, ground service personnel, and air defense troops. In 1952, 26,000 Russian air force personnel were sent to North Korea. According to official Soviet records, Soviet fighters shot down 1,097 UN airplanes;[119] antiaircraft artillery forces shot down 212. The Soviet air force lost 335 fighters and 299 personnel, including 120 pilots.[120]

Between 1950 and 1953, more than 2.3 million Chinese troops participated in the Korean War. In addition, twelve air force divisions

Zhu De and Zhou Enlai meet with CPVF representatives in Beijing. (Reproduced by permission of World Knowledge Press, Beijing, China.)

participated in the war, including 672 pilots and 59,000 ground service personnel. China also sent to Korea 600,000 civilian laborers to work in logistical supply, support services, and railroad and highway construction. In all, 3.1 million Chinese "volunteers" took part in the Korean War. Although the PRC government did not declare war on any foreign country, this was the largest foreign war in Chinese military history.[121]

From October 19, 1950, to July 27, 1953, confronted by U.S. air and naval superiority, the CPVF suffered heavy casualties, including Mao's son, a Russian translator at the CPVF headquarters, who died in an air raid. Chinese soldiers who served in the Korean War faced a greater chance of being killed or wounded than those in WWII and those in the Chinese civil war. According to Chinese military records, Chinese casualties in the Korean War break down as follows: 152,000 dead, 383,000 wounded, 450,000 hospitalized, 21,300 captured, and 4,000 missing in action, totaling 1,010,300 casualties.[122] Among the 21,300 Chinese POWs, 7,110 were repatriated to China in three groups in

September and October 1953 (the armistice was signed in July).[123] The other Chinese prisoners went to the ROC on Taiwan.[124]

The PRC spent a total of about 10 billion yuan (about $3.3 billion) during the war. The Chinese government transported into Korea a total of 5.6 million tons of goods and supplies during the intervention. Between 1950 and 1953, China's military spending represented 41 percent, 43 percent, 33 percent, and 34 percent of its total governmental annual budget.[125] The Korean War was the first time Chinese armed forces engaged in large-scale military operations outside China, and they faced one of the best militaries in the world. The Korean War was the only meaningful reference point for sustained PLA contingency operations beyond China's border. Chinese generals recall their fighting in the Korean War as a heroic rescue operation and an extension of their own struggle against imperialism. Chinese history books portray China as a "beneficent victor" in the Korean War. Peter Hays Gries observes that "to many Chinese, Korea marks the end of the 'Century of Humiliation' and the birth of 'New China.'"[126] Still, after the Korean War, Chinese generals were convinced that the Chinese military was a regional force, not a global one, and that it would fight limited wars in terms of both theaters of war and geopolitical objectives. This would force the PLA to consider the relevance of China's traditional approach.

After the Chinese-American confrontation in Korea, China's position in the Cold War was no longer peripheral to the two opposing superpowers but was, in many key senses, central.[127] In retrospect, China's early Cold War experience—as exemplified in its participation in the Korean War—not only contributed significantly to shaping the specific course of the Cold War in Asia but, what is more important, helped create conditions for the war to remain cold in the 1950s and 1960s.

★ 4 ★

Russianizing the PLA

THE KOREAN WAR transferred the focal point of the global Cold War from Europe to east Asia. After its decision to intervene in the Korean War, China quickly adjusted its position in international affairs and willingly moved to the center of the ideological and military confrontations between the two contending camps headed by the Soviet Union and the United States. The active role that China played in east Asia turned this main Cold War battlefield into a strange buffer between Moscow and Washington. With east Asia standing in the middle, it was less likely that the Soviet Union and the United States would become involved in a direct military confrontation.[1] Some Western historians agree that the alliance between Beijing and Moscow was the cornerstone of the Communist international alliance in the 1950s.[2] Mao Zedong continued his revolution by calling on the people to "learn from the Soviet Union" and launching a series of political campaigns throughout the 1950s. As Chinese society became more radicalized to maintain its identity within the Communist camp, its foreign policy became more active in supporting the worldwide Communist movement to keep up with its new power status.

China's increasing political ambition and rising international position demanded a strong military. The armed forces had to be able to defend China against any foreign invasion, defeat technologically advanced Western forces, keep neighboring countries out of Western imperialist control, and enhance "China's prestige and influence in

113

the international arena."[3] To meet these new goals, the PLA launched a reform movement in the 1950s that continued the modernization it had begun during the Korean War. The 1950s reforms aimed to transform the PLA from a peasant army into a modern, professional force with new capacities. The reform programs, following the Soviet model, included major institutional changes, a centralized command system, technological improvements, advanced training and educational programs, reorganization of defense industries, a strategic missile force, and a nuclear weapon research and development program.

Ironically, these reforms caused the PLA to become more regularized and institutionalized as the CCP and society became more radicalized and ideological. The gap between the army and the party caused a series of political problems, which eventually led to the termination of the reform programs in the early 1960s. Chinese military reform took place only within the greater context of the newly founded republic, constrained by how far the Communist Party was willing to go and what Chinese society at large could support. This chapter examines the widening gap between an increasingly radicalized society and a gradually regularized military during the 1950s. The revolutionary society emphasized ideological factors, the human spirit, irrational decisions, extremist programs, and independence in its development. The military favored technological improvements, institutional control, rational decisions, regular programs, and dependence on Soviet aid. The political gap divided the military leadership and resulted in disagreements about Chinese military modernization.

Marshals Peng Dehuai and Liu Bocheng, like other Chinese military leaders, fought political battles to keep top party and government leaders on their side to help implement their reform plans. As this chapter demonstrates, the military reform achieved certain goals and eventually transformed the PLA, as Ellis Joffe describes, "from a guerrilla army with antiquated equipment and outdated tactics into a fairly modern and professional army."[4] The stories of Generals Zhang Aiping (Chang Ai-ping) and Nie Fengzhi indicate the emergence of a new generation of professional soldiers and accomplished commanders. They thought creatively about the issues of and solutions to the 1954–55 Taiwan Strait crisis and demonstrated that the PLA had significantly improved its operational, logistical, and technological abilities.

Campaigns for Control

China's intervention in the Korean War dragged the country into a fight for which it was unprepared. To cope with the Korean conflict, the CCP needed to strengthen its domestic control more than ever. Following the Soviet experience after the Russian Revolution of 1917, the Chinese Communist regime had adopted several high-handed measures to consolidate its power and fight the war. In the early 1950s, state control depended on radical movements and mass political participation. The radical movements included the campaign to suppress counterrevolutionaries in 1950, the Three Antis (Sanfan) and Five Antis (Wufan) campaigns of 1951–54, and the anti-rightist movement (*fanyou yundong*) in 1957. Little evidence in China links the Korean War to China's domestic politics, but clearly, conflict arose on the home front during and after the Korean War.[5]

After the outbreak of the Korean War, political consolidation intensified and escalated into a nationwide campaign. In late September 1950, Mao asked the new government not to kill a single agent of the enemy but to put the arrested agents in jail. He believed they should be given a means of living and compelled to reform themselves through labor to become new men.[6] Soon, however, the Chinese leaders changed their position, calling for the execution of all enemy elements.[7] The CCP South Central Bureau reported to the Central Committee on November 26, 1950, about the problems of the campaign to suppress counterrevolutionaries in the south. During the campaign, according to the report, some local governments used a lenient policy and let the counterrevolutionaries go without necessary punishments. The bureau suggested a political initiative of killing people (*sharen*): "If they should be executed, they must be executed."[8] Mao wrote that this sounded like "a good plan." Liu Shaoqi (Liu Shao-ch'i), PRC vice president and CCP vice chairman, forwarded these suggestions to all CCP bureaus with this instruction: "This is a good policy. [You are all] expected to follow this plan."[9] The new regime realized the necessity of stamping out all resistance in its effort to consolidate wartime control. The PRC State Council and People's Supreme Court issued a joint order, "Youguan zhenfan gongzuo de zhishi" (Directive concerning the Suppressing of Counterrevolutionaries), in early 1951, specifying that the "death penalty would be meted out not only to assassins and saboteurs but also to their accomplices."[10] In February 1951, the government passed the Regulations concerning Suppressing and Punishing Counterrevolutionaries. In May, Mao urged his party to rely on the masses in rounding up enemies of the revolution and said, "We must implement the party's mass line in suppressing counterrevolutionaries."[11]

The campaign was swift and decisive. Thousands of counterrevolutionaries and alleged counterrevolutionaries were rounded up, tried—sometimes on extremely flimsy evidence—and arbitrarily sentenced. The policy shocked the rural population, most of whom were unaware of the wrath of the revolutionary state. Premier Zhou Enlai claimed at the first national meeting of the Chinese People's Political Consultative Conference in October 1951, "If we had not attached great importance to the uprooting of the remnant forces of the counter-revolutionaries, it would have been impossible to consolidate important measures for the people's cause, such as the movement to resist America and aid Korea."[12] In the formulation and execution of the policy toward the urban opposition, the CCP not only asserted its authority over the society but developed an outline for further social transformation. The top leadership had a firm hand on the campaign, and party functionaries exercised strict oversight at all levels. Senior General Luo Ruiqing, minister of public security, reported directly to Mao and Peng Zhen, a member of the Politburo primarily in charge of political and legal work.

While the campaign to suppress counterrevolutionaries rocked urban China, two other campaigns, the Three Antis and Five Antis, expressed the will of the new regime to impose order in industry and commerce. The Three Antis campaign, which targeted corruption, waste, and obstructionist bureaucracy, reflected the CCP leadership's concerns about the moral decay of the rank and file of the revolution. This policy sought to embrace the war in Korea, which required a solid base and stable economic growth. The Five Antis campaign represented an "all-out assault on the bourgeoisie" in the cities.[13] It began in January 1952, when the CCP apparatus and CYL cells moved swiftly to mobilize employees in private enterprises and business firms against illegal activities. In Shanghai, some fifteen thousand propaganda workers were deployed in private companies to encourage employees to report on their employers' activities and coerce business owners to align with the state. The campaigns created an unprecedented political storm against the bourgeoisie. Under extreme political heat, entrepreneurs moved quickly, if often reluctantly, to comply. In Shanghai, voluntary confessions by business owners amounted to more than one thousand daily. Noncompliance meant humiliation, trial, and even betrayal by their own families. Most private entrepreneurs were found guilty one way or another. In Tianjin, a major port city and industrial center in north China, 10 percent of enterprises were classified as "law-abiding," 64.2 percent as "basically law-abiding," 21 percent as "semi-law-abiding," and 5.3 percent as "serious lawbreakers."[14] The nationwide ratios were 10–15 percent "law-abiding," 50–60 percent "basically law-abiding," 25–30 percent "semi-law-abiding," 4 percent "serious lawbreakers," and 1 percent "totally law-breaking."[15]

The timing of the Three Antis and Five Antis campaigns revealed the growing impatience of the new regime. Official statistics on the human costs of these campaigns are unavailable. Estimates from both inside and outside China have been largely speculative. Zhou Jingwen (Chow Ching-wen) claims that 1.5 million Chinese died during the suppression of the counterrevolutionaries, and another 200,000 or more during the Three Antis and Five Antis movements.[16] These figures are probably not grossly exaggerated. Chinese historian Bai Xi reports the casualties of these movements: 80 percent of the counterrevolutionaries received punishment ranging from incarceration to the death penalty. The government neutralized 2.4 million bandits. As for counterrevolutionaries, 230,000 were put under public surveillance, 1.27 million were incarcerated, and 710,000 were executed.[17] Frederick C. Teiwes concludes that "these campaigns indicated to broad sections of society the full extent of the Party's aims for social transformation. As the emphasis shifted from reassurance to tightening control, many groups that had hitherto been left basically alone were now drawn into the vortex of directed struggle. By the end of the 1950s the CCP had become, for the majority of China's urban population, a force to be reckoned with."[18] The high-handed measures certainly made China a Soviet-style state, if not a police state.

In the rural areas, starting in the early 1950s, the CCP mobilized peasant participation in the Korean War and in political campaigns by offering them membership in local peasants' associations and participation in local elections for village chiefs to seize political control as well as to carry out social transformation. Both the campaign to suppress counterrevolutionaries and the land reform efforts of 1950–53 effectively organized poor peasants. Between 1953 and 1958, peasants were collectivized to establish producers' cooperatives and people's communes. These campaigns extended state power to every corner of rural society, sometimes forcibly. Different areas experienced different levels of peasant backlash. These campaigns, however, as Chinese historian Zhou Xiaohong argues, also incorporated principles of peasant participation in local politics.[19] The CCP's membership increased from 2.7 million in 1947 to 6.1 million in 1953 and to 10.7 million in 1956, when the Eighth CCP National Congress was held in Beijing. At the party congress, Mao was again elected chairman of the Central Committee, with Liu Shaoqi, Zhou Enlai, Zhu De, and Chen Yun as vice chairmen and Deng Xiaoping as secretary-general.[20]

During the 1950s, peasants' demands were highly influenced by the state. An individual peasant's opportunities had less to do with his level of education, knowledge, ability, experience, or sense of responsibility than with his political loyalty and family connections. Only a few in the government and in the party received political power. Many peasants joined the military to gain political power and the opportunity to make decisions about their own lives. It had been the CCP's successes that had empowered Chinese peasants and turned them into the main strength of the Communist forces in World War II and the civil war. Now the PLA could continue to attract peasants by offering them CCP membership and providing them with political training for Mao's "continuous revolution" on their return to civilian life. In December 1952, the Central Committee established the people's armed forces committees (renmin wuzhuang weiyuanhui). Organized from the top down into province, region, county, city, and township levels across the country,[21] these committees connected the PLA with peasants. They provided weapons and training for village militias, informed the masses of security issues, and served as recruitment offices and veteran administrations for the PLA. Chen Jian points out that "Mao's revolution never took as its ultimate goal the Communist seizure of power in China; rather, as the chairman repeatedly made clear, his revolution aimed at transforming China's state, population, and society, and simultaneously reasserting China's central position in the world."[22]

During the 1950s, the PLA experienced major demobilization and reorganization. Its forces were reduced from 6.11 million in 1952 to

4.2 million in October 1953 by deactivating nineteen infantry armies, including seventy-three divisions. After two more large-scale demobilizations in 1954–55 and 1956–58, the PLA forces were reduced to 2.4 million.[23]

On December 16, 1954, the State Council announced the New System of Compulsory Military Service, a peacetime conscription system that replaced the universal military service system that had been adopted for the Chinese civil war.[24] Once selected, army conscripts had three years of mandatory service; navy and air force conscripts served four years. Following the Soviet system, the PLA used two mechanisms for maintaining technical expertise among enlisted personnel: lengthy mandatory service and optional extended service, up to six years. In some cases, volunteers were given the option to serve for an additional eight to twelve years or even to choose the military as a career.[25] The PLA high command intended to transform the Chinese peasant guerrilla army into a Soviet-style professional army. This conscription system lasted for thirty years.

Debates and Demands

During the 1950s, the CCP carried out Soviet-style social and economic reforms. The Chinese Communist revolution established a new socioeconomic system with a mixture of Marxism-Leninism and its Chinese version—Mao Zedong Thought. After the founding of the PRC, the CCP developed an integrated plan for the nation's economic recovery. Mao's social reforms, based on Soviet doctrine, were modified to the Chinese situation. Chinese land reform, for example, followed the Soviet collective ownership model. As a result, China emphasized the new state's revolutionary and Communist nature. Soviet financial, technological, and educational support aided China's reconstruction and economic growth, marking the "closest collaboration" between China and the Soviet Union.[26] In 1953, Mao called for a national movement to learn from the Soviet Union. The chairman remarked, "We are facing tremendous difficulties because we are building a great country. We do not have enough experience. Thus, we must carefully learn from the Soviet success."[27]

Mao asked the PLA to do the same. The chairman said that the Chinese military "must learn all of the Soviet experience and really

Zhou Enlai signs the Sino-Soviet Treaty of Friendship, Alliance, and Mutual Assistance. (Reproduced by permission of Contemporary China Press, Beijing, China.)

master all of their advanced technology in order to change our army's backward condition. We must re-construct our army as the second finest modern army in the world."[28] Mao appraised the Soviet aid on the fifth anniversary of the signing of the Sino-Soviet Treaty of Friendship, Alliance, and Mutual Assistance: "The all-round cooperation between China and the Soviet Union in political, economic and cultural fields has scored extensive development."[29] Naturally, Marshal Peng Dehuai accepted Mao's call for PLA reform, but he failed to deal effectively with different opinions within the military leadership. Their questions revolved around what examples the PLA should copy from the Soviet model.

Marshal Liu Bocheng questioned the following of the Soviet model and suggested that the PLA treasure the Chinese experience and not lose sight of the people's war doctrine. Born in Sichuan in 1892, Liu joined the army when he was very young and served in it his whole life. After the 1911 Revolution, he participated in the campaigns to protect the republic. In a battle in 1916, Liu was struck in the head by two bullets and lost his right eye; he became known as the one-eyed general.[30] He joined the CCP in 1926 and served as chief of staff of the front committee in the Nanchang Uprising in 1927. After the failure at Nanchang, Liu went to the Soviet Union and studied its military for two years. On his return to China in 1930, Liu was appointed chief of staff of the CMC and vice president of the Red Army University. He served as commander of the 129th Division of the Eighth Route Army during the Second Sino-Japanese War and commander of the Second Field Army, with Deng Xiaoping as his political commissar, in the civil war.[31]

After the PRC's establishment, Liu became the vice chairman of the CMC, chairman of the Southwest Military and Political Committee, and vice chairman of the National People's Congress. He was one of China's top military experts both in theory and in practice, with "few equals at home or abroad."[32] He taught Sun Zi's *The Art of War* at the China Academy of Military Science (CAMS) when he served as its president.[33] Deng Xiaoping praised Liu for having made "a great contribution to the shaping and development of Mao Zedong's thinking on military matters. It can truly be said that Comrade Bocheng's military theories constituted an important part of Mao Zedong's military thinking."[34] In the late 1950s, Liu stressed Chinese experience, proposed Chinese ways to build a modern regular army, and opposed copying the entire Soviet model.

But Peng Dehuai believed that only a Soviet-style army could confront the inevitable conflicts with international imperialists and ensure victory in future wars. Peng realized that the success of his 1950s reforms depended on this "successful learning" and the "availability of Soviet assistance."[35] In August and September 1953, Peng defended his reform agenda while chairing a series of expanded CMC meetings. On August 21, he told the CMC executive meeting about the Central Committee's five-year plan for PLA standardization. He pushed for both reorganization and modernization of equipment and training. Peng explained that China had now entered a new international environment and needed a more standardized military. The Soviets provided a proven model.[36]

Peng used the need to establish a more centralized chain of command as an example. Over the previous twenty-four years, Chinese forces had fought mostly guerrilla warfare against Japanese and GMD armies. Guerilla warfare did not require a centralized chain of command. As a result, field commanders enjoyed a great deal of autonomy. During WWII and the Chinese civil war, it was common for field officers to disregard their superiors. These commanders had developed a working structure: they won battles and got things done, but they did not follow orders. Peng pointed out that, as a nation's army, the PLA needed a centralized chain of command. At the next executive meeting, on September 4, he suggested a high command conference before the end of the year to discuss military reform in detail, and Mao and the Central Committee approved.[37]

From December 7, 1953, to January 26, 1954, this unprecedented meeting was held at the Zhongnanhai compound in Beijing. Among the 123 participants were the PLA's top commanders, CMC standing members, and academy presidents. Marshals Zhu, Peng, Chen Yi, Ye Jianying, Liu Bocheng, Nie Rongzhen, He Long, and others engaged in the debate on the PLA's reform. With Mao on his side, Peng silenced any dissenting opinions and signaled the beginning of Soviet-style military reform. The meeting set new principles for the PLA's modernization over the next decade by agreeing that the Chinese must learn advanced military science and technology from the Soviets.[38] In March 1956, Peng instructed the CAMS to launch a political movement against the dogmatism (*jiaotiao zhuyi*) of its own president, Liu Bocheng. Although he offered valid explanations for his positions, Liu was criticized and forced to confess his so-called mistakes and wrong ideas under political pressure. Soon Liu was replaced by Marshal Ye Jianying as CAMS president and political commissar. Then, with Mao's approval, Marshal Lin Biao launched an anti-dogmatist movement across the PLA. The 1958 anti-dogmatist campaign criticized some of the officers and included a top-down purge.[39] Deng simply said, "That was unfair."[40] The political campaigns undermined unity and promoted grievances and rivalry in the military.

After the 1953–54 meeting, Peng ordered all ranks to cooperate and maintain close working relationships with their Russian advisors.[41] From 1954 to 1958, the Defense Ministry systematically introduced Soviet military organization and doctrine as a model for Chinese military modernization. It translated Soviet Red Army regulations, manuals, curricula, handbooks, and research works into Chinese and distributed them to PLA units. From 1954 on, Soviet military advisors were stationed in China and assigned to various levels of all services. Many of them worked side by side with Chinese officers on operational planning and training and taught at the military academies with the help of translators.[42]

Most of the eighty thousand Soviet advisors sent to China each year in the 1950s were military advisors.[43] In Beijing, among 442 chief advisors, 310 were chief military advisors, 72 were economic and technology advisors, 47 were government and foreign policy advisors, and 13 were intelligence and national security chief advisors. The Soviet Military Advisory Group (SMAG) general headquarters in Beijing assigned its advisors to all of the PLA headquarters in the capital and sent many others to PLA regional, army, and divisional commands across the country. For instance, the PLA Navy (PLAN) had 711 Soviet advisors working at navy headquarters, naval bases, and academies.[44] Unlike civilian advisors, who were under the supervision and management of the Soviet Embassy in Beijing, the military advisors were under the direct command of the Soviet high command in Moscow. General Zahalov, deputy chief of the Soviet General Staff, served as head of the SMAG in 1950–51. He was followed by General Kalasovski (1951–53) and General Peterlusovski (1953–57). The last chief of the SMAG was General Dulufanov (1957–60).[45]

During the 1950s reforms, the military significantly improved its weapons and equipment by importing Soviet-made arms. In 1952, the CMC developed the first five-year plan for national defense, emphasizing artillery and tank force development.[46] By the end of 1955, the army had rearmed 106 infantry divisions, 9 cavalry and security divisions, 17 artillery divisions, 17 anti-aircraft artillery divisions, and 4 tank and armor divisions with Soviet weapons. These included eight hundred thousand automatic rifles, eleven thousand artillery pieces, and three thousand tanks and armored vehicles. By 1957, the army had completed its standardization program. The PLAN armed 9 gunboat brigades with two hundred Soviet-made vessels. With Soviet technology and training, the navy established a submarine force in June 1954. By the end of 1955, the navy had five hundred gunboats, three hundred support vessels, and three hundred heavy coastal artillery pieces.[47] The PLAAF armed 33 divisions with Soviet equipment and technology. By the end of 1955, the air force had received five hundred aircraft from the Soviet Union. As Jeanne L. Wilson points out, the Soviet

Union sought to keep China's armed forces reliant upon the Soviets to prohibit any connection with the West.[48] Thus, for example, the Soviet leaders offered fighters and bombers to the PLAAF but did not allow schematics or any type of production information to be passed to their Communist brethren. This forced Chinese military leaders to continue to rely on their northern neighbors for military supplies. Throughout the 1950s, China spent about $2 billion on arms purchases. For Peng, there was no other option to supply his navy and air force.[49]

During his trip to the Warsaw Pact conference in May 1955, Peng made stops at naval and air force bases in the Soviet Union.[50] In Poland, he visited a jet fighter manufacturing complex, the Polish Air Force Fifth Division, a motorized division base, and officer academies.[51] Peng emphasized the importance of Soviet technology in advancing China's military reforms.[52] In late 1955, at the request of Beijing, Moscow increased military aid to China and began to provide schematics and prototypes of some of its equipment. Moscow also assisted in building more than 256 plants throughout China for the development of the Chinese defense industry. The Chinese imported Soviet technol-

Mao Zedong examines a Chinese-made rifle. (Courtesy of the National Military Museum of the Chinese People's Revolution, Beijing, China.)

ogy for the production of small arms and artillery. Having learned from the Soviets, China developed some new weapons systems, including the first Chinese-made submarine, which went into service in 1956. By the end of the 1950s, China could manufacture 100mm antiaircraft artillery pieces, 122mm and 152mm howitzers, medium tanks, and rocket launchers.[53]

The PLAAF relied almost exclusively on Soviet-designed aircraft. From 1951 to 1955, China purchased 5,000 Russian aircraft.[54] Initially, the Soviets delivered the aircraft directly to China. But later the Russians and Chinese coproduced the same models of fighters and bombers in China. The Chinese learned how to reengineer, modify, and produce their own variations in China from the late 1950s to the 1970s. By the end of 1955, the PLAAF had established eleven first-level departments in its administrative command structure and had 4,400 aircraft. In 1957 the air force merged with the surface-based air defense force, a total of eleven antiaircraft artillery divisions. In July 1958, the air force established three surface-to-air missile battalions. In 1956, the PLAAF tested the Qian-5 fighter, a Chinese version of the Russian MiG-17 fighter. By 1959, the nation was manufacturing Qian-6, a modified MiG-19.[55] By the late 1960s, the air force had created fifty air divisions and thirteen air corps.[56]

Institutional Changes and New Officer Corps

In September 1954, the First National People's Congress (NPC) established a new constitution that created a new National Defense Commission under the central government and a new Ministry of Defense under the State Council. Peng became the first defense minister in this new configuration. Thereafter, he reorganized the command system. On October 11, 1954, the PLA established eight department headquarters, which paralleled those in the Soviet army, including the existing headquarters of the General Staff Department (GSD), General Political Department (GPD), General Logistics Department (GLD), and General Officer Corps Department, and four new general departments: equipment, training, finance, and auditing.[57]

As in the Soviet Red Army, the GSD carried out the staff and operational functions of the PLA and implemented modernization plans. Within the defense hierarchy, the GSD conveyed policy directives downward, translated national security and defense policy into specific responsibilities for subordinate departments, oversaw policy implementation on behalf of the CMC, and commanded China's military operations in wartime. The GSD also performed important organizational functions such as procurement, operational planning, and intelligence. Headed by the chief of the General Staff, the department served as the headquarters for the ground forces and contained directorates for the other armed services. The GPD was responsible for ideological indoctrination, political loyalty, morale, personnel records, cultural activities, discipline, and military justice. Organizationally, the GPD provided the PLA with its party structure. The director of the department oversaw a system of political commissars assigned to each echelon of the PLA. One of the political commissar's primary tasks was the supervision of the party organization through party committees at the battalion level and above and through party branches at the company level. After the fall of Marshal Peng, the GPD's role was strengthened. In the 1960s, under the guidance of Marshal Lin Biao, it exerted a considerable amount of political influence throughout the defense establishment. The GLD was the least politically influential of the general departments. Headed by a chief, the GLD supervised production, supply, transportation, housing, pay, and medical services. Before the Korean War, most of this support had come from the civilian populace, usually organized by commissars.[58]

Peng, now defense minister, created a highly centralized command structure by reorganizing the PLA forces from field armies into regional military commands—in other words, from mobile armies, or "nomadic troops," into regional armies, or "habitant troops." In the 1950s, the Chinese military had six grand regional commands: East, North, Northeast, Northwest, Southwest, and South Central. Each region was further divided into several provincial commands.[59] Technology took a larger part of the forces and defense budget throughout the 1950s. While the army's infantry troops decreased from 61.1 percent of total PLA forces in 1950 to 42.3 percent in 1958, its artillery units increased from 20.4 percent in 1950 to 31.9 percent in 1958; its tank units increased to 4.8 percent in 1958; and its engineering units increased from 1.6 percent in 1950 to 4.4 percent in 1958. The air force increased to 12.2 percent of PLA forces and the navy to 5.8 percent by 1958.[60]

As part of his reforms, Peng established a Soviet-style military rank system in 1955. Some of the CCP leaders opposed the new ranking system, since it changed the PLA tradition of equality among soldiers and commanders. Mao, however, approved the system and awarded, for the only time in PLA history, the rank of marshal to 10 top PLA commanders: Zhu, Peng, Nie Rongzhen, Lin Biao, Chen Yi, Xu Xiangqian, Liu Bocheng, Ye Jianying, He Long, and Luo Ronghuan. (In May 1992, the last marshal, Nie Rongzhen, died. Currently, the highest military rank in China is general.) On September 27, 1955, Premier Zhou Enlai appointed 10 senior generals and 57 generals. Then the military regional commands awarded 175 lieutenant generals, 800 major generals, and 32,000 colonels and majors. Between 1955 and 1966, an additional 5 generals, 2 lieutenant generals, and 560 major generals were promoted within the services.[61] Marshal Lin Biao criticized Peng's reform and the PLA ranking system as part of the "Soviet revisionist military structure." As Peng's successor, Lin abolished the ranking system in 1966.

In the early 1950s, as part of the officer training effort, the CMC began a reeducation program to eliminate illiteracy among the officer corps. It created 262 schools at the division and army levels to provide elementary and secondary education for the officers. Illiteracy among the PLA officer corps was reduced from 67.4 percent in 1951 to 30.2 percent in the mid-1950s. Among the rank and file, the percentage who passed the third grade literature test increased from 16.4 percent to 42.1 percent.[62] The PLA also opened up new military academies and colleges across the country. By 1959, it had 129 military academies, including 26 war colleges, 72 technology institutes, and 16 cadet schools, with a total enrollment of 253,000 officer-students. The PLA established a complete officer training system from primary to advanced level. This curriculum and training trend moved away from traditional peasant army and guerrilla warfare tactics toward large-scale joint operations.[63]

The first Chinese naval school was founded in Dalian, Liaoning, in February 1950 with the help of the Soviet navy. It later became the PLA Naval Academy in Dalian and then the Dalian Naval Engineering Institute. Soviet naval advisors selected the campus site, designed facilities, outlined and drafted the entire curriculum, and translated hundreds of Russian naval textbooks into Chinese.[64] In April, another naval academy was founded in Nanjing, also with the help of Soviet naval advisors. On October 8, Mao asked Stalin for help in establishing Chinese submarine forces. On February 7, 1951, the Soviet navy agreed to use two Soviet submarines and crews to train Chinese submariners for two years. According to the agreement, the Soviet navy would sell these two submarines to China after the training. On April 20, 275 Chinese naval officers were sent to the Soviet Pacific Fleet to study submarine navigation and operation at the Russian submarine bases. They worked and lived with the Russian submarine crew for three years.[65] On June 19, 1954, when the Chinese submarine training group finished their training in the Soviet Union, they sailed the two submarines back to China. On July 22, the Chinese navy established its first submarine division at Qingdao, Shandong.

The School for Foreign Language Cadres, founded in the early 1950s in Nanjing, developed several training programs for military intelligence personnel. Its Russian instructors offered training in information collection, analysis, and technology. Some of its graduates continued their study by attending the Moscow Institute of International Relations and receiving further training from the KGB. All of the officer-students also participated in major PLA exercises, such as the anti-landing exercise on Liaodong Peninsula in 1954. The study and training were difficult, and the Russian instructors were hard taskmasters. The class of 1955 was the second class in the school. In the two departments, operations and intelligence, only 319 of 458 students graduated.[66] In his commencement speech as the school's superintendent, Marshal Liu Bocheng acknowledged the many years of tough training it took to complete the programs.[67]

In the 1950s, the PLA sent a large group of young and promising officers to the Soviet Union to study military science and technology, operational tactics, and logistics. Many of them later became the second (1970s–1980s), third (1980s–1990s), and fourth (2000s) generations of Chinese military leaders. For example, General Cao Gangchuan, China's defense minister since 2003, was one of the students who studied in the Soviet Union. Born in 1935 in Wugang, Henan, Cao joined the PLA and CCP in 1956. He studied at the PLA's Dalian Russian Language Special School in 1956–57. In September 1957, he attended the Leningrad Advanced Military Engineering School to further study missile design. After six years of study and training in Russia, Cao graduated from the Soviet Army Artillery Academy and returned to China in 1963. Speaking fluent Russian, he became an instructor at the First Artillery Ordnance Technical School. In the late 1960s, he served as an assistant in the ordnance section of the equipment department of the GLD. He was promoted to staff officer of the comprehensive planning section of the equipment department of the GSD in April 1975.[68] Cao's study in the Soviet Union built a solid background of military technology and personal connections that helped his military career. In September 1988, when the PLA restored the military ranking system, he was given the rank of lieutenant general.

Reorganization and modernization presented opportunities for rapid advancement, especially in the relatively new air force. Lieutenant General Qiao Qingchen was born in 1939 in Zhengzhou, Henan, and joined the PLAAF in 1956 and the CCP in 1960. Qiao became commander of an aviation division in the 1960s, and later deputy political commissar of the Fourth Air Force Army. He rose to major general in 1988 and was promoted to lieutenant general in 1996. By May 2002, he was the chief of the Chinese air force.[69] Of all the services, the air force most closely followed the Soviet doctrine, tactics, and training.[70]

The Soviet Union's massive amounts of weapons systems training and help organizing the defense industry greatly influenced the 1950s reforms. Jonathan Spence states that, during the 1950s reforms, "the shape of a professional army began to emerge, especially with the development of technical arms such as the engineering corps, railway and signals corps, and the 'ABC' corps," so named for its attempt to master the techniques of antiatomic, biological, and chemical warfare.[71] It was apparent that the Chinese military had become regularized, modernized, and ready to take on new challenges, like amphibious landing campaigns against the GMD-held offshore islands during the 1954–55 Taiwan Strait crisis.

From the Land to the Seas

A comparison of the PLA's 1949 Jinmen (Quemoy) landing campaign and its 1955 Yijiangshan landing campaign indicates the tremendous changes in PLA training, planning, operational tactics, and supply that resulted from the 1950s reforms. The failure of the 1949 Jinmen landing demonstrated the serious problems of irregular guerrilla forces in a modern amphibious campaign. The successful 1955 Yijiangshan landing showed the positive impacts of the reforms on the PLA's combined operations and combat effectiveness.

For the PLA, offshore operations became an important and difficult issue in late 1949, the last year of the Chinese civil war, when Jiang Jieshi and his troops retreated from the mainland to the offshore islands, including Taiwan, Hainan, Zhoushan, and Jinmen. Taiwan, which is 13,900 square miles and lies 120 miles from the mainland, was the largest island occupied by GMD forces. Taiwan had a population of some four million people in 1949. Hainan Island, about 13,300 square miles, had a population of one million. Jinmen Island, covering a total of 60 square miles, had a population of forty thousand at that time. It is not in the open ocean but lies in Xiamen (Amoy) Harbor, surrounded by the mainland on three sides. Less than 2 miles away from Xiamen, the largest seaport on the southeast mainland, Jinmen was effectively defended by the GMD troops. In the fall of 1949, the PLA Third Field Army, with 1 million men, in east China and the Fourth Field Army, with 1.2 million men, in south China actively prepared for amphibious operations against the GMD-occupied islands.

After taking over Xiamen on October 17, 1949, the Tenth Army Group of the Third Field Army ordered its Twenty-eighth Army to prepare a landing campaign against Jinmen Island. On October 24, the Twenty-eighth Army attacked Jinmen Island. As the first wave of 10,000 troops landed, they found themselves tightly encircled by the GMD garrison and suffered heavy casualties. GMD air and naval forces destroyed the two hundred small fishing junks collected around Xiamen by the PLA for landing before they could land reinforcements.[72] With no boats, the Tenth Army Group, 150,000 strong, could not reinforce the Jinmen landings. They could only listen helplessly as their comrades pleaded for aid on the radio. Three days later, transmissions ceased. The Twenty-eighth Army lost 9,086 landing troops, including more than 3,000 prisoners.[73]

No existing Chinese record reveals serious discussions at the high command on the Jinmen operation before October 28, 1949, when the bad news reached Beijing: one of the best army groups in the Third Field Army had lost three regiments on the Jinmen beaches. Shocked, Mao drafted a warning to all PLA commanders, "especially those high-level commanders at army level and above," that they "must learn a good lesson from the Jinmen failure."[74] Mao suggested that all concerned armies take time to train for cross-strait operations to better prepare their troops for future landings. On October 31, Mao telegraphed Marshal Lin Biao, Fourth Field Army commander, to halt all amphibious operations on the South China Sea coast.[75] In early November, Mao informed Senior General Su Yu, deputy commander of the Third Field Army, to postpone the attacks on the islands in the East China Sea.[76] Su issued orders to the Seventh, Ninth, and Tenth army groups on November 14 that army group headquarters would no longer order offshore attacks; only the field army headquarters could authorize such an operation.[77]

On December 8, 1949, Jiang Jieshi moved the seat of his government to Taiwan. At Taipei, the new capital of the ROC, Jiang prepared for the final showdown with Mao in the last battle of the Chinese civil war. He concentrated his troops on four major islands: 200,000 men on Taiwan, 100,000 on Hainan Island, 120,000 on the Zhoushan Archipelago, and 60,000 on Jinmen Island.[78] Mao showed extra caution from this point on. He telegraphed the field army commanders again in November that the "cross-strait campaign is totally different from all experience our army had in the past." He asked his commanders to "guard against arrogance, avoid underestimating the enemy, and be well prepared."[79] In December, the high command reorganized the headquarters of the Twelfth Army Group, Fourth Field Army into the headquarters of the PLAN. Senior General Xiao Jinguang, commander of the Twelfth, was appointed commander of the navy.[80]

On November 18, on his way to Moscow, Mao drafted a lengthy telegram to Marshal Lin Biao. This message was the first systematic consideration of PLA amphibious operations by top Chinese leaders.[81] Mao traveled to Russia to gain Soviet financial and material support for the PLA cross-strait attack on Taiwan and other offshore islands. Mao spent two months in Moscow to convince Stalin and negotiate a Sino-Soviet agreement. In February 1950, after signing the Sino-Soviet Treaty of Friendship, Alliance, and Mutual Assistance, Mao and Zhou signed a huge naval order with Stalin. The Soviet Union agreed to arm a new Chinese naval force with ships and equipment worth $150 million, half of the total loan package Stalin granted during Mao's two-month stay.[82]

Returning from Moscow in February 1950, Mao called Su to Beijing to plan attacks on Jinmen and Taiwan with Marshal Nie Rong-

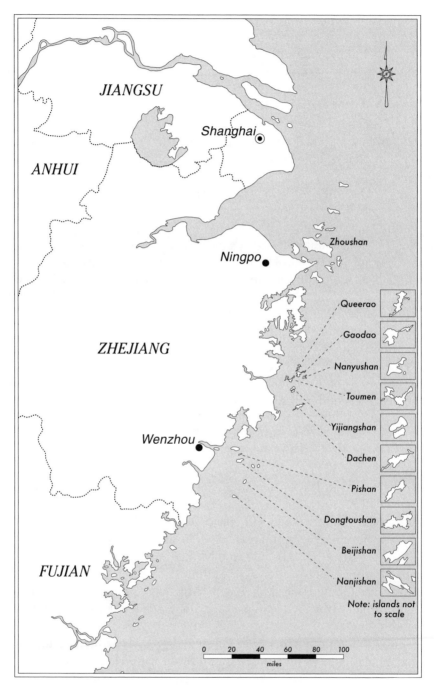

East China Sea Islands

zhen, acting chief of the General Staff. During their discussions, Mao instructed Su to train airborne forces and prepare an additional four divisions for amphibious maneuvers.[83] On March 11, Senior General Xiao Jinguang, PLAN commander, met Senior General Su Yu to discuss the first detailed plan to liberate Taiwan. According to their plan, the Third Field Army and the navy would deploy five hundred thousand troops to attack Taiwan.[84] They planned to make two landing waves. In the first wave, the Third Field Army would land its Seventh and Ninth army groups, including six infantry armies, three hundred thousand troops. The second wave would consist of its Tenth Army Group, including three infantry armies, plus other three armies, about two hundred thousand troops. In the meantime, the Fourth Field Army would prepare its Thirteenth Army Group, including three infantry armies, as a reserve for the attack. Three more armies of the Nineteenth Army Group would be deployed along the coast as a mobile force. Total forces for the invasion of Taiwan would be around eight hundred thousand men. In April, the CMC approved the Su-Xiao plan. The Third Field Army began its landing training in late spring.[85]

In April, Mao also approved the Fourth Field Army's attack on Hainan Island. In April, one hundred thousand men of the Fifteenth Army Group, Fourth Field Army crossed the twenty-mile-wide Qongzhou Strait in the South China Sea and successfully landed on Hainan. The landing forces quickly overran the island. A month later, the Seventh and Ninth army groups of the Third Field Army occupied the Zhoushan Archipelago in the East China Sea. In the late spring of 1950, it was widely expected that the PLA would soon attack Jinmen and Taiwan. By the time Zhoushan fell, the PLA was better prepared for further amphibious operations. The first group of eighty-nine pilots graduated from the pilot training schools in May 1950. The air force organized the first division in Nanjing with fifty Soviet-made fighters and bombers. (The GMD air force on Taiwan had about two hundred fighters and bombers at that time.) Meanwhile, the PLAN expanded to fifty-one medium warships, fifty-two landing boats, and thirty support vessels, totaling forty-three thousand tons. (The GMD navy had a total tonnage of one hundred thousand at that time.)[86]

In early June, as we have seen, the CMC reorganized the PLA forces from field armies into regional military commands. The Third Field Army became the East China Command (ECC) and its four army groups, including fifteen armies stationed in six provinces, including Zhejiang, Fujian, Shanghai, and coastal areas along the Taiwan Strait. The CCP held its third plenary session of the Seventh CCP National Congress in Beijing June 6–9, 1950. Mao urged the liberation of Taiwan and Tibet as the party's central tasks. At the meeting, Senior General Su Yu, then deputy commander of the ECC, reported on preparations for invading Taiwan. After the meeting, Su's forces attacked offshore islands as preparation for the upcoming Taiwan campaign. In June, the ECC landed forces on the Dongshan and Wanshan island groups. Unfortunately for the ECC, the Korean War broke out, and the United States drastically changed its position on Taiwan.

On June 27, 1950, two days after the North Korean invasion of South Korea, President Truman announced that the U.S. Seventh Fleet would be deployed in the Taiwan Strait to prevent a Chinese Communist attack on GMD-held Taiwan. However, as David M. Finkelstein argues, Truman's order to the Seventh Fleet was not just to keep the Communists from invading Taiwan, but also to keep the GMD from attacking the mainland and thus widening the war beyond Korea. Finkelstein makes it clear that "Taiwan was neutralized for purely military-strategic reasons. Washington could not allow the island to be occupied by enemy forces while U.S. ground troops were committed to a land war in Korea."[87] The Seventh Fleet's presence in the Taiwan Strait marked a turning point in the cross-strait situation. What had been part of the Chinese civil struggle transformed into an international confrontation. With Washington's direct involvement in the Taiwan Strait, the PLA now faced a serious challenge.

On June 30, Zhou, premier and CMC vice chairman, postponed operations against Taiwan.[88] On July 31, General MacArthur led a U.S. military delegation, including sixteen generals, to Taiwan. Later, the United States organized a military advisory assistant group in Taiwan.[89] Considering these new developments, the CMC cabled Marshal Chen Yi, commander of the ECC, that there would be no attack on Taiwan until 1952 at the earliest. In November, after Chinese troops intervened in the Korean War, Mao ordered the ECC to postpone all offshore offensive operations. To restrain the Tenth Army Group's desire to revenge its loss at Jinmen, the CMC issued another order to Ye Fei, the army group commander, that there would be no operations against Jinmen until the CPVF achieved a decisive victory in Korea.[90] These orders converted the coastal region from the front line of the Chinese civil war to a rear area of the Korean War.

The Korean War was the largest Chinese security concern in the summer of 1950. Northeast China, bordering Korea, was the most important strategic region in the country, containing the industrial center and communication and supply lines with the Soviet Union. After the outbreak of the Korean War, the CMC moved four of its best armies from central China to northeastern China and reorganized them into the Northeast Border Defense Army in July, as discussed in the previous chapter. On July 13, the CMC appointed Senior Generals Su and Xiao as the commander and deputy commander of the NBDA. These decisions reflected the strategic shift from the Taiwan Strait to Korea. In early October, after the UNF crossed the 38th parallel, the PLA deployed eighteen divisions, totaling 260,000 men, along the Yalu River. The Chinese leaders believed that Korea, not Taiwan, was the place for a Chinese-American showdown. According to Mao's Cold War theory, there would be a clash between the two countries sooner or later. The Chinese military should have its own initiative, advantage, and alternative before this inevitable conflict. In the early 1950s, America intruded in and threatened China's security in three areas: Korea, Indochina, and the Taiwan Strait. Concerned with the regional economy, transportation capacity, and technology gap, the Chinese believed Korea was the place to fight against the United States. Mao also chose Korea instead of Taiwan as the battleground because he believed he had a better chance to win a land war.

The 1954–55 Taiwan Strait Crisis

With the Korean armistice in July 1953 and a settlement on Indochina at Geneva in July 1954, international tensions, especially between the two superpowers, subsided. The post-Stalin Soviet leadership had a different worldview, especially with respect to the Cold War. Moscow changed from a hard-line stand to a moderate and flexible one. The Soviets expected other Communist states to follow and change their positions toward the United States accordingly. Nikita Khrushchev clearly revealed his ideas in a discussion with Chinese defense minister Peng Dehuai in early 1955. Peng visited Khrushchev in Moscow on his way to Poland to attend the Warsaw Pact conference. Khrushchev told

Peng that since the United States was still very powerful, peaceful negotiations should be encouraged to solve international disputes. Peng
voiced agreement with Khrushchev and asserted that China needed
a peaceful period to build up its economy, reform the military, and
strengthen its defenses.[91]

In 1953, Mao adopted a moderate foreign policy of cooperation
with the new Soviet leaders. To avoid a major international crisis in
the Taiwan Strait, Mao curbed an ECC plan to land five armies on Jinmen Island.[92] In December, the CMC telegraphed Marshal Chen Yi,
ECC commander, and instructed the ECC to order all its provincial
commands to keep offshore operations defensive in nature. The high
command wanted no direct engagement with U.S. forces in China's
waters.[93]

Though Beijing welcomed a relaxation of international tensions,
it worried about U.S. policy toward Taiwan. Beijing hoped a victory in
Korea would prompt an American withdrawal from the Taiwan Strait.
But the Korean armistice did not end the Taiwan problem or lead to
the withdrawal of the Seventh Fleet. Instead, America increased its
involvement, dashing Beijing's hopes for an end to the Chinese civil
war. Soon after Eisenhower took office in 1953, he signed an order stating that the Seventh Fleet would no longer be used to prevent Jiang's
forces from attacking the mainland. This strategy was described as "un-
leashing Jiang." Beijing undoubtedly was puzzled about Washington's
future role in the strait. The Seventh Fleet engaged in "routine" exercises with GMD forces[94] and aided Taipei in harassing the mainland
from offshore islands. These efforts included coastal raids, guerrilla operations, leaflet dropping, fishing boat seizures, attacks on PRC coastal
shipping, and the seizure or firing upon of foreign vessels bound for
Chinese ports.[95]

In 1954, Beijing perceived unmistakable indications that Taipei-
Washington collaboration was accelerating. If China did not send a
quick and effective message to the United States, Beijing believed,
American cooperation would legitimize Taiwan in international politics, hindering Beijing's goal to gain full acceptance as a significant
member of the international community. However, facing a changing
international situation, China had exhausted its peaceful maneuvers
before it could solve the problems left behind by the Korean War. Mao
confronted a new and ambiguous situation. With limited alternatives,

he decided to deal with Washington and Taipei separately. That meant China would deal with the United States through diplomatic channels, if possible, and would in the meantime continue its military operations against the GMD-occupied offshore islands.[96]

By the summer of 1954, GMD troops still held eighteen islands off China's coast. The islands are geographically divided into two groups. The first is the Taiwan Strait island group, which has six islands, including Jinmen and Mazu (Matsu), that lie a few miles south of Fujian Province. The second is the East China Sea group, which has twelve islands, including the Dachen Islands, that lie east of Zhejiang Province. In addition, there are a dozen much smaller, uninhabited islands, also very close to the mainland, within hit-and-run range of both the GMD and the PLA.

General Zhang Aiping was in charge of PLA offshore operations along the Zhejiang coast in 1954–55. In 1950, he had become the commander of the ECC East China Sea Fleet, the PLA's first naval force. He was promoted to chief of the ECC General Staff in March 1952. In December 1953, at age forty-three, Zhang became the commander of the Zhejiang Command (ZC), a subdivision of the ECC. Zhang faced a Cold War paradox in 1954. On one hand, he had to follow Beijing's overall policy to reduce international tensions and avoid any conflict with the U.S. Navy. On the other hand, he had to defend the Zhejiang coast. Zhang maintained that he could protect his assigned section of the coast only by attacking GMD-occupied islands. The Zhejiang coast stretched almost 1,400 miles, not including its many islands, and a GMD landing could be effected almost anywhere. The GMD occupied ten islands within a few miles of the Zhejiang coast and had been conducting raids from them since 1949. From 1950 to 1953, for example, the GMD troops raided more than two thousand Zhejiang fishing boats and captured ten thousand fishermen. Zhang simply could not defend the entire coast.[97]

Thus General Zhang developed a new, active defense plan that extended onshore defenses offshore. Instead of waiting for a GMD strike, he planned to attack and occupy the GMD-held islands. To avoid an international crisis, he would attack the smallest island first, a campaign he hoped would draw little attention. He would conduct a piecemeal operation, beginning with the northernmost islands, which were more than two hundred miles away from the Taiwan Strait and at least one hundred miles away from the units of the U.S. Seventh Fleet in the South China Sea. He could then move south successively and attack larger islands, one by one.[98] His plan made PLA strategy more offensive and aggressive.

Beijing was concerned about the PLA's ability to control the air and sea off the Zhejiang coast. When the CMC approved Zhang's plan, it instructed Zhang to restrict attacks to the smaller islands, identify the weakest points of the GMD's island defenses, and practice air, naval, and landing operations.[99] Zhang chaired a commanders' meeting in January 1954 at which he and his officers made several key decisions. The Dongji Islands—the islands farthest from Taiwan, in the northern East China Sea—were identified as the first target. The ZC commanders agreed, first, that amphibious plans would involve air, naval, and land forces. This was the first attempt in PLA history to establish joint operations among all three services in a single campaign. The use of such a combined force would not become a specific and pronounced PLA policy until much later, in the 1980s. Second, amphibious operations would begin with a fight for control of the sea and air to isolate GMD garrisons and offset their superior firepower. Third, the Twenty-fourth Army would concentrate on training for landings. The high command approved the ZC's plan and instructed the ZC headquarters to coordinate its attack in the spring to protect the fishing season in Sanmen Bay and surrounding waters.[100]

General Zhang carried out the naval and air campaign from March through May 1954. His naval force, the East China Sea Fleet, concentrated on Sanmen Bay, with six medium escort ships and ten gunboats. On March 18, the fleet attacked GMD naval forces north of the Dachen Islands, sinking one GMD warship and damaging another. From March 18 to May 20, the East China Sea Fleet engaged in twelve battles with the GMD navy and damaged nine GMD ships. Meanwhile, the Second Division of the PLAAF engaged the GMD air force over the same area. The experienced Second Division had just returned from Korea and was equipped with Soviet-made MiG-15 jet fighters, whereas the GMD still lacked jet fighters, although American F-84s had just arrived in Taiwan.[101] In six air engagements, six GMD fighters were shot down while the PLAAF lost only two. By May, the PLA controlled the skies and waters north of the Dachen Islands. As the situation grew more unfavorable to the GMD, Jiang Jieshi became so

Jiang Weiguo in Taipei. (Author's collection.)

concerned about the successful PLA operations that he made his first visit ever, on May 6–7, to the GMD garrison in the Dachen Islands. He told his troops there to avoid panic under any circumstances. General Jiang Weiguo recalled that his father's visit strengthened the morale on the Dachen Islands by disproving rumors that the GMD high command would evacuate the GMD troops from these islands. The Dachen Islands garrison received reinforcement and more supplies.[102]

The 1955 Landing Campaigns

In early May, the PLA was ready to launch its landing campaign. As General Zhang planned, the Sixtieth Infantry Division would take the Dongji Islands first. With air support provided by the First and Second air force divisions, newly arrived from Shanghai, and with naval support from twelve East China Sea Fleet gunboats, two landing ships and sixteen transports carrying the 180th Regiment of the Sixtieth Division sailed for the islands at 1900 hours on May 15. The troops landed at the Dongji Islands and eliminated the GMD garrison, capturing sixty prisoners. The PLA's amphibious operations had experienced a rapid evolution as a result of its commanders' ability to adjust to changing conditions. With Zhang's success, the CMC decided in July that the ECC and ZC would launch a similar attack in September on the Dachen Islands, the much larger island group off the Zhejiang coast.[103]

General Zhang had learned some lessons from his amphibious campaign. Combining the air, naval, and ground troops in the landing made the operation more complicated than the PLA field generals believed. A combined operation did not merely involve engaging three services in the same battle. It required a different commanding system with better communication and cooperation. In the fall of 1954, Zhang established his joint command, the Zhejiang Front Command (ZFC), in Ningbo for the Dachen campaign. Under his command was a tripartite front headquarters, with air, naval, and landing forces. During the first joint meeting, on August 31, Zhang presented his cautious step-by-step plan for the Dachen campaign. Many other commanders, however, expressed optimism about an immediate landing on the seven islands of the Dachen group at the same time. General Nie Fengzhi, commander of the ZFC air force, disagreed with the majority opinion and favored Zhang's plan.

During the Korean War, Nie served as commander of the Chinese–North Korean joint air force. After returning to China, he served as the commander of the ZFC air force and later the ECC air force.[104] General Nie supported Zhang's piecemeal tactic: one island at a time. The commanders finally agreed with the Zhang-Nie plan and selected Yijiangshan, a half-square-mile islet seven miles north of the major Dachen Islands, as the first target of the landing campaign. The ZFC scheduled the attack on Yijiangshan for September. By September 2, Nie's air force was ready. On September 3, the PLA artillery on the Fujian front began a heavy bombardment of Jinmen and Mazu to reduce reinforcements and supply shipments from Taiwan to these islands.[105]

Back in Beijing, however, Mao had no intention of jeopardizing China's international position with these ongoing amphibious campaigns. He asked the CMC to put the ZFC request on hold because of Indian prime minister Jawaharlal Nehru's September visits to Shanghai and Hangzhou, the provincial capital of Zhejiang. In late September, the ZFC again requested Mao's approval to carry out its landing plan.[106] Only in late October did Mao reluctantly agree.[107]

General Nie began his assault on the Dachen Islands on November

1. For four days, ZFC bombers and fighters raided the Dachen Islands and Yijiangshan, flying more than one hundred sorties and dropping more than one thousand bombs.[108] Nie, following CMC instructions, took care to avoid conflict with American airplanes. He talked personally with all of his pilots about this policy and made it clear that they could not engage U.S. aircraft without his permission. General Nie recalled, "Throughout the whole campaign we had an excellent result with no involvement with foreign air forces."[109] By late November, the ZFC had completed construction of a torpedo-boat base and coastal artillery positions opposite Yijiangshan. The ZFC now dominated both air and sea around the Dachen Islands, and a landing at Yijiangshan seemed imminent.[110]

But again the high command called a halt, this time to await the outcome of negotiations on a U.S.-Taiwan mutual defense treaty, which might or might not include the offshore islands. As we have seen, Mao did not want a war against the United States in the East China Sea. On November 30, Senior General Su Yu, chief of the PLA General Staff, ordered the ZFC to continue its preparations and rescheduled the landing for no earlier than December 20.[111] On December 2, Taipei and Washington agreed on a mutual defense treaty that specified a U.S. commitment to defend GMD-occupied islands.[112] For the PLA, this made conducting any further amphibious operations very difficult, if not impossible, without risking war with the United States.

General Zhang Aiping had his own concerns. A delay of his invasion would create serious problems within his forces because of the ongoing PLA demobilization and reorganization initiatives. On August 1, 1953, Marshal Zhu, commander in chief, had announced that the PLA would begin a complete reorganization to adjust the overstaffed command system and reduce the number of troops. Thereafter, the headquarters of the General Staff decided to reduce PLA troops from 6.1 million to 3.5 million men in 1954.[113] Mao approved the plan on January 5. Meanwhile, the new compulsory military service law replaced the universal military service employed in the Chinese civil war. By the end of 1954, the ECC had lost some three hundred thousand soldiers through retirement and deactivation. Moreover, both the reductions and the compulsory service policy required most of the veterans who had joined in the civil war or the Korean War to leave the army by the Chinese New Year in 1955 because they had long since passed retirement age.[114]

This massive demobilization and reorganization threatened to retire the most experienced soldiers and delay the liberation of the offshore islands in the East China Sea. Zhang coped with the situation in two ways. One tactic was to persuade his veterans to stay until they occupied the Dachen Islands. Zhang held quite a few commanders' meetings and visited veterans on the front. For example, at a political mobilization general meeting that he chaired at Ningbo, he expressed the hope of keeping experienced troops for the upcoming landing. The veterans' representatives responded favorably. Since they had been prepared for this landing campaign, they did not want to leave the job to new recruits. Many veterans asked to delay their retirement until they had conquered the Dachen Islands.[115] Zhang's other approach was to push the high command to approve his plan to speed up his amphibious operations.[116]

On December 16, ZFC commanders met at Ningbo again to discuss the Yijiangshan landing and sent another request to the CMC for approval. Beijing did not reply until December 21. Between December 21 and January 10, the ZFC air force conducted five heavy raids against the Dachen Islands, including 28 bomber and 116 fighter sorties. On January 10, the PLA aircraft raided Dachen Harbor, sinking one GMD tank landing ship and damaging four other ships.[117]

Zhang and Nie decided to launch the attack on January 18, 1955. At 0600 hours on January 17, Zhang moved the ZFC headquarters forward from Ningbo to Linhai, only five miles away from Yijiangshan. Around 1000 hours, however, the General Staff headquarters in Beijing called Zhang again, questioning his decision to attack Yijiangshan. At this time, the high command believed that the ZFC should postpone the attack for anther two or three months, until it was better prepared. At 1700 hours, Zhang received an ECC telegram ordering him to "follow the instruction of the 17th from the General Staff HQs. Withdraw all your troops. Stop the attack on Yijiangshan."[118] Zhang, however, insisted on the fixed schedule and called General Chen Geng, deputy chief of the General Staff in charge of operations. Chen reported directly to Mao. Mao left the final decision to Marshal Peng. Peng approved Zhang's request immediately, sending Zhang a telegram at around 1730 hours via the CMC: "Launch your landing campaign on the 18th according to your schedule."[119]

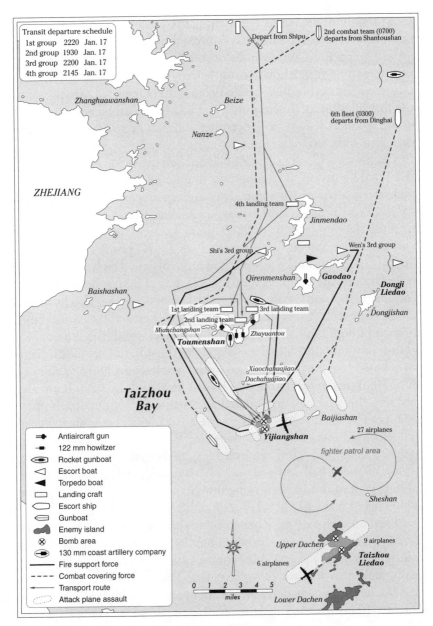

Depart from Shipu

2nd combat team (0700) departs from Shantoushan

Zhanghuawanshan

Beize

6th fleet (0300) departs from Dinghai

Nanze

ZHEJIANG

4th landing team

Jinmendao

Shi's 3rd group

Wen's 3rd group

Qirenmenshan   Gaodao

Dongji Liedao

Baishashan

Dongjishan

1st landing team   3rd landing team

2nd landing team

Mianchangshan   Zhuyuantou

Toumenshan

Xiaochahuajiao
Dachahuajiao

Taizhou Bay

Baijiashan

Yijiangshan

27 airplanes

fighter patrol area

Sheshan

Antiaircraft gun
122 mm howitzer
Rocket gunboat
Escort boat
Torpedo boat
Landing craft
Escort ship
Gunboat
Enemy island
Bomb area
130 mm coast artillery company
Fire support force
Combat covering force
Transport route
Attack plane assault

Upper Dachen   9 airplanes

Taizhou
Liedao

6 airplanes

0 1 2 3 4 5
miles

Lower Dachen

The Yijiangshan Landing Campaign

Throughout the campaign, Beijing tried to avoid any conflict with the American forces in order to continue the civil war on Taiwan without inflaming the Cold War. As records of the telephone calls from the General Staff headquarters on January 17–19 show, the ZFC was instructed that no conflict should occur with U.S. forces. Zhang made sure that the ships of the Seventh Fleet had not returned after they "left for the typhoon season" in November and that there would be no engagement with American forces.[120]

On January 18, 1955, the ZFC launched the Yijiangshan landings. The GMD garrison at Yijiangshan numbered only about one thousand troops armed with some sixty artillery pieces and one hundred machine guns. Zhang's ten thousand attacking troops had overwhelming numerical superiority. At 0800 hours, to begin the attack, fifty-four bombers and eighteen fighters raided key GMD positions, headquarters, and defense works at both Yijiangshan and Dachen. Over the next six hours, the bombers dropped 127 tons of bombs on the islands. Then, at 1220 hours, coastal artillery at Toumenshan began a two-hour bombardment of Yijiangshan. Between 1430 and 1500 hours, three thousand troops landed. The Second Battalion, 180th Regiment landed first, on the south side of the island; the First Battalion, 178th Regiment landed on the east, followed by the Second and Third battalions. By 1730 hours, troops controlled the entire island. By 0200 hours the next day, the PLA had annihilated all remaining GMD pockets of resistance. The GMD lost its entire garrison of 1,086 men, with 567 dead and 519 prisoners. The PLA suffered 1,592 total casualties: the army had 393 dead and 1,037 wounded, nearly 50 percent of its landing troops; the navy had 23 dead and 139 wounded.[121] The navy had one landing craft sunk and twenty-one ships damaged; the air force suffered no losses but had eight bombers and fighters damaged.[122]

Flushed with victory, Zhang pressed an attack on the Dachen Islands. On January 19, two hundred bombers conducted the largest air raid in PLA history. The GMD command on the Dachen Islands was badly shaken by the loss of Yijiangshan. The Eisenhower administration, for its part, persuaded Jiang Jieshi to withdraw his troops from the Dachen Islands with American assistance. Between February 8 and 12, the Seventh Fleet helped the GMD evacuate some twenty-five thousand military and eighteen thousand civilian personnel from the Dachen Islands.[123] On February 22, after the GMD was informed that the United States would not assist in the defense of Nanjishan Island, it was evacuated as well. By February 26, all of the East China Sea offshore islands along the Zhejiang coast were under PLA control.[124]

The field commanders, including Zhang and Nie, based their plans and operations on manpower and human conditions rather than technology and weaponry. Matters such as air control, naval power, and transportation and communication equipment seemed to have been only contributing, not determining, factors in their decision making. Technology did not become the determining issue until much later, when the PLA set up a new strategic guideline,[125] namely, the use of advanced technology to modernize the Chinese armed forces and transform the PLA from a quantity-oriented, manpower-intensive, large-scale army to a quality-oriented, technology-intensive, highly efficient army.

In the wake of the PLA's successful amphibious campaigns against the GMD-occupied islands, the Eisenhower administration looked for "some dramatic steps" to prevent further Chinese Communist aggressions. At the same meeting that decided the Dachen evacuation on January 20, 1955, President Eisenhower and Secretary of State John Foster Dulles agreed that abandoning all the offshore islands would be a "great blow to Nationalist morale and that the U.S. must therefore assist in defending Quemoy and Matsu as long as the PRC continued to threaten Taiwan."[126] To implement this policy, Eisenhower requested authorization from Congress for the United States to participate in the defense of Jinmen, Mazu, and other islands in the Taiwan Strait. On January 29, Congress passed the Formosa Resolution of 1955, which authorized Eisenhower to employ U.S. armed forces to protect Taiwan from a possible PLA invasion. In late February, Dulles made several stops in east Asia to assess the situation in the Taiwan Strait. He concluded that "the situation out there in the Formosa Straits is far more serious than I thought."[127] Upon his return to Washington on March 6, Dulles reported to the president that if the Communists crushed the GMD on Jinmen and Mazu, the results would be catastrophic for Taiwan and for the rest of Asia.

To stop further Chinese Communist invasion of Jinmen and Taiwan, the United States began to make fearsome nuclear threats. On March 6, Eisenhower and Dulles reaffirmed their commitment to the defense of the offshore islands and concluded that this would require drastic measures, including "the use of atomic missiles," by which they evidently meant tactical nuclear weapons.[128] To bolster public opinion, Eisenhower directed Dulles to state in a nationally televised speech on March 8 that the administration considered atomic weapons "inter-changeable with the conventional weapons" in the American arsenal.[129] The president, the U.S. military, and especially the Joint Chiefs of Staff heartily endorsed Dulles's position on the use of nuclear weapons.[130] At a well-known press conference on March 16, Eisenhower himself was direct in answering the question of whether nuclear weapons could be used in the Taiwan Strait: "Yes, of course they could be used." He explained, "In any combat where these things can be used on strictly military targets and for strictly military purposes, I see no reason why they shouldn't be used just exactly as you could use a bullet or anything else."[131] On March 17, Vice President Richard Nixon echoed the president, stating that "tactical atomic weapons are now conventional and will be used against the targets of any aggressive force."[132]

The United States appeared willing to risk a war, even a nuclear war, over the Taiwan Strait against Chinese Communist aggression just one year after the Korean armistice. Beijing backed down in April, when the Chinese premier offered to negotiate with the United States at the Bandung Conference. Zhou Enlai said that the PRC wanted no war with America, that "the Chinese people are friendly to the American people," and that his government was willing "to negotiate with the U.S. for the reduction of the tensions in the Taiwan Strait."[133] The 1954–55 Taiwan Strait crisis was over. On August 1, 1955, Chinese-American ambassadorial talks began in Geneva.

★ 5 ★

Building Missiles and the Bomb

THE POSSIBILITY OF AN AMERICAN nuclear attack on China during the Korean War and the first Taiwan Strait crisis posed new challenges to the Chinese military. Washington's threat of using atomic weapons against Chinese troops in North Korea and northeast China was of immediate concern to Beijing in 1952–53. With no strategic weapons, China had to depend on nuclear protection from the Soviet Union, which had developed atomic weapons in the late 1940s.

After Stalin, Soviet Cold War policy changed, calling for a relaxation of international tensions and peaceful coexistence between the Communist camp and the free world. During the 1954–55 Taiwan Strait crisis, Moscow complained about China's aggressive actions and expressed its unwillingness to use its atomic weapons if the United States retaliated over the PLA's invasion of Taiwan. Beijing felt nuclear pressures from both superpowers: an increasing nuclear threat from the United States and decreasing protection from the Soviet Union's nuclear umbrella. By 1955, it became apparent that China could not ensure its own national defense, avoid international humiliations, or liberate Taiwan without its own nuclear weapons.[1] The PRC could be bullied or even invaded by any Western power equipped with an atomic bomb. A great country like China needed its own nuclear weap-

147

ons to demonstrate its abilities, achievements, and prosperity and to enhance its rising status on the world stage.

This chapter examines how China responded to the nuclear threats, when it started its nuclear capability, and what factors shaped its nuclear, missile, and space programs. In retrospect, it is clear that the Cold War not only triggered these programs but also determined their direction. The stories of Marshal Nie Rongzhen and scientists Qian Sanqiang, Qian Xuesen (Tsien Hsue-shen), and Deng Jiaxian detail the Chinese management of Soviet technology and restrictions, staff shortages, and economic limits. They also offer a perspective on the social norms that shaped innovation and technological development, revealing the complicated interactions between the state and military. The military mobilized civilian professionals and utilized national resources for its strategic weapons programs by centralizing the nation's science and technology development. China's nuclear programs from the mid-1950s to the 1970s were characterized by centralization and bureaucratic power, which guaranteed the program's success. In 1960, the first Chinese-made missile was launched in the northwestern desert, leading China to its first nuclear bomb test on October 16, 1964, and its first hydrogen bomb on June 17, 1967. In less than fifteen years, China became a nuclear power. This was followed by its first satellite launch on April 24, 1970. When he visited China's electron-positron collider on October 24, 1988, CMC chairman Deng Xiaoping said, "It has always been, and will always be, necessary for China to develop its own high technology so that it can take its place in this field. If it were not for the atomic bomb, the hydrogen bomb, and the satellites we have launched since the 1960s, China would not have its present international standing as a great, influential country."[2]

Washington's Threat and Beijing's Plan

The prolonged engagement between the CPVF and U.S. forces in the Korean War created a U.S. nuclear threat against China. American desire to end U.S. participation in the Korean conflict became an issue during the 1952 presidential campaign and triggered the talk of a nuclear option. In May 1952, John Foster Dulles, as a Republican foreign policy spokesman, advocated a U.S. nuclear attack against Communist aggression when he criticized Democratic president Harry Truman's

Korean War policy. Dulles described Truman's approach as "treadmill policies which, at best, might keep us in the same place until we drop exhausted." Dulles suggested the free world needed "to develop the will and organize the means to retaliate instantly against open aggression by Red armies, so that, if it occurred anywhere, we could and would strike back where it hurt, by means of our own choosing."[3] Thereafter, General Dwight Eisenhower, a Republican presidential candidate, was "sympathetic to a foreign policy based on nuclear deterrence, and at no time did he eliminate as an option the use of nuclear weapons in Korea."[4] Throughout his 1952 election campaign, Eisenhower explained that his tougher policy provided for "rolling back" the Communist invaders and using "massive retaliations."[5] At a National Security Council meeting in early 1953, less than a month after taking office, President Eisenhower himself raised the option of nuclear intervention.

The Chinese troops in North Korea thus faced the possibility of a U.S. nuclear attack. Having certainly perceived the direct threat, Beijing began to seriously rethink its nuclear protection and safety. In February 1953, Mao sent a scientific delegation, headed by Qian Sanqiang, to Moscow. Their mission was to persuade Stalin to help China start its own nuclear research. After their arrival on February 24, however, Stalin had a stroke, and he died on March 5. In late 1953, Qian proposed his own plan for China's nuclear program.

In September 1954, when Khrushchev, the new Soviet leader, came to Beijing to join the Chinese leaders' celebration of their republic's fifth anniversary, Mao asked for Soviet technology and materials to assist China's nuclear research and development. Khrushchev, surprised by Mao's request, immediately refused. Khrushchev explained, "It is too expensive to develop nuclear weapons. Our big family has a nuclear umbrella protection. It is not necessary for everybody to develop and own nuclear weapons."[6] The Soviet Union enjoyed its nuclear monopoly within the Communist camp and would not share its nuclear technology with China. Moreover, Khrushchev's promised nuclear umbrella soon proved not to include the Taiwan Strait or any place where China might confront the United States and risk an international crisis or a war.

Beginning in September 1954, China and the United States confronted each other in the Taiwan Strait. After the PLA began shelling Jinmen and Mazu islands on September 3, the Americans' "reaction was quick" in supporting the Chinese Nationalists. According to the CIA, "by the morning of 5 September, three carriers, a cruiser division and three destroyer divisions of the Seventh Fleet were standing by, patrolling the waters in the Formosa Straits at a distance of several miles from Quemoy."[7] In response to the PLA bombardment, the Eisenhower administration in December signed a mutual defense treaty with the GMD government in Taiwan. The treaty, however, did not stop the PLA from landing on several islands along the southeastern coast. That winter, the U.S. Seventh Fleet joined the Chinese Nationalist operations on the offshore islands.

Mao and Marshal Peng believed that a conflict between the PRC and the United States over the Taiwan Strait was inevitable and that it could involve the use of nuclear weapons against China. The Chinese leaders looked for ways to ensure the success of operations in the Taiwan Strait against a U.S. nuclear capability they simply could not match. Mao called the United States' threats "atomic blackmail" during a January 1955 conversation with Carl-Johan Sundstrom, Finland's first ambassador to China. Mao promised that China would "resolutely strike back" if the United States launched such a war.[8] It seems that the Chinese leaders made up their minds to build their own bombs in January 1955, before the Eisenhower administration's nuclear threats in March during the Taiwan Strait crisis (see chapter 4). Some scholars have argued that, in addition to earlier events in Korea, the 1954–55 Taiwan Strait crisis constituted the "proximate cause of the Chinese decision to build a national strategic force. These events galvanized the leadership to act in the winter of 1954–1955 and gave special urgency to the strategic weapons program in the decade thereafter."[9]

Thus the Chinese leaders believed that their country was vulnerable to nuclear coercion. China needed its own bomb. In early January 1955, Mao called an expanded meeting of the CCP Central Secretariat to discuss starting China's nuclear weapons program. On January 14, prior to the meeting, Premier Zhou Enlai held an "unusual seminar" in his office that included leading scientists, such as geologist Li Siguang and nuclear scientist Qian Sanqiang, to discuss the current status of China's nuclear research and "to evaluate the country's manpower and facilities in the nuclear field."[10] At the conclusion of the meeting, Zhou invited the scientists to brief Mao and other top leaders the next day. On January 15, Li and Qian lectured Mao, Liu,

Zhou, Zhu, Chen Yi, Deng, Peng, and other members of the Central Secretariat on nuclear physics and uranium geology. Mao opened the session by saying, "Today we are pupils of yours."[11] During a question-and-answer session, Mao stated that it was definitely time for the party and government to work seriously on the matter.

At the meeting, China's first nuclear weapons plan, Project 02, was approved.[12] Project 02 reflected the Chinese recognition of the superpowers' assertion that nuclear weapons would remain a central feature of international affairs. The leaders were convinced that nuclear development would play an important role in China's military-security concerns. "Today," Mao said at the afternoon meeting of January 15, "the danger of world war and the threat to China comes primarily from the war hawks in the United States. They have invaded Asia and even wanted to launch an atomic war. . . . In today's world, we cannot afford not to have this weapon, if we don't want to be bullied."[13] At the dinner that evening, Mao toasted "to our nuclear development, bottoms up!"

On March 31, when Eisenhower and Dulles once again heightened Chinese fears of a nuclear attack, Mao called for military mobilization and nuclear research. "We are starting a new era of history in which [we will] gain the knowledge and proficiency of nuclear power."[14] Obviously, the Taiwan Strait crisis in 1954–55 and the U.S. nuclear threat in March 1955 justified the Chinese leaders' momentous decision to make their own bombs. Historian He Di stresses that "an even more profound influence of the nuclear threat of the United States on China was the fact that China started to formulate gradually a whole set of deterrence and security strategies to deal with the possible nuclear attack of the United States. Under the guidance of such strategic ideas, national defense construction, weapons development, service establishment, military training and militia organizations had all been adapted to fighting under atomic warfare."[15] Thus the 1954–55 Taiwan Strait crisis may be viewed as the starting point of China's nuclear weapons development program.

In the spring of 1955, China's nuclear program began to "acquire content and direction," and the most important organizational decisions followed that summer.[16] In July, the Politburo appointed three of its members, Chen Yun, Marshal Nie Rongzhen, and Bo Yibo, as national leaders for nuclear research and development. This group contained both civil and military leaders: Chen, as PRC financial chief, and Bo, known for his managerial talent, were vice premiers, and Marshal Nie was CMC vice chairman and acting chief of the General Staff. In 1955, the Three-Member Group established a new ministry under the State Council, the Second Ministry of Machine Building (Dier jijie gongyebu), as well as the Fifth Academy (Wu yuan). The Second Ministry of Machine Building was in charge of atomic and hydrogen bomb development, and the Fifth Academy (China's NASA) was in charge of missile and space technology. The Fifth Academy became, in the 1960s, the Seventh Ministry of Machine Building and then, in the 1980s, the Space and Navigation Ministry. On November 4, 1955, the Three-Member Group drafted China's first plan for its nuclear programs, "Yuanzineng fazhan guihua" (Proposal for the Atomic Energy Cause). November 4 became the national anniversary of the beginning of the Chinese nuclear and strategic weapons industry. In that year, the Three-Member Group also formed the Third Bureau (San ju), the Bureau of Architecture and Technology (Jianshe jishu ju), and other offices in the central government to organize and supervise the nuclear industry. China's budget for research and technology rose from about $15 million in 1955 to $100 million in 1956.[17]

Marshal Nie was appointed to head the nation's nuclear research and development organization. In 1956, Nie worked with the Chinese Academy of Sciences to establish the Nuclear Research Institute, which would be in charge of theoretical analyses, scientific experiments, research design, and problem solving for the industrial ministries. The PLA sent military representatives to the Chinese Academy of Sciences' research institutes, labs, and manufacturing facilities for security, inspection, and quality control. On August 7, the Ministry of Defense set up its Fifth Bureau (Wu ju), for missile development, and on September 5, the General Staff Department established the Missile Testing Range Commission (Bachang dengjian weiyuanhui).[18]

Soviet Aid and the Sino-Soviet Split

Once the U.S. nuclear threats triggered China's nuclear program, the Chinese naturally looked for technology and material assistance from the Soviet Union. The Chinese realized that the United States enjoyed the availability of massive resources and spent roughly ten times as much on its military as China did. Chinese military planners coped with limited economic resources, lack of technology, and, most important, a shortage of experts. Mao had no choice but to solicit Soviet support. Undeterred by Khrushchev's initial refusal in 1954, Mao telegraphed Moscow in February 1955 asking for limited scientific, technological, and industrial assistance "in promoting research in peaceful uses for atomic energy" in China.[19] In another February telegram, Mao warned the Soviet leaders, "Now, at this very moment, the imperialist war bloc is intensifying its creation of international tension, preparing for atomic war, carrying out war provocations, and gravely threatening world peace."[20] Mao's emphases have been interpreted as indicating his "heightened nervousness" about the possible U.S. use of nuclear weapons during the Taiwan Strait confrontation in 1955.[21] Chinese leaders were very disappointed by the Soviet rejection.[22] They realized now that China's nuclear weapons program would have to be put on a path to self-reliance.

After a long delay, in the summer of 1956, the Soviets finally agreed to discuss providing technology and material assistance to China's nuclear weapons program. In August, when Marshal Nie approached Soviet representatives in Beijing and asked for missile technology training, the Soviets agreed to train some Chinese officials for executive management of a future Chinese nuclear research institute. Fifty Chinese were accepted for a year of administrative training in Russia. On August 17, the two governments signed an agreement that the Soviets would aid the Chinese in building their nuclear industries and research facilities. On December 19, the Soviets agreed to assist China's independent management of uranium surveys.[23]

In July 1957, Nie visited V. A. Arkhipov, Soviet chief advisor for advanced technology in Beijing. The Chinese marshal requested more Soviet aid in nuclear and missile technology. On July 20, Nie received word that the Soviet government was willing to negotiate with the Chinese government. In September, Marshal Nie led a delegation to Moscow, including Senior Generals Chen Geng and Song Renqiong, and attended thirty-five days of meetings. On October 15, the Chinese and Soviets signed the New Defense Technical Accord for Soviet aid in nuclear research, missile development, and aviation technology. Thereafter, the Soviet Union supplied China with a prototype of an atomic bomb and industrial equipment for the processing and enrichment of uranium.[24] Meanwhile, Chinese nuclear scientists studied and worked at the Soviet labs.

Why the Soviet shift? In 1957, the Soviet Communist Party faced its most serious political crisis since the death of Stalin. On June 18, 1957, seven of the eleven members of the Standing Committee of the Politburo criticized Khrushchev's economic policy and arbitrary working style and voted to remove him from the party's first secretary position. Even though Khrushchev survived and, by June 29, purged those Politburo members with the help of Marshal Zukov, defense minister, the crisis undermined his leadership. To regain political control, Khrushchev desperately needed all the domestic and international support he could get. In November, he invited Mao to the celebration of the fortieth anniversary of the Soviet National Day in Moscow. To secure Mao's visit and support, Khrushchev silenced the Russian military's opposition and offered China aid and assistance in nuclear and missile technology.[25]

Soviet aid and Sino-Soviet cooperation were necessary for China to start its nuclear and missile programs. In December 1957, China sent its science and technology delegation, headed by Guo Moruo, president of the Chinese Academy of Sciences, to Moscow. The Chinese delegation signed an agreement for more science and technology aid. According to this agreement, the Soviet Union would assist 122 cooperative research projects, including 58 defense industrial enterprises and 3 strategic weapons research institutes that were related to nuclear and missile technology.[26] After these agreements, from 1957 to 1959, the Soviets provided the Chinese with atomic testing data, missile designs and samples, and other research information.

In December 1957, a Soviet-made P-2 surface-to-surface short-range missile arrived in Beijing. In early 1958, Russian nuclear and missile experts began to arrive in Beijing. The Fifth Academy began to copy the Soviet model. As part of the 1950s military reforms, the Soviet Union greatly influenced China's nuclear and missile weapons programs from their inception, although the Soviets refused to offer data on their nuclear-powered submarines and other weapons systems. In 1958, with Soviet help, China completed its first nuclear reactor near Beijing.[27] At that time, the PLA established its first surface-to-surface missile battalion as a strategic force. In late 1958, the PLAAF established three surface-to-air missile battalions; on May 21, 1959, it opened its surface-to-air missile training center; and in March 1964, it established its first surface-to-air missile division.[28]

On October 4, 1957, the news that the Soviet Union had launched the first satellite, *Sputnik,* inspired the Chinese. In 1957, the Chinese Academy of Sciences suggested to top Chinese leaders the possibility of developing its own satellite technology. In early 1958, the Politburo approved the Chinese Academy of Sciences' satellite program and appropriated a special fund of 200 million yuan ($70 million). The academy established three new institutes for satellite research and development, and the leading facility was named the 581 Research and Design Institute (referring to the establishing date, January 1958).[29] In January 1958, the Defense Ministry sent forty thousand engineering troops to northwest China to construct a nuclear testing ground. The first site selected was about one hundred miles northwest of Dunhuang in Gansu. The second site was the Lop Nur area, much farther west, in the Taklimakan Desert of Xinjiang. The CMC decided on the Lop Nur area, nearly one hundred thousand square miles, as the nuclear testing ground. In March 1958, the Twentieth Army Group returned from North Korea to China, and the Defense Ministry transferred them to Nei Monggol (Inner Mongolia) to construct a missile testing ground. Thus, by the late 1950s, China's nuclear, missile, and space programs were fully underway.[30]

Soviet and Chinese leaders, however, soon split on ideological and political issues, including differences over nuclear weapons, because of complicated domestic and international factors. The most important of these factors was whether Beijing should become a new center of the international Communist movement. The Sino-Soviet alliance began to decline.[31] The first ideological conflict came in 1956 when Khrushchev issued a secret report to the Congress of the Communist Party of the Soviet Union, denouncing Stalin as a dictator.[32] In November 1957, when Mao visited Moscow to attend the Russian Revolution anniversary celebration, he attended a meeting of Communist parties from around the world. Mao emphasized that they should not be frightened by the prospect of a nuclear war started by the imperialists but should realize that such a war, although carrying a high price, would end the imperialist system.[33] Chen Jian points out that Mao's statement was "a deliberate challenge to Khrushchev's emphasis on the necessity and possibility of 'peaceful coexistence' with Western imperialist countries," and "it inevitably worried Moscow's leaders."[34] Historian Yang Kuisong makes a further point that the Mao-Khrushchev split resulted from their differing worldviews and visions for the Communist future when Khrushchev departed from Stalinist ideology.[35]

The great Sino-Soviet polemic debate thereafter further undermined the ideological foundation of the Sino-Soviet alliance. In a deeper sense, Beijing's confrontation with Moscow changed the essence of the Cold War. Since its beginning in the late 1940s, the Cold War had been characterized as a fundamental confrontation between two contending ideologies—liberal capitalism and Communism.[36] The great Sino-Soviet split buried the shared consciousness among Communists and Communist sympathizers all over the world that Communism was a solution to the problems created by the worldwide process of modernization. The Great Proletarian Cultural Revolution that began to sweep across China in the 1960s completely destroyed any hope that Beijing and Moscow might continue to regard each other as comrades in arms. The hostility between China and the Soviet Union reached a new height in early 1969, when two bloody clashes occurred on the Sino-Soviet border.[37]

The conflicts between the two Communist parties extended to strategic issues. In Beijing from July 31 to August 3, 1958, Khrushchev proposed a Russo-Chinese joint fleet—a permanent naval force including both the PLA and Soviet navies—and a long-wave radio system between the two countries. Mao denounced the Soviet offer as an attempt to control the Chinese military. In March 1959, supporters of the Dalai Lama launched an armed rebellion in Tibet against the Chinese central government. His independence movement received official support from the Indian government, suddenly raising tensions between India and China. Ignoring the information and suggestions from Beijing, Moscow issued an official statement on September 9, condemning China and defending India's policy toward Tibet.[38]

In June 1959, the Soviet Union met with the United States and Britain in Geneva to discuss partially banning nuclear weapons. On June 20, the Central Committee of the Soviet Communist Party informed the CCP Central Committee that, in order to achieve an agreement to partially ban nuclear tests, the Soviet Union would have to terminate the Sino-Soviet agreement on cooperation in nuclear development. On July 16, the Soviet government informed the Chinese government that it would withdraw all of its nuclear scientists and experts from China. By August 13, 1960, all twelve thousand Soviet experts left China with their blueprints and designs. Among them were more than two hundred who had been working on nuclear research and development programs. The Soviets also stopped shipments of equipment and materials that the Chinese nuclear program desperately needed.[39]

The end of Soviet aid in technology and materials almost scuttled China's four-year-old nuclear and missile programs. Disappointed by the Soviets' unilateral termination of their agreements, some Chinese thought it was the end of China's nuclear research and development efforts. Many Soviet experts believed that China "won't be able to develop its own nuclear weapons within the next twenty years."[40] Still, on July 3, 1960, Nie wrote to Mao and the Central Committee suggesting that China continue its nuclear research and development. Mao proposed a policy discussion on the future of China's nuclear, missile, and space programs without Soviet aid.[41] On July 18, the Central Committee met at Beidaihe to discuss how to deal with the Soviet aid termination.[42] Mao felt that the Chinese must undertake the task of advanced technology themselves and that it was actually good that Khrushchev had refused to give China advanced technology. If he had given it to the Chinese, the expense would have been incredible.[43] At the meeting, the Central Committee agreed that China should continue its nuclear research and development without any interruption. The meeting established Project 596 (symbolizing the time, June 1959, when the Soviets withdrew all technology and personnel) to develop China's own nuclear bomb within eight years.

Overseas Scientists and Students

Although the end of Soviet aid caused serious losses and delays, it did not stop the Chinese nuclear, missile, and space programs. By 1960, the Chinese had established a highly centralized system for strategic weapons, based upon close cooperation between the civil government and the military, a concentration of national resources, and a series of social and political incentives for professionals. These organizations and individuals had a strong impact on China's programs. Marshal Nie Rongzhen was responsible for the whole process. John W. Lewis and Xue Litai point out that after Nie became the head of China's nuclear research and development, he played a vital role in supervising the entire strategic weapons program. When almost everything else in China failed from the late 1950s to the late 1960s, he managed to save the country's nuclear, missile, and space programs, which "stand as a major accomplishment, a marked contrast to China's general fate in that decade."[44]

Nie was one of Mao's closest working colleagues and most trusted marshals. Born in Jiangjin, Sichuan, in 1899, he grew up in an independent peasant family and went through home school at his grandfather's house. During his secondary school years in Jiangjin County, Nie learned about a work-study program in Europe, and he left China in 1919. He became an overseas student activist when he enrolled in a French college. In 1921, he took classes in physics, machinery, and chemical engineering in Belgium, where he joined the CCP in 1922. Selected by the CCP European branch, Nie was sent to the Soviet Union in the fall of 1924 and attended the Oriental University of the Communism and Labor Movement in Moscow. His curriculum included the labor movement, history of Bolshevism, Soviet government, and world revolution. In February 1925, he was transferred to the special class for Chinese officers at the Soviet Academy of the Red Army. While in Red Army uniform, Nie studied and drilled with Red Army officers, learning the Soviet military system from the inside.[45]

On his return to China, Nie worked as a secretary and an instructor in the late 1920s in the Huangpu Military Academy's political department, where Zhou Enlai was the director. With his organizational skills and Soviet military training, Nie served as the second secretary of the CCP's Northern Bureau in the 1930s and commanded the PLA's Northern Military Region in the mid-1940s. In 1948–49, after the CCP leadership moved from Yan'an to north China, closer to the civil war battleground, he worked with Mao on a daily basis. Nie successfully protected the CCP headquarters and PLA high command and personally saved Mao's life during an air raid.[46]

When Mao founded the PRC, Nie was appointed mayor of Beijing, commander of the Beijing-Tianjin garrison, and deputy chief of the PLA General Staff. He ran the General Staff because Zhou, as its chief, was preoccupied with the premiership and foreign ministry and because the entire General Staff was Nie's former Northern Military Region staff, people who worked with Mao in the civil war and then moved to Beijing with him. Nie became acting chief of the General Staff in 1950, vice chairman of the CMC in 1951, and, after 1954, one of the party's eleven top national leaders as a member of the Standing Committee of the Politburo. In 1955, he became one of ten marshals in China (see chapter 4).[47] During the Korean War, as one of the top military commanders and Mao's senior aide in Beijing, Nie took part in high command decision making, planned major military operations, and shared the responsibility of war mobilization and supply. One of the problems he pondered quite often during the Korean War was how to deal with an enemy equipped with superior weaponry.[48] Nie concluded at the end of the war that the Chinese army had suffered from inferior technology. He also believed that, because of China's scientific and technological disadvantage, imperialist countries like the United States could bully or even invade the country, as they had Korea. China needed to change its passive position and avoid such blows by advancing its science and technology.[49]

In the spring of 1955, Nie became one of the three top leaders in charge of the nuclear research and development program. In 1956, when the Three-Member Group became less active, Nie as the vice premier "assumed overall supervision of the entire strategic weapons program."[50] He organized the Aviation Industry Committee for aerospace technology in the same year. Nie worked through the bureaucratic system and created new government offices, research institutes, and testing facilities for defense projects. The number of science and technology research institutes and facilities increased from 40 in 1949 to 380 in 1956 and to 1,300 in 1962.[51] In April 1956, Nie organized more than six hundred scientists and seventeen Soviet advisors to draft a long-term plan (through 1967) for China's scientific and technological development. The six-million-word plan proposed fifty-seven tasks comprising more than six hundred research projects, including twelve key projects. The top three were nuclear research, missile development, and electronic and computer technology. In October, Nie's proposal to develop China's own nuclear weapons with or without foreign aid was approved by the Central Committee. Nie remembered that 1956 was "the most important year" in the development of Chinese science and technology.[52] While he worked closely with the party center, government bureaucracy, and military high command to implement his proposals, he established his own system to protect his new sources.

However, Nie's plan faced a serious human resources shortage. His programs needed more than thirty thousand college undergraduate and graduate students in 1956–57. China had a total of thirty thousand undergraduate students in science and engineering from all colleges and universities each year in the mid-1950s. Only some of the science and engineering bachelor's degree holders could work for the newly established nuclear and missile programs because of other demands for BS degrees. Moreover, in the 1950s, the country had only two thousand or so college professors qualified to offer graduate courses. Most of them worked in the universities and colleges, with approximately two to three hundred working in research institutes. Nie worked with the party and government to deal with the shortage of researchers, especially senior experts. Mao, after reading Nie's report, instructed Zhou to recruit the best Chinese scientists and experts in nuclear science, including those who were studying or working overseas.

Bringing overseas professionals and students back to China was the first step in dealing with the shortage of experts. Nie visited the Ministry of Foreign Affairs when the annual ambassador conferences were held in Beijing. As a former overseas student in Europe, he told the ambassadors to Europe that the country desperately needed Chinese professionals and students who were working and studying in the West to return to their homeland so they could contribute to China's scientific research and development. The Foreign Ministry began bringing Chinese students and professionals back from the West, particularly the United States, even though the PRC had no diplomatic relationship with that country. After World War II, the United States had the most advanced science and technology research projects in the world and was sponsoring a large number of the best students and professionals from China. Mao wanted them back in China as soon as possible and offered to pay them more than his own salary.[53]

China's first recruitment opportunity came in February 1954, when the foreign ministers of the United States, Soviet Union, Britain, and France met in Berlin and agreed to invite the PRC to attend the Geneva Conference in April–July as a fifth power to discuss the Korean and Indochinese issues. This conference represented Beijing's first participation in an important international conference as a major power; the Chinese thus attached significant value to attending. They readily accepted the invitation and sent a large delegation headed by Zhou

Deng Xiaoping and Nie Rongzhen examine a PLA plan. (Reproduced by permission of the PLA Literature Press, Beijing, China.)

Enlai, premier and foreign minister. According to the minutes of the Central Committee meetings in March, direct contact with the United States in Geneva was highly sought.[54]

During the Geneva Conference, five meetings occurred between the PRC and U.S. delegations at the ambassadorial level, between U. Alexis Johnson and Wang Bingnan. On June 3, two days before the first meeting, Zhou instructed Wang to raise the question of Chinese students' having been prohibited from leaving the United States since the outbreak of the Korean War in 1950.[55] At the June 5 meeting, the Chinese delegation used the problem of several dozen American civilians detained in China as leverage to open the negotiations. If Washington changed its policy on Chinese students in the United States and permitted them to return to China, Beijing would consider allowing some Americans to leave China.[56] No agreement, however, was reached between the two delegations at this early stage of negotiations.

Between August 4 and September 10, the two sides continued to discuss the return of their civilians. After fourteen rounds of talks lasting forty days, the two sides finally reached an agreement.[57] On October 18,

1954, the U.S. government permitted 27 Chinese students to return home. On April 8, 1955, 76 more Chinese students living in America received permission to leave. According to the Foreign Ministry's documents, by July 31, 1955, 80 of 103 students on the PRC's list had returned.[58] Additionally, 9 students had made their own way secretly out of America and back to China without U.S. government permission. Among the 89 returning students, 12 were majoring in nuclear physics, 8 in aviation and space technology, 11 in electrical engineering, 8 in civil engineering, 9 in machinery, 14 in chemistry or chemical engineering, 5 in biology, 9 in medicine or pharmacology, and 13 in other majors.[59] In the 1950s, a number of undergraduate and graduate students, doctoral degree holders, and senior researchers, with some world-class experts among them, returned to China from Europe. They eventually worked in nuclear and missile research institutes.

These returning students and experts were absolutely critical to the research and development of China's nuclear and missile technology. Quite a few of the scientists returning from the United States made contributions to Chinese nuclear technology developments. For instance, Ren Xinmin, professor of the State University of New York at Buffalo, became the founder of China's space programs in the 1960s and vice minister of the Seventh Ministry of Machine Building in the 1970s;[60] MIT graduate Tu Shou'e was appointed vice president of the Institute of Strategic Missile Research in 1961 and was chief engineer of China's first missile in 1962;[61] Virginia Institute of Technology graduate Wang Xiji served as chief designer of China's space rockets in the 1960s;[62] and Cheng Kaijia, who received his doctorate from Edinburgh University, became a nuclear expert and one of forty-six prestigious academicians in China. Another prestigious academician was Qian Xuesen (Tsien Hsue-shen), one of the most important Chinese Americans to China's nuclear and missile programs. Premier Zhou later said that China had gotten Qian Xuesen back from America at the Geneva Conference. Had it been the only Chinese achievement at Geneva, the Sino-American ambassadorial talks would have been a success.[63]

Qian Xuesen was born on December 11, 1911, in Zhejiang. In August 1935, he left China on a Boxer Rebellion Scholarship to study at MIT. He then went to the California Institute of Technology to study applied mechanics, including jet propulsion and engineering control theories, on the referral of Theodor von Kármán.[64] After he obtained his PhD in 1939, Qian worked with the U.S. military's intercontinental ballistic missile program (developing the Titan) as a designer and then a director of the Jet Propulsion Laboratory in Pasadena, California.[65] After WWII, he served in the U.S. Army as a lieutenant colonel and was sent to Germany as part of the team that examined captured German V-2 rockets. In 1945, he married Jiang Ying, the daughter of General Jiang Baili, one of Jiang Jieshi's leading military strategists. Soon after Qian became a U.S. citizen in 1950, the FBI alleged that he was a Communist and revoked his security clearance. It became a turning point in his life, since he found himself unable to pursue his career. Qian recalled, "In the early 1950s, McCarthyism began running wild in the United States, and I was persecuted. By that time, I had come to see through my personal experiences what democracy really was."[66] Within two weeks, he announced plans to return to mainland China. The U.S. government wavered between deporting him and refusing to allow his departure because of his knowledge. Qian became the subject of negotiations between the United States and the PRC, and he lived under virtual house arrest. As a result of the Chinese diplomacy at the 1954 Geneva Conference, he and his wife were allowed to leave America on September 17, 1955.[67]

On February 17, 1956, Qian submitted a proposal to the CCP Central Committee requesting the establishment of a ballistic missile program. On April 13, Zhou, vice chairman of both the Central Committee and the CMC, established the State Commission of Aviation Industry (Hangkong gongye weiyuanhui), including Marshal Nie, Qian, and Zhou himself as the leading members.[68] On February 18, 1957, Qian became director of the Fifth Academy under the Ministry of Defense and helped reverse engineer the Soviet P-2 missile, an improved version of the German V-2 rocket. In that year, Qian was made a lieutenant general in the PLA. In 1959, Qian joined the CCP and began work on the Chinese-made short-range missile Dongfeng-01, based on the P-2. In 1964, the first Chinese-designed medium-range missile, Dongfeng-02, had a successful test. In 1965, Qian became vice minister of the Seventh Ministry of Machine Building, then vice chairman of the State Commission on Science, Technology, and Industry for National Defense in 1970, and chairman of the Chinese Association for Science and Technology in 1984. As one of the pioneers of China's space science, he became the "father of Chinese missiles" and the "king of rocketry." Mao met Qian on several occasions. As the chief designer and a major leader, Qian played a key role in the research, testing, and manufacture of carrier rockets, guided missiles, satellites, and aerospace programs.[69]

Through diplomatic efforts and overseas connections, China brought home many of its badly needed nuclear scientists, missile experts, experienced engineers, and graduate students from the West. The second approach to China's expert shortage problem involved sending a large number of the best students to study in the Soviet Union and Eastern Europe. The selection process and overseas studies program went through three periods. In the first period, from 1950 to 1953, the government carried out a policy to "restrict selection and [put] quality before quantity." During these years, 1,700 Chinese students were sent to the Soviet Union and other Eastern European countries. In the second period, from 1954 to 1956, the Central Committee implemented a long-term science and technology plan. The policy change included "selecting carefully while sending as many as possible," with an emphasis on science and engineering. During these years, China sent a total of 5,800 students, including 1,200 graduate students, most of whom majored in science and technology. In addition, Chinese education consuls from the embassy and consulates-general traveled to Russian colleges to ask Chinese students who were majoring in the social sciences, humanities, and some science and engineering fields to switch to majors related to the defense industry, aviation technology, and nuclear science. In the final period, from 1957 to 1958, the government adapted a new policy to "send more graduate students, no undergraduate students."[70] Two years of postbaccalaureate work experience were now required before enrolling in overseas graduate studies.

The third method of dealing with the staff shortage was to establish programs in nuclear science, technical physics, and theoretical physics at the key universities of China. The Ministry of Education made technical physics a new major at Peking University and created an engineering physics degree at Tsinghua University. The ministry selected the best physics students from all the universities to study nuclear science at Peking University.

The fourth method of solving the problem involved shifting professionals from academic research institutes to defense facilities. With the establishment of the Missile Research Institute, Nie needed the best rocket scientists and aviation experts in the country. In March 1956, as vice premier, Nie invited the ministers of education, rail transportation, mineral industry, chemical industry, and other ministries to a recruitment meeting. He asked them to supply several hundred scientists and experts from their ministries. At the meeting, Nie and the ministers agreed on a list of 380 senior and experienced experts to submit to Premier Zhou. Zhou approved the list and ordered the experts and professionals transferred to the missile institute without any major delays.

Through these methods, Nie was satisfied that the expert shortage problem would be solved. In 1961, he reported to Mao that several thousand engineers and technicians with college or graduate degrees worked in the Fifth Academy. It also had several hundred scientists, missile experts, and senior specialists. This concentration and centralization of the nation's human resources would guarantee the design and manufacturing of China's medium-range missile in 1962 and its first test in 1963.[71]

Professional Careers and Political Security

For scientists and technicians, defense facilities and nuclear programs offered better career opportunities and political protection than academic institutes and civilian enterprises could. The newly established missile institute, for example, soon expanded to several branch institutes working separately on strategic and tactical missiles. The nuclear program's rapid development created new positions, offered promotions, and provided the experts opportunities to do things in their own ways. They started by imitating Russian missiles and then developed their own models.[72] Marshal Nie also selected several thousand technicians from among PLA veterans and employed them at the institute. The country's science and advanced technology researchers increased from 650 in 1949 to more than 9,000 in 1956 and to 94,000 in 1962. Within the 1962 total were 2,800 researchers and associates, 7,700 assistant researchers, and 50,000 interns and junior researchers in training.[73]

Qian Sanqiang, the founder of China's nuclear program and head of the nuclear institute, recalled that his excitement and success resulted from top leaders' support. "In 1949 I felt an overnight change, a total change in everything around me."[74] Born in 1913 in Zhejiang, Qian Sanqiang graduated from Tsinghua University in 1936 with a physics degree. At twenty-four, he earned a governmental scholarship from the China-French Foundation for Education and enrolled in a PhD program in Paris. He studied nuclear science under Nobel laureates Frédéric and Irène Joliot-Curie. In May 1948, in the middle of the Chinese civil war, Qian, his wife, and their six-month-old daughter returned to China. He headed the ROC's Nuclear Research Institute in Beijing. This organization had only five people: Qian, two researchers, one assistant, and one staff member. Qian complained that the ROC government provided no long-term plan and did not coordinate communication or exchanges among nuclear experts around the country. Qian failed to gain GMD official support for his effort to assemble a national research team.[75]

In March 1949, two months after the PLA took over Beijing, Qian received a notice from the CCP government to attend an international conference in Paris. Having studied in Paris, Qian thought attending the conference would provide a good opportunity for him to contact his former professors and buy new books and equipment in France. He requested $200,000 for his purchases. Four days later, he received a call summoning him to the central government office at Zhongnanhai. Li Weihan, minister of the CCP United Front, greeted Qian with the good news that he had received $50,000. He was touched by the CCP's prompt response and immediate support. As we have seen, the government moved rapidly into the reorganization of national science and technology research and development. In November 1949, one month after the founding of the PRC, the Chinese Academy of Sciences was founded with twenty-two research institutes and two hundred researchers. In 1950, the academy received an annual budget of 2.87 million yuan (about $1 million). The new Modern Physics Research Institute received a large part of the 1950 budget as a designated key area, and it changed its name to the Nuclear Research Institute.[76] Receiving official support from the top, Qian and others were excited and ready to work at the Nuclear Research Institute. As the nation's center for nuclear research, this institute recruited the best scientists, experts, and professors in the field, including those just returning from overseas.[77]

In October 1958, Qian visited Deng Jiaxian in Beijing. Deng had received a PhD in nuclear physics from Purdue University in the summer of 1950, when he was only twenty-six years old. His young age earned him the nickname Dr. Kid. On August 29, 1950, Deng left

America for China on the passenger steamer *President Wilson*. In 1958, at the age of thirty-four, fluent in both English and Russian, he accepted Qian's invitation to work at the Nuclear Research Institute. Deng was in charge of theory research and bomb design and earned a monthly salary of 204 yuan (about $60). His wife, Xu Luxi, was not happy about the secret and dangerous nature of his work in nuclear research. For twenty-eight years, her husband spent little time at home with her and their two children, even on holidays and birthdays, because of his job. She recalled that she was not as excited as other Chinese citizens following the nuclear tests.[78] She worried about her husband. Deng never talked with his wife about his work until he was diagnosed with cancer in the 1980s. In 1979, a nuclear bomb test failed. As the head of the design division, Deng traveled to the testing area to look for the unexploded nuclear warhead. Inadequate protection from the strong radiation caused serious health problems for the researchers and crew. In 1985, Deng Jiaxian was diagnosed with late-stage rectal cancer; he died on July 29, 1986, at the age of sixty-two.[79]

As we have seen, Mao launched several political campaigns targeting intellectuals and academics, and the society became more radicalized from the late 1950s through the 1970s. In 1957, for example, the anti-rightist movement targeted non-party members and those who were not interested in Communist politics. In schools and in the mass media, party committees and branches mobilized the masses to identify "rightists" among faculty members, researchers, and educated employees. Many intellectuals and professionals, criticized as rightists, lost their positions and were even separated from their families. Some of them were jailed, sent to the remote border areas, or even executed. These efforts were called *babaiqi* (taking out white flags).

The military academies and facilities, however, were usually not implicated to the same degree as their civil counterparts.[80] The Defense Ministry and the PLA tried to reduce the political pressures on the defense industry and nuclear programs throughout the movement.[81] Most nuclear and missile experts faced less criticism and fewer accusations and avoided the investigations and political purges in 1957–58. For students who had returned from overseas, when their Western training and work experience brought suspicion, they had to stay in the military and work for the strategic weapons programs for the sake of their own political safety and family security.

During the anti-rightist movement, Nie, as vice premier and CMC vice chairman, quietly transferred most of the civilian employees at the nuclear and missile research institutes into military service. In October 1958, he founded the Commission on Science, Technology, and Industry for National Defense (COSTIND) of the CMC and served as its chairman. The COSTIND was a highly centralized top military authority in charge of the defense industry and weapons development. Within this civil-military hierarchy, Nie transferred the Nuclear Research Institute from the Chinese Academy of Sciences to the Second Ministry of Machine Building under the newly founded COSTIND. The Motion Research Institute was renamed the Missile Research Institute after its transfer to the Fifth Academy under the COSTIND. Qian Xuesen recalled that he survived because "I strongly believed that science must integrate with politics. It can be said the most important thing since my return to the motherland was about integrating science with politics."[82] He became a lieutenant general in the PLA in 1957 and survived all the political movements thereafter.

Political security was a major concern for Chinese intellectuals from the late 1950s through the 1960s. Thousands of scientists and researchers became active servicemen through the militarization of their research institutes. Most were willing to join the PLA to acquire political security for themselves and their families. The fear factor of Mao's harsh, endless political campaigns against intellectuals worked.

The military could also utilize civilians' technical knowledge in its nuclear and advanced weapons research without offering them higher salaries or better living conditions. Nevertheless, many young and middle-aged scientists and experts joined the military and gained a higher social status for themselves and their families. Defense research and military service became very attractive to senior scientists in China from the late 1950s to the early 1970s. Nuclear research and development also brought academic and commercial research and experience to strategic weapons programs. On August 1, 1958, the first Chinese computer was developed in Shanghai. Soon the designers—and the computer—joined the military to work in its nuclear research program. In September 1959, a second computer began operating. In October, it was moved to the Nuclear Research Institute of the Second Ministry of Machine Building.[83] Quite a few of the scientists and engineers who returned from the United States contributed to Chinese computer technology developments.

During the Great Proletarian Cultural Revolution (1966–76), the worst political disaster in PRC history, Nie again militarized the satellite and space research institutes to protect the researchers and save the programs. In March 1967, after gaining approval from Mao and Zhou, he sent PLA troops to all the research institutes and nuclear testing facilities. In addition to the Nuclear Research Institute, he transferred the 581 Research and Design Institute and other facilities from the Chinese Academy of Sciences to the Seventh Ministry of Machine Building, under his COSTIND. The space programs survived the Cultural Revolution. On April 24, 1970, in the middle of the political disaster, China launched its first satellite into space.[84]

The Atomic Bomb versus the Rice Bowl

From 1959 to 1961, China experienced a serious economic depression known as the three hard years. Serious shortages of food, fuel, and other daily needs claimed more than thirty million lives. This disaster resulted from the massive failure of Mao's Great Leap Forward movement, an effort to industrialize through labor power and collectivization instead of technology and private enterprise. Total grain production decreased from 200 million tons in 1958 to 144 million tons in 1960. The government first blamed the decreased production on the weather and called the situation a natural disaster.[85] The main culprit later became the Soviet Union, when the ideological split between China and its main ally was made public in 1961. The Chinese people were told that the Soviet Union had betrayed them by withdrawing all aid and terminating all contracts between the countries.

To cope with the economic problems, the CCP Central Committee held a meeting at Beidaihe in July 1961. The committee members debated whether to continue the nuclear and missile programs, since the country faced bankruptcy. China seemed to be falling prey to the guns-versus-butter debate. Some leaders argued that the weapons programs were too expensive and siphoned resources from other industries. Others believed that China should focus on tanks, airplanes, and other conventional weapons and abandon the nuclear and missile programs. Marshal Nie, however, insisted that China continue its nuclear and missile programs. China could make progress without further Soviet aid. He pointed out that the Missile Research Institute had several thousand scientists, experts, engineers, and technicians who held bachelor's degrees and were capable of designing short- and medium-range missiles. The Nuclear Research Institute also employed several thousand experts, scientists, engineers, and technicians in 1960–61. Nie believed that China could manufacture its own bomb in three to five years. Cancellation of China's nuclear program would be a disastrous waste and validate the Soviet opinion that China was unable to build its own bomb.[86]

The Central Committee reached an agreement that China would continue its nuclear and missile programs. Mao said, "We have to make up our mind to focus on the most sophisticated technology. Khrushchev refused to give us advanced branches of science. It is great! We would not be able to pay him back if he had given them to us."[87] Marshal Chen Yi supported the idea but commented that they would have to sell their pants to continue the programs. He told Nie that, as the foreign minister, "I cannot be very firm at the negotiating tables without that bomb." Thus the leaders agreed that the nuclear and missile programs should continue.[88]

With this approval, Nie and his staff adjusted their plans and came up with a new guideline to "shorten the list, line up the items, and focus on the importance."[89] The missile program's first priority was to develop medium-range surface-to-surface missiles within three years and long-range ones in five years. The second priority was to design and build surface-to-air missiles to deal with American U-2 spy planes. As for nuclear research, it should emphasize producing nuclear fuel and designing and testing a bomb within four years. The last major problem was the refinement and enrichment of uranium.[90]

In 1958–60, General Chen Shiqiu led forty thousand special engineering troops to Lop Nur to begin construction of the nuclear testing site. They established a huge testing ground with launch sites, an airport, a railroad, and warehouse facilities. On September 9, 1960, the first Chinese missile, modeled on the Soviet P-2, was launched successfully in Nei Monggol, though it was short range and not suitable for carrying a nuclear warhead.[91] On November 5 and December 6 and 16, China tested three missiles of its own design, C-1059, two of which were surface-to-surface missiles. In June and July 1964, there were three successful medium- and long-range surface-to-surface missile tests of China's own models. In December, China began to manufacture its surface-to-air missile, Hongqi-01 (Red Flag 1). By October 1966, the improved Chinese medium-range missiles were capable of carrying nuclear warheads.[92]

Unfortunately, the weapons programs suffered from communication and cooperation gaps between research and manufacturing and between military and civilian officials. To strengthen the leadership of China's nuclear and missile programs, on November 17, 1962, the Central Committee organized the Special Commission in charge of nuclear research and development. The commission consisted of fifteen top leaders, including seven vice premiers, five vice chairmen of the CMC, and some ministers. Zhou served as the chairman.[93] On November 29, the Special Commission held its second meeting to centralize the structure, coordinate defense and civilian industries, and concentrate materials and manpower. By December, the committee had transferred 126 senior experts and scientists and 6,000 college

Zhou Enlai, Nie Rongzhen, He Long, and Chen Yi at a Special Commission meeting. (Reproduced by permission of the PLA Literature Press, Beijing, China.)

graduates to the weapons program. It also transferred 1,108 pieces of equipment and machinery to the program. Under this new centralized structure, an atomic bomb design was completed in 1963.[94]

In the summer of 1964, China's first atomic bomb was ready for testing. A crew of ten thousand staff, medical personnel, workers, troops, and logistic groups gathered at the testing ground and waited for Beijing's orders. At its eighth meeting, the Special Committee was briefed by General Zhang Aiping and Liu Xiyao, vice minister of the Second Ministry of Machine Building. Zhou asked Zhang and Liu whether it was all right not to test the bomb at that time. The Chinese government had received information that the United States would attack China's nuclear labs and testing facilities if nuclear tests were conducted. The Special Commission discussed the situation and submitted to the Central Committee on September 16 two proposals: one to conduct the test as scheduled, and the other to postpone the test. Mao opted for the first proposal. He said that the atomic bomb was made for scaring people and might never be used. Since it would scare people, it should be exploded early.[95]

Zhang and Liu Xiyao then suggested at a Special Committee meeting that testing be scheduled for October 1, the country's founding day. The Central Committee rejected their suggestion and requested a later date, between October 15 and 20. Their concerns centered on the chances of a successful first test. At the meeting, Marshal He Long asked Liu Xiyao, Liu Jie (minister of the Second Ministry of Machine Building), and the others, "Can you guarantee the explosion?" No one responded. He asked the question again, and again there was silence. Zhou also worried about security and secrecy: the country would face a bigger risk if the West knew the first nuclear test had failed.[96] Finally, Beijing decided to test its bomb at 1500 hours on October 16. On October 14, the bomb was placed in a metal container on the top of a 335-foot-high steel tower. The next day, the Central Committee gave its order to "shoot the basket"—a go-ahead order. The final assembly took place in the afternoon of October 15, when five engineers put together the explosive triggering device. By midnight, the assembly was completed. The next morning, all personnel moved into the control center, about fourteen miles from the tower. At the control center, General Li Jue gave the control key to Zhang Zhenhuan, who issued the orders at 1440 hours: "Electric power! Generator! Counting!" When it counted down to zero, Zhang ordered, "Fire!" The key controller pushed the red button. There was a very short silence, but it seemed very long to everyone in the control center. Then a strong flash was followed by a sunlike fireball over the tower, an earthshaking explosion, and a great mushroom cloud. China had completed its first nuclear test.[97]

Zhang, Liu Xiyao, and other officers at headquarters also saw the mushroom, but Zhang wanted to make sure it was a nuclear explosion before he reported it to Beijing. He asked the scientists at the headquarters, "Is this a nuclear explosion?" Wang Xinchang said it was. Zhang then called Minister Liu Jie's office in Beijing. Liu Jie and others had been waiting with some trepidation. When the phone rang, the person who answered was nervous and dropped the phone. Liu Jie picked up the phone and listened to Zhang's briefing. He then called Premier Zhou, who was waiting in his office; Zhou in turn reported to Mao immediately. Zhou called Liu Jie back and said, "Chairman Mao instructs us to double check whether it was indeed an atomic explosion in order to convince the foreigners."[98] After receiving another assessment report from Lop Nur, Liu Jie reported to Zhou in the affirmative.

China's first nuclear bomb had an estimated yield of more than twenty-two kilotons of TNT, about twice the power of the Hiroshima bomb. Direct expenses for nuclear bomb research, development, manufacturing, and testing from 1955 to 1964 were estimated at 2.8 billion yuan ($1 billion). The annual cost of nuclear research and development was 280 million yuan ($100 million), about 5 percent of China's annual defense budget. The indirect expenses of the first nuclear bomb were estimated at more than 8 billion yuan ($2.6 billion); its development and manufacturing involved nine hundred research institutes, universities, civil industrial factories, and transportation and communication enterprises across the country.[99] The total cost was thus about 10.8 billion yuan ($3.6 billion). Historian Shen Zhihua compares the spending by China and the Soviet Union: In 1947–49, the latter spent 14.5 billion rubles (about $11.6 billion) on its first nuclear bomb. In 1951–55, it planned a budget of 64.8 billion rubles ($51.8 billion) for nuclear and missile research and development. Shen points out that China made its first bomb at a much lower cost.[100]

China conducted its second nuclear test on May 14, 1965, this time by dropping the bomb from an airplane. That summer, Premier Zhou visited the nuclear test site at Lop Nur to inspect a missile launch experiment. After returning to Beijing, on August 9–11, Zhou held the thirteenth meeting of the Special Commission to discuss the combination of nuclear warheads and missiles to produce strategic nuclear weapons.[101] A week later, Zhou, Nie, and others began to organize China's strategic missile force, the Second Artillery Corps (Dier paobing). The fourteenth meeting of the committee was held December 29–31. Participants discussed tactical nuclear weapons, surface-to-air missile production, and strategic and tactical missiles. Committee members named 1966 the missile year (*daodannian*).[102] Plans for nuclear submarines, satellites, and an antimissile defense system were established.

After the third nuclear test on May 9, 1966, China began to test rockets carrying warheads. The first carrier rocket was successfully tested on June 29.[103] On June 6, General Wu Kehua was appointed commander of the PLA Second Artillery Corps. From the beginning, the corps maintained the arsenal for both conventional and nuclear-armed missiles. On October 25, 1966, the first combined test of a missile carrying a nuclear warhead was conducted at Lop Nur. The next test, on December 28, yielded an explosion estimated to be equivalent to 3.3 megatons of TNT.[104] Marshal Nie stayed at the testing range for thee months and supervised both tests. On June 17, 1967, China tested its first hydrogen bomb. At about 0700 hours that day, Marshal Nie and other commanders came to the testing front headquarters. By 0800 hours, the bomber took off on its way to ground zero. Upon reaching the target, however, the pilots were so nervous they failed to open the cargo bay and drop the bomb. The headquarters ordered them to try again. The bomber flew back to ground zero and dropped the bomb at 0820 hours. This test was successful and yielded an explosion equal to about 3 megatons of TNT.[105]

In 1968, Second Artillery regiments were divided into short, intermediate, long range, and intercontinental units.[106] (The Second Artillery Corps retains operational control of China's land-, air-, and sea-based nuclear missiles today. Political control over the nuclear forces is exercised by the chairman of the CMC, and the corps comes under the operational control of the GSD.[107]) On September 23, 1969, China conducted its first underground nuclear test. In that year, the first group of operational nuclear warheads and missiles was delivered to the Second Artillery Corps. Thereafter, the Chinese military possessed nuclear and strategic weapons. By the 1970s, China had become an independent nuclear weapon producer and continued to develop and build more advanced strategic weapons. In 1980 it tested its first intercontinental ballistic missile; two years later, it tested its first submarine-launched ballistic missile. PLA officials admitted the short-comings of their missile force but expressed little doubt that missile technology was one area in which China would make great strides in the late 1970s and the 1980s.[108]

What has not been made clear is China's relatively benign nuclear doctrine. Unfortunately, no official Chinese document confirms its doctrine; from the beginning, much has been inferred. In the 1950s, Mao pledged that China and its people were not afraid of nuclear weapons and that China would not be afraid to fight a nuclear war to defend itself after nuclear weapons had become available. China's nuclear weapons were for self-defense purposes. In 1964, China adopted a no-first-use policy—that is, it would not use nuclear weapons first under any circumstances.[109] China also supported "nuclear disarmament, the 'Fissile Material Cut-off Treaty' (FMCT), security assurance to non-nuclear-weapon states, and prevention of an arms race in outer space."[110] As David Shambaugh points out, however, "China has consistently taken the 'high ground' on global nuclear disarmament but has itself been unwilling to enter into negotiations to reduce its own stockpiles until the other declared nuclear powers reduce their inventories to China's level first."[111] Alastair I. Johnston notes a change in China's nuclear doctrine from minimum deterrence to limited deterrence (youxian weishe).[112] China is now clearly in line with limited deterrence based on its second-strike force that will attack only if the nation suffers a nuclear attack by another country.

Adopting a policy of limited deterrence required China's nuclear forces to survive and be flexible. China's nuclear modernization plan, which would eventually bring mobile missiles on board, was consistent with that policy. Further, China was not attempting to reach nuclear parity with either the Soviet Union or the United States: to do so would mean spending itself into bankruptcy. China's main goal was to avoid being subjected to the nuclear blackmail it had experienced in the Taiwan Strait in the 1950s. The problem of Taiwan and frequent crises in the Taiwan Strait with the GMD and the United States were used to justify China's nuclear modernization, but it would take place only within the greater context of a changing China and a changing world.

★ 6 ★

Crises and Politics

IN THE 1950S, AS CHINESE society became more radical during the anti-rightist and Great Leap Forward movements, the Chinese military experienced tremendous institutional changes. Defense Minister Peng Dehuai utilized Soviet technology, the officer reeducation and promotion system, and bureaucratic regulations to train a new "professional generation" of the PLA.[1] Obviously, a gap existed between the military reform programs and Mao's continuous revolution, which included political movements against intellectuals and emphasized *zhengzhi juewu* (political spirit). To Mao, the revolution that brought the CCP to power was the key to continued success. Mao imposed unprecedented, radical methods to mobilize the Chinese masses to forge a new revolutionary generation. The young Chinese, who were "born in New China and raised under the red flag," had little experience with class struggle. They should be trained and ready to carry on the revolution.

PLA officers did not fully understand Mao's political intentions or his solutions to military and international problems.[2] Some generals were uneasy with or puzzled by Mao's directives in the second Taiwan Strait crisis (1958). Generals Ye Fei and Nie Fengzhi indicated that they had no idea what Mao wanted to do during the crisis. Neither did Marshal Peng. Mao drafted orders in Peng's name and made decisions by himself, with little or no counsel. Some generals complained about the lack of communication between Beijing and the field headquarters. Unhappy with the gap between the party and the military, Mao demanded a supportive relationship between the party center and the PLA high command, like the one that existed during its previous military struggles. In the meantime, however, he could not tolerate the military leaders' criticism of his domestic policy. When Peng questioned Mao's Great Leap Forward movement, the marshal was purged at the party's Lushan conference in the summer of 1959.[3] That fall, 1,848 generals and officers were dismissed or jailed as rightists or as members of Peng's "anti-party clique."[4]

After Peng's fall, Marshal Lin Biao became the defense minister, serving from September 1959 to September 1971. He promoted Mao's ideology of the people's war. He became the second most powerful party leader, and Mao made him his successor in 1969. Chinese military historians consider Lin's fourteen-year tenure as defense minister destructive to the PLA. This chapter, however, argues that Chinese military modernization did not completely stop after the high command shakeup in 1959. The PLA continued to improve its commanding system, combat effectiveness, and logistics supply until 1967. Its experience in the 1962 Sino-Indian War demonstrated the positive results of the 1950s reform. Sergeant Li Weiheng's story in this chapter also attests to the reform's benefits. The debate in the PLA between the people's war and modernization continued until the Great Proletarian Cultural Revolution (1966–67), when all of Lin's opponents were removed from their posts in the PLA.

The 1958 Taiwan Strait Crisis

Before his fall, from August to October 1958, Marshal Peng faced a major international crisis in the Taiwan Strait involving the armed forces of the PRC, ROC, and United States.[5] In the summer of 1958, when a serious Middle Eastern crisis diverted American attention, it seemed a good opportunity to renew PLA attacks in the Taiwan Strait.[6] On July 16, the Chinese government strongly condemned the U.S. armed interference in Lebanon.[7] On July 17, the CCP Central Committee, hoping the United States was distracted by the Lebanese crisis, decided to shell Jinmen to crack down on Jiang Jieshi's army's frequent harassment along the Fujian coast across from Jinmen and Mazu.

On the evening of July 18, Mao spoke at a decision-making meeting attended by CMC vice chairmen and leading air force and navy officers, emphasizing that Jinmen and Mazu were China's territory and that shelling the GMD troops was an internal Chinese matter and would not give the United States an excuse to attack mainland China. Mao believed that the shelling would last for two to three months.[8] Later that night, the CMC held an urgent meeting attended by the heads of the PLA branches. Defense Minister Peng conveyed Mao's instructions and told the chiefs that the GMD planned to create a tense situation in the Taiwan Strait that would necessitate a PLA response. The bombardment of Jinmen would begin on July 25, and air force units would be deployed in Fujian and eastern Guangdong by July 27.[9]

The air force chief issued operational orders the next day. After extensive preparations, on July 27, forty-eight MiG-17 fighters arrived at the air bases at Liancheng in Fujian and Shantou in Guangdong.[10] General Nie Fengzhi was appointed commander of the Fujian Front Command (FFC) air force that summer. Over the next year, the PLAAF would deploy twenty-three fighter regiments, totaling 520 aircraft, mostly MiG-17s, on the front. In response to the initial PLAAF buildup across the strait, Jiang Jieshi announced in July 1958 that all the GMD troops on Taiwan, Penghu (Pescadores), Jinmen, and Mazu were "on emergency alert."[11] After the PLA deployed its air force in the two southern provinces at the end of July, its fighters challenged the GMD air force over the Taiwan Strait. Between July 29 and August 22, the PLA fighters downed four GMD fighters and damaged five, while the PLA lost one fighter.[12] Thereafter, the PLA controlled the airspace along the Fujian coast.

On July 19, General Ye Fei, commander of the FFC, received instructions from the General Staff to prepare a large-scale bombardment to block transport between Jinmen and Taiwan. Ye had commanded the Tenth Army Corps in 1949 in the failed invasion of Jinmen, where he lost nine thousand men. Thereafter, he never missed an opportunity to seek revenge for Jinmen. At a planning meeting in Xiamen on July 20, Ye discussed how to blockade this GMD-occupied island group with his artillery.

The Jinmen island group, lying less than 2 miles off Xiamen, with three sides surrounded by the mainland, was about 140 miles away from Taiwan. At that time, the GMD had six infantry divisions and two tank battalions with 308 heavy artillery pieces stationed among the nine islands of the Jinmens. Some eighty-eight thousand troops and fifty thousand residents totally depended upon supplies from Taiwan, requiring at least four hundred tons of supplies per day. Transportation and logistics thus were the critical vulnerabilities of the Jinmen garrison.[13] If the PLA cut off or restricted the flow of supplies, it could undermine the garrison's effectiveness.

At Ye's planning meeting, the FFC commanders agreed that an effective blockade could force the GMD garrison to withdraw from Jinmen to Taiwan. Shore batteries, bolstered by naval attacks on cargo ships, and air raids on the harbor and airport could isolate the Jinmen garrison as long as the United States did not intervene.[14] The commanders also realized, however, that their artillery pieces were mixed and inferior in quality to the GMD's, which consisted mainly of American-made 155mm howitzers. Although the PLA had some Soviet-made 152mm and 122mm howitzers, the bulk of their pieces were Japanese-made howitzers from WWII and American-made 105mm howitzers from the Chinese civil war. To maximize their firepower, the commanders planned to deploy thirty-two artillery battalions and six naval coastal artillery companies in three locations: seventeen artillery battalions in Lianhe would shell Jinmen; fifteen artillery battalions in Xiamen would target Little Jinmen and the west side of Jinmen; and the naval artillery troops would shell the ships in Xiamen Harbor. Meanwhile, three other artillery divisions from outside regions were transferred in succession to Fujian.[15]

General Ye received another CMC order on July 25 that FFC artillery units on the Fujian front should be "prepared for an operational order at any moment."[16] Two days later, however, as his forces prepared to shell Jinmen, Ye received a copy of a letter from Mao to Peng and General Huang Kecheng, vice defense minister and secretary general of the CMC. Because of his intense preoccupation with the shelling, the chairman reportedly could not sleep at all on July 26. It seemed to Mao, as reflected in his letter, that it would be "more appropriate to withhold the attack on Jinmen for several days" and to wait for "the best scenario," one in which Jiang's army would attack some major cities on the mainland and make the Jinmen attack appear to be retaliatory. Mao emphasized, "We must persist in the principle of fighting no battle we are not sure of winning." He asked his defense minister to discuss

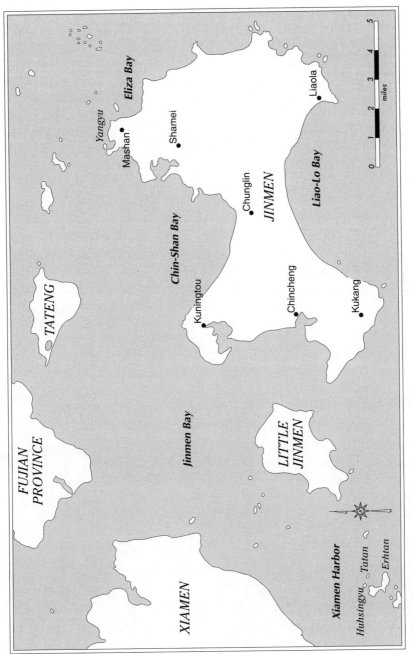

Jinmen Islands

these ideas carefully with other top military commanders. "If you agree [with the above points]," Mao told Peng, "telegraph this letter to Ye Fei and ask him to think about it very carefully. Let me know his opinion."[17] Ye called an urgent meeting after receiving Mao's letter on July 27. The leading FFC commanders discussed Mao's points and agreed that postponing the bombardment of Jinmen would allow them to be better prepared. Ye telegraphed their views to Peng the same day and ordered the artillery units to make further preparations for the bombardment.[18]

In the third week of his wait-and-see policy, Mao finally decided to go ahead. He instructed Peng on August 18 to prepare to start the bombardment, which would deal "with Jiang directly and the Americans indirectly."[19] To avoid conflicts with U.S. aircraft, Mao insisted that PLA airplanes not go beyond the airspace of Jinmen and Mazu in pursuit of GMD airplanes. Mao called a meeting on August 20 at Beidaihe, where he was chairing the Politburo Standing Committee meeting from August 17 through 30. Marshals Peng and Lin Biao and General Wang Shangrong, chief of the operations department of the General Staff headquarters, attended the meeting at Mao's summer house. Mao told Peng, "You want a fight, while I want to wait. The opening show is yours. You can start it."[20] Peng reported the PLA's readiness and plans for shelling Jinmen. Mao, however, needed more details and summoned Ye to Beidaihe from the FFC headquarters on August 21. During Ye's report, Mao looked carefully at the maps and asked, because Ye had deployed so many artillery pieces (almost ten thousand) along the front, whether he would kill American military advisors.[21] Ye immediately answered yes. Mao fell into a deep silence for more than ten minutes. He then asked Ye whether he could avoid hitting Americans, but Ye said no. In the meantime, Lin wrote a note to Mao suggesting that Wang Bingnan, the PRC representative at the Sino-American ambassadorial talks in Warsaw, inform the Americans of the shelling. But Mao rejected this suggestion.

Ye recalled that he had no idea what Mao wanted to do. Neither did Marshal Peng, who had been requesting an invasion of Jinmen.[22] The next day, August 22, Mao decided to begin the shelling at 1200 hours on August 23. Mao outlined a strategy for the shelling of Jinmen: "Take one step first, and look carefully before taking another step." The chairman decided that the PLA shelling would continue for three days. The next step would depend on Taiwan's response and Jinmen's

PLA batteries in Fujian shell Jinmen Island in 1958. (Courtesy of the National Military Museum of the Chinese People's Revolution, Beijing, China.)

situation. Mao predicted that the GMD garrison would show some intention of withdrawing from the islands if the PLA could successfully cut it off. He reemphasized caution and preparation and asked Ye to remain at Beidaihe to command the shelling.[23] Ye did not understand why Mao wanted him two thousand miles away from his command. Perhaps Mao thought it would give the top-level commanders a unified focus and control of the bombardment.[24]

By the evening of August 21, Ye had already sent his last preparation order to his forces. By August 23, all his artillery units were ready. There would be no spotting rounds. The massive surprise bombardment would, he hoped, shock the GMD garrison. The shelling targeted Jinmen's command headquarters, artillery positions, radar sites, harbor facilities, and ships in harbor.[25]

At 1730 hours on August 23, Ye issued the final order to shell the Jinmen island group. The first barrage was delivered by 459 artillery pieces from twenty-four artillery battalions that fired some twenty-four thousand shells onto the islands in just thirty-five minutes. In eighty minutes, the PLA fired more than thirty thousand shells onto the islands and killed some six hundred GMD troops, including three vice commanders. The next day, the shelling continued, sinking one transport ship and damaging two others. The GMD also lost two fighters in air engagements with the PLA fighters. One PLA plane was shot down by its own antiaircraft artillery.[26] By August 25, the PLA's heavy shelling had totally cut the Jinmen island group off from Taiwan.

Three days later, however, Taiwan employed a new strategy: it changed from daytime to nighttime shipments and anchored at smaller surrounding islands instead of on Jinmen Island itself.[27] To achieve a total blockade, Peng ordered Ye to isolate Jinmen Island from the surrounding islands. Beijing sent two more artillery divisions, the Second and Sixth, to Fujian as reinforcements. On the fifth day, PLAAF searchlight units arrived to assist nighttime shelling. The units began their operations on September 2, turning on their long-range lights every fifteen minutes throughout the night to spot artillery. They made GMD nighttime shipments extremely difficult.[28] The PLA continued its overwhelming shelling and silenced GMD counterbattery fire. But Chief General Hao Bocun, the GMD garrison commander on Jinmen, remembered that the bombardment did not destroy GMD artillery pieces.[29]

Hao Bocun and the author in Taipei. (Author's collection.)

On the eighth day, at the end of August, PLA General Han Xian-chu proposed bombing the Jinmen island group by air. Ye, who had returned to Fujian, opposed Han's proposal. Ye remembered Mao's closely considered precautions: no landing on Jinmen, no conflict with the United States, and no killing of Americans. Without a planned landing, air raids were unnecessary. Moreover, air raids would require both bombers and fighters over Jinmen and surrounding waters. It would be very difficult to avoid a conflict with U.S. aircraft in such an operation. But Han was the FFC commander, and Ye was his political commissar. Ye cabled both opinions to Beijing. Mao agreed with Ye.[30]

After ten days of shelling, the Jinmen garrison had received only a very small percentage of its regular supplies through a limited and ineffective airlift and some nightly shipping. The PLA was ready to make further moves. Ye recalled, "The Jinmen garrison collapsed and we could have taken it as easily as crossing the street if we had launched a landing attack. But we could never know what was in Chairman Mao's mind."[31] On the evening of September 3, Mao suddenly ordered that the shelling of Jinmen stop for three days to gauge the American response.[32]

U.S. Escorts and the PLA's Setback

On September 7, seven American warships (two cruisers and five destroyers) escorted two GMD supply ships sailing to Jinmen. Ye saw the combined American-Taiwanese fleet on the radar from his headquarters as soon as it left Taiwan, and he immediately reported this development to Mao in Beijing. Mao responded with an order, passed through the General Staff headquarters, to shell the combined fleet. Ye asked whether to fire on the American ships. Mao's instruction was to shell only Taiwanese ships and not to open fire until the fleet reached the harbor. More worried than confused, Ye asked Mao whether to return fire if the American ships fired at his positions. Mao's answer was loud and clear: no returning fire without his order. Afraid of misunderstanding the order, Ye repeated his question to the General Staff headquarters, which confirmed Chairman Mao's order not to return fire. Ye became very nervous because the American ships were so close to the Taiwanese ships. He also had a difficult time conveying Mao's order to his field commanders, though they would have followed Mao's commands without any question or hesitation.[33] Since the commanders did not have enough time to identify the American ships, the small flotilla reached Jinmen unmolested.[34]

The next day, September 8, Taiwan sent another American-Taiwanese fleet to Jinmen using a similar escort pattern, with four GMD landing ships and five American ships (one cruiser and four destroyers). Around 1200 hours, the combined fleet reached Jinmen Bay. Mao gave the order to open fire at 1243 hours. Thirty-six artillery battalions and six coastal artillery companies fired 21,700 shells.[35] The American ships turned southward quickly and moved out of the PLA artillery's range. They stayed six to twelve miles away from Jinmen without firing a shot, while the GMD ships suffered heavy losses.[36] Taiwan tried the escort tactic again on September 11, with four American ships escorting four GMD transport ships and seven GMD warships. At about 1500 hours, when the fleet was getting close to Jinmen, the PLA used forty artillery battalions and six coastal artillery companies to shell the combined fleet. The GMD, having learned a hard lesson on September 8, turned around immediately, without waiting for the Americans. The American-Taiwanese fleet retried it two days later but again could not get to Jinmen because of the fierce PLA fire.[37]

Taiwan then employed a different transportation vessel—an LVT (landing vehicle, tracked), a small amphibious vehicle that American troops had successfully used in WWII that could land and unload almost anywhere.[38] On September 14, the GMD sent seventeen fully loaded LVTs from large transport ships outside Jinmen; fifteen reached the island. From September 14 to October 5, GMD transport from Taiwan to Jinmen gradually resumed, using LVTs. By October 5, some 170 tons of supplies arrived per day, about 40 percent of the daily needs of the island garrison, a significant increase from the 5 percent it had received since late August.[39]

Meanwhile, U.S. planes began escorting GMD shipments to Jinmen, as did GMD F-86 fighters equipped with new air-to-air missiles, their first use in combat. These became a huge tactical obstacle for PLA pilots. The PLAAF discovered that the GMD had air-to-air missiles only when, on September 24, PLA fighters were shot down by the missiles in an engagement with GMD fighters.[40]

The blockade of Jinmen was becoming more and more difficult to sustain. Ye and his commanders became nervous as the CMC put more pressure on its field generals. On September 15, after receiving reports of problems associated with stopping the LVTs, the CMC ordered the FFC to improve the accuracy of its artillery to sink or neutralize these small vessels before they could reach the beach. On September 24, the CMC reiterated that the FFC must develop new methods to stop Taiwan's increasingly successful shipments to Jinmen. Meanwhile, the CMC transferred more artillery troops from Guangzhou and other regions to Fujian as reinforcements. By the end of September, fourteen artillery regiments, seven artillery battalions, and fourteen artillery companies were engaged in the bombardment of Jinmen.[41]

Despite forty days of shelling, new tactics, and reinforcements, the PLA's blockade of Jinmen was not fully effective, and Taiwan showed no signs of withdrawing its garrison. The PLA high command now had to decide on its next step. Early on October 5, Mao wrote to Peng and General Huang Kecheng, "Our batteries should not fire a single shell on October 6 and 7, even if there are American planes and escort ships. If the enemy bombs us, our forces should still not return fire. We will cease our activities, lie low, and wait and see for two days. Then we will know what to do." Mao asked Peng and Huang to "carry out the above order immediately and pass this letter as an order to Ye Fei and Han Xianchu."[42] Mao and the CMC decided to slow down the shelling of Jinmen.

Chinese leaders seemed willing to accept that the PRC would not fight the United States over the offshore islands if the Americans committed to their defense. Such was the outcome of the test shelling of Jinmen. Mao, however, had to find an excuse for slowing down the bombardment. On October 5, the CMC issued an instruction, drafted by Mao, that rationalized the slowdown in shelling by claiming that, although the PLA could have seized Jinmen, it would have been merely a short-term victory. China would leave Jinmen linked to Taiwan to avoid giving the United States a pretext for instigating a "two Chinas plot." The nation's unification and the liberation of Taiwan were much more important over the long run than was the recovery of a few off-shore islands. The problem of the offshore islands could eventually be solved along with the Taiwan problem.[43] A month earlier, Mao had described the "noose strategy": Beijing would leave the islands, including Jinmen and Mazu, in Jiang's hands as a burden on America. Beijing, however, could use its treatment of the islands as a noose to serve its own goals in the international arena. China could bombard Jinmen to tighten the pressure on America, or stop the bombardment to relax the tension.[44] Mark A. Ryan, David M. Finkelstein, and Michael A. McDevitt view this new policy as another example of Mao's tendency to "rationaliz[e] constrained options as successes." They point out that "the 'noose policy' has every appearance in retrospect of an elaborate and self-serving ex post facto rationalization—a fig leaf designed to obscure the fact that any serious PLA attempt to retake the offshore islands of Jinmen and Mazu may well have triggered a sizable U.S. retaliation, including nuclear strikes."[45]

Thus, by October 5, the tension in the Taiwan Straits began to ease, though small-scale shelling of Jinmen continued as part of Mao's noose policy. Mao told top PLA commanders that America had concentrated a large force in the Taiwan Strait, including six of its twelve aircraft carriers, three heavy cruisers, forty destroyers, and two air force divisions. Such strength should not be underestimated. PLA policy toward Jinmen, therefore, would be to shell without landing and cut off without killing. Bombardment of Jinmen would continue to hamper communication and transportation but would not totally bottle up the enemy on the island.[46] Mao said that the bombardment of Jinmen made the Americans very nervous. Mao pointed out that Dulles was putting his neck into the noose of Jinmen-Mazu by defending all of Taiwan, Penghu, Jinmen, and Mazu. "It is good for us to get the Americans there," said Mao. "Whenever we want to kick them, we can. Thus we have the initiative, and the Americans do not."[47]

Early on October 6, Mao drafted "Gao Taiwan tongpao shu" (Message to Compatriots in Taiwan), which was published in the name of Defense Minister Peng later that day. The message announced that the PLA would stop shelling Jinmen for seven days to allow GMD troops to receive supplies. It pointed out that both sides considered Taiwan, Jinmen, and Mazu to be Chinese territories and that all agreed there existed only one China, not two. The message formally proposed negotiations to peacefully resolve the thirty-year Chinese civil war.[48] Seven days later, Mao drafted a defense minister directive, also published under Peng's name, that announced suspension of the shelling for another two weeks "to deal with the Americans. We must draw a very clear line between Chinese and Americans for our national interests."[49] These two statements marked an important turning point in Mao's policy toward the offshore islands. Limited military operations now mixed with

Cold War politics in the Taiwan Strait. Attempts at forcible military takeover of the offshore islands gave way to political struggle against Taiwan in the international arena. On October 25, "Zaigao Taiwan tongpao shu" (Second Message to Compatriots in Taiwan), also drafted by Mao and issued in Peng's name, announced that Beijing had ordered PLA batteries on the Fujian front not to shell Jinmen on even-numbered days, while a continued shelling on odd-numbered days would be limited by certain conditions. Mao admitted, "Militarily it sounded like a joke, since such a policy was unknown in the history of Chinese or world warfare. However, we are engaged in a political battle, which is supposed to be fought this way."[50] Ultimately, the PLA shelling would not stop until January 1, 1979, the date on which the PRC and the United States normalized their diplomatic relations. The bombardment of Jinmen was the longest sustained artillery campaign in world military history.

From August 23 to October 6, 1958, the PLA shelled the Jinmen island group and surrounding waters with 474,900 rounds. The PLA claimed to have sunk twenty-one GMD gun ships and transport ships and damaged another seventeen, shot down eighteen GMD airplanes, and inflicted more than one thousand GMD casualties.[51] The PLA bombardment in the 1958 Taiwan Strait crisis demonstrated a Chinese military paradox with some important implications. Prior to the crisis, a gap existed between Mao's political considerations and the PLA's operational goals on the ground in Fujian. While emphasizing loyalty and discouraging policy debates, the PLA generals had to find their own ways to fight and win their battles. Their operations had the unintended impact of helping to bring about the major international crisis of 1958. The relationship between Mao and Peng became more complicated toward the end of the crisis, when Mao began to communicate less frequently with Peng. Peng would be purged a year later at the Lushan conference, which was, as Joffe describes, "the most serious leadership struggle since the establishment of the Communist regime."[52]

The Fall of Peng

Peng should have realized that his relationship with Mao was weakening in the late 1950s. While emphasizing professionalism and institutional control, Peng had opposed Mao's cult of personality in the army.

In 1954, he forbade the erection of statues of Mao at military bases. In 1955, when he read in a manuscript the line "The victory of the CPVF won the war under the correct leadership of the CCP and of Comrade Mao Zedong," he crossed out "and of Comrade Mao Zedong."[53] After Khrushchev attacked Stalin's cult of personality in 1956, many CCP and PLA leaders felt it necessary to do the same in China. Mao, concerned about his reputation and popularity in the party and army, questioned Peng's loyalty. All available evidence indicates that the Mao-Peng relationship was troubled during the 1950s. Clearly, Mao was concerned about Peng's increased power in the military, the result of his reorganization of the PLA during the 1950s reforms.

In September 1954, when a new Ministry of Defense was created under the State Council, Peng became the first defense minister. The new constitution also established the National Defense Committee, a body subordinate to the National People's Congress, with Mao as committee chairman. Among the fifteen vice chairmen were the ten marshals: Zhu, Peng, Lin, Luo Ronghuan, Liu Bocheng, He, Chen Yi, Xu Xiangqian, Nie Rongzhen, and Ye Jianying. Eighty-one additional committee members formed the state's consulting body in military affairs, which did not direct or command the armed forces. On September 28, the same day the National Defense Committee was created, the Politburo passed the Resolution on the Establishment of the CCP Central Military Commission (CMC). The Politburo believed that the Chinese armed forces had a tradition of Communist Party command. As in the past, the PLA must be under the command of the CCP Politburo and Central Secretariat. The CMC exercised de facto authoritative policymaking and operational control over the military.[54] The CMC, as the highest command, issued orders to all services. Any public directive or statement was issued by the Ministry of Defense. The CMC had the same makeup as the National Defense Committee: Mao was the chairman of the CMC, and the ten marshals plus Zhou Enlai and Deng Xiaoping were its members. Thus the military was under party control.[55]

One critical difference between the two institutions was the existence of the CMC General Office, which served as the central coordinating unit for the party. This office facilitated and supervised personal interactions among the senior members of the PLA leadership, managed the external activities of the Ministry of Defense, coordinated bureaucratic interactions among the core military agencies, supervised the daily operations of the CMC departments, and oversaw the CMC ad hoc subcommittees. The General Office also served as the key coordination and evaluation point for strategic research and assessments developed within the defense bureaucracy.[56]

Peng apparently based his military reforms on Mao's political support—there was no clear agreement among the military leaders. When Mao began to criticize the post-Stalin leaders of the Soviet Union in the late 1950s for ideological and political reasons, Peng lost ground in both the party and the army. The first conflict between the two Communist parties came in 1956 when Khrushchev denounced Stalin as a dictator in his secret report to the Congress of the Communist Party of the Soviet Union. Mao launched a massive campaign in 1957–58 criticizing the post-Stalin leaders in Moscow as "revisionists" and "social imperialists" who betrayed the CCP and the world Communist movement. The conflicts between the two Communist parties extended to issues on foreign policy, economic cooperation, military aid, and other exchange programs. Mao terminated China's Sovietization movement in the late 1950s.[57]

On November 18, 1957, when Mao attended the celebration of the fortieth anniversary of the Russian Revolution in Moscow, he pledged that China would catch up with Great Britain in steel and other major areas of industrial production within fifteen years. In early 1958, the second plenary session of the Eighth CCP National Congress officially authorized Mao's Three Red Banners (Sanmian hongqi), including the Great Leap Forward and people's communes. The movement instated a bold advance on a large scale. All the industrial production targets for the second five-year plan were doubled, and agricultural production targets were raised by 20 to 50 percent. Only three months later, at the Beidaihe conference of the expanded Politburo in August, these targets were doubled yet again. These rash advances are historically known as the Great Leap Forward. This movement's consequences were more disastrous than those of earlier programs. In 1958, tens of millions of people were mobilized in a nationwide movement of steelmaking, an extremely costly operation in terms of labor, capital, and raw material. In the countryside, peasants were organized into people's communes and forced to eat at community mess halls. Large numbers of rural hands were moved away from grain fields to work in urban industries. Many of the able-bodied men left behind were put to work on backyard furnaces for steel production. Consequently, the grain harvest was dismal, leading to the widespread famine of the three hard years. The civil-military tension increased at this juncture, with widespread dissatisfaction with the Great Leap Forward inside and outside the leadership.[58]

In the summer of 1959, a political storm arose that shook the foundations of both the party and the PLA. From July 2 to August 16, CCP elites gathered at Mount Lushan for a series of meetings of the Politburo and Central Committee. The original agenda of the expanded Politburo session was to discuss how to correct leftist mistakes in implementing the economic policies of the Great Leap Forward. On July 14, Peng wrote his now-well-known letter to Mao to emphasize the problems that had appeared during the Three Red Banners movement. Peng maintained that the leftist mistakes were rooted in "petty bourgeois fanaticism." The party center was too slow to realize the severity of the problems in 1958, he said, and it was wrong to continue the Great Leap Forward in 1959. Peng asserted that the problems were not only economic but also political. For instance, relations between workers and peasants and between urban and rural populations were distorted. Despite his criticisms, Peng apparently tried to disconnect Mao from these problems.[59]

Peng's criticisms probably would have been tolerated if they had been raised by another military leader, but Mao was worried about Peng's disloyalty and his military power. On July 23, Mao, addressing the whole conference, rebuked Peng. Mao equated Peng and his supporters with the rightists of 1957 and accused him of being the leader of a "military club" and prohibiting "civil-military collaboration." Mao told Peng, "All [I] ask[ed] of you was not to set up [your own] center this time." At the July 31 Politburo Standing Committee meeting at Lushan, Mao summarized his relationship with Peng: "It was said at the Second Plenary Meeting of the Eighth Party Congress that [we should] be ready to deal with a split. It had specific meaning. It meant you [Peng]. . . . Yesterday we were friends, and today, enemies."[60] Fang Zhu points out that Mao feared that Peng would use "his military power to defy Mao's authority in the party leadership." Peng's criticism was perceived "as a sign of military disloyalty to Mao's personal authority." Zhu believes, however, that Peng "never intended to threaten the party center or Mao Zedong. There was no sign of his plotting any military action against anyone."[61] Yet Mao considered Peng a threat. He accused Peng of forming a "right opportunist clique" and conducting "unprincipled factional activity" in the party and army, charges that were often raised against those thought to have pro-Soviet political positions. Peng was dismissed from all of his positions in the army and party and thereafter lived under virtual house arrest. He wrote many long, personal letters to Mao and the CCP Central Committee, appealing for suspension of his disgrace. These letters brought even more criticism and troubles for him in the 1960s.[62]

Marshal Lin Biao, the new defense minister, terminated most of the programs that Peng had initiated. Although Peng's reform efforts did not create modern armed forces, they did have a major impact on military institutionalization, structural improvement, technology applications, and strategic weapons research and development, as evidenced by China's successful tests of atomic and hydrogen bombs. Peng supposedly cried in his cell when he heard the news of the first nuclear test in 1964.

The Rise of Lin

After the PRC was founded in 1949, the CCP had nine years of successful socialist reform and construction. But then, inflated self-confidence and self-destructive elements engendered inside the party a kind of joyous arrogance. Like the social reforms of the period, the 1950s military reforms failed when the CCP transformed its leadership from a Leninist to a charismatic style of leadership, the cult of Mao. An exaggerated estimation of accomplishments further stirred unrealistic thinking and opened a broad avenue for impetuous violations of the laws of economics. A number of radical leftist theories evolved and finally gained prominence inside the CCP. At the same time, worship of the top leader and arbitrary decisions by key individuals grew. Mao had already set himself up as an absolute authority and was increasingly impatient with any disagreement. Odd Arne Westad explains the cult of Mao's personality as "the ideal of complete adherence to his instructions." Ultimately, "the belief in the myths and visions he developed became the center of the party's existence."[63] Marshal Lin played a very important role in creating the cult of Mao after he emerged as the top military leader.

The military leaders split between the rightist or pragmatic group and the leftist or radical group, according to their loyalty to Mao. After the criticisms of Peng at the Lushan conference in 1959, the Central Committee directed the high command to hold an expanded CMC meeting in Beijing from August 18 to September 12, 1959. All the army, provincial, and regional commanders, more than 1,500 officers, attended. Following the party's political disputes, the meeting criticized Peng's reforms as the "capitalist military line" and the root of "all rightist and dogmatist evils." The participants allied with Mao, not Peng and his "military club." To prove their political loyalty, they denounced "rightists and opportunists" in their own units. A top-down purge went through the PLA. Less than six months later, 1,848 high- and middle-ranking commanders and officers who had questioned the Great Leap Forward and people's communes or expressed their support or sympathy for Peng had been dismissed, criticized, or jailed.[64] The overextended political struggle and large-scale purge had convinced the rank and file that professionalism was wrong and dangerous, while the radical leftist line was safe.

Lin, who had been in charge of the administration of the CMC since September 1959, emphasized politics in command, promoted Mao's cult of personality, and carried out a leftist policy for the PLA. In October 1960, Lin launched a mass political campaign in the PLA to study Mao Zedong Thought, which he called the "peak of modern thought."[65] Reading classes replaced training and drills in all the services. In May 1964, he organized the compilation of *Mao zhuxi yulu* (Quotations from Chairman Mao), known worldwide as the "little red book," to guide the soldiers and later the Chinese people to participate in the Cultural Revolution. Fang Zhu describes this process as the "Maoization of the PLA."[66] Lin brought the people's army back by emphasizing the people's war principle and military-civilian integration. In 1966, he published *Renmin zhanzheng shengli wansui* (Long Live the Victory of People's War), which emphasized the PLA's guerrilla warfare experience. That same year, Lin abolished the Soviet-style system of military ranks established by Peng in 1955. Lin blamed this system for having changed the PLA tradition of equality among soldiers and commanders.[67] "Non-professionalism" and "irregularity" formed Mao's legacy of military involvement in civilian activities and civilian participation in war.

Soon the whole nation was fired up to imitate the PLA's unconditional dedication to Mao. A large number of PLA officers and soldiers were dispatched to people's communes to promote the study of Mao Zedong Thought. People's communes, designed by Mao and officially endorsed by a Central Committee resolution in August 1958, were a high point of the radical movement in rural areas. According to the resolution, rural communes could best mobilize peasants' production capabilities and would play a major role in facilitating socialist construction and accelerating China's transition to Communism. Consequently, communes began to emerge all over the countryside. By the end of 1958, there were twenty-six thousand people's communes; by 1960, there were seventy-four thousand. Almost all peasant households were organized into people's communes. Although communes varied in size, each had an average of five thousand households, or between fifteen thousand and twenty-five thousand people. By 1965, 150,000 officers and soldiers had been sent to the people's communes and production teams or villages in Shandong, and 100,000 in Guangdong. Their missions were to bring the PLA's experience of studying Mao Zedong Thought to the peasants and to establish centralized control at the village level.[68]

The establishment of communes represented a radical effort to create large-scale, self-contained rural communities and led to a highly centralized rural economy. Based on Mao's notion of self-reliance, each commune was to be capable of producing its own basic necessities, complete with its own education and medical systems, agricultural production, and industry. Virtually replacing the existing townships and county-level administrations, communes functioned as the new rural political and economic units and integrated almost all aspects of peasants' lives. The people's communes were supposed to, and did on many occasions, provide more effective means of organizing an extensive labor force for large-scale construction and water-control projects. People's communes were divided into production brigades consisting of several originally separate villages, which were in turn divided into smaller work units known as production teams. A production team was in practice a reconstituted village and was often directly in charge of work assignments and the recording of work points gained by peasants. Work points were tallied at year's end and converted mainly to payment in kind, usually in the form of grain, and partially to payment in cash. A significant change brought about by the commune system was the incorporation of rural women into the workforce.

Caught up in the fervor of creating economic miracles during the Great Leap Forward, many communes plunged into agricultural disaster. Intent on pleasing their superiors or demonstrating their revolutionary enthusiasm, some overzealous rural cadres resorted to foolhardy planting techniques that killed crops before they reached maturity. Unable to meet unrealistically high quotas, cadres often submitted inflated reports of productivity. Exaggerated reporting of grain production left Chinese peasants poorly prepared for the three hard years (1959–61), when bad weather, combined with seriously flawed policies, resulted in severe food shortages and massive famine.[69]

In the 1960s, all the organizations of state power that had extended their reach into local communities underwent dramatic transformations. In the wake of the three hard years, the economic and political system continued to diverge from Mao's ideal path of socialist construction. Mao found that, to stabilize post-famine China, he had to stabilize his position within the party. In September 1962, he announced the slogan "Never forget class struggle," at the same time accusing various people within the party of disagreeing with his views.[70] In 1963, under this slogan, the party commenced the socialist education movement, also known as the Four Cleanups (Siqing) movement, in the villages. From the very beginning of the movement, local cadres, as agents of the state within the villages, were victims of the conflict between state and society. Mao and Liu Shaoqi, heads of the party and government, respectively, had very different goals for the movement and very different opinions about the role of local cadres. Although many local cadres had diligently carried out the directives of the state by implementing collectivization and compelling villagers to turn over their grain to the state, Mao now wanted to implicate them as agents of the landlord class. As sociologist Huang Zhongzhi explains, "Chairman Mao skillfully transformed the struggle against his political opponents within the Party into class struggle."[71] Everyone was either on the revolutionary path, led by Mao, or on the counterrevolutionary path, led by Liu Shaoqi. Historian Zhou Xiaohong points out that, after 1966, large-scale rural political participation became Mao's method for reconstructing the nation by destroying those taking the counterrevolutionary path.[72]

Local cadres received the worst of it under this mandate for mass villager participation. Villagers had grown to resent local cadres because of their role as agents of the state and because of their tendency to "eat a lot, take a lot." Villagers had previously used complaints, posters, and demonstrations to protest cadre abuses of power; now that they had the official support of the party, their protests became much more open and, in some cases, violent as they released their long-accumulated dissatisfactions.[73] In the 1950s, they had been encouraged to participate in the social reforms that overthrew the old social and economic order, thereby contributing to the process of state-building and state expansion. But in the 1960s, they were told to turn around and attack local officials in the very organizations that they themselves had helped the state to build. This kind of participation escalated during the Great Proletarian Cultural Revolution. According to Mao, the entire government structure had become dominated by Liu Shaoqi and other "capitalist roaders." The masses were therefore justified in attacking the government and replacing existing government organizations with new ones, including allowing military participation in civil administrations.[74]

When the civil government's control declined in the early 1960s, the military's penetration was swift and deep. Fang Zhu's work shows that the PLA sent its political instructors to the political departments of most businesses and organizations in Henan and to 70 percent of the state's political departments in that province. In 1963, eight thousand officers were transferred from the PLA to finance and commerce departments in Hubei. In Liaoning, 70 percent of the enterprises had on staff PLA officers and soldiers, who served either as party branch secretaries or political instructors.[75] With this large-scale military participation in civil administration, for a short period, officers and soldiers participated in the management of factories, people's communes, and government offices at different levels.[76]

Even though the people's communes turned out to be an economic disaster, they functioned effectively to organize local militias, recruiting the best young men in the villages. In the early 1960s, about four thousand militia divisions were organized and armed by the PLA across the country (an estimated 60 million members), including male peasants between eighteen and forty-five and female peasants between eighteen and thirty-five.[77] Usually, a militia company was established at the production team level, a militia battalion in each people's commune, and a militia regiment in each county. Militia units were also established in each factory, college, institute, and government facility. The PLA itself experienced a significant increase in numbers as well. Having expanded its involvement in civil government and international conflicts, the PLA reached 6 million strong, the largest in its history, with a significant increase in its navy, air force, and certain services, like engineering corps and railroad corps. From 1958 to 1965, the PLAN increased 51.6 percent and the PLAAF 41.8 percent.[78] Meanwhile, a large number of new party members were recruited among the services. In 1961 alone, more than 229,000 PLA members reportedly joined the party. At the same time, the PLA sped up its war preparations because international tensions had intensified along China's border with India.[79]

The 1962 Sino-Indian War

The brief relaxation of international tensions ended in the 1960s, when the Cold War between the two superpowers intensified. In August 1961, Khrushchev ordered construction of the Berlin Wall in Germany. In October 1962, the United States learned of the Soviets' deployment of missiles in Cuba. President John F. Kennedy forced a showdown by ordering the U.S. Navy to stop the shipment of Soviet offensive weapons and equipment to Cuba. The world held its breath for several days during the Cuban Missile Crisis.[80] Meanwhile, U.S. forces increased their presence in South Vietnam, which was viewed as a prelude to a U.S. invasion of China. Again, the changing international environment had a strong impact on Chinese strategy.[81]

In addition to the perceived U.S. threat from the southwest, there was increasing tension along the Chinese-Russian border in the northwest and northeast. In 1962, minorities in northwestern China revolted in the Xinjiang Uygur Autonomous Region, and more than sixty thousand residents fled to the Soviet Union. The Soviets increased their forces along the border. That same year, Jiang Jieshi called for a return to the mainland and increased GMD military harassment along the southeastern coast. Last but not least, in October 1962, the Sino-Indian War broke out along the Tibetan border.

In 1951, the Chinese central government and Tibet signed the Agreement on Measures for the Peaceful Liberation of Tibet. The

PLA entered Tibet to safeguard its borders with India and Nepal. The agreement affirmed Tibet's political, social, and religious autonomy. In 1959, however, the central government accused the Buddhist spiritual leader, the Dalai Lama, of organizing a separatist movement in Tibet. PLA troops suppressed the rebellion. The fourteenth Dalai Lama escaped into India. The central government then imposed policies to abolish the traditional economic and political systems of Tibet. In 1961, an election was held to uproot the Tibetan leaders. In September 1965, the First People's Congress of Tibet was convened, at which the Tibet Autonomous Region and its regional government were officially established. Tibet became one of the twenty-nine provinces and autonomous regions of the PRC.

The Sino-Indian War arose over border disputes along the Himalayan Mountains in Ladakh and Aksai Chin in the west and in the North East Frontier Agency in the east.[82] Part of the difficulties in the east concerned the McMahon Line, a border based on a 1914 British-Tibetan agreement. Tibet had served as a buffer between the PRC and India since 1951, when Beijing recognized the autonomy of the Tibetan government. As a result of the PLA's suppression of the Tibetan rebellion in 1959, Chinese-Indian relations reached their lowest point since the founding of the PRC.

The Indian government granted sanctuary to the Dalai Lama, who denounced China's "aggression" in Tibet and continued to be "active in exile."[83] Armed clashes escalated during the summer of 1959. On August 25, a small group of Indian troops crossed into the Longju area north of the McMahon Line and exchanged fire with a Chinese border patrol. On October 21, another small-scale incident occurred along the border of the western sector at Kongka Pass. Each side claimed that the other had fired first. Premier Zhou suggested a "mutual withdrawal" in the North East Frontier Agency to 12.4 miles behind the McMahon Line.[84] Prime Minister Jawaharlal Nehru and the Indian government instead expanded the Indian armed forces and reinforced the border areas to pressure the Chinese through India's forward policy. According to Cheng Feng and Larry M. Wortzel, India's forward policy, formulated in 1960–61, placed "continuous pressure and forward movement on Chinese forces" along the disputed border.[85] Nehru also turned to the Soviet Union for more economic aid and military support.

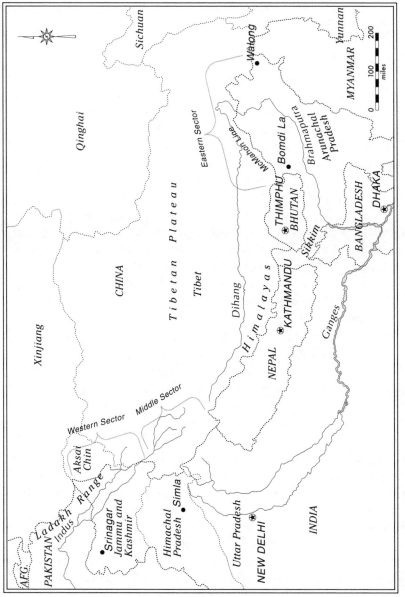

China-India Border Sectors

PLA troops fight Indian troops in 1962. (Reproduced by permission of World Knowledge Press, Beijing, China.)

In 1962, the CCP Central Committee and CMC instructed the PLA to mobilize the frontier troops and plan a counteroffensive campaign. The PLA employed four regiments in Tibet, about thirteen thousand men, and one regiment in Xinjiang, about seven thousand men. Large-scale attacks began on October 20 against the Indian garrisons in Ladakh and Aksai Chin and the North East Frontier Agency. In the east, the PLA troops crossed the border and destroyed defense points of the Indian Army. On October 22, the PRC Defense Ministry announced that the PLA operation would not be limited by the "illegal McMahon Line."[86] By October 28, the PLA's Tibet regiments had wiped out forty-three strongholds on the Indian side of the McMahon Line. In the west, Xinjiang's regiment crossed the border and took over thirty-seven Indian strongholds by traveling more than six hundred miles along the border. The Indian troops, ill prepared and poorly supplied, fell back under the PLA assaults. The Nehru administration, however, did not give up. While requesting military aid from the West, including the United States, Nehru reinforced the border areas with an additional thirty thousand men in November. His defensive effort still focused on the east. In early November, the Indian troops launched their own counteroffensive along the eastern border.[87]

Facing the Indian attacks, the CMC deployed more troops to the border. By mid-November, the PLA had eight infantry and three artillery regiments along the eastern border, four regiments at the middle section of the eastern border, and one regiment in the west. The troops in the east encircled the Indian troops and cut their supply lines by November 17. The next day, the eastern troops launched an all-out attack on the Indian troops. By November 21, the PLA had eliminated the Indian presence along the eastern border. In the west, the PLA also attacked the Indians. By November 21, the PLA had accomplished its goal. On November 22, the Chinese government announced a cease-fire along the Chinese-Indian border. After December 1, Chinese forces began pulling out of Indian territories and returning to the old boundary, the "traditional" border. According to Chinese reports, between October 20 and November 21, India lost 8,700 troops, including 4,800 killed and 3,900 captured. Total PLA casualties were 2,400 dead and wounded.[88]

The 1962 Sino-Indian War validated the PLA's warfare doctrine and its basic principles of war, including "discipline, surprise, flexibility, mass, and maneuver."[89] But no Tibetan people's war existed at this time. In Tibet and Xinjiang, the PLA faced new social and political issues, such as religion, minorities, geopolitics, and independence movements. In contrast to the wars of the 1930s and 1940s, the Sino-Indian War was fought in the middle of a hostile population—Tibetans. The Tibetans and the Indian troops shared religions and ethnic traditions and had close political connections and similar languages. Unlike the North Koreans in the Korean War, the Tibetan and Uygur people did not provide much support, even moral support, to the Chinese troops. The few Tibetan and Uygur soldiers in the PLA could not bridge the social, cultural, and political gaps between the Chinese troops and the local people.[90]

Sergeant Li Weiheng recalled that he and his comrades felt as if they were entering a foreign country when they went to Tibet. Religious and linguistic barriers, separatist propaganda, and a backward economy had created a seemingly irreparable rift between the troops and local Tibetans. As a radar operator on the front line, Li was stationed on the top of a hill overlooking a small Tibetan village. Chinese

PLA troops pursue Indian troops into India. (Reproduced by permission of World Knowledge Press, Beijing, China.)

soldiers and Tibetan villagers rarely interacted. Li recalled that one of the regulations for the PLA troops in Tibet was to refrain from talking to the Tibetan people without permission. Any communication between the village and the radar company had to be conducted by Li's company commander through village chiefs, one of whom spoke Chinese. During his six months of service in Tibet, Li visited the village only twice.[91]

One day, Li recalled, one of the Chinese soldiers had a bad *puna*, or high-altitude illness. Their medic could not reduce the soldier's high fever. The captain and his guards rushed to the village to find a Tibetan medicine man. He refused to go to the radar station and insisted on seeing the soldier at his home. Li and four others carried the soldier to the medicine man's house. Heavily armed, Li stood outside the house while two machine gunners stayed in their truck. Li could feel the hostility around them. Children vanished into their homes when they arrived.

No women could be seen. Several Tibetan men sat in front of the house with knives in their hands, staring at Li without saying a word. Li felt lucky that all firearms had been collected from the Tibetans after their rebellion of 1959. Nobody could legally have a gun. However, Li kept thinking that these Tibetans might attack, and for three tense hours he waited. On their way back to the station, the men who had been inside the house voiced similar feelings.[92]

Li's second mission to the village was different. During the war, a temporary POW camp was built at the bottom of the hill. Indian prisoners of war arrived in large numbers, more than the camp guard unit could handle. Ordered to assist in guarding the prisoners, Li and his platoon moved down the hill to the POW camp. He was surprised to see many Tibetan villagers visiting the Indian prisoners, bringing water, food, and milk. The Tibetans and Indians seemed to have the same religion and similar traditions. Li even saw the old medicine man visiting sick and wounded Indian soldiers. Li and his platoon complained to the camp commander. The commander, however, had a dilemma. He had been instructed that no Tibetan man should have contact with the Indian soldiers, but he had had difficulty feeding the large number of prisoners. As a compromise, he had decided to allow Tibetan women and children to visit the Indian prisoners. The problem did not last long, since all the prisoners were repatriated within two months of the war's end. As a prison guard, Li encountered many Tibetan villagers and learned something about Buddhism and Tibetan culture, and a few Tibetan words.[93]

The PLA's experience in India demonstrated that the Chinese troops were much better prepared for a foreign war than they had been ten years before in Korea. The improved logistics supply, communication and transportation, and chain of command all reflected positive results of Peng's reform efforts. The technology and professionalism that had developed in the mid-1950s were maintained after the fall of Peng in 1959 and the Sino-Soviet split in 1960. Before long, however, the new high command, including radical leaders like Marshal Lin, "subverted the programs of the professional military for ideological and political reasons."[94] The PLA's poor performance in the Vietnam War in 1965–70 showed its outdated tactics, lack of training, and antiquated organization.

$$\bigstar \ 7 \ \bigstar$$

Border Conflicts and the Cultural Revolution

SINCE THE FOUNDING OF THE PRC in 1949, China has involved itself in two wars in Vietnam. During the French Indochina War (the First Indochina War), from 1949 to 1954, it assisted the People's Army of Vietnam (PAVN) against French forces.[1] China sought to secure its southwestern border by eliminating the Western power's presence in Vietnam. The PLA's military assistance to Vietnam maintained Beijing's brooding influence in Vietnam, Laos, and Cambodia throughout the Cold War. The PLA's second involvement occurred from 1965 to 1970, when China sent 320,000 troops to aid North Vietnam against American forces in the Vietnam War (the Second Indochina War).[2] Through its war efforts in North Vietnam, Beijing tried to break a perceived U.S. encirclement of China. But China was not interested in a "more powerful" Vietnam on its southern border. Some Vietnamese Communists complained about China's limited assistance to the Viet Minh.[3]

This chapter traces the rise and fall of the Sino-Vietnamese alliance through the two episodes of Chinese involvement in Vietnam. It examines the changing international strategic environment and external conflicts that influenced the Chinese military's organization and strategy. It begins with Mao's continuous revolution, his central theme in shaping Chinese foreign policy and security strategy. The CCP supported Ho Chi Minh, the leader of North Vietnam, in his war against the French forces in 1946–54. The stories of Senior General Chen Geng and General Wei Guoqing show that Chinese economic and military aid to Ho and the PAVN increased until the end of the French Indochina War. The PLA continued to support Ho's regime against the U.S. Air Force and Navy in the Vietnam War in 1965–70.[4] The PLA's deployment successfully deterred any U.S. invasion of North Vietnam, as the United States feared provoking China. The stories of Lieutenants Chen Pai and Wang Xiangcai detail the PLA's operations and tactics in the Vietnam War. In 1968, Chinese influence over North Vietnam decreased as Soviet influence grew.[5] The PLA withdrew its antiaircraft artillery units in March 1969 and its support troops by July 1970.

The 1960s was the most controversial as well as the most crucial decade in Chinese military history. By 1969, the Soviet Union had replaced the United States as Beijing's leading security concern, prompting changes in China's strategic thought. Thereafter, the high command prepared to repel a Soviet invasion. In 1969–71, the PLA clashed with the Soviet forces along the Sino-Soviet border. As a result of its frequent engagements, the PLA increased to more than six million men, the highest point in its history. The Soviet threat and conflicts pushed the Chinese leaders to improve their relations with the United States. Their strategic needs eventually led to the normalization of the Sino-American relationship in the early 1970s.[6]

During the Cultural Revolution in the late 1960s, the PLA moved to the center of domestic politics. Marshal Lin Biao became the second most powerful leader in the country, next to Mao. Their relationship, however, turned into a political struggle that included an attempted assassination of Mao by Lin's son. Lin died while fleeing China in 1971. After Lin's death, in 1972–74, Mao launched a purge of Lin's followers and programs in the PLA.[7]

This chapter examines the impacts of domestic political developments, the changing international strategic environment, and external conflicts on the makeup of the military leadership. The stories of Marshal Lin and Colonel Feng Shangxian demonstrate changes and distorted relations between the military and party during the Cultural Revolution. Internal factors, including domestic politics, played an important role in changing the Chinese military. Interactions between and within the state and the military also functioned as driving forces of changes in the PLA. Three soldiers describe their experiences in the wars against the two superpowers, the United States in the Vietnam War and the Soviet Union along the Chinese-Russian border.

The French Indochina War, 1946–54

The CCP's involvement in Vietnam began before WWII. Ho Chi Minh (1890–1969) founded the Indochinese Communist Party (ICP) in China in 1930. He organized a Communist revolutionary movement among Vietnamese exiles in Hong Kong in 1931–33. From 1938 to 1941, Ho worked with the CCP as an advisor to the Chinese Communist forces. When Japan occupied Vietnam in 1941, he resumed contact with ICP leaders in Indochina. At the eighth plenary session of the ICP, he helped to found a new Communist-dominated independence movement in Vietnam, the Viet Nam Doc Lap Dong Minh Hoi (League for the Independence of Vietnam, popularly known as Viet Minh), to fight the Japanese. For years, Vietnamese leaders, both Communist and non-Communist, had worked in the southern Chinese province of Yunnan. Throughout WWII, the Viet Minh consolidated its popular base, particularly in the northern border areas. In the meantime, with Allied support, Ho's guerrilla force along the Vietnamese-Chinese border grew to five thousand men under the command of General Vo Nguyen Giap.[8]

The sudden surrender of Japan in August 1945 created a power vacuum in Vietnam. Giap entered Hanoi with one thousand Viet Minh troops on August 18. On September 2, Ho proclaimed the independence of Vietnam and founded the Democratic Republic of Vietnam (DRV) in the north with himself as president. Virtually all key posts in the new government were held by members of the Viet Minh. In the meantime, however, France reasserted its prewar colonial control over Vietnam. With British help, the French returned to Vietnam. In March 1946, France and the DRV reached a compromise that the DRV was a "free state" in the French Union.[9] Soon Viet Minh and French soldiers clashed in the north. In December, the French Indochina War broke out between Ho's force and French forces.[10]

After the founding of the PRC, as a Communist state bordering Vietnam, China actively supported the Vietnamese Communist war against France. In October 1949, when Ho Chi Minh sent his representatives to Beijing requesting a large amount of military and financial aid, the Chinese government agreed.[11] In January 1950, Ho secretly visited Moscow and Beijing to seek additional aid for his war against the French, who had occupied most cities and strategic points in Vietnam. The CCP Central Committee decided to send Chinese military advisors and war materials to Vietnam. On January 17, the first group of eight Chinese advisors, headed by Luo Guibo, chief of the General Office at the Revolutionary Military Committee of the Central Government, left Beijing for Vietnam to lay the groundwork for further aid.[12] On January 18, the PRC became the first nation to establish diplomatic relations with the DRV. In March, Luo and Chinese advisors began work at Viet Minh headquarters.[13] In April, the CMC instructed its Southwest Regional Command to supply arms, ammunition, and equipment to the PAVN on a regular basis. The regional command assigned a truck regiment to aid transportation in the border area.[14]

Chinese leaders then organized the Chinese Military Advisory Group (CMAG) to Vietnam. In early April 1950, Liu Shaoqi, vice president of the PRC, summoned General Wei Guoqing to the Zhongnanhai compound in Beijing and told him about the CMAG. "Under the request of President Ho," Liu said, "the Central Committee has decided to send the military advisory group to Vietnam to help their Anti-French War. You are the head of the military advisory group."[15] Wei was ready to accept his new appointment. On April 14, Liu telegraphed Hanoi to introduce Wei to Ho as an army group commander.[16]

Wei was born in 1913 into a poor peasant family of the Zhuang minority in Donglan County, Guangxi, bordering with Vietnam. He joined the Chinese Red Army in 1929 and the CCP in 1931. He became a captain and then a battalion commander in the Seventh Army under the command of Deng Xiaoping. Wei served as a regimental commander in the Long March. He was a brigade commander and political commissar of the New Fourth Army during WWII. In the Chinese civil war, he became the political commissar of the Tenth Army Group of the Third Field Army. After his army group took over Fuzhou, the capital of Fujian, in September 1949, Wei was appointed director of the Military Administrative Committee of Fuzhou. In February 1950, the Central Committee ordered him to leave Fuzhou for a new appointment. Between February and April, without knowing anything about this new appointment, Wei studied international relations, diplomacy, and the new republic's foreign policy in Beijing.[17]

Shortly after accepting his new appointment, Wei submitted his plan to the high command. On April 17, the CMC ordered its Second, Third, and Fourth field armies to select experienced officers to organize the CMAG. In May, 281 officers reported to the CMAG, including 59 commanders and officers at the battalion level or above. On June 27, two days after the Korean War broke out, Mao, Zhu, and Liu met with Wei, Mei Jiasheng, Deng Yifan, and other high-ranking advisors at Zhongnanhai. Mao told the military advisors that he was not the one sending them to Vietnam. "It is President Ho Chi Minh who has asked me for [your assistance]," the chairman said. "Who would have thought our revolution would succeed first? We should help them. It is called internationalism. You will help them to win the battles after you get to Vietnam."[18] Liu and Zhu also spoke at the meeting. In July, the CMC approved a party committee of the CMAG with Wei as the secretary and Deng Yifan as the deputy secretary. At the CMAG head-

Ho Chi Minh and Vo Nguyen Giap meet with Chen Geng and Luo Guibo in Vietnam in 1950. (Courtesy of Colonel Yan Guitang, member of the CMAG.)

quarters, political, operational, technical, and medical advisory teams were organized.[19]

On July 7, Senior General Chen Geng joined the CMAG as the CCP Central Committee's representative and entered Vietnam. Born in Hunan in 1903, Chen joined the CCP in 1922 and enrolled in the Huangpu Military Academy in 1924. He studied military science in the Soviet Union in 1926. After his return, he became a battalion commander and participated in the 1927 Nanchang Uprising. Then he served as regiment and division commander of the Red Army. During WWII, Chen became the commander of the 386th Brigade, 129th Division, Eighth Route Army. During the Chinese civil war, he was appointed commander and political commissar of the Fourth Army Group. After the founding of the PRC, he became the commander of the Yunnan Military District and governor of Yunnan Province. Senior General Chen was one of the most experienced and dedicated generals of the PLA. In his telegrams to Chen in June 1950, Liu Shaoqi authorized Chen as the "representative of the CCP Central Committee" in charge of military advice in Vietnam.[20]

On August 11, Wei led the CMAG, about 250 officers, accompanied by Hoang Van Hoan, the Vietnamese ambassador to China, into Vietnam. The next day, the PAVN held a welcome meeting, and General Giap, commander in chief of the PAVN, made a speech in Chinese. After their arrival, Wei, Chen, Mei, and top advisors served at PAVN headquarters, including in the General Staff Department and the Bureaus of Political Affairs and General Logistics. The other advisors served at the headquarters of the 304th and 308th divisions and at the headquarters of the 148th, 174th, and 209th regiments, according to their rank and expertise. Zhai argues that personality was "an important factor in shaping Beijing's attitude toward revolution in Vietnam." The CCP and PLA leaders did not ignore "the close personal ties and revolutionary solidarity that they and Ho Chi Minh had forged in the years of common struggle in the past." In deciding to assist the Viet Minh in 1950, Mao "stressed the importance of reciprocating friendship."[21] The PRC offered Vietnamese Communists a Chinese model. In the new republic, the CCP mobilized vast sectors of the population, especially the peasantry. The Communist Party could therefore spread its net more widely than anywhere else to encompass a broader segment of the population.[22]

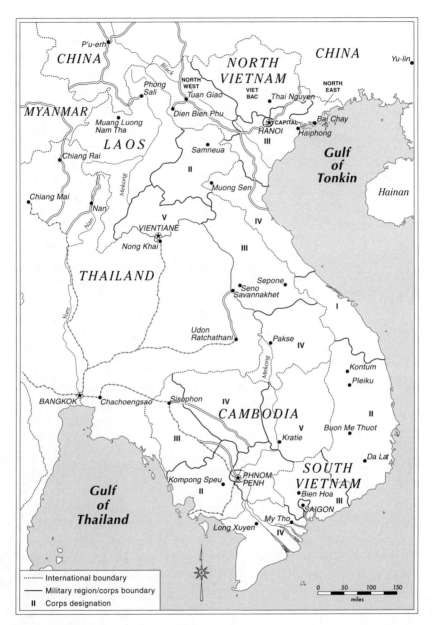

China, Vietnam, and Southeast Asia

The Chinese advisors participated in the PAVN's battle planning, operations, and assessments in the Bianjie campaign in the fall of 1950, offensives on the Red (Hong) River delta from December 1950 to June 1951, the Dien Bien Phu campaign of 1954, and many other battles. Chinese advisors and Vietnamese commanders, however, often had sharp disagreements about how to conduct the battles. In some cases, Chen called Ho or even Mao in Beijing to explain why his plan was best for the PAVN. He even threatened Giap repeatedly that he would resign if the Vietnamese did not accept his plan.[23] Chen left Vietnam for the Korean War on November 1, 1950.

Vietnamese troops had experience with traditional guerrilla warfare and small-scale operations, but the Chinese advisors believed that the PAVN should engage in large-scale offensive campaigns and fight mobile battles to drive the French troops out of Vietnam. To fight this type of war and eliminate more enemy troops, the PAVN needed more regular units. In 1950, the PAVN had only three infantry divisions. In May 1951, the Chinese advisors established and armed the 316th, 320th, and 325th infantry divisions and the 351st Artillery and Engineering Division. By the end of 1952, the PAVN had three more infantry divisions, all equipped with Chinese arms and supplies. In 1951–52, the CMAG also provided many training sessions for PAVN middle- and high-ranking commanders, logistics officers, and medical personnel. The Chinese advisors wrote the curriculum, drafted the training manuals, and organized routine drills and joint exercises. They trained the Vietnamese on mobile tactics, offensive operations, and tactics against defense works.[24]

The Chinese also trained the Vietnamese inside China by opening an officer academy; communication, technology, and mechanic schools; and driver training centers in Guangxi and Yunnan.[25] The PAVN sent entire units to China for training and rearming. For example, in 1951, the PAVN 308th Division and 174th and 209th regiments traveled to China for training and to receive new arms, weapons, and equipment from the PLA. By 1954, the Chinese had provided military and technology training for fifteen thousand Vietnamese officers and soldiers in China.[26]

Although Giap was graceful about the Chinese efforts to reorganize his troops, he worried about the problems caused by the PAVN's expansion and concentration. For instance, the rapid increase of the

PAVN troops caused a serious shortage of grain in the northern provinces. Giap turned to the CMAG for help. In an urgent telegram to the CCP Central Committee, the CMAG reported on May 15, 1951, that "troops are starving, even though we had transferred three regiments to the central areas and reduced office and logistics personnel daily grain [rations] down to 700 grams." It asked the Chinese government to send between 1,500 and 2,000 tons of rice to Vietnam before the end of June.[27]

To supply the Vietnamese, the PLA General Logistics Department set up an office at Nanning to handle military aid, economic assistance, and supply transportation. William J. Duiker points out that, "during the years following the signing of the Sino-Vietnamese agreement in 1950, Chinese aid had been steady but relatively modest in size, averaging about 400 to 500 tons of military materiel each month." However, by July 1953, his French sources indicate, China had increased aid to at least 10,000 tons per month.[28] Obviously, after the Korean armistice was signed in July 1953, China shifted its attention and its efforts against the Western imperialists from Korea to Vietnam. According to Chinese records, from 1950 to 1956, China shipped 155,000 small arms, 58 million rounds of ammunition, 3,600 artillery pieces, 1.08 million artillery shells, 840,000 hand grenades, 1,200 vehicles, 1.4 million uniforms, 14,000 tons of food, and 26,000 tons of fuel to Vietnam.[29] From August 25, 1953, to March 7, 1954, the Chinese government shipped goods, matériel, medicine, and fuel to Vietnam worth 3.2 billion yuan ($14.4 billion). In 1954, the Chinese imports increased and included trucks, gasoline, generators, and more than 4 million yards of cotton material.[30] By the end of 1954, China had armed five Vietnamese infantry divisions, one artillery division, one antiaircraft artillery division, and one security regiment.[31]

During the 1952 rainy season, the Chinese assisted the PAVN in launching its first large-scale political education and thought reform movement. The CMAG held a series of political conferences for PAVN medics and field hospitals in April. The CMAG did a second series for recruitment and mobilization in August. The third training conference series, in September, focused on psychological warfare. And the fourth conference series provided training for divisional and regimental commanders during the same month. China and North Vietnam began mail delivery across the border at the CMAG's suggestion.[32]

In late November 1953, the PAVN high command and the CMAG planned a response to the French occupation of Dien Bien Phu. The Central Committee of the Vietnamese Workers' Party (which had absorbed most of the Viet Minh's leaders in 1951) approved the plan on December 6. From December 1953 to early March 1954, the PAVN encircled the 15,000 French troops at Dien Bien Phu. In the meantime, the PLA sent to Dien Bien Phu one Vietnamese rocket battalion and one 75mm recoilless gun battalion, which had been equipped and trained in China. On March 13, the PAVN launched attacks to isolate French strongholds. By late April, the French troops held only three points. On May 6, the PAVN launched its final attack. The newly arrived Chinese-manufactured six-rocket launchers played an important role in the final assaults. The next day, the French surrendered. After eight years of fighting, Ho and the PAVN finally defeated 120,000 French troops in the French Indochina War.[33]

After Dien Bien Phu, the Geneva Conference on Indochina started, including France, North Vietnam, China, the Soviet Union, the United States, and four other countries. Zhou met Ho Chi Minh in Guangxi, on the border with Vietnam. Accompanied by General Wei and other top Chinese advisors, the premier pressured Ho to accept a peace settlement in Indochina at the Geneva Conference. Mao instructed Zhou to ask Wei to "not operate any large-scale military movement in July. Any decision on when you can have a big battle must depend totally upon the situation at the Geneva Conference." Clearly, Mao wished to secure the southern border of China. He tried to avoid international conflicts in Indochina because any external crisis then would only be a distraction.[34]

In July, the Indochina settlement was signed in Geneva by the Viet Minh, French, Chinese, Soviets, and Americans. According to the 1954 Geneva Accord on the restoration of peace in the Indochinese region, as a temporary arrangement, the PAVN would withdraw from southern Vietnam to the area north of the 17th parallel, paving the way for the French departure and a mandatory national election.[35] The election was to be held in July 1956 to produce a united national government. The PAVN's withdrawal started in August 1954 and was completed in May 1955.

After the Geneva Conference secured the Vietnamese Communists' power in North Vietnam, Ho strengthened his social and political reform efforts. In 1959, the DRV government passed a new constitution stating that the DRV was a people's state, an alliance between the workers and peasants, led by the Vietnamese Workers' Party, which resulted from Ho's reorganization of the ICP. According to the constitution, a national congress would take place every five years; in practice, however, congresses were convened on an ad hoc basis to approve decisions already passed by the party's Central Committee and Bo Chinh Tri, the top decision-making body. The latter enabled senior party and military leaders to handle day-to-day issues between plenary sessions of the Central Committee. Ten members met about once a week.[36]

After the Geneva Conference, China tried to scale back its military involvement in North Vietnam to reduce international tension. In 1954, for instance, Wei Guoqing planned to continue training in China for the PAVN artillery troops, but Mao turned Wei's proposal down. He forwarded Wei's report to General Huang Kecheng, vice chairman of the CMC, in April 1954, adding, "Expecting a possible cease-fire in Vietnam . . . training the [Vietnamese] new artillery force is no longer appropriate within the boundaries of our country. It may be better to transfer all the used training artillery batteries and other equipment into Vietnam's boundaries at an early date. Please ask Wei Guoqing for another plan."[37] In September 1955, the CMAG returned to China, but China continued to provide weaponry, equipment, and military training to North Vietnam. Between 1955 and 1963, Chinese military aid totaled 320 million yuan (about $106 million). China's massive support of North Vietnam helped Ho intensify guerrilla warfare in South Vietnam in the early 1960s.[38]

PLA Operations in Vietnam, 1965–70

After the Republic of Vietnam (ROV; South Vietnam) was founded in Saigon in 1955, the Communist leadership in Hanoi rejected the Nationalist government in South Vietnam and called for national reunification by its Communist forces. ROV president Ngo Dinh Diem cooperated with the U.S. government and suppressed a large number of suspected Communists. Under U.S. pressure, the Diem regime tried a land reform program in 1956 that called for breaking up large landholdings and offering farmland for purchase to the previous tenants at low interest rates. But implementation was hampered by landlord resistance. After a few years, only 10 percent of peasant families had received any land under the program. In 1957–58, angry southern rebels launched antigovernment rebellions in rural areas. To grasp the opportunity to lead the southern mass movement, the Viet Minh organized the National Liberation Front (NLF) in December 1960 as an umbrella organization to mobilize the masses against the Diem government. Now the southerners joined the northern Communist revolution against the ROV government and U.S. involvement in South Vietnam. In February 1961, the People's Liberation Armed Forces (PLAF) formed under a united military command with Tran Luong as the head. Soon he was replaced by several northern generals of the PAVN, veterans of the war against France. Diem labeled the NLF and PLAF the Viet Cong, or Vietnamese Communists.[39]

As the PLAF increased its activities, Diem requested more American aid. By the end of 1961, there were 3,205 U.S. "advisors" in Vietnam. During the next year, the figure jumped to 9,000. At the time President John F. Kennedy was assassinated in November 1963, the American forces totaled 16,700. A few weeks before the JFK assassination, Diem was killed in a military coup. As president, Lyndon Johnson continued Kennedy's policies and kept many of his advisors. By 1964, the ROV government, under new president Nguyen Van Thieu, suffered strong resistance and lost control of 40 percent of the South Vietnamese countryside. On August 2 and 4, in the Gulf of Tonkin, North Vietnamese boats supposedly attacked American warships, giving Johnson a good opportunity to seek congressional support for military action against North Vietnam. The Gulf of Tonkin Resolution, which passed on August 7 with little debate, authorized President Johnson to escalate U.S. intervention in South Vietnam. At the same time, the United States shifted its war efforts increasingly toward North Vietnam. The Johnson administration finally decided to escalate the war in February 1965 by sending the first U.S. combat troops and launching Rolling Thunder, a massive bombing campaign against North Vietnam. However, as David Kaiser points out, "The administration tried to sell the idea that a demonstration of American power might lead to early negotiations, rather than acknowledge the true scope of the administration's plans and the task it had undertaken."[40] But the Johnson administration had one major fear: Chinese intervention that would convert a regional war into a Cold War showdown.

The U.S. bombing of North Vietnam in 1964–65 made the DRV desperate for help. In April 1965, Le Duan, first secretary-general of the North Vietnamese Communist Party, and General Vo Nguyen Giap, defense minister, rushed to Beijing to ask China to provide increased aid and to send troops to Vietnam. On behalf of the Chinese leadership, Liu Shaoqi, then president of the PRC and vice chairman of the CCP, replied to the Vietnamese visitors on April 8, "It is the obligation of the Chinese people and party" to support the Vietnamese struggle against the United States. "Our principle is," Liu continued, "that we will do our best to provide you with whatever you need and whatever we have."[41] In April, China signed several agreements with the DRV government delegation concerning the dispatch of Chinese support troops to North Vietnam.

On May 16, Ho Chi Minh met with Mao Zedong in Changsha, Hunan. Ho requested that China send antiaircraft artillery troops to Vietnam. In early June, Van Tien Dung met with Luo Ruiqing and specifically requested that China send two antiaircraft artillery divisions to defend Hanoi and the areas north of Hanoi in the event of an American air strike. Luo agreed.[42] On July 24, the Vietnamese General Staff telegraphed the PLA General Staff to formally request that China send "the two antiaircraft artillery divisions that have long completed their preparations for operations in Vietnam. The earlier the better. If possible, they may enter Vietnam on August 1." The next day, the Chinese General Staff cabled the Vietnamese General Staff that China would send two antiaircraft artillery divisions and one regiment to Vietnam immediately, and that these units would take the responsibility of defending the Bac Ninh–Lang Son section of the Hanoi-Youyiguan Railway and the Yen Bay–Lao Cai section of the Hanoi–Lao Cai Railway, two main railways linking China and North Vietnam.[43]

In July 1965, China began sending troops to North Vietnam, as well as surface-to-air missiles, antiaircraft artillery, and railroad, engineering, mine-sweeping, and logistics units. Chinese forces operated antiaircraft guns and surface-to-air missile sites and built and repaired roads, bridges, railroads, and factories. Chinese participation enabled Hanoi to send more PAVN troops to South Vietnam to fight the Americans. Between 1965 and 1968, China sent twenty-three divisions, including ninety-five regiments, totaling some 320,000 troops. The peak year was 1967, when 170,000 Chinese soldiers were present in North

Mao Zedong makes a toast to Ho Chi Minh in Beijing in 1965. (Reproduced by permission of the PLA Literature Press, Beijing, China.)

Vietnam. Among the Chinese were 150,000 antiaircraft artillery troops, who engaged in 2,150 encounters.

On August 1, the first wave, including the Sixty-first and Sixty-third divisions, entered North Vietnam from Yunnan and Guangxi. On August 9, the Sixty-first Division was put into action in Yen Bay against American F-4 fighter-bombers for the first time. According to Chinese records, the Sixty-first Division shot down one F-4, the first American plane to be downed by Chinese antiaircraft units. The troops of the Sixty-third Division entered the Kep area and engaged in their first battle with the Americans on August 23.[44]

Later, eleven PLA divisions operated in the east: the Nineteenth, Thirty-first, Thirty-second, Thirty-third, Thirty-fourth, Thirty-fifth, Thirty-seventh, Sixty-second, 163rd, 168th, and 170th divisions. Six divisions operated in the west: the Sixth, Sixty-first, Sixty-seventh, 164th, 165th, and 166th divisions. Following their experience during the Korean War, the Chinese used Vietnam as a training ground and rotated their antiaircraft artillery troops there. Each division operated in Vietnam for six to eight months. Before entering Vietnam, they were familiarized with the Americans' air force, aircraft, and weapons systems. The men learned some English words that they might need if ever confronted by downed American pilots. They also learned some Vietnamese words and cultural aspects.

By March 1969, the PLA had sent sixteen divisions, including sixty-three regiments, of its antiaircraft artillery force to North Vietnam.[45] These units, which entered Vietnam in eight stages, were mainly from the artillery forces, the air force, and the navy and, in some cases, the Kunming and Guangzhou regional commands. They were deployed to defend strategically important targets, such as critical railway bridges on the Hanoi-Youyiguan and Hanoi–La Cai lines, and to provide cover for Chinese engineering troops. There is no evidence that any of these units were engaged in operations south of Hanoi or in the defense of the Ho Chi Minh Trail.

Lieutenant Wang Xiangcai was one of the Chinese soldiers in Vietnam. He was born in a small village, Mingshui, Heilongjiang, in 1944. As the first of six in the family, he dropped out of school to help his father in the cornfield during the day and his mother at night, taking care of his younger brothers and sisters during the three hard years. In the fall of 1964, the country's economy turned around, and Wang's village had the first good harvest in five years. His father thought about sending his brothers and sisters back to school, and his mother began to visit a matchmaker in the village to try to arrange his marriage. At twenty, however, Wang wanted to achieve his childhood dream of being a manufacturing worker in a city. His chance came that year when a PLA recruiting team paid its annual visit to his village. The recruiting officers told Wang and other young men in the village that the army was a big school and they would learn a trade through their service. After their time in the military, they would have choices for retirement, like returning to their village or working in the city. Wang and six other young men became village heroes when they signed up for service. His parents supported his decision, and his brothers and sisters were envious.[46]

After the new-recruit orientation in the spring of 1965, Wang Xiangcai was assigned to the Fourth Company, First Battalion, Third Regiment of the First Antiaircraft Artillery Division in the Shenyang Regional Command. Wang recalled that the division, though well trained and experienced from the Korean War, had old weapons and equipment. It still had the same guns used in the Korean War, including Russian-made 100mm, 75mm, and 67mm antiaircraft artillery pieces, and 37mm antiaircraft machine guns. Wang, however, enjoyed "drilling in the morning, riding on the truck, talking to the men across the countryside, and eating in the mess hall."[47]

Wang's favorite part of the daily routine was the one hour of "political study," or "motivational education." Wang called it "reading and writing class." He enjoyed picking up books again after having left school early. The company political instructor taught world history and Chinese literature to help the soldiers understand Communist theory and Mao Zedong Thought. Under this instruction, Wang learned more Chinese characters and grammar so he could write essays to express his own understanding of the Chinese revolution, exchange ideas with others, and build his loyalty to the party. His first paper, six pages long, was an application essay for CCP membership.[48]

When Wang became a CCP member and a corporal in July 1965, Chinese troops were beginning to participate in the Vietnam War. His division received the order in October and left for North Vietnam in the summer of 1966. The division assembled in early September at Ningming, Guangxi, about thirty miles from the Chinese-Vietnamese border. During their four-week orientation, Wang and his comrades had to take off their Chinese uniforms. They could display no Chinese badges, no red star cap insignia, no PLA rankings, and no Chinese names. They put on Vietnamese light green uniforms and gray caps without ranks. Wang recalled that the men laughed at each other because they could pass as Vietnamese soldiers if they did not talk.[49]

On September 28, 1966, Wang and his regiment left China and entered Vietnam. He had no idea where they were going, knowing little about what was going on in North Vietnam. He recalled he was nervous and "a little" scared. He, however, as a Communist Party member, believed that his cause was just and that he had the support of his country. These beliefs were all he needed to go into battle and win the fight. He did not think much about his own survival since he was convinced that he could make it as long as his company and his comrades did well.[50]

On the morning of September 30, Wang's battalion received a call from the regiment headquarters at about 0920 hours that six F-105 fighter-bombers were headed in their direction. At 0935, the battalion's first outpost, about thirty miles south, called in to report that four F-105s, at middle speed and an altitude of eighteen thousand feet, were flying from southeast to northwest. Five minutes later, the second outpost, about ten miles south of the bridge, called, "Four 105s are coming!" The same message was passed on from the battalion headquarters to the company commanders. "Ready," the voice of the captain of the Fourth Company rang out from the loudspeakers on the hill. Wang recalled that the approaching jets' engines sounded like rolling thunder. The captain shouted, "100mm's, 75mm's, fire!" The big guns opened fire with huge conflagrations before Wang could see the American planes. Although Wang had learned a lot about the American fighter-bombers, he did not realize that they were so noisy and fast. The hill shook, the sky smoked, and the air smelled of burning gunpowder. He barely heard the captain's order, "37mm's, fire!" Wang looked hard into the sky but could not see the airplanes. He pulled the trigger anyway. The 37mm antiaircraft machine gun roared and sent bullets flying into the sky. The battle made Wang excited and wild. He kept firing until he heard the captain's cease-fire order. Wang, sweating and out of breath, realized that the whole battle took only minutes. The Chinese soldiers jumped out of their positions and cheered with an inexplicable joy when they knew the American fighters had gone. Even though the American airplanes had only been passing through the area, it was the Chinese soldiers' first taste of real combat.[51]

Wang recalled that he hated the heat and jungle in North Vietnam as much as he did the air strikes. All of his men were "polar bears" from north China, and the weather in Vietnam was too hot for them. In October, Vietnam's dry season began. The troops often operated in temperatures between 100 and 110 degrees Fahrenheit. Wang recalled that they sweated all day long. The next spring, the endless monsoon rains arrived, keeping them constantly wet. Some of them became sick. Common afflictions included bacterial and fungal infections, such as jungle rot, malaria, hepatitis, and ringworm. Exposure to the jungles of North Vietnam proved as harsh and deadly as the American bombs. In an environment infested by snakes, mosquitoes, ants, and leeches, the Chinese had to face discomfort, pain, and even death. When Wang accompanied one of their men to the field hospital, he was surprised to see that the hospital was full of sick Chinese soldiers.[52]

In the spring of 1967, Wang and his regiment returned to China after an eight-month tour in North Vietnam. He became a sergeant in 1967 and a lieutenant in 1968. After he retired, a local veteran administration office offered him a job as a manufacturing worker in Harbin, the provincial capital of Heilongjiang. As for his service in the military, Wang still complains that he has received no medal or honor. Nor do his files mention his Vietnam War experience—there exists no recommendation or appreciation from the Vietnamese government to this Chinese soldier.[53]

The DRV government and the PAVN officially denied the involvement of any foreign Communist troops in the Vietnam War during the 1960s. In fact, however, in addition to the Chinese troops, the North Vietnamese invited antiaircraft missile troops from the Soviet Union. They knew that the Soviet Union and China were rivals in the Communist camp, competing for leadership in the Asian Communist movement, which included Vietnam. Each claimed to be a key supporter of the Vietnamese Communists' struggle against the American invasion. So the Vietnamese brought troops from both nations into North Vietnam, increasing the competition between the Chinese and Soviet Communists. The Chinese high command ordered its troops to intensify their training to shoot down more American airplanes than the Soviets did. Lieutenant Chen Pai said that the Chinese troops had two enemies in Vietnam: "the American imperialists in the sky, and the Soviet revisionists on the ground."[54]

Chen Pai did two tours in 1966–67 as a Chinese-Vietnamese translator at the headquarters of the Sixty-third Antiaircraft Artillery Division, Guangzhou Military Region. His division deployed two regiments at Thai Nguyen along the Long Son–Hao Binh provincial border to protect local roads and bridges. The rest of the division was positioned along a sixty-mile section of Route 1, from north to south through Long Son, to provide air defense of the province's cities, railroads, and highways. Speaking both Vietnamese and Chinese, Chen worked closely with the PAVN officers at the division headquarters. He knew the problems between the two Communist giants in Vietnam. He recalled that the Communist troops spied on each other and fought over the recovery of American aviation technology. Whenever an American plane was shot down, both tried to reach the crash site first. According to their agreements, neither Soviet nor Vietnamese troops could enter Chinese "operating areas." If the Soviets or Vietnamese got there first, they would guard the site, and the Chinese could not interfere in their "operations."[55]

Chen recalled that the Chinese troops were instructed by the division command to check on crashed planes and to capture any surviving pilots in order to evaluate the air defense and improve Chinese antiaircraft performance. In fact, the PLA wanted American aviation technology. After the Sino-Soviet split in 1960, the Chinese lost their only source for air force modernization. Their participation in the Vietnam War opened up a new window of opportunity to learn from the U.S. Air Force, the most advanced in the world. The command instructed its troops to search for pilot logbooks, codes, records, and training manuals as well as instrument panels, communication devices, radar equipment, electronic systems, weapon controls, missiles, launchers, and cameras. Chen accompanied several groups of Chinese defense engineers, technology experts, and weapon designers from Beijing to crash sites and POW camps to interrogate American pilots. The agreements requested that all captured pilots be turned over to the PAVN within two hours, and all weapons and equipment within twenty-four hours. The Vietnamese command, however, knew that the Chinese and Russians were researching and pirating the American high-tech equipment and shipping it back to their countries. The Vietnamese were not allowed to stop Chinese or Soviet military vehicles or to search Chinese or Russian military personnel.[56]

Chen also remembered that the Vietnamese officers complained incessantly about the Chinese rotation system. The Vietnamese believed that it took a couple of months for a Chinese antiaircraft artillery unit to get used to the weather, terrain, American air raids, and other combat conditions. By the time the unit became combat effective and able to shoot down American airplanes, in the fourth or fifth month, it had to prepare for its departure. Then the new unit would repeat the same cycle. Vietnamese officers believed the Chinese did not shoot down enough American airplanes to protect North Vietnam.[57]

Nevertheless, the PAVN could exchange military intelligence with the Chinese and Russians and also request combat information from them. Within twenty-four hours of each engagement, the Chinese and Russians had to provide routine paperwork, counting ammunition and assessing results, to the PAVN officers. The information included the number of American planes shot down, American pilots captured, Chinese or Russian casualties, and civilian casualties, as well as bridge or road damage, technical problems, communication failures, and any other problems. Each army had its own system of counting American airplanes. The PAVN numbers were based on local militia reports at crash sites. The Chinese and Russian numbers were based on their combat unit reports after each engagement. The dual system produced conflicting information about how many American airplanes were shot down in North Vietnam.[58]

As we have seen, the direct engagement of the Chinese and Soviet armed forces in North Vietnam enabled Hanoi to send more troops to South Vietnam. The level of infiltration from the north was significantly increased, and the main force units of the PAVN began to stream south. Hanoi's main risk was that a further deterioration of security in the south would lead to increased U.S. involvement, a development neither Hanoi nor its allies in Moscow and Beijing desired. By the mid-1960s, the PAVN units were conducting guerrilla operations and a people's war to assist the PLAF in fighting the ROV army and the U.S. armed forces in South Vietnam. By 1968, the PAVN had extended its operations, and its troops in the south reached a total of four hundred

A PAVN general in Vietnam. (Photo by the author.)

thousand men. Ho Chi Minh died in 1969. Le Duan became the secretary-general of the North Vietnamese Communist Party, and Ho's other position, president of the DRV, went to Ton Duc Thang. In the late 1960s, the PAVN extended its operations into Cambodia and Laos. Then the struggle in South Vietnam began to take on the signs of an open military confrontation between North Vietnam and the United States.[59]

The Tet Offensive of 1968 became a turning point in American domestic politics and public opinion toward the war in Vietnam. "The changes the Tet Offensive brought were decisive," Marilyn B. Young states. "Because Tet was reported as an American defeat, they claim, politicians lost heart, rejected making an increased effort, and took the first steps on the slippery slope toward withdrawal and admitted defeat."[60] After the Tet Offensive, President Johnson's political career was derailed. On March 31, 1968, he announced a halt in the U.S. bombing

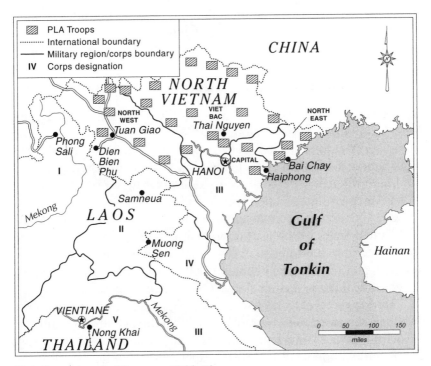

PLA Operations in Vietnam, 1965–70

of North Vietnam. The announcement, intended as a new peace ges-
ture, evoked a positive response from Hanoi. In May, peace talks between the United States and North Vietnam opened in Paris.[61]

China knew nothing about the U.S.-DRV peace negotiations until
much later. In response to Johnson's speech that announced the cessa-
tion of bombing, Hanoi announced on April 3 its readiness to discuss
with the Americans the end of the bombing. Zhou Enlai immediately
asked Ho, who was in Beijing for medical treatment, about Hanoi's decision. Ho said that he knew nothing about it. In April, Beijing began
to criticize Hanoi for making a major compromise with the United
States. After the Paris negotiations began on May 13, Beijing continued to criticize Hanoi for conducting negotiations with Washington.[62]
Between 1968 and 1971, while Beijing refrained from participating in
the Paris peace talks, Moscow was enthusiastic about the negotiations.
After Ho died in September 1969, Hanoi began to move closer to the
Soviet Union for waging war against the United States and the Saigon
regime. In July 1970, the PLA withdrew all of its troops from Vietnam.
At that moment, none of them dreamed they would return eight years
later as an invading force.

Sino-Soviet Border Conflicts, 1969–71

In the late 1960s, the Soviet Union was the PLA's big headache not
only in Vietnam but also along the Chinese-Russian border. As we
have seen, Beijing's defense strategy and national security concern had
shifted from the United States to the Soviet Union, which Marshal Lin
and his lieutenants considered a more immediate threat to the PRC.
They saw the United States as a declining power because of its failures in Vietnam and serious problems in other parts of the world. As
the United States withdrew from Vietnam, the Soviet Union filled the
power vacuum, replacing the United States as the imperialist aggressor
in the region. Therefore, China, like other Asian countries, became a
target and victim of the new "Soviet socialist imperialist" policy.[63]

Lin's conception made sense to PLA soldiers and commanders,
who saw increased Soviet hostility as a direct threat to their country. In
1960, the Soviet Union unilaterally ended six hundred bilateral contracts and withdrew all the Soviet experts from China. In 1961, the
Soviets canceled all projects of scientific and technical cooperation,

including the joint nuclear programs. Obviously, the Soviet Union did not want to see a strong and prosperous neighbor. In 1962, Soviet agents instigated the migration of tens of thousands of Chinese citizens from Yili prefecture to the Soviet Union. In 1966, the Soviet government ordered all Chinese students to leave the country within a week. After the Soviet Red Army invaded Czechoslovakia in 1968, its troops broke into the Chinese Embassy and "savagely" beat Chinese diplomats.[64] As the tension mounted, the Soviet Union deployed a large number of Red Army troops along the Soviet-Chinese border.

Border disputes between China and Russia have a long history, dating back to the eighteenth century. Following China's alliance with the Soviet Union in 1949, both countries accepted the territorial status quo along their 4,150-mile border and, in 1951, signed the Border Rivers Navigation Agreement. When the Sino-Soviet split began to occur in the 1960s, the border issue resurfaced. China claimed some border territories as its own and sent PLA troops into these areas. Soviet forces expelled the Chinese, but until the late 1960s, fighting was usually avoided. By the end of 1968, the Soviet Union had increased its troops along the Sino-Soviet border from seventeen divisions to twenty-seven divisions. In 1968–69, the PLA apparently felt directly threatened by the Soviet Union.[65]

In October 1968, Lin warned the army and the country that Soviet forces would invade China soon. Thereafter, the country became militarized and prepared for an invasion. While planning to defeat the invading troops by a people's war, Lin instructed the PLA to confront the Soviets wherever an invasion occurred. Beginning in March 1969, small-scale border skirmishes erupted at Zhenbao (Damansky) and Bacha islands in Heilongjiang, northeast China, and at Taskti and Tieliekti in Xinjiang, northwest China.[66]

In the first clash, on March 2, forty Chinese soldiers patrolled Zhenbao Island, one of the disputed uninhabited islands (0.74 square mile) in the middle of the Ussuri River. The Soviets dispatched seventy border troops to the island, but the Chinese refused to leave. Each side blamed the other for opening fire at 0900 hours. With two hundred reinforcements, the Chinese attacked and killed thirty Soviet soldiers, losing only six of their own. After a twelve-day standoff, on March 15, more than one hundred Soviet troops and six tanks counterattacked. Heavy artillery pieces shelled both shores. More than forty Chinese soldiers were killed. The Soviets lost eight men and one T-62 tank, which sank in the river when artillery fire shattered the six-foot-thick ice cover.[67]

For the rest of the year, sporadic fighting continued in many places along the border, and both nations stood on the brink of war, with the Soviets threatening nuclear retaliation. Among the border incidents, on June 10, fifty Soviet soldiers attacked the Chinese in Taskti. On July 8, the fighting in Heilongjiang extended to Bacha Island in the Amur (Heilong) River. On August 13, more than three hundred Soviet troops, supported by twenty tanks and two helicopters, engaged in Tieliekti and annihilated all the Chinese troops in the battle. The border conflicts did not escalate into a total war between the two Communist countries. Zhou met with Soviet premier Aleksey Kosygin in Beijing on September 11, 1969. But the border clashes continued along the Chinese-Russian border until the late 1970s.[68] Reportedly, Moscow's leaders considered using a "preemptive nuclear strike" against China.[69]

A PLA soldier aims at a Soviet tank. (Reproduced by permission of the PLA Literature Press, Beijing, China.)

By the early 1970s, the Soviet Union had deployed up to forty-eight divisions, nearly one million troops, along the Russian-Chinese border. China prepared for total war, including possible Russian nuclear attacks. Beijing demanded a reduction in the number of Soviet troops on the Sino-Soviet and Sino-Mongolian borders as one of the three conditions for a normalization of relations with Moscow. Mao also intended to undermine the rising power of the Soviets in Asia by playing the "American card" and opening a new relationship with the United States.[70]

At that time, I was an eighth grader. In my school years in Beijing, millions of city residents dug antiaircraft shelters and underground works. I was impressed by the scale and deliberation of some underground hospitals and schools in suburban areas when my school organized training tours. In 1969, the CMC established the PLA Heilongjiang Production and Construction Corps (PLA-HPCC), which as a paramount military organization and a state-run enterprise had six divisions, totaling 1.2 million troops. The corps recruiting officers visited our middle school and called for a massive enlistment. They offered a full-time government job and a monthly salary of 36 yuan (about $10), a very attractive offer to many youths in the cities. During the Cultural Revolution, no full-time jobs were offered for years. Along with more than half of the ninth-grade class, I signed up for service in the PLA-HPCC. I was seventeen.

In September, we were sent to the Eleventh Regiment, Second Division, PLA-HPCC in Luobei, about thirty miles from the Chinese-Russian border. At the train station, I was assigned to the First Engineering Company in the regiment with most of my classmates. We were a little disappointed when we put on uniforms without red stars and found we had to work on road and bridge construction most of the time. The PLA-HPCC was a semi-military corps, farming in peacetime and fighting in wartime. The Second Division had eight regiments. I enjoyed daily morning drills and military training, which included shooting, grenade practice, and demolition training, a couple of hours every day. I did not enjoy night patrol. In 1970, our company was upgraded to a standard combat unit. Only six of the twenty-three companies in the Eleventh Regiment earned this designation. Wearing red stars and red flags, we were proud to be PLA soldiers. Everyone became more serious in training, and we seemed to become adults over-

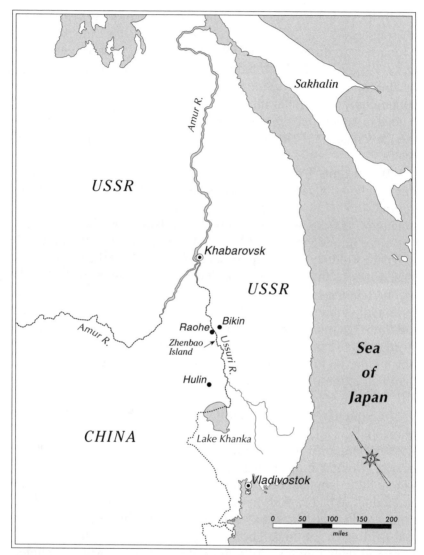

The Sino-Soviet Border

night. That spring, our company shifted to a new location, about ten miles from the Chinese-Russian border. The first mission came when our company joined a search for Russian spies. My platoon searched bushes along the Amur River, the Chinese-Russian border. We walked along the river bank and combed the bushes inch by inch. I looked at the other shore, several hundred yards away, across the river that separated the two countries. It was a very quiet and peaceful morning. I did not see any Russian soldiers or tanks. Where were the one million troops and eight thousand tanks? We had been told they were along the border. I saw a small fishing village on the other side of the river and heard some dogs barking. I was a little bit nervous and sweated all day, though there was no action at all.

During the missions and training, we looked up to our platoon and squad leaders for confidence, solutions, and answers. They were all CCP members, our role models and caretakers. Although we all wanted to join the CCP, we had to join the CYL first. It took about one year for most of the men to become CYL members. Then, in the second year, about 30 percent joined the CCP. In 1972, when I left the PLA-HPCC's Eleventh Regiment, 60 percent of the men in my company were CCP members. That spring, along with a couple dozen others, I was transferred to Daqing to protect the country's largest crude oil field, which produced more than half of the national total. In early 1973, I retired from the PLA but remained at the Daqing oil field as a petroleum worker.

The Cultural Revolution and the Fall of Lin

By the mid-1960s, questions about Mao's Great Leap Forward policies and dissenting opinions in the party and government had spread to some extent. With Marshal Lin's cooperation, Mao responded to the opposition with a new effort to mobilize support beyond the party, to include soldiers and students: the Great Proletarian Cultural Revolution. As Fairbank describes it, "The public scene was soon filled with mass meetings, parades, and propaganda displays exalting Mao as 'the red sun in our hearts.' Tremendous excitement, even hysteria, among millions of youth led to exhaustion, apathy, and further surges of effort. Out of it all came a purge of the party by the leader."[71] On May 16, 1966, the Politburo issued a circular, drafted by Mao, that pointed out a need to purge the "bourgeois representatives who wormed their way into the party, government, and army."[72] Fang Zhu considers the meeting a "turning point" in the Cultural Revolution. After the meeting, "the Maoists gained control over the party leadership."[73] On May 28, the Politburo organized the Central Committee's Cultural Revolution Leading Group, the body that would guide the national movement. In August, when Jiang Qing, Mao's wife, became its chair, the Cultural Revolution Leading Group gradually replaced the Politburo as the party's authority for the Cultural Revolution.[74]

In the summer of 1966, the Cultural Revolution became a nationwide political struggle with extensive purges. Mao used mass organizations such as the Red Guard to publicly attack, or "paoda" (bomb), the CCP and PRC hierarchy officials, including PRC president Liu Shaoqi and CCP secretary-general Deng Xiaoping. The Red Guards, mostly college, high school, and middle school students, were empowered by Mao; they called for "bombing the headquarters" and "learning revolution by making revolution," claiming "rebellion is justified." From June to August 1966, all high schools and colleges dismissed classes and allowed students to participate in the new revolution. There were three months of "red terror"—or "tianxia daluan" (great chaos under the heavens), as Mao called it. The Cultural Revolution was contrived from top to bottom. Lin Biao, Jiang Qing, and other leftists took advantage of the revolutionary enthusiasm and naïveté of the students, inflaming them with a lot of demagogic mummery. In a letter to Jiang Qing on July 8, Mao wrote, "Complete confusion leads to complete stability. The task today for the entire Communist Party, for the entire nation, is to fundamentally destroy the rightists."[75]

On August 12, 1966, at the eleventh plenary session of the Eighth CCP National Congress, Lin became the vice chairman of the CCP, second only to Mao. At the meeting, Mao described the Cultural Revolution as a political struggle, a class struggle inside the party. "This is repression, terrorizing," Mao told the Standing Committee members of the Politburo, and "the terrorizing comes from the Central Committee." More specifically, he added, "There are ox demons and venomous spirits sitting here among us . . . to rebel is justified!"[76] On August 18, at a mass meeting celebrating the Cultural Revolution, Lin exhorted the youthful Red Guards to "smash" the Four Olds: "the old concepts, culture, customs, and habits of the exploiting classes." On August 20, Red Guards in Beijing took the lead in an unprecedented assault against the Four Olds. It quickly swept the country. Coming out of the schools, the Red Guards blanketed the land in a revolutionary red terror. Instigated by Lin and spurred on to a frenzy by the

Cultural Revolution Leading Group, it degenerated into a wild spree of home searches, property destruction, free-for-all fights, and even murder. By the end of the year, social stability had vanished. Industry, agriculture, and commerce were badly disrupted, causing widespread public resentment. Disturbances and conflicts increased. At the same time, because understanding and concepts varied among the numerous Red Guard organizations, they developed serious factional differences and constantly argued heatedly among themselves. China's vast land rumbled and seethed. It had indeed reached the "ideal" stage of Mao's "great chaos under the heavens" so earnestly sought by the revolutionary seer.[77]

On August 23, at the CMC Standing Committee meeting, Lin called for "three-month turmoil" in the PLA. On October 5, the CMC and General Political Department issued an urgent instruction to all military academies and institutes to dismiss their classes and allow their cadets to become fully involved in the Cultural Revolution. Throughout the fall, with PLA logistical support, some eleven million Red Guards came to Beijing for a succession of mass rallies and then dispersed over the country.[78] In 1967, encouraged by Mao and Lin, Red Guards began a direct attack on government officials at various levels and demanded that all government and party officials accused of being counterrevolutionaries and capitalist roaders be removed from their positions.

In early 1967, some marshals and generals in Beijing tried to stop the Maoists' attempt to involve the PLA in the Great Proletarian Cultural Revolution. Their efforts failed, and they were branded the February Countercurrent. Mao asked them to leave their posts and conduct self-critiques. In March 1967, Lin mentioned several times the need to identify "a small handful in the army" and burn them to death. It was then that the Cultural Revolution Leading Group moved into power, replacing the Politburo. Lin used the Cultural Revolution mass movements to purge the military leaders who did not agree with his strategy and policy. He mobilized PLA soldiers and commanders in Beijing to look for "bourgeoisie agents in the PLA." Then, with Mao's approval, Lin dismissed and jailed many marshals and generals.[79] Among the marshals was He Long, Lin's longtime rival, who was labeled the "biggest bandit" and later died in prison. In early 1968, the Central Committee dismissed and jailed General Yang Chengwu, chief of the

General Staff, and General Yu Lijin, chief of the air force. Lin then appointed loyal followers to these positions. Most marshals and generals lost their positions and were jailed or publicly criticized.

In Beijing, all the PLA headquarters were paralyzed. Commanders and officers were expelled from their positions. In the course of the cruel questioning sessions, many were tormented or beaten to death. For instance, in the General Political Department, Lin's followers and leftists on July 25 called for "zalan yanwangdian" (destroying the GPD hell) and the overthrow of General Xiao Hua, director of the GPD. Thereafter, forty top officers in the GPD were purged, and most of them died in prison.[80] In the navy, there was a "struggle between the two headquarters," the leftist headquarters and the rightist headquarters. In July 1967, the PLAN headquarters issued the "little white book," *Haijun liangge silingbu luxian douzheng dashiji* (Chronicle of the Struggles between the Two Headquarters in the PLAN). On October 28, the PLAN Party Committee circulated the confession of Yuan Yifen, commander of the South Sea Fleet, and concluded that Yuan "had made serious mistakes and took the wrong side."[81] General Yuan was soon dismissed and jailed. From 1967 to 1969, more than 80,000 officers were accused and purged. Among them, 1,169 died of torture or starvation or were executed. Many military institutes were shut down, and research programs were cancelled. The number of military academies was reduced from 125 to 43. Many defense works were destroyed, and regular training stopped. The PLA suffered the "most serious damage since the founding of the PRC."[82]

At local levels, the regional and provincial commands were either paralyzed or divided into two or more factions. For example, the Wuhan Regional Command had an armed clash with the Hubei Provincial Command on July 20, 1967, because of their different opinions about the local, factional mass organizations. Their armed conflict brought the entire province into a civil war. During and after the incident, more than 180,000 officers, soldiers, and civilians were killed or wounded in the streets of Wuhan.[83] Many officers brought the same attitudes and problems back into the PLA, and in many of its units this led to the rise of two opposing factions.

During the turmoil, Lin devoted his energy to a futile effort to build up his personal following in the PLA by distributing favors, in terms of appointments and promotions. He appointed General Li Zuopeng, his longtime lieutenant, as the political commissar of the navy. Li selected Zhang Xiuchuan, Wang Hongkun, Xiao Yun, and Shi Fengxiang from his personal circle for positions in the naval headquarters, political department, and security department in Beijing. Then they traveled to the naval bases and regional fleets to build personal loyalty to Lin and Li and to develop their network in the service. In early 1969, for example, they appointed Feng Shangxian political commissar of Lüshun Naval Base after Feng came back from Vietnam.[84]

In September, Shi Fengxiang, now deputy director of the navy's political department, visited Lüshun Naval Base and praised Feng Shangxian as one of the best naval officers. Shi emphasized loyalty to Li's network at the base commanders' meeting: "We in gray uniform must obey the gray, not the yellow" (the army uniform).[85] He also visited submarines 138 and 139 and told the crews, "You are the Red Guards underwater." He explained, "Before my trip, Li Zuopeng asked me to visit the Submarine Division." Shi told the submariners that Li had a special feeling about them.[86] Feng built his personal network by setting up "model officers" and "outstanding sailors" who, in turn, provided unquestioning support to Feng's control of the base. Feng identified those who were loyal to him by asking that all officers and sailors "zhandui" (line up) with the "proletarian headquarters." Feng launched political campaigns against officers who refused, forcing them to retire early or leave the base. By January 1967, there were more than five thousand posters criticizing the officers all over the base.[87]

Since early 1967, the situation across the country had worsened, as the Cultural Revolution entered the phase of a total takeover of the authorities. The Red Guards took over government offices at all levels, jailed the officials, and administered provincial and local affairs. But, as we have seen, different factions within the Red Guards had contradictory political orientations and different plans, leading to violent conflicts within the Red Guards, in many places resembling civil war. To stop the national turmoil, Mao ordered the PLA to control the situation with Three Supports and Two Militarizations: support leftist masses, manufacturing production, and agricultural production; and impose martial law with military administration and civilian training. Mao employed the PLA to restore social and political order and to prevent civil war. On January 23, the Central Committee, CMC, State Council, and Cultural Revolution Leading Group issued a joint directive about the PLA's new tasks. On March 19, the CMC ordered all PLA units to fully engage in the Three Supports and Two Militarizations to stop the armed conflicts and stabilize the social order across the country. Thereafter, tasking headquarters were established at regional and provincial commands, and tasking offices were opened at the army and divisional levels. Moving to center stage, under Lin's command, the Chinese military replaced civilian governments at the provincial, district, county, and city levels through military administrative committees from 1967 to 1972. The PLA used its officers as administrators for schools, factories, companies, villages, and farms.[88] More than 2.8 million officers and soldiers participated in the tasks. By February 1967, the military administration took control of nearly seven thousand enterprises of mass media, defense, law enforcement, foreign affairs, transportation, finance, and other pivotal activities. By 1967, PLA administrative teams had taken over all universities, colleges, high schools, and elementary schools across the country. The military teams also organized professors, teachers, administrators, and students for military training and daily drills. The PLA takeover promoted military-civilian integration and contributed to another increase in military service. By the mid-1970s, the PLA numbered more than 6 million troops.[89]

Between 1967 and 1971, the PLA became the dominant political force in the country. By September 1968, each province had established a provincial revolutionary committee to replace the governor's office, a provincial congress, and a provincial court. The majority of the provincial committee members were from the military: about 98 percent in Hubei, 97 percent in Yunnan, 95 percent in Shanxi, 84 percent in Liaoning, 81 percent in Guangdong, and 78 percent in Beijing. Lin's power grew to an unprecedented level. At the CCP Ninth National Congress in April 1969, the Central Committee and the entire party recognized Lin as Mao's "close comrade in arms and successor."[90] As Fairbank, Reischauer, and Craig point out, "In the end, the attack on the government and party gave civil power to an increasing number of army men, who were brought into key administrative positions and often continued to terrorize intellectuals and bureaucrats." They conclude that the Chinese Cultural Revolution is "generally seen as 'ten lost years' in China's modern development. The wanton destructiveness of ignorant teenagers; the reign of terror against members of the intellectual and official establishments; the harassment, jailing, beating, torture, and often killing perpetrated against something like a million victims were an enormous human and cultural disaster."[91]

In 1970, the Cultural Revolution took an unexpected turn. A new political struggle between Chairman Mao and Marshal Lin erupted, a struggle that would rip a great hole in a political arena that was already tattered. Lin and Mao differed in strategy, foreign policy, and domestic politics.[92] For instance, when Mao proposed that the PRC constitution be amended to eliminate the post of head of state, Lin made a counterproposal that Mao assume the presidency. Mao repeatedly turned the offer down and said, "I cannot do this job. The suggestion is inappropriate." On the surface, this was only a question of whether to retain the post, but it concealed a host of contradictions.[93]

The contradictions burst forth at the second plenary session of the Ninth Central Committee at Lushan in August–September 1970. In his opening speech as the second party leader, Lin again advocated creating the office of head of state. His generals voiced their support. The military leaders overplayed their hand in the party. Mao called an expanded meeting of the Politburo and sternly criticized Lin and the military, thus dooming Lin. The session ended on September 6, when Mao's concluding speech struck the party leaders like a bolt of lightning. After the stormy meeting at Lushan, some of Lin's lieutenants were criticized, compelled to make self-criticisms, or removed from office. Mao compared Lin to Peng Dehuai and Liu Shaoqi a year later:

> I thought their surprise attacks and underground activities were planned, organized, and programmed. Their program was to set up a state chairman, advocate "genius," oppose the line put forth by the Ninth Party Congress, and overthrow the three items on the agenda of the Second Plenum of the Ninth Central Committee. A certain person was very anxious to become the state chairman, to split the party, and to seize power. . . . The struggle at the 1959 Lushan Conference with P'eng Te-huai was a struggle between the two headquarters. The struggle with Liu Shao-ch'i was also a struggle between the two headquarters. The struggle at this Lushan Conference was again a struggle between the two headquarters.[94]

Zhu considered the Lushan conference in 1970 only a prelude to the Mao-Lin showdown a year later. "By disagreeing with Mao during the plenum, for whatever reason, Lin had provided Mao with hard evidence of his political ambition. The relationship between the two men had deteriorated to the point of open confrontation."[95]

In Mao's eyes, what the Lushan conference revealed was not a simple political error but the ambitions of Lin Biao. Angry and disappointed, Mao considered Lin's ambitions and personal influence in the military to be dangerous. Mao had never expected that Lin would challenge his authority and openly stand up against him as an equal. Mao decided to deal with Lin. He took steps to weaken the influence of Lin's followers on national and local government officers by methods colloquially called "reng shitou" (throwing a few stones), "chan shazi" (mixing in sand), and "wa qiangjiao" (digging away at the foot of the wall). In August and September 1971, Mao traveled around the country, talking to key people, both military and civilian, stressing how serious the situation had become. In the Mao-Lin struggle, most of the military leaders chose Mao and denounced Lin.[96]

Lin and his family realized that Mao was directing his political struggle against them. Following Peng, Liu, and Deng, Lin would be the next victim of Mao's brutal political movement. Lin's son, Lin Liguo, planned to assassinate Mao on his way back from Shanghai. Mao realized the danger and returned to Beijing early on September 12. Lin Liguo's plot failed. Lin Biao had taken a fatal step from which there was no return. On September 13, 1971, at the urging of his wife and son, Lin and his family fled. Lin commandeered a plane at the Shanhaiguan Airport. They flew north, heading for the Soviet Union. For unknown reasons, the plane crashed in Mongolia. Lin, his family, crew members, and others on board, eight in total, were killed in the crash.[97]

The Lin incident was the most troubling political event since the inception of the Cultural Revolution. Five days after the plane crash, Central Committee leaders, with Mao's approval, notified committee members of Lin's treasonous flight. Ten days later, Mao informed military officers and commanders at the divisional level and above. On September 24, the Central Committee dismissed all the key members of Lin's group from their positions. On October 3, Mao dissolved the Executive Office of the CMC, formerly controlled by Lin, and created a new CMC office under Marshal Ye Jianying. The next day, Mao chaired the first meeting of the new office. He said that Lin had controlled the armed forces for more than ten years and that many problems existed in the military. The PLA must be unified and prepared for war.[98] On October 6, the Central Committee issued a report regarding the "criminal activities of the Lin Biao clique." Lin was accused of forming an "anti-revolutionary clique," conducting a military coup, planning the assassination of Mao, and betraying his country. In mid-October, the document was sent to all local CCP branch secretaries. On October 24, the Central Committee made it available to all CCP members.[99]

After Lin's death, Mao launched a nationwide movement to criticize Lin and Confucius (*pilin pikong*), labeling Lin a "closet Confucianist," a "bourgeois careerist," a conspirator, and an "ultra-rightist." Historians are surprised to see that "these obviously contradictory criticisms were heaped on a man who had been a brilliant general and one of Mao's closest friends." June Grasso, Jay Corrin, and Michael Kort state that "Lin Biao was blamed for nearly everything that went wrong in China during the late 1960s."[100] Since Lin had promoted the Mao cult and the Cultural Revolution, his death brought great joy to China's millions. But cool scrutiny raised doubts about the entire course of action, orientation, and policy that had been followed since the advent of the Cultural Revolution. Mao himself certainly knew better. A person who worked closely beside him later recalled, "After Lin Biao crashed, the Chairman became very ill. Lin's betrayal had a serious effect on his health. We heard him quote the old adage: 'At 73 or 84, if Death doesn't invite you, you should go to its door!' We felt badly. He was very depressed."[101]

As in the past, Mao's political criticism was followed by a top-down purge and shakeup in the military. During the movement to criticize Lin and Confucius in 1972–73, most of Lin's generals were purged, and his military programs were terminated. On December 22, 1972, the CMC ordered the chiefs of eight regional commands to exchange their positions within ten days. By January 1973, the CMC had completed its thorough reorganization of all services and departments. Thereafter, Marshal Ye Jianying took charge of the PLA's daily affairs with the consultation of Premier Zhou Enlai. This Zhou-Ye system replaced the Lin-Jiang system of 1966–71. A new power struggle now began between Zhou-Ye and Jiang Qing, who continued to dominate the media and preach class struggle. The Cultural Revolution lasted until Mao's death in September 1976.[102]

After Lin's death in 1971, the continuing threats from the Soviet Union, together with the fading status of Mao's continuous revolution at home, created the motives for Beijing to pursue a rapprochement with the United States. Both President Richard Nixon and his national security advisor, Henry Kissinger, saw that an improvement in the relationship with China would be beneficial to the United States: in the short term, it would help get America out of the Vietnam War, and in the long term, it would dramatically enhance the strategic position of the United States in a global confrontation with the Soviet Union.[103] All of this paved the way for Nixon's historic visit to China in February 1972.

★ 8 ★

Survivor and Reformer

PRESIDENT RICHARD NIXON'S 1972 visit to China profoundly reshaped the Cold War world. First and foremost, it ended the confrontation between the United States and China that had lasted for almost a quarter century, thereby opening a new chapter in relations between the world's most powerful nation and its most populous nation.[1] Within the context of this Sino-American rapprochement, Beijing's relations with Japan also improved. In September 1972, only months after Nixon's visit, China and Japan established formal diplomatic relations. In 1978, the two countries went further and signed a treaty of friendship and cooperation.

Consequently, a new, crucial feature of the Cold War in east Asia as well as in the world emerged: international politics became dominated by a specific "triangular structure."[2] Taking the "Soviet threat" as an overriding concern, Beijing and Washington established a "quasi strategic partnership."[3] To the crises of Vietnam's invasion of Cambodia in 1979 and the Soviet Union's invasion of Afghanistan in 1980, Beijing's and Washington's reactions were compatible—both condemned Hanoi and Moscow. Both also emphasized the interrelatedness of the events in Cambodia and Afghanistan, and both provided various types of support to resistance movements in these two countries.[4] In January 1979, China and the United States established formal diplomatic relations. In February 1979, China invaded Vietnam with two hundred thousand PLA troops.

241

From 1972 to 1989, the PLA experienced tremendous ups and downs that corresponded with international as well as domestic politics. With the Great Proletarian Cultural Revolution sweeping across China, the PLA moved to the center of national politics in 1966–71. Then, after Lin Biao's death and a series of purges, it moved out of the political arena. Mao brought back some of the government officials who had been purged during the Cultural Revolution. Among others, Deng Xiaoping was rehabilitated by Mao and appointed as a member of the Central Committee in 1973. As a survivor of the Cultural Revolution, Deng announced new military reforms in 1975 and tried to "repair the damage" done to the PLA during the Cultural Revolution.[5] But soon Deng was dismissed by Mao again. After Mao's death in 1976, Deng returned once more and launched unprecedented reforms in 1978. He opened China to the outside world to bring the Four Modernizations, including the modernization of defense, to the country.

This chapter examines the military reforms in the late 1970s and the 1980s led by Deng Xiaoping, the second generation of Chinese leadership. Deng knew the PLA's social and political problems. He sharply criticized its poor performance and declining morale during the Chinese-Vietnamese conflicts. The personal accounts of Colonel Zhi Zhanpeng of the 1979 Sino-Vietnamese War and Private Xu Xiangyao of the 1984–85 Sino-Vietnamese border conflicts suggest strong implications for the PLA's reform aspirations. This chapter highlights the gap between Deng's goals and the limited resources available for military reforms in the 1980s. Many of these shortcomings became evident during the 1989 Tiananmen Square incident.

Deng's Return, Reform, and Restraints

Between 1972 and 1989, the PLA's fortunes fluctuated with Deng Xiaoping's political career. During the Cultural Revolution, Deng was purged along with Liu Shaoqi as the head of the "bourgeoisie headquarters within the party" and ousted from the CCP and PLA hierarchy in 1966. Thereafter, Deng and his wife were placed under house arrest in Beijing for two years and then sent to Jiangxi to work in a tractor repair factory.[6] After Lin's death, in 1973, Mao brought Deng back to power as his vice premier. Deng was appointed as a member of the Central Committee and then chief of the PLA General Staff, vice chairman of the CMC, vice chairman of the Central Committee, and member of the Politburo Standing Committee in 1975.[7]

Deng announced new economic and military reforms in 1975. In contrast with previous reforms, Deng's movement was not aimed at an American or a Soviet threat but instead addressed serious problems within the PLA. At a General Staff meeting in January 1975, Deng criticized the PLA for losing many of its "fine traditions" and being a "seriously bloated" organization. "An over-expanded and inefficient army is not combat-worthy."[8] At an expanded meeting of the CMC in July, he summed up the PLA's problems with five words: "bloating, laxity, conceit, extravagance, and inertia." While blaming these faults on "sabotage by Lin Biao and his followers," Deng called for immediate reforms to solve the problems by consolidating the PLA. The new chief made his goal very clear. "This meeting will decide on a new size and organizational structure for the army, with a view to making it less unwieldy. But this is not our only task. We must also solve the four other problems, all of which have to be handled in connection with the first one."[9] Deng began his reform by demobilizing six hundred thousand troops. Having criticized the Cultural Revolution for exacerbating the PLA's problems, Deng made a strategic transition from Mao's people's war doctrine to a new doctrine of people's war under modern conditions.[10]

Maoists, including Mao's wife, Jiang Qing, criticized Deng's reforms, arguing that they were restoring old bourgeois lines and returning (fan'an) to rightist ways. In April 1976, Mao and leftists accused Deng of criticizing both the Cultural Revolution and Jiang Qing and dismissed him from the government. The new reform movement seemed to be over before it had even started. The interdependencies between military reforms and political changes played an important role in PLA history. In the meantime, Mao gave Marshal Ye Jianying command of China's armed forces.[11]

On September 9, 1976, Mao died. The power struggle in the party surfaced between the Maoists, or the Gang of Four—Jiang Qing, Zhang Chunqiao, Yao Wenyuan, and Wang Hongwen—and the old guard, including Chen Yun, Xu Xiangqian, Ye, Nie Rongzhen, and Wang Zhen. Real control, however, remained in the hands of Ye, who was vice chairman of the CCP Central Committee, a member of the Standing Committee of the Politburo, vice chairman of the CMC, and minister of defense. On October 6, Ye ordered security troops to arrest the Gang of Four and Mao Yuanxin, Mao Zedong's cousin.[12]

After the demise of the Gang of Four, Deng staged his second comeback in 1977. He won an intense struggle in the post-Mao succession by removing the Maoists and gaining firm control of Beijing. He then ended the Cultural Revolution and led China from a period of political turmoil to one of economic development by denying the need for any continuous domestic class struggle, the underlying impulse of Mao's Cultural Revolution. In 1978, he emerged as the new leader, launched new reform policies, and opened China up to the outside world. He represented a new generation of Chinese leadership.[13]

In 1978, Deng made his historic speech, "Jiefang sixiang, shishi qiushi, tuanjie yizhi xiangqiankan" (Emancipate the Mind, Seek Truth from Facts, and Unite as One in Looking to the Future), at the third plenary session of the Eleventh CCP Central Committee. His speech declared that China would open itself to the world so as to bring the Four Modernizations to China: industry, agriculture, science and technology, and national defense.[14] He told a press delegation from West Germany, "Due to the interference of Lin Biao and the Gang of Four, China's development was held up for ten years. In the early 1960s, we were behind the developed countries in science and technology, but the gap was not so wide. However, over the past dozen years, the gap has widened because the world has been developing with tremendous speed. Compared with developed countries, China's economy has fallen behind at least ten years, perhaps 20, 30, or even 50 years in some areas."[15] Deng was determined to lead China onto the road of economic prosperity by deprogramming Mao's system and convincing people that reality is the only criterion for judging whether a theory represents the truth. Deng stressed that Marxism was a century-old theory imported from the West. To expect Marxism to reflect China's reality in the twentieth century would simply be unrealistic. Deng defended the market economy as having no contradiction with socialism, because it is simply an economic tool that may serve any ideological cause.[16] In Deng's system, Marxism and Mao Zedong Thought became means to support the reform rather than ends that the party must abide by.

Deng introduced capitalist management in 1979 by establishing special economic zones, where trade could be conducted without the central government's authorization. He later expanded the experience to the rest of the country. By 2000, private enterprise accounted for roughly 40 percent of the economy. A direct outcome of this change was that privately owned enterprises pushed state-owned enterprises to become more competitive. The state-owned enterprises must either shake off inertia or disintegrate into privately owned companies. Deng did not intend to send socialism to Mao's bier. Deng believed that both planned and market economies were ways to "liberate productivity." In January 1980, while speaking at a CCP leaders meeting, Deng emphasized economic development. "Any deviation from this pivotal task endangers our material base. All other tasks must revolve around the pivot and must absolutely not interfere with or upset it. In the 20-odd years since 1957 we have learned bitter lessons in this respect."[17] He considered the reform movement a revolution—the second revolution of the country, comparable to the founding of the PRC in 1949. "China is now carrying out a reform. I am all in favor of that. There is no other solution for us."[18]

In September 1982, Deng called for "constructing a socialist country with Chinese characteristics" at the opening ceremony of the Twelfth CCP National Congress.[19] In 1987, he laid out three stages of achievement for China's modernization: sufficiency, relative affluence, and the living standard of a medium-level developed country. In terms of income figures, the first step was to reach a per capita gross national product of $500 by 1990, doubling the 1980 figure of $250. The second step was to reach a per capita gross national product of $1,000 and achieve relative comfort (xiaokang) by the turn of the century. The third step was to quadruple the $1,000 figure in thirty to fifty years.[20] In a 1987 speech to high-level officials, Deng pointed out that both planned and market mechanisms were instruments to serve economic growth. He believed it best for China to develop a socialist market economy, rather than a capitalist market economy. Deng explained that in a capitalist society individualism prevails, whereas the socialist market economy leads to common prosperity. Even if some individuals or regions get rich ahead of others, this does not lead to polarization, because the socialist system has the strength of working effectively for common prosperity.[21] Deng claimed that China had opened its door and would never close it again. The heart of his program was a commitment to economic development.

A pragmatist rather than an ideologue, Deng tried to bring China back into the international system to seek maximum opportunities for its economic and technological development. He signed numerous treaties with Western governments and joined many international organizations.[22] He met Presidents Ronald Reagan and George H. W. Bush in Beijing during their state visits to China. Deng also began negotiations with the British to resume Chinese sovereignty over Hong Kong, and with the Portuguese to return Macau to China. He developed a theory of "one country, two systems" to apply to these territories, as well as to Taiwan, for peaceful national reunification. Soon a rapid increase of cross-strait trade, visits, and exchanges occurred, and multilevel official negotiations began between Beijing and Taipei in the 1980s.[23]

The open-door economic policy reflected a fundamental change in China's developmental strategy. Beijing wanted broad and generous U.S. support for the Four Modernizations. The desire to get greater access to U.S. economic assistance and technology provided impetus for Beijing to work to improve relations with Washington.[24] The normalization of Sino-American relations on January 1, 1979, led to the rapid creation of an institutional and legal framework for expanded economic cooperation. These efforts paid off; the United States granted most favored nation trade status to China in July 1979 and gradually loosened trade restrictions, shifting the PRC to the category of friendly, non-allied, in May 1983. The improved relationship was seen in the Sino-U.S. communiqué of August 17, 1982, signed by President Ronald Reagan during his visit to China.[25]

China's fast economic development was premised on a stable international environment. Reducing tension was part of Deng's endeavor to construct such an environment. In other words, peace and development were consistent with Deng's foreign policy, which emphasized a nonconfrontational approach toward the West in general and the United States in particular, and good relations with China's neighbors, including Taiwan.[26] Deng adopted a low-profile foreign-policy posture to buy time for China's economic takeoff and military upgrading. He summarized the foreign policy guidelines as "observe patiently, respond sensibly, consolidate our own footing, be skilful in hiding one's capacities and biding one's time, be good at the tactics of low-profile diplomacy, never take the lead, and take proper initiatives."[27]

To avoid any erratic or provocative actions by the PLA, Deng continued the modernization and professionalization of the military in the wake of the 1979 Vietnam incursion. Deng had a similar background to Mao's, having worked extensively in the military and in the CCP's rural base areas in the past. Popular and trusted, Deng had been one of the most influential and senior commanders in the PLA. In 1982, Deng uprooted Hua Guofeng, chairman of the CMC, and reinstalled himself as the chief of the PLA General Staff. The high command faithfully supported Deng's leadership. To oversee the reform, the Military System Reform Leading Group was established within the CMC in February 1982. The group asked the PLA to promote a revolution of military affairs in a distinctively Chinese way, according to the reality of the Chinese armed forces.[28]

The PLA viewed Deng's economic reforms as favorable and necessary for military restructuring. General Xiong Guangkai, deputy chief of the General Staff, believed that a growing national economy needed a strong national defense, and that a strong national economy could support and contribute to a strong military.[29] From May 23 to June 6, 1985, the CMC held a landmark conference that became the starting point of Deng's 1980s military reform. Like Deng's efforts in the mid-1970s, the mid-1980s reform was not aimed at fighting a foreign invasion or a world war, but instead targeted the problems within the PLA by downsizing its troops and commanding system.[30]

To reduce the PLA, Deng, now the chairman of the CMC, argued that a new world war was not inevitable and nuclear war no longer seemed imminent. His remarks outlined a major change in China's strategic thinking and worldview. He told the Chinese military that peace and development were the two leading trends in international affairs. The PLA needed to contemplate a new and different international environment and participate in China's ongoing reforms.[31] In 1985, Deng explained his new strategic thoughts to the high-ranking commanders. First, the Chinese armed forces should expect a local, limited war rather than a total or nuclear war. Second, the next war needed a professional army with modern technology. This was another strategic transition from Mao's people's war doctrine to the new doctrine of people's war under modern conditions.[32]

The mid-1980s reform followed Deng's new doctrine of fighting a limited, local war and emphasized the development and employment of new technology and improved weaponry. Deng downsized the PLA forces by one million troops over the next two years. Theoretically, the money saved from the troop reduction would be available for upgrading defense technology.[33] However, the PLA did not get what it wanted in terms of a bigger budget and new technology. According to Deng, national economic growth was a prerequisite for the PLA's technology improvement. Deng emphasized that "only when we have a good economic foundation will it be possible for us to modernize the army's equipment. So we must wait patiently for a few years."[34] He believed that defense building must be subordinated to serve national economic development but that the two causes should be promoted in a coordinated manner. You Ji points out, "Many senior officers attribute the PLA's slow modernization progress to Deng's decade-long suppressive policy of 'jundui yaorennai,' meaning the armed forces must refrain from demanding too large a budget."[35] PLA generals still talk about the debt the party center and government owe to the military.

The transition to a market economy dramatically changed the structure of Chinese society, especially rural society. After 1978, the concept of Mao's people's communes weakened considerably. Deng was the first Communist leader to encourage people to get rich. With his slogan "To be rich is glorious," Deng won the endorsement of the people, particularly peasants. Small Chinese farmers were determined to improve their living standard, and they succeeded, leading directly to the collapse of the entire commune system. The state retreated substantially from grassroots rural society.[36]

Long-dissatisfied peasants started to redistribute land to households on the condition that each household submit a certain amount of output to the government. This practice achieved great success immediately because individual farmsteads regained complete control of their inputs and outputs. The practice was officially accepted nationwide after a short pioneer experiment in some areas and then was promoted as the household production responsibility system in 1979. The production contracting system simply gave villagers control rights to production. Redistribution, or the fear of redistribution, prevented peasants from leaving their village, resulting in a decline in interest in serving in the military. A peasant family needed as many household members as possible to receive a larger piece of land. Parents also wanted to keep their sons on the farm to help them succeed in competitive market farming. In the early 1980s, with a sizable piece of land and able hands, some of the peasants in the southern provinces got rich quick and became *wanyuanhu* (10,000-yuan families), with an annual income of about $3,000, compared to the peasant's national average annual income of about $60. Colonel Wang Lilin recalled that, until 1984, the PLA had not missed its enlistment goals since 1949. In the mid-1980s, the army's recruitment fell short three years in a row. Not only was the PLA short on numbers, Wang complained, but it was also losing the best youths to the labor market.[37] Many young farmers, especially those who were hardworking and had ambition, decided to engage in market farming or small business. They saw their future in the marketplace, not on the battleground.[38]

Moreover, village leaders and local governments intended to keep the educated young people with leadership potential in their villages for political consideration. Following the collapse of the people's commune system, the state's grip on society loosened, and weakened local governments found themselves unable to carry out their responsibilities. Villages, especially in backward areas, were trapped in a state of disorder. Confronted with these grassroots-level problems, the state began deliberating on how to fill the organizational power vacuum left by the dissolution of the people's communes. At the time, the state could draw on party and governmental organizational resources. At the National Conference on Village Political Tasks in 1982, the party reemphasized the need to strengthen its role in grassroots-level organizations. Between 1983 and 1985, the upper half of the commune administration was transformed into township governments, but the lower half—composed of production brigades and teams—was not able to recover from the changes wrought by the household responsibility system. The state administration had two choices. One was to invest in strengthening formal state structures at the local level. The other was to unload part of the responsibility for organizational rebuilding onto local communities and allow them to implement self-governance and institute village democracy.[39]

For the first time, peasants needed to produce their own leadership, win elections against corrupted cadres, and carry out their own policies to benefit their villages. Villagers had long been dissatisfied with the parasitic nature of local cadres. This dissatisfaction was the core motivation behind many villagers' decision to leave their homes during the Maoist period. Now the successful peasants wanted to work in their villages rather than serve in the military. As a result, peasants gained control rights over production, the opportunity for social mobility, and the power to participate in village governance. Peasants now had choices: farm to improve their living, or leave the village for new opportunities.[40]

Labor migration from rural to urban areas emerged as a nation-wide phenomenon in the mid-1980s. Before then, the household registration system had successfully confined people to their place of birth. Rural-to-urban migration occurred only on an extremely small scale, under the auspices of the government, including the veteran administrative arrangement. Beginning in the late 1970s, economic reforms improved food supply to the cities and abolished the food rationing system for urban residents. As the old apparatuses of migration control became less effective, rural people began to spontaneously migrate to urban areas without obtaining government approval. Since the mid-1980s, a large number of migrants have successfully entered cities without official approval. By the late 1990s, the estimated total was about twelve million. They caused some problems with employment, housing, public education, healthcare, transportation, and law enforcement in the cities, whose governments continued to deny permanent residency to rural people. The urban-rural segregation caused serious concerns and hostility between the government and migrants.[41]

In this new environment, PLA recruiting officers faced unprecedented problems. With new opportunities available, many young peasants considered joining the army the last choice on their list. The decline of interest in the service had a negative impact not only on the quantity but also on the quality of the troops. Beginning in the mid-1980s, the recruiting officers either did not have enough recruits or had some sign-ups they did not really want.[42] Even though the military lowered the physical and political requirements for new recruits, the enlistment rates continued to decline. More negative social factors emerged: high divorce, particularly among officers, and difficulty finding a job after retirement from the military. These problems had a negative impact on China's wars with Vietnam from 1979 to 1987.[43]

The 1979 Sino-Vietnamese War

The PLA's problems became evident during the Sino-Vietnamese War of 1979. Mentally and physically, the Chinese troops were not ready to undertake such a large-scale foreign invasion. Even as the tension mounted between the two countries, many in the rank and file still thought of Vietnam as one of their friends. Despite Chinese–North Vietnamese cooperation in the French Indochina War (1946–54) and Vietnam War (1963–73), there existed a number of serious differences between the two Communist parties. When China pressed Ho Chi Minh to accept the Geneva Accord in 1954 to split the country into a Communist north and non-Communist south, the North Vietnamese thought the control of the whole country was within their reach. Once the war against the Americans was underway, Hanoi rejected China's counsel that North Vietnam conduct Maoist guerrilla warfare rather than conventional warfare. Vietnamese Communist leader Le Duan once bluntly declared that Vietnam's military strategy should be one of offense, not defense, and that Vietnam must make its own decision.[44]

In the early 1960s, the growing rift between China and the Soviet Union put North Vietnam in an awkward position. The Vietnamese had to move carefully between their patrons to avoid offending either of them. The Chinese became less willing to facilitate the transport of Soviet aid across China. A Soviet proposal in 1965 to establish an air corridor over China was abruptly refused by Mao, who considered it a pretext for Soviet intrusion. China did permit a railway corridor for the delivery of Soviet supplies, but the Vietnamese saw this as less advantageous to their national liberation struggle. From 1965 to 1968, China pressured North Vietnam to continue to fight instead of holding peace talks, generating further differences with the Vietnamese. In 1968, North Vietnam entered into negotiations with the United States without consulting China. After Ho's death in 1969, North Vietnam moved closer to the Soviet Union, which further provoked Beijing. Although China continued to provide support to Vietnam, relations worsened. Hanoi considered the marked improvement of relations between China and the United States in 1972 in the wake of Nixon's visit as tantamount to betrayal on China's part. Leaders in Beijing, based on geopolitical considerations, had decided that they could not stand by while Vietnam was engaged in a war that might endanger Chinese security. The Chinese "tightened their belts" to contribute to North Vietnam's survival. Their continuing military, economic, and diplomatic aid was crucial to the victory of the North Vietnamese.[45]

As the American menace receded after 1973, border disputes and differences over Indochina caused a rapid deterioration in the Vietnam-China relationship. In the Chinese view, North Vietnam was an ingrate challenging China under Soviet protection. China lamented the loss of Chinese lives and the expenditure of so many resources for so little in return. For the Vietnamese, the Chinese "northern threat" replaced America as the enemy. The Vietnamese charged that the Chinese intended to keep Vietnam in the war in order to exhaust the United States. On November 15, 1976, Pham Van Dong, Vietnam's premier, asked for more economic assistance from China. On February 24, 1977, Li Xiannian, CCP vice chairman, declined the Vietnamese request when Nguyen Tien, vice foreign minister, visited Beijing. Premier Dong was not happy when Nguyen told him of the Chinese rejection on March 17. References to Chinese aid have disappeared from Vietnamese historical writings, and China is now portrayed as having been an impediment to reunification. One of the Vietnamese party leaders told a Swedish reporter, "Vietnam borders China in the north, which is a powerful country. This neighboring relationship has both positive and negative impact. By any means, the political and cultural pressures from the north must be eliminated."[46] The deteriorating relationship, along with Vietnam's persecution of its ethnic Chinese and its invasion of Cambodia in late 1978, induced China to take military action in 1979.

After the border conflicts began in 1974, tension mounted between the countries. At least 100 border skirmishes occurred in 1974 alone. In 1978, Chinese sources reported 1,100 border incidents, in which about three hundred Chinese troops and civilians were killed or wounded. That same year, the PLA reinforced the border with twenty infantry divisions.[47]

Both international and internal factors played important roles in the changes in China's security concerns. After Mao's death in 1976, the Chinese leadership's worldview changed. Deng intended to stabilize China's relations in southeast Asia and create a "peaceful international environment" in order to focus on reforming the economy and opening up to the Western world. When Vietnam challenged China's goal by sending troops to Cambodia and clashing with the PLA along the Chinese-Vietnamese border, Deng decided to punish Vietnam. This course of action served as a warning to some neighboring countries while pleasing others, like Thailand, which was worried about

Vietnam's aggressive foreign policy. China's invasion of Vietnam in 1979 and several major attacks along the Sino-Vietnamese border in 1981 and 1984 also expressed Beijing's concerns on other issues, such as Vietnam's expelling some two hundred thousand Chinese Vietnamese refugees into China and challenging China's claims on the South China Sea islands.[48]

On December 20, 1977, Vietnam sent 200,000 troops into Cambodia. Joining the international community, Beijing denounced the invasion and asked for an immediate and full withdrawal of Vietnamese troops from Cambodia. On December 25, China closed the border. The next day, the PLA began to deploy 220,000 troops along the Vietnamese border. In the east, along the Guangxi-Guangdong border, about 110,000 troops, including five armies, moved into their positions under the command of General Xu Shiyou. In the west, along the Yunnan border, more than 100,000 men were deployed under the command of General Yang Dezhi. On July 8, 1978, the PAVN Politburo issued the "Outline of the New Tasks of the PAVN," which warned of a possible invasion by "a foreign country" while its troops fought in Cambodia. The Vietnamese military intelligence was accurate. By November 20, Chinese troops from the Guangzhou Regional Command were combat ready. On December 8, the CMC issued an order of deployment and re-formation. On December 13, the CMC ordered the troops to move into the border area. By the end of the month, all the Chinese troops had moved into their positions along the border. On January 8, 1979, the PAVN occupied Phnom Penh, the capital of Cambodia.[49]

China saw a good opportunity for invasion, not only because Vietnam's national defense was weakened but also because an attack could be morally justified. On January 28, Deng Xiaoping paid a state visit to America. He told President Jimmy Carter that Asia "is very unstable." At the meeting with the Senate Foreign Affairs Committee on January 30, a senator asked whether China would attack Vietnam since the Beijing-supported government in Cambodia had been overthrown and the country was in a serious crisis. Deng answered, "We will not allow Vietnam to make so many troubles [in Asia]. In order to protect our country and world peace, we probably have to do something that we don't want to."[50] In early February, on his way back to China, Deng told the Japanese prime minister in Tokyo, "To deal with the Vietnamese, it seems [there will be] no effect by any other means than a necessary lesson." Deng wanted to teach Vietnam "a lesson."[51] Chen Jian points out that "Beijing's leaders used force only when they believed that they were in a position to justify it in a 'moral' sense."[52]

On February 17, 1979, the CMC ordered the attack. Deng set up three principles for the Chinese invasion: limited attack, quick victory, and avoidance of "mission creep." The Chinese operation can be divided into three phases. The first phase, from February 17 to 26, was an attack on all fronts in two major directions. In the east, the Guangxi troops—five armies, more than one hundred thousand men—under the command of General Xu crossed the borders in fourteen places. On February 20, his troops encircled Caobang, which was defended by the PAVN 346th Division. The PLA Fifty-fifth Army took the city on February 25, but the Vietnamese division headquarters had escaped. Xu, upset, yielded to Bian Guixiang, commander of the Fifty-fifth Army. Serious communication problems arose because of poorly manufactured equipment and untrained operators. Xu's attack order to the Sixty-seventh Regiment, for example, somehow changed to a hold-

Infantry troops ride on tanks in Vietnam. (Courtesy of Dr. Shao Aiqin, field doctor for Chinese troops in North Vietnam.)

and-defend order when it passed through the army and division headquarters. The regiment thus never joined the general attack on Lang Son. In the west, the Yunnan troops—five armies, about one hundred thousand men—under the command of General Yang concentrated on the Lao Cai region by crossing the Red River in six different places. By February 20, the Yunnan troops took over Lao Cai with strong artillery support. Then they moved farther south, toward Cam Duong, a major mining city in the north. The Vietnamese troops reinforced Cam Duong. On February 25, the Yunnan troops captured the city and its mines.[53]

The second phase of the Chinese operation, from February 27 to March 5, was a focused attack on Lang Son, one of the major cities in the north and the provincial capital. The city was well connected by railroads, highways, and rivers and defended by a large number of Vietnamese troops. On February 27, the Guangxi troops attacked the city's defenses. Xu concentrated more than three hundred artillery pieces and issued an order that "no house stands in Lang Son."[54] At about 0750 hours, the Chinese bombardment began. Having failed to stop the Chinese attack, the PAVN 308th Division withdrew from Lang Son. By March 2, the Chinese troops occupied the northern part of the city. By March 4, they took over the city and threatened Hanoi, only eighty miles away. The Vietnamese government gathered troops for the defense of its capital. The Chinese invaders, however, did not press on but stopped at Lang Son.[55]

The third phase was the Chinese withdrawal from Vietnam, from March 6 to 16. The CMC ordered all troops to move out of Vietnam on March 5. On their way back, Chinese troops looted North Vietnam, removing industrial machinery, equipment, and government property, and destroying the remainder. Many artillery and tank units fired indiscriminately at Vietnamese towns. Some units that had suffered heavy casualties retaliated by burning villages, bridges, and anything else they could ignite.

Some Chinese soldiers called it a "painful, little war." Vietnamese troops avoided battle and instead harassed PLA forces. Some Chinese officers described it as a "ghost war," since the enemy troops were almost invisible, or a "shadow war," since it seemed they were fighting against their own shadows. The Vietnamese troops employed the same tactics, made the same moves, and used the same weapons as the Chinese. They knew exactly what the Chinese were trying to do. They exploited almost every problem and weakness the Chinese had. The Chinese troops had to fight their own problems first before they could fight the Vietnamese. Deng's border war taught the PLA a hard lesson.[56]

During the first phase of the Chinese operation, Lieutenant Zhi Zhanpeng was a platoon commander of a tank regiment in the Forty-third Army, in the east. His company had ten 59-M battle tanks. At 0500 hours on February 17, when the Chinese artillery pieces began shelling the Vietnamese positions, Zhi and his overwrought crew awaited orders in their tank. "Our radio did not work at all. With a lot of noises, we couldn't hear the captain's order." Zhi complained, "We had to look outside for signals." At about 0530 hours, three red flares rose in the sky to signal the general attack order. Zhi started the engine. Tanks and infantry troops rushed to the border without a formation. Nobody followed the plan. "Our guns kept firing all the way without aiming or stopping," Zhi recalled. "Everyone was so nervous, or should we say excited, that our charge was in a big disorder without cover, infantry-tank cooperation, nor any communication." He saw many soldiers fall. One of their tanks got hit by a Russian-made forty-rocket launcher. The 59-M tanks proved to have many problems, including weak armor protection, poor mobility, and lack of communication. When the Vietnamese destroyed a dam and flooded a country road, the tanks could not drive through the water and mud. Still, by 0715 hours, the tank company occupied the enemy position with two Chinese infantry companies.[57]

The next morning, the tank company advanced along a mountain road to attack a village in conjunction with an infantry company. More than 120 soldiers rode on the tanks, as the Russian troops had in WWII. To avoid falling off, the soldiers tied themselves to the tanks with their backpack belts. "It was such a bad idea," Zhi sighed. On the way to the village, the Chinese column was ambushed twice by Vietnamese fire from the forest. More than 40 infantry soldiers died before they could untie themselves and jump off the tanks. The tanks then shelled the village heavily. Zhi felt good when he saw the houses explode and the village burn to the ground. During the attack, however, the company lost another tank. The Chinese troops killed and wounded 46 Vietnamese soldiers, captured seven machine guns and thirty-one automatic rifles, and destroyed thirty-three houses.[58]

On February 19, the tank company took a break because all the tanks had some damage or technical problems. By noon, the captain was very glad to know that his men had fixed most of the problems. He gave a bottle of *baijiu* (hard liquor, Chinese whiskey) to each tank crew. Some of the men caught a water buffalo outside the village. They killed it and made beef braised with ginger in brown sauce. The men were ecstatic, as they had not had any meat for several days.[59]

Wang Tonggui, the first gunner of the Second Platoon, got drunk and lost control of himself. He began crying, threw away the bottle, and hit his head on a tree again and again. He told the company political instructor, who tried to calm him down, that his fiancée had left him after she learned he was going to war. The instructor tried to convince Wang that he would find a better girl after they won the war. The instructor told the company that twelve men had gotten divorced or lost their girlfriends before their deployment. These women were afraid

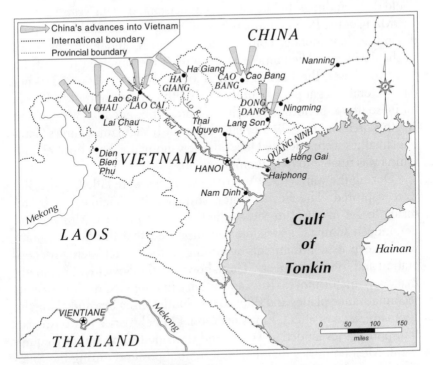

The Sino-Vietnamese War, 1979

of being widowed or living with a disabled veteran for the rest of their lives. "Selfish and near sighted," the instructor said, loud and clear, "they were not the women for Chinese soldiers." Zhi still remembers what the instructor said: "You are the heroes. You are the most beloved men in our country."[60]

After lunch, the company party branch held a meeting to discuss six applicants for party membership, including one who had been killed the day before. The party members voted unanimously to accept all six applications. Then the men wrote their wills and loyalty oaths one more time. By March 18, when the company left Vietnam, they had lost four tanks and seventeen men, and twenty-two others had been wounded. In addition, four men had been disciplined for robbing a store and filling their tanks with jewelry, watches, and other luxury goods.[61] The charges against three of them were dropped because they either turned in the robbed goods or burned them before they returned to China. Colonel Zhi said that he did not quite understand at the time how his comrades could do such things, but he came to understand it many years later.[62]

Many of the PLA's commanding officers were shocked by the poor discipline, low morale, combat ineffectiveness, and high casualties in the 1979 Sino-Vietnamese War. During the nineteen days of the first two phases, the PLA suffered 26,000 casualties, about 1,350 per day.[63] Gerald Segal points out that in Vietnam, "in contrast to Korea, Chinese troops performed poorly. In Korea, they adequately defended North Korea, but in 1979 they failed to punish Vietnam. China's Cambodian allies were relegated to a sideshow along the Thai frontier, and China was unable to help them break out."[64]

During the war, 37,300 Vietnamese troops were killed, and 2,300 were captured. The Soviet Union surprised the Vietnamese by refusing to get involved in the conflict. On February 18, Moscow had denounced China's aggression and promised that the Soviet Union would keep its commitments according to the Soviet-Vietnam cooperation and friendship treaty. Then, however, the Soviet Union did not make any major moves. Russian military intelligence did increase its reconnaissance planes and ships in the South China Sea and along the Vietnamese coast after China's invasion. On February 24, two Russian transport planes landed at Hanoi and unloaded some military equipment. Most countries maintained a neutral position during the Sino-Vietnamese War.[65]

The brief war was a grievous misfortune for both China and Vietnam, not only because it resulted in material and human losses for both nations but also because it brought years of earlier cooperation to a dispiriting conclusion. The war showed that American belief in the domino theory was misplaced, since two Communist countries, one of which had just attained national liberation, were now in conflict with each other. Each valued its own national interests much more than the common Communist ideology. On February 27, 1979, Deng told American journalists in Beijing that "Vietnam claims itself as the third military superpower in the world. We are eliminating this myth. That's all we want, no other purpose. We don't want their territory. We make them to understand that they can't do whatever they want to all the times."[66]

Hanoi believed, however, that the Vietnamese army had taught the Chinese army a lesson. One PAVN general said that China lost militarily and beat a hasty retreat: "After we defeated them we gave them the red carpet to leave Vietnam."[67] As Henry J. Kenny points out, "Most Western writers agree that Vietnam had indeed outperformed the PLA on the battlefield, but say that with the seizure of Lang Son, the PLA was poised to move into the militarily more hospitable terrain of the Red River Delta, and thence to Hanoi." Kenny, however, points out that Lang Son is less than twelve miles from the Chinese border but is twice that distance from the delta. Moreover, at least five PAVN divisions remained poised for a counterattack in the delta, and thirty thousand additional PAVN troops from Cambodia, along with several regiments from Laos, were moving to their support.[68] Thus the PLA would have taken huge losses in any southward move toward Hanoi.

Continued Border Conflicts

The Chinese withdrawal from Vietnam in March 1979 did not end the border conflicts. For the next decade, PAVN units, along with a rearmed and retrained militia, maintained as many as eight hundred thousand troops in northern Vietnam. Across the border, more than two hundred thousand Chinese troops faced them. In May and June 1981, the PLA attacked Vietnam again after many small border conflicts. The Chinese troops occupied and defended several hills.[69]

The largest offensive campaign after 1979 took place in April–May

1984, when the PLA overran PAVN positions in the mountains near Lao Son. The attack began on April 2 when the Chinese artillery heavily shelled the Vietnamese positions in the area. The bombardment continued until April 27. On April 28, the infantry troops from Yunnan Province charged the Vietnamese defensive positions at Lao Son, including hills 395, 423, and 662. The Chinese forces eliminated two Vietnamese companies of the 122nd Regiment, 313th Division and occupied hill 662, the highest position in the Lao Son mountains. Within a few days, the Chinese troops controlled most of the mountain and had eliminated about 2,000 Vietnamese troops. On April 30, the Chinese forces attacked the Vietnamese positions on Yen Son Mountain. By May 15, the Chinese occupied most of the positions on the two mountains and built defensive works against the PAVN counterattacks. During this five-week offensive campaign, 939 Chinese soldiers were killed in action, and 64 Chinese laborers were killed.[70]

Beginning on July 12, the Vietnamese launched counterattacks. The Chinese troops held their positions for three years, until April 1987. They constructed defensive works, launched small-scale attacks, defeated Vietnamese troops, and defended their positions on these two mountains. The Chinese maintained a large force with two armies, usually including two artillery divisions, four infantry divisions, and several tank regiments, in the Lao Son area. Artillery played a major role in the 1984–87 defenses. A typical battle at Lao Son began with a small Vietnamese infantry unit (usually a company) charging the Chinese positions. The Chinese defenders called in their artillery support. After the Vietnamese located the Chinese artillery positions (it took only a couple of minutes), the Vietnamese artillery began counterbattery fire. Then the Chinese artillery targeted the Vietnamese artillery positions. During the artillery exchanges, the Vietnamese withdrew. Finally, the shelling stopped, and the battle was over. The Chinese artillery divisions were equipped with 130mm guns, 152mm howitzers, and forty-barrel rocket launchers. The infantry regiments used 85mm guns and 100-D mortars. Chinese tanks also took part in several battles.[71]

Private Xu Xiangyao joined the PLA in his village in Hebei on March 19, 1984. After a few weeks of intensive training, he was assigned to an infantry company in the Thirteenth Army. That summer, his regiment moved south by train. Inside their boxcar, one of twenty-one, no one talked. "We were so nervous and scared," Xu recalled of

PLA artillery positions against the PAVN in 1984. (Reproduced by permission of the PLA Literature Press, Beijing, China.)

his ride in the number 9 car. After three days on the train, their worries about going to the Sino-Vietnamese border were confirmed when the train stopped at Kunming, the capital of Yunnan Province. About 120 CA-10 trucks picked up thousands of men at the station and took them to the border. Many recruits cried on the road. The next morning, a mass rally replaced the daily drill. "Comrades, you are going to the Lao Son front," a deputy commander of the Thirteenth Army told the newly arrived regiment. "It's time for you to shed blood for your country. The entire country is watching you. Our people depend on you." Before he finished his speech, cries of lamentation rose. Some of the men screamed, "Mom, Dad!" Xu was shocked and did not shed any tears. The commanders obviously were used to these reactions. They walked down from the platform, shaking hands and saying to the men, "Go ahead, cry! You can cry now, but no more crying later in battle." Xu joined the crowd and cried. He asked his friends to tell his parents if he should fall. "I really regretted joining the army at that point," Xu said.[72]

In the afternoon, the men wrote their wills and letters to their parents. Then they replaced all their weapons with brand new AK-56 assault rifles, a Chinese version of the Soviet AKM. Loaded magazines and five grenades not only added a lot of weight to their gear but also built up some confidence. At dinner, when the army commanders toasted the troops with tears, only a few cried. "We thought we had to go to a war and die anyway. Why don't we fight bravely and die with honor?" Xu explained. Willing acceptance of the cruel facts and adaptation to the rapidly changing situation saved Xu and many men in Vietnam. On their way to the border, many peasants, students, and local people organized rallies along the road, cheering, singing, and dancing for the troops. Proud and excited, the men felt they were heroes. Feeling good, they began to talk, laugh, and make jokes on the last part of their journey to Vietnam.[73]

After crossing the border at Hekou, the men became quiet and serious again. Forty trucks had stopped at Hekou, and the rest continued south toward Lao Son. When the eighty trucks finally stopped, it was 0400 hours. Xu became nervous and scared again because he knew they were close to the front. At about 0600 hours, the regiment had a general assembly, including infantry battalions, tank companies, medical teams, engineering corps, and reconnaissance units. After Colonel Zhao, the regiment commander, gave a brief talk, the regiment added three hundred rounds to each soldier's AK-56 rifle. Then all the men received a little metal box that looked like a candy tin with a ring. Colonel Zhao told his men that it was their "guangrong dan" (personal glory bomb). "Keep it in your left pocket," the commander said. "If you are wounded, disabled, or about to be captured by the Vietnamese, you can use it. Just pull the ring; it will explode for an immediate, heroic death. You will be remembered as a revolutionary martyr." None of the men said anything, since they knew they would commit suicide rather than surrender in shame. The glory bomb brought back the fears of danger and death, but the haughty tank men seemed to be having fun with it, joking and laughing as if this suicide device were just for the infantry.[74]

In the rotation, the Thirteenth Army replaced the Fourteenth Army at Lao Son. Xu's regiment was deployed along the second defense line, which was pretty quiet that summer. The weather and boredom became his worst enemies. For the soldiers from north China, Vietnam's weather was too hot and wet in the summer and too hot and dry in the fall. "There were only two kinds of people with their clothes on: females and officers," Xu recalled, laughing. The soldiers also endured intense boredom. Combat occupied a minority of their time. The exhausting yet mind-numbing tasks of digging foxholes (or *maoerdong*, a hole shaped like a cat's ear) and cleaning weapons took up most of their time. By October, when the regiment was rotated out, combat and disease had taken their toll: it had lost one-third of its men, 150 dead and 500 wounded. After returning to China, Xu was promoted to staff sergeant. Among the problems Xu recalled were inferior weapons and aging commanding officers who still used the tactics of the human wave and guerrilla warfare from their Korean War experience.[75]

In April 1987, the CMC reduced the scale of the PLA's operations in Vietnam, though the Chinese maintained routine patrols at Lao Son and Yen Son. From April 1987 to October 1989, there were only eleven attacks, most of them simply artillery bombardments. To give more troops combat experience, the CMC began to rotate troops into the Lao Son and Yen Son areas. Many PLA units, including infantry, artillery, antiaircraft, and reconnaissance troops, moved into Vietnam from Guangxi and Yunnan provinces. Deng once said of this policy, "Let all of our field armies touch the tiger's butt."[76] By the end of the 1980s, China and Vietnam had normalized their diplomatic relationship. In 1992, all Chinese troops withdrew from the Lao Son and Yen Son areas and returned to China. In 1993, to develop trade between the two countries, the PLA troops in Guangxi and Yunnan began large-scale mine-clearing operations along the Chinese-Vietnamese border.

The high command had certainly learned lessons from the 1980s border conflicts. It moved away from the people's war theory by introducing new strategies and tactics and emphasizing officer training. The PLA stopped its traditional method of selecting officers from the enlisted ranks. Instead, it recruited high school graduates to attend military academies. The Infantry Academy of Shijiazhuang, for example, had a record high annual graduation of ten thousand officers in the early 1980s. Despite improvements in technology and officer training, PLA morale remained low in the 1980s because of many "material problems": "weapons stockpiles were deteriorating; . . . military property and facilities were inadequately protected; and military installations had been vandalized."[77] The Chinese military suffered more damage and casualties at the end of the decade, when the country faced a serious political crisis and the party ordered PLA troops to open fire on students in Tiananmen Square in Beijing.

The 1989 Tiananmen Square Crackdown

Deng's reform movement brought tremendous changes to China, a second revolution comparable to Mao's 1949 revolution. For the first time, the country began to establish a market economy and participate in the international community. Mao had led China's military and political rise; now Deng put China on track for economic growth. Described in the West as a "mountain mover," Deng was one of very few world leaders to be twice named *Time* magazine's Man of the Year (in 1978 and 1985). Jing Luo, however, points out that "without Mao's systematic failure, there would not have been Deng's systematic reform. In reality, Deng's reform may be understood as following Mao's blueprint in the opposite direction."[78] In 1987, Deng refused to become chairman of the CCP, premier of the State Council, or president of the PRC. Along with conservative senior party members, he resigned from the Central Committee to ensure continuity of his reform policies. Though officially retired, Deng remained at the center of China's reforms in the late 1980s and early 1990s, when the third generation of Chinese leaders came to power.[79]

The economic and military reforms in the 1980s were, in Deng's words, comparable to "crossing the river by feeling the stones." Unfortunately, the economic growth did not contribute significantly to China's democratic transformation or to its social stability. Arguably, the economic development and modernization led instead to political instability.[80] The magnitude of China's social transformation carried within itself seeds of social instability. During the 1980s, new problems emerged. Official corruption, abuses of power, and theft of public property were rampant in spite of the government's efforts to control them. The reforms accentuated the sharp disparities that existed between rich and poor. In addition, the relatively slow pace of economic change for farmers and millions of layoffs in urban areas made the traditional pillar classes feel deprived by the change. Deng's reform strategy contrasted starkly with Mikhail Gorbachev's strategy for the Soviet Union; Deng focused on liberal economic reform while discouraging and even stifling political reform.[81] To ensure stability, Deng insisted on the Four Cardinal Principles: keeping to the socialist road, upholding the people's democratic dictatorship, sticking to the CCP's leadership, and adhering to Marxism-Leninism and Mao Zedong Thought. Deng believed that, although China must keep its door open to the world, stability must be stressed; to guarantee stability, the party must be in control.[82]

Increasing political dissatisfaction, highlighted by antigovernment minority revolts, pro-democracy student activities, and widespread complaints of corruption among party and government officials, threatened stability.[83] Unable to solve some of the economic and social problems and unwilling to carry the reform into the political arena, Deng and other Chinese leaders found themselves challenged by pro-democracy demonstrations during the spring of 1989.

After Hu Yaobang, the former CCP secretary general, died on April 15, 1989, student mourning activities on Beijing campuses soon became a citywide and then a nationwide pro-democracy demonstration asking for political reforms across the country and protesting against corruption and power abuse. Deng denounced the movement later that month.[84] The negative attitude and harsh judgment of the government caused more dissatisfaction, not only among students but among other citizens as well. In May, hundreds of thousands of students and citizens joined and continued their demonstrations at Tiananmen Square (Beijing's Washington Mall), which had become a traditional site for popular protests since the May 4 movement in 1919. The demonstrations spread to 116 cities across the country. On May 6–16, the Beijing students encamped at Tiananmen Square and began a hunger strike to show their determination to promote democracy and to root out corruption.[85]

On the afternoon of May 19, the CCP established martial law in Beijing and ordered a large number of PLA troops to move into the city. Most generals did not know much about the student demonstrations, and the announcement came as a total surprise. Some of them felt "varying degrees of sympathy for the students," and some thought "the measure might be too drastic, and besides their views had not been solicited."[86] On May 20, a group of generals signed a letter addressed to Deng Xiaoping and the CMC: "We request that troops not enter the city and that martial law not be carried out in Beijing."[87] Among the signers were Generals Ye Fei, Zhang Aiping, Xiao Ke, Yang Dezhi,

Chen Zaidao, Song Shilun, and Li Jukui. Deng sent top military leaders to visit these generals, and Yang Shangkun, the PRC president, made some phone calls. Thereafter, Zhang Liang says, "the mini-revolt was pacified."[88]

In the meantime, under the Martial Law Force Command, troops from twenty-two divisions of thirteen PLA armies moved toward Beijing: the Fifteenth, Twentieth, Twenty-fourth, Twenty-sixth, Twenty-seventh, Twenty-eighth, Thirty-eighth, Thirty-ninth, Fortieth, Fifty-fourth, Sixty-third, Sixty-fifth, and Sixty-seventh armies. The deployment reflected the uncertainty and anxiety of the party elders about each army's loyalty and connection to the party center, which had been divided. Many troops were stopped in the suburbs or blocked in city streets by the crowds and failed to reach their destinations.[89]

Thus martial law was not effective at all. The students remained at Tiananmen Square, and the demonstration on May 23 was the largest since the declaration of martial law. On May 24, at Deng's behest, the CMC held an expanded meeting, attended by all the top military commanders and political commissars, to make sure that the top officers were unified in their support of the party center. Yang Shangkun explained Deng's views on the political crisis and ordered the senior commanders to unify their units' understanding of the party's position. After the meeting, all three general departments, all service arms, and the military regional commands publicly expressed their support for the party center. They expressed "total loyalty and submission to the authority of the CMC under the leadership of Deng Xiaoping and Yang Shangkun."[90]

By the end of May, the party prepared for a final crackdown. On June 2, party elders Deng Xiaoping, Li Xiannian, Peng Zhen, Yang Shangkun, Bo Yibo, and Wang Zhen met with the Standing Committee of the Politburo. They decided to "put a quick end to the turmoil and restore order in the capital." That meant to clear Tiananmen Square. After initial clashes between the troops and citizens in Beijing, the leaders called an emergency meeting on June 3 and further decided that they confronted a "counterrevolutionary riot" that would have to be put down by force. Deng did not attend the meeting, but he agreed that PLA soldiers should open fire on the protesting students.[91]

The emergency meeting issued orders to the PLA Martial Law Force Command at 2100 hours on June 3 to put down the counter-

Yang Shangkun, Yu Qiuli, Yang Dezhi, Zhang Aiping, and Hong Xuezhi at an expanded CMC meeting. (Reproduced by permission of Contemporary China Press, Beijing, China.)

revolutionary riot in Beijing. The troops were to arrive at Tiananmen Square by 0100 hours on June 4 and clear the square by 0600 hours.[92] Late on the evening of June 3, the troops forced their way through the streets, followed by tanks and armored vehicles. They clashed with some of the citizens and students who tried to stop the troops from entering central Beijing. At least two hundred civilians were killed, and the troops also suffered some casualties.[93] The next morning, the troops ended both the protest and the occupation of Tiananmen Square.

Some soldiers, however, had refused to fire upon the unarmed students and civilians. Some dropped their weapons and deserted. Some high-ranking military officials followed their orders only reluctantly, if at all. General Xu Qinxian, for example, feigned illness to avoid commanding his troops against the demonstrators in Beijing.[94]

The Tiananmen Square incident was a major setback to China's reform movement. Viewed from this perspective, the political crisis in 1989 can be understood as a conflict between the inherent totalitarian tendency of a one-party state and the need to recognize the indispensable roles played by various functional groups in achieving economic growth and modernizing society.

Throughout the rest of 1989, no one in the military could voice any disagreement with the party. According to PLA documents, as many as 3,500 PLA commanders were investigated after the Tiananmen Square incident. Many of them were newly promoted officers, products of the 1980s reforms. The party believed its investigations and punishments necessary because 111 PLA officers had "breached discipline in a serious way," and 1,400 soldiers "shed their weapons and ran away."[95] The majority were reprimanded or charged thereafter. High-level military officials who lost their positions in the aftermath included Generals Hong Xuezhi, deputy secretary-general of the CMC; Guo Linxiang, deputy director of the General Political Department; Li Desheng, political commissar of the NDU; Li Yaowen, political commissar of the PLAN; Zhou Yibing, commander of the Beijing Military Region; Xiang Shouzhi, commander of the Nanjing Military Region; Wan Haifeng, political commissar of the Chengdu Military Region; Li Lianxiu, commander of the People's Armed Police; and Zhang Xiufu, political commissar of the People's Armed Police. The most important of these was General Xu Qinxian, who was court-martialed and imprisoned. From 1989 to 1993, the penetration of politics into the military broke through all nonparty barriers. Political restraints and suppression significantly slowed down the military reforms.

After the Tiananmen Square incident, Western countries joined an all-out demonstration against Beijing's military suppression of the student-led movement. Most Americans supported the George H. W. Bush administration's policies, which suspended official bilateral exchanges with Beijing and participated in economic sanctions imposed on China by other Western industrial countries. Deng, however, continued his economic reform, with a new theory of "building socialism with Chinese characteristics."[96] Health problems, however, soon reduced his political role; by the mid-1990s, Parkinson's disease, lung ailments, and other problems had made him almost blind and deaf. Deng died in Beijing on February 28, 1997.[97]

One scholar points out that "if Mao Zedong is remembered as the founder of the People's Republic of China, as well as the source of wave after wave of nerve-wracking political campaigns, Deng Xiaoping is remembered for deprogramming Mao's system and for leading

China onto the road of economic prosperity."[98] Deng proved that a market economy and new technology worked in China and that Chinese people needed materially better lives. His reform, however, succeeded only with the high costs of loss of political control by the party, decentralization of the government, increased societal stratification and inequality, and decreased status of the military. The PLA believed that it had sacrificed for Deng's reform more than it had gained from it in 1978–95. With loyalty and patience, the military had waited for its turn to come, as Deng promised. After Deng Xiaoping, they expected a big payback from the new leader in Beijing, Jiang Zemin, the third generation of Chinese Communist leadership.

★ 9 ★

Technocrats and the New Generation

THE PLA EXPERIENCED a remarkable change in the last decades of the twentieth century. It transformed from a peasant army to a professional army under its new commander in chief, Jiang Zemin. After the Tiananmen Square incident in 1989, Jiang became the chairman of both the CCP and CMC. In the 1990s, Jiang, as part of the third generation of military leaders, launched another round of military reforms known as the Two Transformations. First, the PLA would be changed from an army prepared for "local wars under ordinary conditions" to an army prepared to fight and win "local wars under modern high-tech conditions." Second, the PLA would change from an army based on quantity to an army based on quality.[1] This comprehensive reform and modernization effort cut across every facet of PLA activity. China military experts point out that the 1990s reform affected "such areas as doctrine, operational concepts, and warfighting techniques; the acquisition of modern weapon systems and integration of new technologies; as well as reforms to the weapons research, development, and acquisition processes."[2] Jiang's doctrine of fighting local wars under modern, high-tech conditions became the new guideline for the PLA's institutional reform under the third-generation high command.[3]

This chapter examines how the PLA restructured its relationship to a changing society and reacted to social issues such as privatization of state-owned enterprises, social stratification, health and retirement problems, and family-planning policy. Obviously, the military did not want to be victimized again by reform and social transition. It intended to participate in policymaking, and it demanded larger budgets for new technology by putting pressure on Jiang Zemin. To win military support for his new leadership, Jiang campaigned for a bigger defense budget. As a result, the PLA enjoyed a double-digit increase in annual military spending from 1990 to 1995. The PLA also increased its representation in the Politburo from none at the Fourteenth CCP National Congress in 1995 to two of eleven members at the Fifteenth CCP National Congress in 1997. The rise of the PLA led to the use of force in the Taiwan Strait during the 1995–96 missile crisis.

Taking Over and Reshaping the PLA

The 1989 Tiananmen Square crisis convinced both reformers and conservatives that neither could win without national disaster. Unwilling to have a final showdown, they agreed to a continuation of reform as long as it proceeded more slowly. Both sides approved Deng's choice of successor, Jiang Zemin, former mayor of Shanghai, who supported reforms but also stressed the Four Cardinal Principles. When each side balanced its political position and blamed the other for the 1989 crisis, however, the PLA was caught in the middle and made to shoulder the blame for killing civilians at Tiananmen Square. Some high-ranking officers believed that they were the victims of Deng's reforms. First, during the 1980s, the military budget had shrunk. Second, with industrialization and the transition to a market economy, recruitment had become a problem and morale was low. Third, low salaries and poor benefits for PLA officers led many to leave the service for more lucrative opportunities. In 1988, for example, a PLA officer earned only about half the salary of an average urban worker.[4] Worst of all, the party had employed the army to deal with the social and political crisis and to bring order to the state, as it had during the Cultural Revolution in the 1960s.[5]

The PLA saw new hope when Jiang came to power in 1989. Jiang had no prior experience in high command or military service, but he became a very popular commander in chief. The rank and file liked

Jiang, even when he suffered setbacks. Educated and pragmatic, Jiang provided moderate leadership. He shared power with the military and others through a bureaucratic institution of collective leadership.[6] He developed his own theory for the party, military, and state—the Three Represents. Addressing the local cadres during his visit to Guangdong on February 25, 2000, he stated that the CCP should represent "the development of China's advanced productive forces, the orientation of the development of China's advanced culture, and the fundamental interests of the broadest masses of the Chinese people."[7] The Three Represents thereafter became the most important requirements for officials and officers during Jiang's era, 1990–2004.

Jiang, a technocratic leader, was born on August 17, 1926, in Yang-zhou, Jiangsu.[8] He earned an electrical engineering degree at Shanghai Jiaotong University. During his college years, Jiang participated in CCP-led student movements and, in 1946, joined the CCP. After the founding of the PRC, he served as an associate engineer and deputy director of a factory. In 1955, he went to the Soviet Union and worked for a year as a trainee at the Stalin Automobile Works. After returning

Jiang Zemin, the third generation. (Courtesy of Xinhua News Agency, Beijing, China.)

home, he served as a deputy division head, deputy chief power engineer, director of a branch factory, and deputy director and director of factories and research institutes in Changchun, Shanghai, and Wuhan. Speaking some English, Russian, and Romanian, he served as deputy director and then director of the foreign affairs department of the First Ministry of Machine-Building Industry. Jiang Zemin's uncle Jiang Shufeng said that as a student of Leninism and Maoism, Jiang Zemin emphasized the employment of theories and dialectic in a practical way, using them for solving problems rather than defending principles.[9]

After Deng launched the reform movement of 1978, Jiang became the first planner of Shenzhen, China's first special economic zone. His successful experience won him election as a member of the Twelfth CCP Central Committee in 1982 and mayor of Shanghai, China's largest city, in 1985. Jiang planned a series of key infrastructure projects using overseas capital. The city raised $3.2 billion from the international market, of which $1.4 billion was poured into such key projects as the city's subway, bridges, airport, and telephone service. In 1987, Jiang became a member of the Politburo at the first plenary session of the Thirteenth CCP Central Committee. In June 1989, at the fourth plenary session, Jiang was elected a member of the Standing Committee of the Politburo and general secretary of the CCP Central Committee. In November, at the fifth plenary session, he became chairman of the CMC.[10]

As the PLA's first civilian commander in chief, Jiang developed an institutionalized authority that enabled him to assume the top post as CCP and CMC chairman and PRC president. "These formal titles, however, were not necessarily sufficient for Jiang to command the PLA," Bin Yu argues. Thus as CMC chairman, Jiang made a concerted effort to befriend the PLA, leading to the military's eventual acceptance of his leadership.[11] In the early 1990s, Jiang granted the PLA high-level autonomy so that PLA interests would be well looked after. Throughout the decade, Jiang campaigned vigorously for enlarging the military. You Ji points out that "although the military is never satisfied with the amount of money it receives each year, the double-digit growth of the military budget does distinguish the period of Jiang's leadership in the 1990s from that of Deng in the 1980s." The PLA was able to act as a fairly autonomous "interest group" for the first time in its history. You Ji argues, "The rise of cohesive corporate spirit and professionalism nurtures China's new brand of technocrat/officers who are forward looking, ready to learn Western military science and technology, and increasingly indifferent to the party's factional politics, though not immune from the nationalist drive."[12] Several traditional beliefs guided the policies of the third generation of leadership. First, Jiang's administration believed in a "rich country and a strong military" as the ultimate goals of its economic and military reforms. Second, Jiang believed it important to establish social stability through the reforms. This would be achieved by his "soft landing" and other gradual, moderate policies. Third, to protect China's stability, military buildup was necessary to deter any external threat and push the Western powers into negotiating on terms favorable to China. Fourth, successful negotiations would bring in foreign investment and the world market. Fifth, drawing lessons from the Tiananmen Square incident, Jiang emphasized raising the people's standard of living.[13]

At the Eighth National People's Congress in March 1993, Jiang was elected president of the PRC. By 1997, Jiang had established an unprecedented institutionalized authority that enabled him to preside over a vast central bureaucracy encompassing the party, state, and military. He traveled widely and visited military units, even those in remote areas, during holidays. Yu explains that Jiang "managed to gain support and loyalty from almost all sectors of the PLA: [from] younger officers for his policy of nurturing a highly educated, well-trained, and professionalized officer core; from the rank-and-file for improving living conditions; from older generals for being promoted to retirement or semi-retirement."[14]

Having built up his credibility in the PLA, Jiang reshaped the Chinese military throughout the 1990s. In July 1991, he set forth the Five Phrases as new principles to guide further military reform: "good political attitude, well-trained combat skills, excellent character, strict discipline, and guaranteed logistics support."[15] From 1991 to 1995, the high command retrained all the commanders and officers at the regimental level and above with Jiang's principles. At an expanded meeting of the CMC in 1994, Jiang added the Four Educations to the officer training programs. In October of that year, Jiang signed "Zhongyang junwei guanyu budui jiaoyu yu guanli de jueding" (CMC Decisions on PLA Control and Education). In December 1995, "Zhongguo renmin jiefangjun junshi xunlian dagang" (PLA Combat Training Guideline) was issued, emphasizing technology training for all the services. In November 1996, Jiang called for the Two Transformations of the PLA. In December 1997, the CMC established a three-step grand plan for the PLA's modernization from 1998 to 2040.[16]

In April 1992, Jiang streamlined and restructured the PLA to consolidate it following the 1-million-man reduction that had occurred since 1985, from 4.24 million to 3.19 million men. In 1997, at the Fifteenth CCP National Congress, Jiang announced his plan to reduce the PLA by another 500,000 men over three years.[17] On July 28, 1998, the PLA stated that it had accomplished its reduction goal and that it would maintain the current 2.5 million troops.[18] By that spring, the PLA had created a unified General Armaments Department alongside the GSD, GPD, and GLD in a major overhaul of its command and control, logistics, and armament mechanisms. In the spring of 1999, the CMC concentrated resources on developing six key strategic heavy group armies as the "pockets of excellence."[19] They completed their reorganization in 2001. By the end of the 1990s, the PLA's institutional reform had made some major changes in the personnel system, organization, and sustainability system. The personnel reforms were the cornerstone of the PLA's transformations from an army based on quantity to one based on quality and from a peasant army to a professional one with more urban and educated recruits.[20]

Impact of Urbanization and Globalization

Jiang's reform privatized state-owned enterprises, decentralized state control, solicited foreign investment, and applied Western technology. From 1991 to 1997, China's gross domestic product rose an average 11 percent each year. After 1992, state-owned enterprises were given greater autonomy to cope with markets at home and abroad and to issue stocks that could be bought and sold on the stock exchanges that had been set up in Shenzhen and Shanghai. In the early 1990s, most foreign investment had come from overseas Chinese via Hong Kong and Taiwan, but by late in the decade, multinational groups, including corporations based in Japan and the United States, began to surpass the earlier investors. Foreign investment was a central component of Jiang's policy. In the 1990s, China was second only to the United States in direct foreign investment received. In 2002, China became the top recipient in the world. In the first years of the new century, while countries around the world entered hard economic times, China still prospered. In 2000 and 2001, the gross domestic product rose 8 percent and 7.3 percent.[21]

Foreign investment accelerated rural industrialization by establishing various industries in the countryside that absorbed a large proportion of the low-wage rural labor force. This industrialization generated a substantial portion of the capital needed for construction of urban projects and stimulated local policymakers to devote great efforts to planning and building modern cities. Foreign investors also directly contributed to the building of new urban centers by getting involved in the development of the real estate sector and urban infrastructure. China experienced rapid urbanization in the 1990s: the rural landscape (characterized by farmland and scattered villages) changed into an urban one (characterized by factory compounds and commercial, financial, and technological facilities). The number of Chinese cities increased from 223 in 1981 to 663 by the end of 2000.[22]

Many of China's rural residents have shifted from agricultural production to nonagricultural economic activities, thereby acquiring an urban way of life, including access to modern utilities. In the 1960s, 84.2 percent of China's total workforce was in agriculture. In 1978, this composition was 67.4 percent; it dropped to 55.8 percent in 1988, 44 percent in 1999, and an estimated 40.3 percent in 2004.[23] In the 1990s, the PLA had great difficulty recruiting soldiers, even from poor and remote rural areas, where there had been a tradition for young farmers to escape their unproductive collective farming. Land redistribution campaigns, however, had given many peasants their own land, and they were now less willing to leave their farms. Newly privatized local businesses also competed with the army for manpower. To deal with the changing society, in December 1998, the Chinese government revised its Military Service Law. The previous statute required Chinese citizens to serve three years in the army or four years in the navy or air force. The new law reduced the service time to two years for all military branches.[24]

Generally speaking, the PLA viewed China's economic reforms as favorable and necessary for military reform. In remarks made on April 16, 2003, General Xiong Guangkai brought to the attention of the rank and file that "we will, on the premise of making economic development our central task, appropriately increase the input in national defense and army building along with the incremental growth of the aggregate national strength; thus providing a solid material basis for modernizing national defense and the armed forces depends on development." He used a popular Chinese saying: "Caida qicu" (He who has wealth speaks louder than others).[25] Elsewhere, Xiong described economic globalization as a "double-edged sword." The general explained that globalization "plays a positive role in promoting world economic development. However, one must not underestimate its negative impact as it may pose more challenges to under-developed countries." He criticized those who put undue emphasis on the positive effects of economic globalization, thinking that countries that participate in globalization can take a free ride and automatically reap benefits from the free flow of essential factors of production. Xiong used the Asian financial crisis to prove that "hidden perils harmful to economic security may arise from the blind opening-up to foreign countries, the blind pursuit of globalization, and unguarded absorption of foreign capital."[26]

China's decision to participate in the global market has had a demonstrably powerful effect on domestic administrative structures, economic institutions, and legal norms. For example, once the decision to open up was made, administrative decentralization, enterprise reform, and the creation of a legal framework to protect commercial transactions and property rights were needed to enhance China's competitiveness in the world market. The realization that rapid economic development and technological modernization would require large infusions of foreign capital similarly meant that the new leadership in Beijing had to pay greater attention to foreign concerns, in particular to ways of improving the local investment climate. Under such conditions, they had little choice but to liberalize prevailing commercial norms and practices.

The rapid expansion of free enterprise demanded more free labor. As a result, a free labor market opened up to both urban and rural laborers in the 1980s. In the 1990s, as many as seventy million rural laborers migrated to the cities and coastal areas seeking work. In Beijing, Shanghai, Guangzhou, and Tianjin, between one and two million transients camped in railway stations and other public places. Some official estimates suggested that more than one hundred million peasants had left the countryside by 2000, leaving behind at least an equal number of peasants underemployed in their home communities, which provided few stable job opportunities.[27] Since many peasants who moved into urban areas could not find jobs, they become part of a mobile or "floating" population. Tianjin, for example, had a large floating population, about one million. The national floating population was estimated at twenty-seven million.[28] Mostly peasants, they travel from place to place, following economic opportunities. Neither city nor rural governments have any control over this large population.[29]

China's new social mobility presented a new challenge to the military. Between 1949 and 1985, Chinese society was fragmented into three major groups: farmers, workers, and soldiers. Disparities in political prestige, income, and education were obvious and unchangeable. Military service was a major channel for farmers and workers to take up other professions, move to new locations, or make their way into the elite group. The PLA enjoyed its popularity, and its recruiting officers always had more volunteers than they needed. In the late 1980s, the social changes diminished the rigid boundaries between the social groups. The loosening of government control over people's mobility opened occupations to farmers that had originally been available only to urban residents.[30] By the 1990s, the rapid changes in the traditional social strata were largely perceived as contributing to the healthy growth of the society. They increased opportunities for the general public and helped make available social mechanisms of choice and award that did not exist in the past.

At the end of the 1980s, the military changed its recruitment quotas, a set of figures determined by population demographics, by increasing urban conscripts to 26.5 percent and reducing rural conscripts to 73.5 percent of total new recruits. As we have seen, the size of the PLA was reduced, to 2.5 million troops in 1998. This downsizing facilitated a natural reduction in bureaucracy and enabled the PLA to more quickly reequip its troops. In 2002, the PLA changed recruiting quotas again. Urban conscript requirements increased to 33.2 percent while rural requirements fell to 66.8 percent.[31]

Demographic Changes and New Social Structures

Some strategists worried about the ongoing privatization that was a result of the economic reform and globalization. From 1982 to 2004, the Chinese constitution was revised five times to legalize the status of the private sector in China's socialist state economy. In 1982, the constitution recognized "self-employment" as a "supplement" to the state economy. In 1988, revisions were made to allow the "existence and growth of private economy." The new constitution recognized "private economy" as "a complement to the socialist state economy." It established that "the State protects the lawful rights and interests of the private sector of the economy, and exercises guidance, supervision and control over the private sector of the economy."[32] Further revisions in 1993 included allowing a household responsibility system to replace people's communes and allowing private management of state enterprises. Its revised article 8 reads, "In rural areas the responsibility system, the main form of which is a household contract that links remuneration to output, and other forms of cooperative economy . . . belong to the sector of socialist economy under collective ownership by the working people."[33] The legal status of the private economy was established and clearly noted in the 1999 constitution: "Non-state economy, self-employment, private economy etc. are an important component in the socialist market economy."[34] In 2004, article 13 of the constitution was amended to read, "The State protects the rights of citizens to own lawfully earned income, savings, houses and other lawful property" and "The State, in accordance with the law, protects the rights of citizens to private property and to its inheritance."[35] For the first time, the socialist state economy was redefined as a socialist market economy. As the centralized state economy declined, the state lost its central gravity in terms of manpower and resources. There is now competition over resources between the market zone (*shichang*) and the war zone (*zhanchang*), and between peacetime construction and wartime readiness.[36]

Rural areas typically are less well off than urban areas. In 2001, the per capita annual net income of rural households was 2,366 yuan (less than $300), whereas the per capita annual net income of urban households was 6,659 yuan ($850). The distribution is even more uneven for ethnic minorities.[37] In Guizhou, a relatively low-income province, twenty-one of the thirty-one poverty-stricken counties (*pinkun xian*) are in minority regions, accounting for half of the total minority population in the province. Partly because of this inequality, agricultural laborers are also the most mobile. They make constant efforts to squeeze into other social strata. As many as 24 million workers are estimated to have been laid off by cash-starved and unprofitable state-owned enterprises in the past decade. An estimated 30 million or more workers in state-run firms are surplus workers, and there are 100 million to 150 million surplus workers in China's agriculture. Industrial cities in northeast and central China are already seriously affected by frequent worker demonstrations.[38] The current unemployment rate in China is between 18 and 23 percent.[39]

In the 1990s, Chinese society restructured itself in response to the rapid economic reforms. Government policies and a market-oriented economy were the two major forces that brought about the new structure. Among the new groups is a booming, but not yet fully developed, middle class, including managers, specialists, professional technicians, private enterprise owners, and administrators. Their composition of China's workforce increased from 8.2 percent in 1978 to 20 percent in 1988 and to 30.3 percent in 1999.[40] Of those in this new middle class, private enterprise owners are gaining wealth most quickly. Relatively small in number, the "social middles" are not yet forceful enough to compromise and stabilize the new socioeconomic structure.

Major demographic changes also took place in the 1990s. First, the country completed its demographic transition from high birth and death rates to low birth and death rates with an interstitial spurt in population growth.[41] Since the implementation of the one-child family planning policy, the average fertility rate has dropped from 6 children per family in the 1970s to 2 per family in 2000 and to about 1.44 per family in 2002.[42] This decrease is largely attributable to the compulsory use of long-term birth control and the wide availability of abortion. Violators of the family planning policy pay a heavy fine of about 3,000 yuan (about $375), equivalent to the average annual income in rural areas, and lose all benefits.[43] The transition from a high to a low fertility rate did not come alone but was intertwined with a group of other demographic shifts, including other fertility, family-household, and age transitions. The family-household transition can be described as one from "family building by fate" to "family building by design."[44]

Although China's divorce rate is lower than most Western countries', the incidence of divorce in China seems to be increasing. In 1985, the divorce rate was 0.9 per thousand. Ten years later, it had doubled.[45] Another indication of family-household structural change is the age at first marriage, which has been increasing steadily for men. In rural areas, it went up from eighteen in the 1950s to twenty-one in the 1980s and to twenty-two in the 1990s. In urban areas, it went up from nineteen in the 1950s to twenty-two in the 1980s and to twenty-five in the 1990s.[46] Because of the late marriage trend and the female-male imbalance, most of the one million military conscripts are neither married nor engaged. Lieutenant General Qin Chaoying said that many conscripts did not have girlfriends at home during their service. Afraid of becoming "unmarriageable males," many of them wanted to leave the service after their second conscript year.[47] Qin's latter observation is confirmed by a Hebei Military District study. The district command sent out a survey to conscripts in three of its regiments looking for potential volunteers and noncommissioned officers. About 32 percent of the conscripts responded that they would take early retirement, before the completion of their service, if such an offer were available.[48] Only 19 percent of respondents thought about continuing in the service after their second year and changing their status from conscript to volunteer. Qin believed that the volunteer rates were even lower among the troops in the cities and developed coastal areas than among the Hebei troops stationed in the rural areas between Cangzhou and Langfang.[49]

The symptoms of an "only-child" society had appeared by the 1990s and were affecting the PLA by the end of the decade. According to defense analyst Zhang Zhaozhong, the PLA has many soldiers who grew up without siblings.[50] In the early 1990s, the only-child soldiers began to serve in the PLA. Their numbers have increased ever since. They made up 20.6 percent of the Chinese forces by 1996, 31.2 percent by 1997, and 42.5 percent by 1998.[51] A frequently asked question is whether these soldiers' combat training and fighting ability are in any way affected by their only-child status. A study done by the political department of a group army in Shenyang Military Region yielded mixed results. It found little significant difference between only-child soldiers and soldiers with siblings, especially those from rural areas, in their personality, training records, and service achievement. In technological training, only-child soldiers seemed to outperform soldiers with siblings in verbal tests, communication, and computer skills. The study attributes these findings to two factors. First, as only children became the norm in the late 1990s, social attitudes toward them may have changed, and so these young men may have been less spoiled than those who grew up in the 1980s, the beginning stage of the one-child policy. Second, in the "furnace of revolution" and in a "teamwork atmosphere," the army may have reduced parental influences and any feelings of self-importance through political works and education provided by division, regiment, and battalion, and through group-oriented experiences in their company, platoon, and squad. The study did identify some problems in the "only-child army." Some of the only-child soldiers were less cooperative with peers and more egocentric than soldiers with siblings. In some units, their performance in personal drills and detachment training was good, but their performance in tactics coordination training was poor. Some were reluctant to participate in high-risk training because they were afraid of injury.[52]

The Hebei Military District survey provided a mixed report on only-child officers as well. In general, it found that the only-child officers were better educated, with at least a high school diploma, and had broad knowledge. Believing in competition and self-improvement, they were eager to learn and open to new ideas. Many of them were interested in technological improvement and military reforms. The survey also found that some of the only-child officers were liberal and democratic, emphasizing individual competition and equal opportunity. Some disliked political control and described the party system as "controlling," "demanding," or "oversimplified and crude." They projected a new and contrasting spirit. Nevertheless, their retention level has been lower than that of officers with siblings in recent years.[53]

The low retention rate of only-child officers may be partially the result of the aging of the Chinese population and the new four-two-one family-household structure (four grandparents, two parents, and one child). The task of supporting aging parents and even grandparents falls directly on the shoulders of only children.[54] In today's China, children, spouses, and kinship ties are still seen as primary sources of economic support for the elderly. The urban elderly are, however, less financially dependent on their adult children than are those in rural areas.[55] Although the Hebei Military District survey does not explain why the only-child officers have a low retention rate, it is reasonable to assume that the lack of a social welfare and retirement system pressures only-child officers to retire early and accept a better-paying job outside the military in order to support their parents and grandparents now and themselves later.[56]

The aging population has become a real pressure in the new century. The government is therefore starting to reform the strict one-child policy. In large cities, like Shanghai, the experimental policy allows one-child couples to have another child. Some cities allow couples to have two children as long as the births are at least five years apart. In rural areas, some villages have abolished birth permits (a quota system) and allow couples to decide on their own when to have a baby. The government also encourages local officials to initiate and fund their own pilot projects on family planning, expecting to achieve both population reduction and stability. The first Family Planning Law, adopted in September 2002, allows provinces and municipalities to set up local regulations. Couples meeting special provisions may be allowed a second child.[57] Some local governments already had laws to that effect. For example, the Anhui provincial government recently passed regulations allowing thirteen categories of couples to apply to have a second child, and some can have a third or even a fourth child. An officer at the GPD believes that a two-child program will be safely and quickly implemented in the entire country.[58]

Military Buildup and the 1995–96 Missile Crisis

China's post-Deng civil-military relations registered a qualitative change. When Deng was commander in chief, the military was powerful vis-à-vis other political institutions but was subject to strongman-style control. Under this personalized party leadership, the interests of the military were repeatedly violated. Deng, for example, ordered troops and tanks into Tiananmen Square, causing lasting negative repercussions on the PLA. Many senior officers attributed the PLA's slow modernization progress to Deng's decade-long military budget restraints.[59]

To further the PLA's interests, the high command undertook to protect the new leadership with Jiang at the center. Under these conditions, the PLA never challenged Jiang's position as its commander in chief; he had earned political support from his armed forces. In the early 1990s, Jiang began to offer special promotions to young and middle-aged generals. Veteran generals who disagreed with the policy were silenced. For example, Jiang removed General Liu Huaqing, who had criticized Jiang, from his posts as member of the Standing

Committee of the Politburo and vice chairman of the CMC. General Zhang Wannian was designated Liu's successor and a candidate to enter the next Politburo; he voiced his firm support for Jiang's September 1995 speech on politics. The essential point was that being correct meant siding with Jiang and the center. Zhang's endorsement of Jiang's speech on behalf of the PLA exerted great weight in China's political arena, where Jiang's speech on politics was compared to Deng's speech on the "truth discussion" in 1979.

General Zhang Wannian was born in Longkou, Shandong, in 1928. He was enlisted in 1944 and joined the CCP one year later. Zhang served as squad leader, platoon leader, deputy company instructor, and staff officer during the Chinese civil war. In 1950–56, Zhang became the head of the operation section of the 369th Regiment, 123rd Division, Forty-first Army. In 1956–58, he served as deputy commander and chief of staff of the 368th Regiment. After three years of study at the Nanjing Military Academy, he served as commander of the 367th Regiment in 1961–66, section chief of the operation section of the Guangzhou Regional Command in 1966–68, commander of the 127th Division in 1978, and deputy commander of the Forty-third Army in 1981. In 1981–82, Zhang was appointed commander of the Forty-third Army. As a career soldier, Zhang moved up from a company commander to a regiment, division, and army commander. He served as deputy commander of Wuhan Regional Command in 1982–85. Between 1985 and 1992, he was deputy commander and commander of the Guangzhou and Ji'nan regional commands. In 1990–95, he was a member of the CMC, chief of the General Staff, and vice chairman of the CMC. In 1997, Zhang became a member of the Central Secretariat of the Fifteenth CCP Central Committee and of its Politburo. Zhang and other generals became interested in flexing military muscle to get a greater budgetary allocation. The ideologues could capitalize on the Taiwan Strait crisis to reconstruct nationalism as a new ideological base for legitimization, and the preparation for action in the strait served to justify the bureaucrats' lurch toward enhanced central control.[60]

General Chi Haotian also became a member of the Politburo of the Fifteenth CCP Central Committee in 1997. He was born in Zhaoyuan, Shandong, in 1929. He joined the PLA in 1945 and the CCP in 1946. During the Chinese civil war, Chi served as squad leader, deputy company instructor, instructor, and deputy battalion political instructor. During the Korean War, he served as battalion instructor and deputy director of the political section of the 235th Regiment, Seventy-ninth Division of the CPVF's Twenty-seventh Army. After the Korean War, he was political director of the regiment until 1958, when he enrolled in the PLA's General Senior Infantry Academy. He transferred to the PLA Military Academy to study integrated warfare. After he received a college diploma from the academy, he was promoted to head the political department of the Seventy-ninth Division in 1966. He became deputy political commissar of the division in 1967 and deputy director of the political department of the Twenty-seventh Army in 1969. In 1970–77, Chi took the posts of political commissar of the Eightieth Division, Twenty-seventh Army and deputy political commissar of the Beijing Regional Command. Between 1977 and 1987, he was deputy chief of the General Staff and political commissar of the Jinan Regional Command. From 1987 to 1992, he was a member of the CMC and chief of the General Staff. Chi became the defense minister in 1992 and vice chairman of the CMC in 1995.[61]

The organizational reform resulted in changes in the structures of headquarters at all levels. The administrative reforms focused on reducing headquarters personnel by 20 to 50 percent. The sustainability reforms encompassed both logistics and the defense industry. In relation to logistics, high priority was accorded to modernizing and improving combat service support functions that were consistent with the new operational concepts. Since the PLA emphasized joint operations to ensure victories in local wars under modern, high-tech conditions, joint logistics, rather than service-focused logistics, became essential. Despite a decade of extensive reform, the Chinese armed forces still face some difficulties in their modernization, just as other sectors of Chinese society do.

The Second Artillery Corps had problems in the areas of high-tech applications and urban reserve training. Missile technology had changed rapidly, and China's strategic missile force struggled to close the gap between China and other nuclear powers. The corps established substantial reserves of trained missile troops in the 1990s to keep up with new missile technology. Its efforts, however, did not reach the goal of high-tech training because the reserves lacked high-tech backgrounds. Since the corps did not have tech-ready reserves, most of its training was at a low-tech level.[62] The reserves were not ready for combat, and the missile equipment was waiting for those who could master the technology. The corps felt pressure when Jiang Zemin said, "We [would] rather let our men wait for the new equipment, not allow the equipment to wait for the men."[63]

The tension mounted in the Taiwan Strait and led to the third Taiwan Strait crisis in 1995–96. The crisis began when ROC president Lee Teng-hui made a trip to Cornell University in June 1995. The Jiang administration had tried to isolate Taiwan and had opposed the U.S. State Department's approval of Lee's visit. General Chi convinced Jiang that a show of force was necessary to condemn the United States for ruining Sino-American relations.[64] From July 21 to 26, the PLA conducted a missile test in an area only thirty-six miles north of an ROC-held island. At the same time, the CMC also concentrated a large force in Fujian. In mid-August, the PLA conducted another set of missile firings, accompanied by live ammunition exercises. The CMC also ordered naval exercises in the same month. In the fall, the high command launched one wave after another of military exercises, including a joint amphibious landing exercise in November.[65] Even though there had been military activities along the strait in the past, this was the first time in many years that they were announced publicly. Beijing's military aggression not only reversed what some observers had called a period of significant rapprochement across the Taiwan Strait but also created the most serious international crisis since Beijing and Taipei engaged in military conflict over the islands of Jinmen and Mazu in the 1950s.

During the short period of crisis, cross-strait tensions rose drastically, as if war were imminent. Taipei was on high alert and declared that it had made all necessary preparations to deal with a possible invasion. In December 1995, to respond to the PLA activities, the United States sent an aircraft carrier, the *Nimitz*, through the Taiwan Strait. Between January and February, the PLA concentrated one hundred thousand troops along the coast across the strait from Taiwan to send a stronger signal to both Taipei and Washington. Still, the Clinton administration and the Pentagon believed that Beijing would not attack Taiwan or other offshore islands in the winter of 1995–96.[66]

In March, the ROC was preparing for its first presidential election in Taiwan since 1949. Lee ran on the GMD ticket. Beijing intended to discourage the Taiwanese from voting for Lee because he had tried to separate Taiwan from China through the independence movement. Jiang again employed the military, this time to threaten the Taiwanese voters. On March 8, the PLA conducted its third set of missile tests, firing three M-9 surface-to-surface missiles just twelve miles from Taiwan's major seaport cities, Chi-lung (Keelung) and Kao-hsiung, through which more than 70 percent of the island's commercial shipping passed. Shipping was disrupted by the proximity of the missile tests. Flights to Japan and trans-Pacific flights were prolonged because airplanes needed to detour away from the flight path of the missiles.[67]

On March 8, the United States announced that it was deploying the *Independence* carrier battle group to international waters near Taiwan. To respond to the U.S. naval deployment, China announced that more live-fire exercises were to be conducted, near Penghu Island, on March 12–20. The Chinese deployed 150,000 troops, three hundred airplanes, guided missile destroyers, and submarines. On March 11, the United States deployed the *Nimitz* carrier battle group to the Taiwan area. The *Nimitz* steamed at high speed from the Persian Gulf to the Taiwan Strait to join the *Independence* carrier battle group to monitor Chinese military actions. This was the largest U.S. naval movement in the Asia-Pacific region since the Vietnam War and the first transit by U.S. warships in the area since 1976. China and the United States seemed on the brink of war again in the Taiwan Strait. By sending two carrier battle groups to the Taiwan Strait, the United States showed its readiness to fight over Taiwan.[68]

Fortunately, the third Taiwan Strait crisis did not evolve into a war between China and the United States. China's intimidation was counterproductive and aroused more anger than fear in Taiwan. According to a Taiwanese survey, China's missile test in March boosted Lee Teng-hui 5 percent in the polls, earning him a majority of the voters. He was elected president on March 23, 1996. The PLA offensive activities in the 1995–96 Taiwan Strait crisis also reinforced the argument for further U.S. arms sales to Taiwan and led to the strengthening of military ties between the United States and Japan.[69] Nonetheless, as Robert Ross points out, Beijing and Washington had tried to protect their strategic positions through the crisis, and both had reached their goals with certain strategic benefits.[70]

The high command in Beijing learned an important lesson from

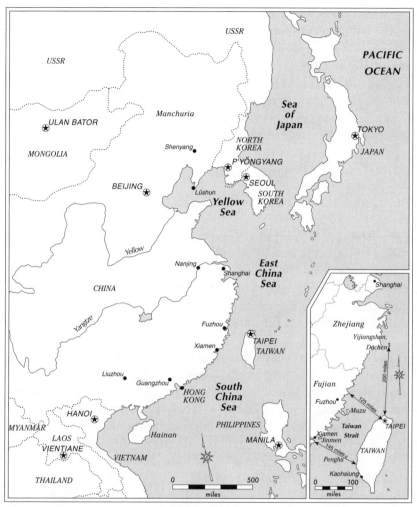

China and Taiwan

the 1995–96 crisis: that the United States would not watch a PLA attack on Taiwan with folded hands. The PLA therefore had to be prepared to deal with a major U.S. military intervention in the Taiwan Strait. In 1997–2001, the PLA sped up its modernization by developing better technology and purchasing more Russian equipment. While addressing the PLA delegation to the Tenth National People's Congress in March 2003, Jiang stated, "We should energetically push forward a Revolution of Military Affairs with Chinese characteristics, so as to ensure that our armed forces keep up with the current rapid development of science, technology, and RMA." The chairman made the PLA's information-based capability the key to China's military modernization. He also said that promoting a revolution of military affairs with Chinese characteristics would bring about profound changes in every aspect of the Chinese armed forces.[71]

The Fourth Generation

After Jiang retired, Hu Jintao became the new leader. He and his generals emerged from protracted service within the government and military. Almost all of their predecessors had been products of political or military crises of the CCP: Mao in the Long March of 1934–35, Peng during the Korean War of 1950, Lin in the Lushan political struggle of 1959, Deng toward the end of the Cultural Revolution about 1973–76, and Jiang after the Tiananmen Square incident of 1989. But Hu does not fit the pattern. At fifty, when he entered the Standing Committee of the Politburo of the Fourteenth CCP Central Committee in 1992, Hu was the youngest member in this top decision-making body. He was reelected to the Standing Committee of the Politburo and became a member of the Central Committee's Secretariat in 1997. In November 2002, when Jiang Zemin retired, Hu became chairman of the CCP at the Sixteenth CCP National Congress. In March 2003, at the Sixth National People's Congress, Hu was elected president of the PRC.

Like the previous generation of China's leadership, Hu and his cabinet members are technocrats.[72] Born in 1942 in Taizhou, Jiangsu, Hu studied hydroelectric engineering at Tsinghua University, where he joined the CCP in 1964. He wanted to be an expert on hydropower, and he has said that he originally had no intention of going into politics.[73] After his graduation in 1965, Hu stayed at Tsinghua University as a researcher until the beginning of the Cultural Revolution. In 1968, he was sent to work in Gansu, where he served consecutively as technician, office secretary, and deputy party secretary in an engineering bureau. In 1974, he was transferred to the Gansu Provincial Construction Committee and served as party secretary. He was deputy chief of the committee's design management division from 1975 to 1980, when he

Hu Jintao, the new commander in chief. (Courtesy of Xinhua News Agency, Beijing, China.)

was promoted to deputy director of the committee and later secretary of the Gansu Provincial Committee of the CYL. During the Eleventh CYL National Congress in 1982, Hu was elected member and first secretary of the Secretariat of the CYL Central Committee as well as president of the All-China Youth Federation. In 1985, at forty-three, Hu was appointed CCP secretary of Guizhou Province, the youngest of his rank in the country. In 1988, he became party secretary of Tibet. During his four years there, Hu sent PLA troops to the Tibetan streets to crush the independence movement and Buddhist rebellions.

Jiang Zemin gave up command of the Chinese military in September 2004 at the fourth plenary session of the Sixteenth CCP National Congress. Hu then became the new civilian commander in chief of the PLA. Hu nurtured a relationship with the PLA by supporting the growing military professionalism with an emphasis on educational credentials and a merit-based system of officer promotion. He selected top military leaders who had college degrees and formal overseas training. To upgrade the officer corps and the air force, the new military leaders had 85 percent of the officer corps obtain a college education; by 2005, all air force pilots and naval commanders of warships had college educations.[74] An examination of their data reveals a trend toward military professionalism in the PLA.

Hu also reaffirmed the PLA's modernization with an emphasis on updating its semi-mechanical equipment to modern technology and digital facilities. As General Xiong explained, the task of PLA mechanization had not yet been completed. In the coming years, he believed, the mechanization efforts would try to keep pace with the building of an information-age force, which in turn would be boosted by mechanization. "We shall promote both processes to eventually succeed in fulfilling the dual tasks of mechanization and informationization," Xiong said. "No distinct line should be drawn between the two and we should never depart from our country's actual situation and the realities of our armed forces."[75] To prepare for the "new era of information warfare," the PLA had to reform virtually all aspects of its gigantic institution.

After taking over the office of commander in chief, Hu Jintao stated that the PLA should resort to different warfare means in future conflicts, including a high-tech approach to circumvent enemy strengths and to confront the enemy in ways it would not be able to match. Thus China would "not be intimidated by a military superpower," and China's foreign policy would "not be constrained by its military weakness."[76] According to Hu and his new high command, the PLA should make a "leap-over" transition from an army with mechanical and semi-mechanical equipment to an army equipped with digital facilities. General Zhang Zhen, vice chairman of the CMC, referred to the "leap-over" idea when he spoke at a joint warfare seminar. Zhang said he believed that the next war would take place in an urban area, even in one of the major cities where China centers its technology.[77] The new high command gave top priority to the technological development of the navy, air force, and strategic forces "to strengthen the capabilities for winning both command of the sea and command of the air, and conducting strategic counter-strikes."[78]

Hu had to operate against the backdrop of Jiang's legacy. He knew that his taking over the CMC chair did not eliminate the need to define the new style, scope, and depth of his own ties with the military. Hu's leadership in the PLA actually started in 1999, when he became vice chairman of the CMC. His elevation to the number two position in the CMC was more than a procedural and symbolic promotion, given his deep involvement in the decommercialization of the PLA. When Jiang decided to unlink the PLA from commercial activities, Hu was assigned to do the dirty work, shutting down or taking away military-operated hotels, trade companies, factories, high-tech corporations, and other businesses. This process was guaranteed to be unpopular among PLA officers. That the PLA went along with these decisions suggests its acceptance of Hu as future commander in chief.

To deal with the problems left behind by Jiang, Hu made certain important changes in the military regulations. In December 2003, "Zhongguo renmin jiefangjun zhengzhi gongzuo tiaolie" (Regulations on the Political Work of the PLA) was revised and promulgated. It maintains that political work is the fundamental guarantee of the party's absolute leadership over the armed forces and assurance for its accomplishment of missions.[79] In February 2004, the CMC released "Guanyu jiaqiang jundui gaozhongji ganbu jiaoyu guanli de ruogan guiding" (Provisions on Strengthening the Education and Management of High- and Middle-Ranking Officers of the PLA), which refined the systems for officers at the regimental level and above to do self-study and self-review and to receive thematic education. On March 14, at the second plenary session of the Tenth National People's Congress, the new leaders revised the PRC constitution. In April, the CMC established the Regulations on the Work of the CCP Armed Force Committees. The new regulations further defined the duties and responsibilities of the party committees and improved the decision-making procedures of the PLA.

Hu then removed some of the old-guard generals and improved the chain of command by announcing a reduction of two hundred thousand troops by the end of 2005 and a rebalancing of the ratio between officers and men. Streamlining the structure, he reduced the number of officers in deputy positions, filled officers' posts with noncommissioned officers, and adopted a system of civilian employees. By 2006, the PLA had reduced 15 percent of its staff officers at the group army level and above.[80] The high turnover rate of PLA elites reflects an effective institutional mechanism by which top civilian leaders prevent the emergence of military strongmen and the stagnation of the military establishment. The average age of PLA top officers significantly decreased after the large-scale military leadership turnover in 2002. The average age of the members of the CMC decreased from sixty-eight in 1998 to sixty-three in 2003. The average age of the military leaders on the CCP Central Committee decreased from 62.3 at the Fourteenth CCP National Congress in 1992 to 58.6 at the Sixteenth CCP National Congress in 2002.[81]

Hu still faces tremendous difficulties in China's economic and political reforms in the midst of continuous social transition. Even though Hu and Jiang had some disputes over specific issues, they reached a consensus on the key objectives: China's economic growth and social stability. In the first decade of the new century, some Chinese analysts worry about the country's macroeconomic instability and potential problems. At a recent conference, researchers pointed out that macroeconomic instability has successfully been contained through government control of the right policy levels. Still, economic and social liberalization have drastically undermined the role of authority and old-style administrative edicts.[82]

Conclusion

CHINESE MILITARY REFORM is an outcome of social and economic changes that are not only related but interdependent. China's foremost task in its drive toward military modernization should be the successful completion of market economy reforms. To build a modern army, it must achieve sustainable industrial economic growth. In the past thirty years, with an annual growth rate of 8.6 percent, the Chinese government was able to double its defense budget, purchasing new weaponry and importing advanced technology from Russia and the West to narrow the technology gap between the PLA and major Western armed forces. Taking an eclectic attitude toward Western technology, the Chinese military made changes in imported weapon systems and tried to fit them into whatever they needed, letting all things serve their purpose. Their approaches, such as third-party purchase, copy and learn, and "leap-over," will define the unique problem-solving characteristics of Chinese military modernization for many years to come.

The new leadership in Beijing is not abandoning the deliberate approach to military reform that the previous generation employed with success. Yet the importation and adoption approach may keep the PLA forever behind the Western armed forces and make its modernization totally dependent on economic success. Any economic recession will slow down or stop China's military modernization. Chinese analysts worry about problems such as unemployment, limited natural resources, energy costs, a weak financial system, state-owned enterprises, and a decline in foreign investment. These problems, though they are not likely to occur simultaneously, will cause serious troubles in the country's economy. Some Western analysts have expressed concern that these problems will lead China to adopt a more aggressive foreign policy, even military expansionism.

To keep the military under control, a continuing coalition between the PLA and the CCP is necessary. At the National People's Congress in 2005, Hu Jintao's vision for "harmony and innovation" became government policy for China's further development. To achieve a harmonious China, the country must build on its long and rich traditions and preserve them in innovative ways. The PLA needs to follow the fundamental principle and system of absolute party leadership of the armed forces. In other words, the PLA should support the Hu administration by showing its loyalty to the party center. The high command should promote social harmony in various ways, and the rank and file should value social harmony, share the new ideas, and live with them as social norms. In this socioeconomic climate, the concept of harmony is becoming increasingly valuable and pertinent to Chinese society as well as the rest of the world.

The PLA still belongs to the party, since the latter controls the resources and personnel management for the military budget and professional careers under the current leadership. The party center can channel the military elite's interests and the individual consciousness, prejudice, and conflicts of the rank and file through the existing strong political institution. Since the state has adapted well to economic and social changes and effectively responded to the rising demands and expectations of the PLA, its political institutions may be able to manage some of the discontent and differing opinions within the PLA in the near future.[1] These activities are still within the boundaries of the party center's control. In the meantime, the PLA should also provide new military capabilities, because there are disharmonious factors and unstable elements in China and in the world. As we know, in the past two decades, disparity in wealth, an unsettled social political infrastructure, and international conflicts have resulted in a new set of uncertainties and challenges for China's sustained development.

Social problems and domestic difficulties will slow China's ascendancy in military reform and global politics to some extent. To build a modern army, China must build a confident and democratic society, and this will not be possible without drastically improving its political system. The task will be both costly and complex to execute. Few countries in history have successfully achieved such tumultuous transformation under the uncertain circumstances China is currently facing. Unlike Japan during the Meiji restoration in the mid-nineteenth century, China is being forced to undergo wholesale reforms led by the elite and by citizens who have become knowledgeable about the world community and vocal about their wishes and desires. The new leadership can hardly afford any illusion that the Chinese public will allow it a leisurely reform drive. The Chinese people, like most global villagers today, demand instant satisfaction. Meeting the public's growing, impatient expectations while maintaining the basic political structure acceptable to the old ideological leadership will require very creative politics.

Our historical overview shows the changing characteristics of the PLA in recent years. The analysis includes three elements that affected the process by which the Chinese military moved from a peasant army to a professional one. The first facet is the human resources that were available for military revolution and reforms. Our stories about peasant soldiers help us to better understand how their values, duties, and concerns affected the military as an institution. The organization was firmly entrenched in Chinese tradition and society. The PLA was one of the few entities in the PRC that enjoyed some praise and recognition of the past. It takes time for a major transition and significant changes to occur. The second element includes the pressure for reform and the limits on it, including outdated technology, poor living standards, lack of education and professional training, and an authoritarian government. The third element is the way the military compromised on difficult changes while shaping Chinese people's attitude toward, and the international view of, the PLA and China. The objective of this analytic process is to effectively present national interests, security concerns, perceived threats, and international conditions.

All three—Chinese resources, problems and limits, and military problem solving—describe unique characteristics of Chinese military culture. This analysis provides a new interpretation in which a balanced examination of social and military history defines the unique characteristics of the Chinese military from its high command to ordinary soldiers. These characteristics are not the same as the Eastern traditional ones or the Western modern ones; they are the unique Chinese characteristics between tradition and modernization. In the near future, Chinese generals may be able to act effectively as independent forces, to have an impact when their concerns and interests converge with the concerns and interests of others in the system. Whether or not the military leaders of the new generation are eventually accepted by the party and government as leading actors, they will shape part of the domestic and foreign policymaking context.

The continuous efforts toward military modernization show that the standard image in the West of Chinese military reforms during the second half of the twentieth century—as a period of reactivity, anxiety, and self-doubt—is misleading. To some extent, Western, Russian, and Japanese expansionism helped engender various forms of reform movements and nationalism, causing some Chinese leaders to question inherited values and leading to advocacy of rapid modernization. But reports of military leaders who found themselves swept away by a hegemonic nationalist discourse, which are often included in conventional accounts of the reform period, are exaggerated. Nor did the leaders feel the need to make a choice between "traditional" Chinese ideas and "modern" Western ones.

Perhaps the most important factor, and the most influential in the long term, is the significant improvement in China's international standing, related primarily, but not only, to a reduction in global and regional threats of conflict. Chinese strategic analysts and military experts have an optimistic view of national security today and opportunity in the near future. While factors of insecurity and instability remain, the Chinese enjoy a favorable surrounding security environment, something seldom seen since the founding of the PRC. It seems possible for the PLA to avoid a major war for a fairly long period of time. Relaxation is still the general trend in international security.

For the PLA, there are more opportunities and challenges, and more hopes and difficulties, ahead. The new leadership will seek a growing role on the global political stage while assuring the international community that China does not pursue a policy of military and political hegemony in a conventional sense. The world community may be willing to accept China as a counterbalance to the United States or Japan. However, while China is repositioning itself by creat-

Poster of a PLA soldier. (Courtesy of Xinhua News Agency, Beijing, China.)

ing a new center of gravity in the Asia-Pacific region, its new demands will create potential problems. A possible source of crisis is the highly sensitive and increasingly dangerous issue of Taiwan's independence, as Taiwan may make bolder moves toward independence before the end of Chen Shui-bian's second term in 2008. In a broader historical perspective, China's Taiwan policy will be directed not necessarily by Communist ideology but by the Chinese nationalism that has been in the making since the late nineteenth century, when Taiwan was ceded to Japan after the First Sino-Japanese War. The PLA needs to develop its own theory and tactics of modern warfare to deal with a possible crisis. The new theory and tactics should be based on the new international environment and China's needs for its own development.

Notes

Introduction

1. The annual symposium on arms control, cosponsored by Tsinghua University, the Ford Foundation, and the MacArthur Foundation, was held July 10–16, 2004. The participants came from twenty-nine institutes, colleges, and military academies across the country. See http://learn.tsinghua.edu.cn/homepage/2000990313/teaching.htm.

2. Sun's advisor, Professor Niu Jun at Peking University, was one of my colleagues at the Institute of American Studies, Chinese Academy of Social Sciences, where I worked in the early 1980s.

3. Cheng Li, *China's Leaders: The New Generation* (Lanham, MD: Rowman & Littlefield, 2001), table 2.1, 36. Li's data include commanders, vice commanders, commissars, vice commissars, directors, and deputy directors of political departments at the regional command level and above. Also see David Shambaugh, *Modernizing China's Military: Progress, Problems, and Prospects* (Berkeley: University of California Press, 2002), 175–77.

4. Jiang Zemin, chairman of the CMC, launched a military reform known as the Two Transformations. First, he said, the PLA should be transformed from an army that fights "local wars under ordinary conditions" to one capable of fighting and winning "local wars under high-tech conditions." Second, the PLA should begin the change from labor intensive to technology intensive; that is, from an army based on quantity to one based on quality. Jiang quoted in PRC State Council Bureau of Information, "China's National Defense, 1998," in *White Papers of the Chinese Government, 1996–99* (Beijing: Foreign Languages Press, 2000), 2:387.

5. Li Hongchun, "Daxue biyesheng zenyang baokao feixingyuan" (Guideline for College Graduates to Apply for PLAAF Pilot), *Zhongguo kongjun*, no. 5 (2004): 12.

6. *Jiefangjun bao*, "Tsinghua daxue de 'guofangsheng'" (National Defense Students at Tsinghua University), November 19, 2003, 5.

7. Jiang Zemin, speech to the PLA delegation to the Tenth National People's Congress, Beijing, reprinted in *Jiefangjun bao*, March 10, 2003, 1–2.

8. Mark A. Ryan, David M. Finkelstein, and Michael A. McDevitt, "Pat-

terns of PLA Warfighting," introduction to *Chinese Warfighting: The PLA Experience since 1949*, ed. Mark A. Ryan, David M. Finkelstein, and Michael A. McDevitt (New York: M. E. Sharpe, 2003), 3.

9. See, for example, Andrew Scobell, *China's Use of Military Force: Beyond the Great Wall and the Long March* (Cambridge: Cambridge University Press, 2003); Shambaugh, *Modernizing China's Military*; You Ji, *The Armed Forces of China* (New York: I. B. Tauris, 1999); and Ellis Joffe, *The Chinese Army after Mao* (Cambridge, MA: Harvard University Press, 1987).

10. See, for example, Ryan, Finkelstein, and McDevitt, *Chinese Warfighting*; David A. Graff and Robin Higham, eds., *A Military History of China* (Boulder, CO: Westview Press, 2002); Hans van de Ven, ed., *Warfare in Chinese History* (Leiden, The Netherlands: Brill, 2000); and James R. Lilley and David Shambaugh, eds., *China's Military Faces the Future* (New York: M. E. Sharpe, 1999).

11. For the "China threat" group, see Jed Babbin and Edward Timperlake, *Showdown: Why China Wants War with the United States* (Washington, DC: Regnery, 2006); Gordon G. Chang, *The Coming Collapse of China* (New York: Random House, 2001); Bill Getz, *The China Threat: How the People's Republic Targets America* (Washington, DC: Regnery, 2000); Richard Bernstein and Ross H. Munro, *The Coming Conflict with China* (New York: Knopf, 1997); and Nicholas Kristof and Sheryl Wudunn, *China Wakes: The Struggle for the Soul of a Rising Power* (New York: Vintage Books, 1994).

12. Solomon Karmel, *China and the People's Liberation Army* (New York: St. Martin's, 2000), 3–5, 8.

13. George Z. Hong, "'The China Uniqueness'—Puzzles and Interpretations of China's Development," *American Review of China Studies* 6, no. 1 (2005): 1–4.

14. The research efforts of military historians in China, like those of their Western counterparts, are constrained by the unavailability of primary sources. Few researchers have been able to explore the official documents of the PLA because most remain closed to historians. Thus many military historians employ a social historical approach in their research.

15. Among the recent publications on the social history of Chinese soldiers in the Korean War are He Ming, *Jianzheng: Chaoxian zhanzheng zhafu qianfan Jieshi daibiao de riji* (Witness: Diary of a Representative for the Explanatory Task to Repatriate Chinese POWs) (Beijing: Zhongguo wenshi chubanshe, 2001); Ge Chumin, ed., *Laozhanshi yishi* (Personal Stories of Veterans) (Beijing: Zhongguo duiwai fanyi chuban gongsi, 2000); Tan Zheng, *Zhongguo renmin zhiyuanjun renwulu* (Veterans Profile of the CPVF) (Beijing: Zhonggong dangshi chubanshe, 1992); and Hu Qinghe, *Chaoxian*

zhanzheng zhong de nuren (Women in the Korean War) (Jinan, Shandong: Huanghe chubanshe, 1992).

16. Sun Lizhou, interview by the author, Beijing, July 2004.

17. After reporting to the recruitment center, Sun Lizhou was assigned to the Third Department (Zongcan sanbu) of the PLA General Staff Department (GSD) in Beijing. He was not very happy about this assignment. The Third Department is responsible for communication and information, signals intelligence, surveillance, satellite management, and foreign languages training. Sun wanted to work in the Second Department (Zongcan erbu), which is responsible for foreign military affairs, military diplomacy, human intelligence collection, and multisource analysis. Ibid. For details on the GSD, see Shambaugh, *Modernizing China's Military*, 128–31.

18. The slogan of building a "rich country and strong military" was coined during the self-strengthening movement of the Qing Dynasty in the 1860s and 1870s. During the movement, the Manchus established a modern navy and a new, German-style army.

19. The party documents include CCP Central Archives, comp., *Zhonggong zhongyang wenjian xuanji, 1921–49* (Selected Documents of the CCP Central Committee, 1921–49) (Beijing: Zhonggong zhongyang dangxiao chubanshe, 1989–92), vols. 15–18; CCP Central Archives, CCP Central Archival and Manuscript Research Division, and CCP Organization Department, comps., *Zhongguo gongchandang zuzhishi ziliao, 1921–97* (Documents of the CCP Organization's History, 1921–97) (Beijing: Zhonggong dangshi chubanshe, 2000), vols. 1–14; Sichuan Party History Research Committee, comp., *Nanfangjiu dangshi ziliao* (Party History Records of the CCP Southern Bureau) (Chongqing, Sichuan: Chongqing renmin chubanshe, 1986); Jiangsu Party History Research Committee, comp. *Zhonggong zhongyang Nanjingjiu: Zhonggong lishi ziliao* (Nanjing Bureau of the CCP Central Committee: CCP Historical Documents) (Beijing: Zhonggong zhongyang dangshi chubanshe, 1990); and Xinhua News Agency, *Xinhuashe wenjian ziliao huibian* (A Collection of Documentary Materials of the New China News Agency) (Beijing: Xinhuashe, n.d.).

20. The Archives of the PRC Ministry of Foreign Affairs, formerly the Archives Section of the General Office of the Foreign Ministry, have 330,000 volumes of documents, which are mainly in paper form, with some microfilms, photos, audio tapes, videotapes, and compact discs. They record China's foreign policy and diplomatic activities since the founding of the PRC in 1949. The archives declassified about 10,000 volumes of the documents in 2004 and 20,000 volumes in 2006.

21. Chinese leaders' papers include *Mao Zedong junshi wenji* (Collected Military Papers of Mao Zedong) (Beijing: Junshi kexue chubanshe, 1993);

Mao Zedong junshi wenxuan: Neibuben (Selected Military Papers of Mao Ze-dong: Internal Edition) (Beijing: Jiefangjun zhanshi chubanshe, 1981); *Zhu De junshi wenxuan* (Selected Military Papers of Zhu De) (Beijing: Jiefangjun chubanshe, 1986); *Peng Dehuai junshi wenxuan* (Selected Military Papers of Peng Dehuai) (Beijing: Zhongyang wenxian chubanshe, 1988); *Liu Bocheng junshi wenxuan* (Selected Military Papers of Liu Bocheng) (Beijing: Jiefangjun chubanshe, 1992); *Nie Rongzhen junshi wenxuan* (Selected Military Papers of Nie Rongzhen) (Beijing: Jiefangjun chubanshe, 1992); *Xu Xiangqian junshi wenxuan* (Selected Military Papers of Xu Xiangqian) (Beijing: Jiefangjun chubanshe, 1992); *He Long junshi wenxuan* (Selected Military Papers of He Long) (Beijing: Jiefangjun chubanshe, 1989); and *Chen Yi junshi wenxuan* (Selected Military Papers of Chen Yi) (Beijing: Jiefangjun chubanshe, 1996).

22. *Jianguo yilai Mao Zedong wengao, 1949–76* (Mao Zedong's Manuscripts since the Founding of the State, 1949–76) (Beijing: Zhongyang wenxian chubanshe, 1989–93); *Jianguo yilai Liu Shaoqi wengao, 1949–52* (Liu Shaoqi's Manuscripts since the Founding of the State, 1949–52) (Beijing: Zhongyang wenxian chubanshe, 2005); *Selected Works of Deng Xiaoping*, 3 vols. (Beijing: Foreign Languages Press, 1994).

23. Part of the research effort resulted in a translated and edited volume: Xiaobing Li, Allan Millett, and Bin Yu, trans. and eds., *Mao's Generals Remember Korea* (Lawrence: University Press of Kansas, 2000).

24. For understandable reasons, some interviewees asked that their names not be used.

25. Some of their stories about the Korean War are included in Richard Peters and Xiaobing Li, *Voices from the Korean War: Personal Stories of American, Korean, and Chinese Soldiers* (Lexington: University Press of Kentucky, 2004).

26. At the National People's Congress in 2005, Hu Jintao's vision of "harmony and innovation" became government policy for China's further development.

1. Peasants and Revolutions

1. The first recorded battle in China occurred about 3000 B.C., when many clans along the Yellow (Huanghe) River entered a stage of patriarchal society. The people had already acquired the skills of making stone and bone instruments and weapons through grinding. They made bows and arrows for hunting and protection. After four tribal confederations emerged in China, conflicts over land, slaves, and water resources evolved into large-scale warfare. See National Military Museum of the Chinese People's Revolution, comp.,

Zhongguo zhanzheng fazhanshi (History of Chinese Warfare) (Beijing: Renmin chubanshe, 2001), 1:29–30; Shi Duqiao, *Zhongguo jindai junshi sixiangshi* (History of Military Thought in Modern China) (Beijing: Guofang daxue chubanshe, 2000), 2; and Zhang Xiuping, Mao Yuanyou, and Huang Pumin, *Yingxiang zhongguo de yibaici zhanzheng* (The One Hundred Battles That Shaped China) (Nanning: Guangxi renmin chubanshe, 2003), 1–3.

2. Edward L. Dreyer, "Continuity and Change," in Graff and Higham, *Military History of China*, 25; John K. Fairbank and Merle Goldman, *China: A New History* (Cambridge, MA: Harvard University Press, 1998), 30.

3. In this work, "peasants" includes landowners and tenant farmers.

4. PRC Bureau of Statistics, *Zhongguo tongji nianjian, 2000* (China's Statistical Yearbook, 2000) (Beijing: Zhongguo tongji chubanshe, 2001), 715–16, 718.

5. Fairbank and Goldman, *China*, 102.

6. Jonathan D. Spence, *The Search for Modern China*, 2nd ed. (New York: Norton, 1999), 14.

7. Kate Xiao Zhou, *How the Farmers Changed China: Power of the People* (Boulder, CO: Westview Press, 1996), 237.

8. The story of Mulan, the teenage girl who took her father's place in the army when northern barbarians invaded China, is not based on historical records. It is from a classic narrative poem, "Mulan shi," popular in north China since the sixth century. Although the poem may be fictional, Chinese women did participate in warfare in the past. For more on "Mulan shi," see Tianjin Normal College Department of History, comp., *Zhongguo jianshi* (A Concise History of China) (Beijing: Renmin jiaoyu chubanshe, 1980), 157.

9. Classical Confucianism includes four books and five classics (*sishu wujing*). The four books are the *Kongzi* (Confucius), the *Lunyu* (Conversations), the *Daxue* (Great Learning), and the *Zhongyong* (Doctrine of the Mean). The five classics are the *Yijing* (Classic of Changes), the *Shujing* (Classic of History), the *Shijing* (Classic of Poetry), the *Chunqiu* (Spring and Autumn Annals), and the *Liji* (Record of Rites). For Confucius's books, see *The Essential Analects*, trans. Edward Slingerland (Indianapolis, IN: Hackett, 2006), and *Analects, the Great Learning, and the Doctrine of the Mean*, trans. James Legge (New York: Dover, 1971).

10. Among the recent English versions are Sun-tzu, *The Art of War*, trans. John Minford (New York: Viking, 2002); Sun-tzu, *The Art of Warfare*, trans. Roger T. Ames (New York: Ballantine Books, 1993); and Ralph D. Sawyer, trans., *The Seven Military Classics of Ancient China* (Boulder, CO: Westview Press, 1993).

11. Michael S. Neiberg, *Warfare in World History* (London: Routledge, 2001), 12.

12. "After the Spring and Autumn Period, ancient Chinese armies were normally much larger than those in Greece. As early as the third century B.C. one Chinese army contained almost 1 million men. In a 295 B.C. battle, 240,000 men died. Most of these men were peasants who had been transformed into infantrymen. The Chinese, like the Greeks, instilled intense discipline and wrote the first drill manuals. The Chinese delayed introducing cavalry until the third century in part because horsemanship required the rider to abandon noble robes in favor of barbarian short trousers and shirts." Ibid.

13. Hu Wenyan et al., *Zhongguo lishi* (Chinese History) (Beijing: Renmin jiaoyu chubanshe, 1986), 38–39; David A. Graff, "State Making and State Breaking," in Graff and Higham, *Military History of China*, 46–47.

14. Hu Guangzheng, *Zhongwai junshi zuzhi tizhi bijiao jiaocheng* (Teaching Text for Comparative Study on Chinese and Foreign Military Organizations) (Beijing: Junshi kexue chubanshe, 1999), 63; Robin Higham and David A. Graff, introduction to Graff and Higham, *Military History of China*, 4–5.

15. Liu Zhan, *Zhongguo gudai junzhishi* (History of the Military System in Ancient China) (Beijing: Junshi kexue chubanshe, 1992), 21–22; National Military Museum, *Zhongguo zhanzheng fazhanshi*, 1:120–21; Wu Ziyong, *Zhanzheng dongyuanxue jiaocheng* (Teaching Text for War Mobilization) (Beijing: Junshi kexue chubanshe, 2001), 22; Michael Loewe, *Everyday Life in Early Imperial China* (Indianapolis, IN: Hackett, 1968), 75.

16. In the seven lunar months of 209 B.C., Chen Sheng and Wu Guang, together with nine hundred other peasants, were drafted and sent to Yuyang (near present-day Beijing) to perform military duties. When they passed through Daze (southwest of present-day Suxian, Anhui), there was a sudden downpour that kept them from arriving on time. Since, according to the Qin law, late arrival for military duty was punishable by death, they decided that they might as well start a rebellion. They staged an armed uprising at Daze and quickly occupied Chenxian (present-day Huaiyang, Henan). Chen and Wu announced the establishment of a new regime, Zhangchu, with Chen as king and Wu as military commander. They called upon all the peasants in China to revolt against the Qin regime. It was this kind of violence, spearheaded by peasants who had nothing as weapons other than hoes and clubs, that eventually toppled the Qin Dynasty. After the deaths of Chen and Wu, Liu Bang (256–195 B.C.), one of the peasant leaders, eventually overthrew the Qin and established the Han Dynasty. Tianjin Normal College, *Zhongguo jianshi*, 87–90; Graff, "State Making and State Breaking," 46–47.

17. Tianjin Normal College, *Zhongguo jianshi*, 94–95.

18. Ibid., 127–28.

19. Chen Jian, *Mao's China and the Cold War* (Chapel Hill: University of North Carolina Press, 2001), 300n44.

20. I am indebted to John K. Fairbank, Edwin O. Reischauer, and Albert M. Craig for the phrase "dynastic cycle." They point out that "the Chinese have traditionally interpreted their culture and their past as a series of dynastic cycles." John K. Fairbank, Edwin O. Reischauer, and Albert M. Craig, *East Asia: Tradition and Transformation*, rev. ed. (Boston: Houghton Mifflin, 1989), 83.

21. Hu et al., *Zhongguo lishi*, 93–94.

22. Tianjin Normal College, *Zhongguo jianshi*, 170.

23. National Military Museum, *Zhongguo zhanzheng fazhanshi*, 1:216–19; Tianjin Normal College, *Zhongguo jianshi*, 171; Dreyer, "Continuity and Change," 32–33.

24. Higham and Graff, introduction, 11–12.

25. Neiberg, *Warfare in World History*, 23.

26. Confucianism as a philosophy focuses on individual moral conduct, family relations, and moral government in the context of the society. The Chinese worldview is a blend of Confucian, Daoist, and Buddhist thought. For detailed discussions of traditional thought, see Benjamin I. Schwartz, *The World of Thought in Ancient China* (Cambridge, MA: Harvard University Press, 1985), 118–19, and Dreyer, "Continuity and Change," 22–23.

27. Neiberg, *Warfare in World History*, 10, 12–13. For more Chinese military writings and traditions, see Sun Zi, *Art of Warfare*, and Sawyer, *Seven Military Classics*.

28. Neiberg, *Warfare in World History*, 30.

29. Tianjin Normal College, *Zhongguo jianshi*, 241–42.

30. National Military Museum, *Zhongguo zhanzheng fazhanshi*, 1:350.

31. Fei Hsiao Tung, *Chinese Village Close-up* (Beijing: New World Press, 1983), 127.

32. Ibid., 24–25. For the detailed Confucian perception of the family, see Confucius, *Analects*, 26–27, 149–51.

33. Clark W. Sorensen, "Asian Families: Domestic Group Formation," in *Asia's Cultural Mosaic: An Anthropological Introduction*, ed. Grant Evans (New York: Prentice Hall, 1993), 93–94.

34. Clark W. Sorensen, "Ancestors and In-Laws: Kinship beyond the Family," in Evans, *Asia's Cultural Mosaic*, 119–20.

35. Zhou, *How the Farmers Changed China*, 2.

36. Hu et al., *Zhongguo lishi*, 170; Frederic Wakeman Jr., *The Fall of Imperial China* (New York: Free Press, 1975), 66–69.

37. The village militia was called *yiyong* or *minzhuang* in some areas. The number of Ming troops reached four million by the late Ming. See Hu Guangzheng, *Zhongwai junshi zuzhi tizhi bijiao jiaocheng*, 63–64, 95, and David C. Wright, "The Northern Frontier," in Graff and Higham, *Military History of China*, 74–76.

38. Dai Yi, *Jianming qingshi* (Concise History of the Qing) (Beijing: Renmin chubanshe, 1980), 1:9–11; Hu et al., *Zhongguo lishi*, 171; Wakeman, *Fall of Imperial China*, 80; Spence, *Search for Modern China*, 16–21.

39. National Military Museum, *Zhongguo zhanzheng fazhanshi*, 1:419–20; Spence, *Search for Modern China*, 21–25; Rhoads Murphey, *East Asia: A New History*, 4th ed. (New York: Longman, 2007), 144.

40. Hu et al., *Zhongguo lishi*, 171–72.

41. Dai Yi, *Jianming qingshi*, 1:108–10; Spence, *Search for Modern China*, 36; Wakeman, *Fall of Imperial China*, 212.

42. The population of China increased from 150 million in 1600 to 300 million in 1800 and to 432 million in 1851. Fairbank, Reischauer, and Craig, *East Asia*, 241–42.

43. Hans van de Ven, "Military Mobilization in China, 1840–1949," in *War in the Modern World*, ed. Jeremy Black (London: Routledge, 2003), 37.

44. Tianjin Normal College, *Zhongguo jianshi*, 340; Immanuel C. Y. Hsu, *The Rise of Modern China*, 6th ed. (Oxford: Oxford University Press, 2000), 225–26.

45. Hu et al., *Zhongguo lishi*, 204; Fairbank and Goldman, *China*, 206–7; Spence, *Search for Modern China*, 172–73.

46. Hong Xiuquan, *Yuandao jiushige*, quoted in Tianjin Normal College, *Zhongguo jianshi*, 342. For more on *Yuandao jiushige*, see Wakeman, *Fall of Imperial China*, 144–47, and Hsu, *Rise of Modern China*, 227–28.

47. National Military Museum, *Zhongguo zhanzheng fazhanshi*, 2:570–71; Maochun Yu, "The Taiping Rebellion," in Graff and Higham, *Military History of China*, 136–37.

48. National Military Museum, *Zhongguo zhanzheng fazhanshi*, 2:575; Wakeman, *Fall of Imperial China*, 150–52; Hsu, *Rise of Modern China*, 232.

49. *Tianchao tianmu zhidu* quoted in Tianjin Normal College, *Zhongguo jianshi*, 351–52. For more on *Tianchao tianmu zhidu*, see Hsu, *Rise of Modern China*, 233–34, and Spence, *Search for Modern China*, 176–77.

50. National Military Museum, *Zhongguo zhanzheng fazhanshi*, 2:581–52; Yu, "Taiping Rebellion," 137–38.

51. Tianjin Normal College, *Zhongguo jianshi*, 370–71; Wakeman, *Fall of Imperial China*, 147–54; Hsu, *Rise of Modern China*, 242–43.

52. Yu, "Taiping Rebellion," 140.

53. National Military Museum, *Zhongguo zhanzheng fazhanshi*, 2:591; Hsu, *Rise of Modern China*, 246–47.

54. Tianjin Normal College, *Zhongguo jianshi*, 345; Spence, *Search for Modern China*, 178–79.

55. Hu et al., *Zhongguo lishi*, 204; Fairbank and Goldman, *China*, 210; Spence, *Search for Modern China*, 179–80.

56. See, for example, Shi, *Zhongguo jindai junshi sixiangshi*, 160, and Zhang Yutian, *Zhongguo jindai junshishi* (Military History of Modern China) (Shenyang: Liaoning renmin chubanshe, 1983), 565.

57. Mao Zedong, "Chinese Revolution and Chinese Communist Party," in *Selected Works of Mao Tse-tung* (Beijing: Foreign Languages Press, 1977), 2:308.

58. Ibid., 2:324.

59. Richard S. Horowitz, "Beyond the Marble Boat: The Transformation of the Chinese Military, 1850–1911," in Graff and Higham, *Military History of China*, 163.

60. Wakeman, *Fall of Imperial China*, 229.

61. Horowitz, "Beyond the Marble Boat," 164–66.

62. Ibid., 171.

63. Li quoted in Shi, *Zhongguo jindai junshi sixiangshi*, 357.

64. Fairbank, Reischauer, and Craig, *East Asia*, 222–23; Bruce A. Elleman, *Modern Chinese Warfare, 1795–1989* (London: Routledge, 2001), 141.

65. The 1900 Boxer Rebellion was a mass movement against foreign missionaries and establishments in north China. Foreigners gave the name "Boxers" to the Yihequan (Righteous and Harmonious Fists; later Yihetuan, Righteous and Harmonious Militia), originally a secret organization in which peasants in Shandong and Hebei provinces resorted to religion in their anti-Qing struggle. It used martial arts training to organize the masses for armed struggle against Qing officials. As Western influence, especially Christianity, expanded in north China, it quickly became the target of Yihetuan's resentment. Toward the end of the nineteenth century, the number of Western missionaries in China, including Catholic and Eastern Orthodox missionaries, was more than 3,300, and the number of Chinese converts exceeded eight hundred thousand. In 1899, the society went public in Shandong Province. Its members burned churches, killed missionaries, and chased out converts. In 1900, the main forces of the Yihetuan were shifted to Zhili, where they joined forces with local groups. Very quickly, they moved toward Tianjin and Beijing. More Western missionaries and their family members were killed in the capital city. As the Yihetuan struck against the Westerners without mercy, eight nations—Russia, Britain, Germany, France, the United States, Japan, Italy, and Austria—formed an alliance to launch a war against the Yihetuan as well as the Qing regime, which had used the movement's antimissionary policy to seize popular leadership and had declared the movement legal. On June 10, 1900, more than two thousand allied forces landed at Dagu and moved toward Tianjin and Beijing. On July 14, the allied forces captured Tianjin. On August 14, now at nearly twenty thousand men, the allied forces occupied Beijing. The Qing government fled to Xi'an, and the Boxer Rebellion ended. On September 7, 1901, the Qing government signed a peace treaty with eleven

countries whereby China had to pay reparations of 450 million taels of silver over thirty-nine years. The treaty also provided that an area in Beijing be designated a legation quarter where foreign troops could station permanently for the protection of foreign embassies, and that the allied nations be allowed to station troops at twelve strategic points along the railway between Beijing and Shanhaiguan, Hebei. Hu et al., *Zhongguo lishi*, 249–52; Wakeman, *Fall of Imperial China*, 216–20.

66. Fairbank, Reischauer, and Craig, *East Asia*, 726–27.

67. Hsu, *Rise of Modern China*, 462–65.

68. Fairbank, Reischauer, and Craig, *East Asia*, 746; Compilation Committee of ROC History, *A Pictorial History of the Republic of China* (Taipei, Taiwan: Modern China Press, 1981), 1:107–8.

69. Zhao Shaoquan, *Xinbian zhongguo xiandashi* (New History of Modern China) (Nanchang: Jiangxi renmin chubanshe, 1987), 1:1–2; June Grasso, Jay Corrin, and Michael Kort, *Modernization and Revolution in China: From the Opium Wars to World Power*, 3rd ed. (Armonk, NY: M. E. Sharpe, 2004), 75–77.

70. Fairbank, Reischauer, and Craig, *East Asia*, 750.

71. Peter Zarrow, *China in War and Revolution, 1895–1949* (New York: Routledge, 2005), 86.

72. Edward A. McCord, "Warlordism in Early Republican China," in Graff and Higham, *Military History of China*, 175.

73. Joseph W. Esherick, *Reform and Revolution in China: The 1911 Revolution in Hunan and Hubei* (Berkeley: University of California Press, 1976), 250–51.

74. He Li, *From Revolution to Reform: A Comparative Study of China and Mexico* (Lanham, MD: University Press of America, 2004), 19.

75. Lucien Bianco, *Origins of the Chinese Revolution, 1915–1949* (Stanford, CA: Stanford University Press, 1971), 112.

76. For more on Mao, see Jung Chang and Jon Halliday, *Mao: The Unknown Story* (New York: Knopf, 2005); Jonathan D. Spence, *Mao Zedong* (New York: Viking, 1999); Philip Short, *Mao: A Life* (New York: Henry Holt, 1999); and Shaun Breslin, *Mao: Profiles in Power* (New York: Longman, 1998).

77. CCP Central Archival and Manuscript Research Division, *Mao Zedong nianpu, 1893–1949* (A Chronological Record of Mao Zedong, 1893–1949) (Beijing: Zhongyang wenxian chubanshe, 1993), 1:1–4; Edgar Snow, *Red Star over China* (New York: Grove Press, 1944), 121–23.

78. I borrow the phrase "plough culture" from Clark W. Sorensen, who describes it as a "highly productive type of cropping system using ploughs and draft animals on permanent fields. The basic unit of production has usually been the peasant household." Sorensen, "Asian Families," 93.

79. Short, *Mao*, 27.

80. CCP Archival and Manuscript Research Division, *Mao Zedong nianpu*, 1:2–6; Li Zhisui, *The Private Life of Chairman Mao: The Memoirs of Mao's Personal Physician* (New York: Random House, 1994), 7; Snow, *Red Star over China*, 123–26.

81. Xu Yan, *Junshijia Mao Zedong* (Mao Zedong as a Military Leader) (Beijing: Zhongyang wenxian chubanshe, 1995), 6; Breslin, *Mao*, 21–22.

82. Deng Rong, *Deng Xiaoping and the Cultural Revolution: A Daughter Recalls the Critical Years*, trans. Sidney Shapiro (Beijing: Foreign Languages Press, 2002), 55.

83. CCP Archival and Manuscript Research Division, *Mao Zedong zhuan, 1893–1949* (Biography of Mao Zedong, 1893–1949) (Beijing: Zhongyang wenxian chubanshe, 1996), 1:12–13; Breslin, *Mao*, 20.

84. Xu, *Junshijia Mao Zedong*, 6.

85. Timothy Cheek, *Mao Zedong and China's Revolution: A Brief History with Documents* (Boston: Bedford/St. Martin's, 2002), 7; Breslin, *Mao*, 22.

86. Tony Saich, ed., *The Rise to Power of the Chinese Communist Party: Documents and Analysis* (New York: M. E. Sharpe, 1996), xix.

87. Ibid., xxvi.

88. Deng, *Deng Xiaoping and the Cultural Revolution*, 190.

89. CCP Party History Research Division, *Zhongguo gongchandang lishi dashiji, 1919–87* (Major Historical Events of the CCP, 1919–87) (Beijing: Renmin chubanshe, 1989), 9; Saich, *Rise to Power*, 4–5.

90. Xu, *Junshijia Mao Zedong*, 10.

91. Harold R. Isaacs, *The Tragedy of the Chinese Revolution*, 2nd ed. (Stanford, CA: Stanford University Press, 1961), 33.

92. Saich, *Rise to Power*, xx, xxviii.

93. CCP Party History Research Division, *Zhongguo gongchandang lishi dashiji*, 14.

94. R. Keith Schoppa, *Revolution and Its Past: Identities and Change in Modern Chinese History*, 2nd ed. (Upper Saddle River, NJ: Prentice Hall, 2006), 180–81; Zhang Guotao, *Wo de huiyi* (My Recollections) (Beijing: Dongfang chubanshe, 2004), 1:118; William Wei, "'Political Power Grows out of the Barrel of a Gun': Mao and the Red Army," in Graff and Higham, *Military History of China*, 230–31.

95. Schoppa, *Revolution and Its Past*, 180–81.

96. CCP Party History Research Division, *Zhongguo gongchandang lishi dashiji*, 20–21; Saich, *Rise to Power*, 76–79.

97. Shanghai University et al., *Xinbian zhongguo xiandashi*, 1:99; Paul J. Bailey, *China in the Twentieth Century*, 2nd ed. (Malden, MA: Blackwell, 2001), 99.

98. CCP Party History Research Division, *Zhongguo gongchandang lishi dashiji*, 24–25.

99. National Military Museum, *Zhongguo zhanzheng fazhanshi*, 2:801–2; Chang Jui-te, "The National Army from Whampoa to 1949," in Graff and Higham, *Military History of China*, 194.

100. The HMA's official name in 1924–26 was Guomindang zhongyang lujun junguan xuexiao (GMD Central Infantry Officer Academy). In January 1926, the GMD Central Committee changed its name to Zhongyang junshi zhengzhi xuexiao (Central Military and Politics Academy). Because it is located on Changzhou Island, near the famous Huangpu Harbor of Guangzhou, it is known as the Huangpu Military Academy. Compilation Committee of ROC History, *Pictorial History*, 1:239–40.

101. Sun Yat-sen, "Lujun junguan xuexiao kaixue yanshuo" (Speech at the Opening Ceremony of the Army Officer Academy), June 16, 1924, in CAMS Military History Research Division, *Zhongguo renmin jiefangjun de qishinian, 1927–97* (Seventy Years of the PLA, 1927–97) (Beijing: Junshi kexue chubanshe, 1997), 7.

102. Edward L. Dreyer, *China at War, 1901–1949* (New York: Longman, 1995), 182–83, 191.

103. Grasso, Corrin, and Kort, *Modernization and Revolution in China*, 89–90; Bailey, *China in the Twentieth Century*, 104–5.

104. CCP Archival and Manuscript Research Division, *Zhou Enlai nianpu, 1898–1949* (A Chronological Record of Zhou Enlai, 1898–1949) (Beijing: Zhongyang wenxian chubanshe, 1990), 5–24; CAMS Military History Research Division, *Zhongguo renmin jiefangjun de qishinian*, 6. For more on Zhou, see Kuo-kang Shao, *Zhou Enlai and the Foundations of Chinese Foreign Policy* (New York: St. Martin's, 1996), and Ronald C. Keith, *The Diplomacy of Zhou Enlai* (New York: St. Martin's, 1989).

105. Chang and Halliday point out that Zhou's support of and loyalty to Mao resulted from his unwillingness or inability to be number one. For discussion of the early Zhou-Mao relationship, see Chang and Halliday, *Mao*, 72, 74, 94, 112.

106. Xu, *Junshijia Mao Zedong*, 10; Scobell, *China's Use of Military Force*, 61.

107. National Military Museum, *Zhongguo zhanzheng fazhanshi*, 2:802; Saich, *Rise to Power*, xx.

108. Xu, *Junshijia Mao Zedong*, 10–11; Saich, *Rise to Power*, xxi.

109. CCP Party History Research Division, *Zhongguo gongchandang lishi dashiji*, 28–29; Saich, *Rise to Power*, 144.

110. National Military Museum, *Zhongguo zhanzheng fazhanshi*, 2:806–7; Compilation Committee of ROC History, *Pictorial History*, 1:263–66.

111. National Military Museum, *Zhongguo zhanzheng fazhanshi*, 2:814–15; Schoppa, *Revolution and Its Past*, 194–95.

112. Dreyer, *China at War*, 356.

113. CCP Party History Research Division, *Zhongguo gongchandang lishi dashiji*, 44–45.

114. Chang and Halliday, *Mao*, 40–44.

115. Mao Zedong, "Report on an Investigation of the Peasant Movement in Hunan," in *Selected Works of Mao Tse-tung*, 1:23.

116. CCP Party History Research Division, *Zhongguo gongchandang lishi dashiji*, 43–44; National Military Museum, *Zhongguo zhanzheng fazhanshi*, 2:816; Bailey, *China in the Twentieth Century*, 108–9; Grasso, Corrin, and Kort, *Modernization and Revolution in China*, 95.

117. Wang quoted in Shanghai University et al., *Xinbian zhongguo xiandashi*, 1:254.

118. Ibid., 1:254–45; Compilation Committee of ROC History, *Pictorial History*, 1:278–80.

119. Zarrow, *China in War and Revolution*, 241.

120. Ibid., 240.

121. Cai Hesen, "Dangnei jihui zhuyi de lishi huigu" (History of the Party's Opportunists), *Dangshi yanjiu ziliao* 4, no. 2 (2001): 508.

122. CCP Central Archives, *Zhonggong zhongyang wenjian xuanji*, 3:340.

123. On July 20, 1927, the CCP Central Committee reorganized its leadership with an emergency standing committee to replace Chen Duxiu, who was released from his position as chairman of the Central Committee. CCP Party History Research Division, *Zhongguo gongchandang lishi dashiji*, 47.

2. The Formative Years

1. CCP Archival and Manuscript Research Division, *Mao Zedong nianpu*, 1:208; Mao Zedong, "Comments on the Report of the Comintern Representative," August 7, 1927, in Saich, *Rise to Power*, 317. Mao said it again in 1938: "Every Communist must grasp the truth, 'Political power grows out of the barrel of a gun.'" Mao Zedong, "Problems of War and Strategy," in *Selected Works of Mao Tse-tung*, 2:224.

2. CAMS Military History Research Division, *Zhongguo renmin jiefangjun de qishinian*, 31; NDU War History Division, *Zhongguo renmin jiefangjun zhanshi jianbian* (A Brief History of the PLA Revolutionary War) (Beijing: Jiefangjun chubanshe, 2001), 20; Elleman, *Modern Chinese Warfare*, 217.

3. CAMS Military History Research Division, *Zhongguo renmin jiefang-*

jun de qishinian, 152–53; Maurice Meisner, *Mao's China: A History of the People's Republic* (New York: Free Press, 1977), 33.

4. Han Huaizhi and Tan Jingqiao, *Dangdai zhongguo jundui de junshi gongzuo* (Contemporary Chinese Military Affairs) (Beijing: Zhongguo shehui kexue shubanshe, 1989), 1:18; Bailey, *China in the Twentieth Century*, 137.

5. Han and Tan, *Dangdai zhongguo jundui de junshi gongzuo*, 1:35; Xu Yan, "Chinese Forces and Their Casualties in the Korean War," trans. Xiaobing Li, *Chinese Historians* 6, no. 2 (Fall 1993): 46.

6. Zhang, *Wo de huiyi*, 1:594–95; Meisner, *Mao's China*, 27.

7. Zhang, *Wo de huiyi*, 1:604–5; Elleman, *Modern Chinese Warfare*, 217.

8. CAMS Military History Research Division, *Zhongguo renmin jiefangjun de qishinian*, 19–21; Bailey, *China in the Twentieth Century*, 109–10.

9. Han and Tan, *Dangdai zhongguo jundui de junshi gongzuo*, 1:18; Dreyer, *China at War*, 156.

10. CAMS Military History Research Division, *Zhongguo renmin jiefangjun de qishinian*, 21.

11. Zhang, *Wo de huiyi*, 2:170–72; Elleman, *Modern Chinese Warfare*, 219.

12. CCP Archival and Manuscript Research Division, *Zhu De nianpu, 1886–1976* (A Chronological Record of Zhu De, 1886–1976) (Beijing: Renmin chubanshe, 1986), 8–15; Dreyer, *China at War*, 157; Shum Kui-kwong, *Zhu De* (St. Lucia: University of Queensland Press, 1982), 3. For more on Zhu, see William W. Whitson with Chen-hsia Huang, *The Chinese High Command: A History of Communist Military Politics, 1927–71* (New York: Praeger, 1973), and Fang Zhu, *Gun Barrel Politics: Party-Army Relations in Mao's China* (Boulder, CO: Westview Press, 1998).

13. According to *Zhu De nianpu*, Zhu graduated from the academy on October 11, 1911. CCP Archival and Manuscript Research Division, *Zhu De nianpu*, 16. Other Chinese sources, however, say that Zhu had an early graduation in August. See, for example, Wu Dianrao, *Zhu De* (Beijing: Kunlun chubanshe, 1999), 12–13.

14. CCP Archival and Manuscript Research Division, *Zhu De nianpu*, 22–31; Shum, *Zhu De*, 4–5.

15. CCP Archival and Manuscript Research Division, *Zhu De nianpu*, 17–32.

16. Wei, "Mao and the Red Army," 234.

17. CCP Archival and Manuscript Research Division, *Zhu De nianpu*, 47–49; Wu, *Zhu De*, 38.

18. CCP Party History Research Division, *Zhongguo gongchandang lishi dashiji*, 50.

19. National Military Museum, *Zhongguo zhanzheng fazhanshi*, 2:821–22; CCP Party History Research Division, *Zhongguo gongchandang lishi dashiji*, 51; Chang and Halliday, *Mao*, 50–51.

20. Mao, "Report on an Investigation of the Peasant Movement," 1:23–62.

21. CAMS Military History Research Division, *Zhongguo renmin jiefangjun de qishinian*, 22–23.

22. Mao Zedong, "The Struggle in the Chingkang Mountains," November 25, 1928, in *Selected Works of Mao Tse-tung*, 1:99.

23. Mao used one of his favorite novels, *Shuihu zhuan* (The Water Margin), to describe his decision to go to the Jinggang Mountains. In this Chinese classic, heroes fight corrupt and greedy officials in the Song regime, which suppresses the rebels. The rebels get together at Liang Mountain to continue their struggle.

24. Yang Kuisong, *Zouxiang polie: Mao Zedong yu Moscow de enen yuanyuan* (Toward the Split: Interests and Conflicts between Mao Zedong and Moscow) (Hong Kong: Sanlian shudian, 1999), 14.

25. Chinese historians call Jinggangshan "geming yaolan" (the cradle of the revolution). See CAMS Military History Research Division, *Zhongguo renmin jiefangjun de qishinian*, 31; NDU War History Division, *Zhongguo renmin jiefangjun zhanshi jianbian*, 20; and Elleman, *Modern Chinese Warfare*, 217.

26. CCP Central Archives, *Zhonggong zhongyang wenjian xuanji*, 4:232.

27. Wei, "Mao and the Red Army," 234.

28. These rules and points went through some changes before being finalized in 1947 as follows. The Three Main Rules of Discipline: (1) obey orders in all your actions; (2) don't take a single needle or piece of thread from the masses; and (3) turn in everything captured. The Eight Points for Attention: (1) speak politely; (2) pay fairly for what you buy; (3) return everything you borrow; (4) pay for anything you damage; (5) don't hit or swear at people; (6) don't damage crops; (7) don't take liberties with women; and (8) don't mistreat captives. PLA General Headquarters, "Instruction on the Re-issue of the Three Main Rules of Discipline and the Eight Points for Attention," in *Selected Works of Mao Tse-tung*, 4:155–56.

29. Mao, "Struggle in the Chingkang Mountains," 1:83.

30. The captain's letter is cited in CCP Archival and Manuscript Research Division, *Mao Zedong nianpu*, 1:223.

31. Mao, "Struggle in the Chingkang Mountains," 1:82.

32. Ibid., 1:73–104.

33. Mao Zedong, "A Single Spark Can Start a Prairie Fire," in *Selected*

Works of Mao Tse-tung, 1:124; CCP Archival and Manuscript Research Division, *Mao Zedong nianpu*, 1:243.

34. Li Baozhong, *Zhongwei junshi zhidu bijiao* (Comparative Study of the Chinese Military System) (Beijing: Shangwu yinshuguan, 2003), 350.

35. Mao Zedong, "Why Is It That Red Political Power Can Exist in China?" in *Selected Works of Mao Tse-tung*, 1:72n8.

36. In this failed CCP-organized uprising, more than four thousand men were killed, including a couple of Soviet officers. The uprising used 100,000 yuan (approximately $30,000) of Soviet financial aid.

37. National Military Museum, *Zhongguo zhanzheng fazhanshi*, 2:829–30.

38. CCP Central Archives, *Zhonggong zhongyang wenjian xuanji*, 4:233.

39. Mao, "Struggle in the Chingkang Mountains," 1:81–82.

40. Mao Zedong to Lin Biao, June 14, 1929, in *Mao Zedong junshi wenji*, 1:80–81.

41. Mao, "Problems of War and Strategy," 2:224; Dreyer, *China at War*, 5.

42. Saich, *Rise to Power*, 499n18.

43. "Resolution on the Peasant Question," July 9, 1928, in Saich, *Rise to Power*, 369–76.

44. "Ganyu hongjun qingkuang de baogao" (Letter from the Fourth Army to the CCP Central Committee), in *Mao Zedong junshi wenxuan*, 1:5–6.

45. Xu, *Junshijia Mao Zedong*, 22–24.

46. Qian Haihao, *Jundui zuzhi bianzhixue jiaocheng* (CAMS Graduate School Curriculum: Military Organization and Formation) (Beijing: Junshi kexue chubanshe, 2001), 37–38.

47. For the First All-China Soviet Congress and the constitution of the Chinese Soviet Republic, see Saich, *Rise to Power*, 514–15, 552–56.

48. Mady W. Segal, Xiaolin Li, and David R. Segal, "The Role of Women in the Chinese People's Liberation Army," *Minerva* 10 (March 1992): 48.

49. Qian, *Jundui zuzhi bianzhixue jiaocheng*, 38; National Military Museum, *Zhongguo zhanzheng fazhanshi*, 2:835.

50. Li, *Zhongwei junshi zhidu bijiao*, 350.

51. For details of Jiang's five offensive campaigns, see NDU War History Division, *Zhongguo renmin jiefangjun zhanshi jianbian*, 67–103, and Zarrow, *China in War and Revolution*, 288.

52. Gen. Jiang Weiguo (Nationalist Army, ret.; president, Taiwan Strategic Society), interview by the author, Taipei, Taiwan, May 1994.

53. Ibid.

54. Mao pointed out that, at the time of the first counteroffensive campaign in Jiangxi, "the principle of 'luring the enemy in deep' was put forward

and, moreover, successfully applied." Mao Zedong, "Problems of Strategy in China's Revolutionary War," in *Selected Works of Mao Tse-tung*, 1:213; Mao Zedong, telegram to the Central Committee, "Guanyu er-yu-wan yin xuandi ruodian qiandi qiyibu de yijian" (Proposal to Identify the Weak Enemy and Eliminate It in Hubei, Henan, and Anhui), September 30, 1932, in *Mao Zedong junshi wenji*, 1:305–6.

55. Yang, *Zouxiang polie*, 41–42.

56. Mao Zedong to the CCP Jiangxi Provincial Committee, November 20, 1930, in *Mao Zedong junshi wenji*, 1:185.

57. NDU War History Division, *Zhongguo renmin jiefangjun zhanshi jianbian*, 121; Zarrow, *China in War and Revolution*, 288.

58. Mao Zedong, "On Tactics against Japanese Imperialism," December 27, 1935, in *Selected Works of Mao Tse-tung*, 1:153–78; Chang and Halliday, *Mao*, 157.

59. Mao, "On Tactics against Japanese Imperialism," 1:160.

60. Zhang, *Wo de huiyi*, 2:377; Chang and Halliday, *Mao*, 157.

61. CAMS Military History Research Division, *Zhongguo renmin jiefangjun de qishinian*, 128.

62. Recently, Zhang's memoir, *Wo de huiyi*, was published in the inner circle of Beijing. His accounts of the Long March and his "separation plot" are different from those of CCP and PLA official history. Zhang, *Wo de huiyi*, 2:416–23.

63. Ibid., 2:541–45; Chang and Halliday, *Mao*, 162–71.

64. Minister Ma Zhaoxiang, interview by the author, Beijing, April 2000.

65. Hu Yaobang appointed Ma vice minister of the Education Ministry in the early 1980s. Ma Changzheng (son of Ma Zhaoxiang), interview by the author, Beijing, July 2004.

66. Ibid.

67. Segal, Li, and Segal, "Role of Women," 48.

68. Shang Fang, "Li Zhen: The First Chinese Woman General," in National Women Association Organization Department, comp., *Zhongguo nujiangjun* (Chinese Women Generals) (Shenyang: Liaoning renmin chubanshe, 1995), 1, 10.

69. Ibid., 10.

70. Xinghuo Liaoyuan Composition Department, *Zhongguo renmin jiefangjun jiangshuai minglu* (Marshals and Generals of the PLA) (Beijing: Jiefangjun chubanshe, 1992), 2:402.

71. Mao, "On Tactics against Japanese Imperialism," 1:160.

72. CAMS Military History Research Division, *Zhongguo renmin jiefangjun de qishinian*, 131–33.

73. Yang, *Zouxiang polie*, 53.

74. NDU War History Division, *Zhongguo renmin jiefangjun zhanshi jianbian*, 194–95.

75. Meisner, *Mao's China*, 34.

76. Joseph Stalin, telegrams, September 27 and October 18, 1936, quoted in Yang, *Zouxiang polie*, 192.

77. Zhang, *Wo de huiyi*, 462–63.

78. Yang, *Zouxiang polie*, 193.

79. Mao, "Problems of Strategy in China's Revolutionary War," 1:337–41.

80. Chang and Halliday, *Mao*, 213.

81. Yang, *Zouxiang polie*, 58.

82. Qian, *Jundui zuzhi bianzhixue jiaocheng*, 39.

83. NDU War History Division, *Zhongguo renmin jiefangjun zhanshi jianbian*, 258.

84. Ibid., 257–58; Elleman, *Modern Chinese Warfare*, 205–6.

85. Iris Chang, *The Rape of Nanking: The Forgotten Holocaust of World War II* (New York: Basic Books, 1997), 4.

86. ROC Defense Department Bureau of Historical and Political Compilations, *Gu Zhutong jiangjun jinianji* (Recollection of General Gu Zhutong's Works) (Taipei, Taiwan: Guofangbu shizheng bianyiju, 1988), 57–58, 275–76; National Military Museum, *Zhongguo zhanzheng fazhanshi*, 2:942.

87. Dreyer, *China at War*, 7.

88. The literature on CCP military operations behind enemy lines during the Second Sino-Japanese War is rich in China. See, for example, Chih Feng, *Behind Enemy Lines* (Beijing: Foreign Languages Press, 1979), chaps. 2–5.

89. Li, *Zhongwei junshi zhidu bijiao*, 229.

90. Jiang Shufeng, interview by the author, Beijing, July–August 1992. Jiang Shufeng helped Wang Zhelan and Jiang Zemin until Wang's death on August 10, 1985.

91. Saich, *Rise to Power*, lii.

92. CAMS Military History Research Division, *Zhongguo renmin jiefangjun de qishinian*, 195, 197.

93. Wan Qing, interviews by the author, Beijing, July 1999 and April 2000.

94. Edgar Snow, *Red Star over China*, 69–70, 474–75.

95. Mao Zedong, "On Protracted War," in *Selected Works of Mao Tsetung*, 2:109–94.

96. Ibid., 2:183, 186.

97. Mao, "Problems of Strategy in China's Revolutionary War," 1:190.

98. CAMS Military History Research Division, *Zhongguo renmin jiefangjun de qishinian*, 236–39; Zarrow, *China in War and Revolution*, 324–25.

99. Mao, "Problems of War and Strategy," 2:226.

100. Liu Xiaoyuan, *A Partnership for Disorder: China, the United States, and Their Policies for the Postwar Disposition of the Japanese Empire, 1941–1945* (Cambridge: Cambridge University Press, 1996), 3.

101. Ibid., 200.

102. NDU War History Division, *Zhongguo renmin jiefangjun zhanshi jianbian*, 484.

103. Mao Zedong, "On Coalition Government," political report to the CCP Seventh National Congress, April 24, 1945, in *Selected Works of Mao Tse-tung*, 3:205–70.

104. NDU War History Division, *Zhongguo renmin jiefangjun zhanshi jianbian*, 484.

105. Qian, *Jundui zuzhi bianzhixue jiaocheng*, 39.

106. CAMS Military History Research Division, *Zhongguo renmin jiefangjun de qishinian*, 256.

107. Compilation Committee of ROC History, *Pictorial History*, 2:255–56.

108. CAMS Military History Research Division, *Zhongguo renmin jiefangjun de qishinian*, 259; Zarrow, *China in War and Revolution*, 330–31.

109. Patrick Hurley, "Aide Memoirs," and Hurley to President Roosevelt, September 25, 1944, Patrick Hurley Papers, University of Oklahoma Library, Norman.

110. Compilation Committee of ROC History, *Pictorial History*, 2:259.

111. Mao Zedong, "The Situation and Our Policy after the Victory in the War of Resistance against Japan," in *Selected Works of Mao Tse-tung*, 4:14.

112. Lanxin Xiang, *Recasting the Imperial Far East: Britain and America in China, 1945–1950* (Armonk, NY: M. E. Sharpe, 1995), 142.

113. CAMS Military History Research Division, *Zhongguo renmin jiefangjun de qishinian*, 274.

114. CAMS Military History Research Division, *Zhongguo renmin jiefangjun quanguo jiefang zhanzhengshi* (History of the PLA in the Chinese Civil War) (Beijing: Junshi kexue chubanshe, 1997), 1:11–72; Qian, *Jundui zuzhi bianzhixue jiaocheng*, 39.

115. Qian, *Jundui zuzhi bianzhixue jiaocheng*, 39–40.

116. CCP Central Committee document quoted in Li, *Zhongwei junshi zhidu bijiao*, 231.

117. CAMS Military History Research Division, *Zhongguo renmin jiefangjun de qishinian*, 266–67.

118. NDU War History Division, *Zhongguo renmin jiefangjun zhanshi jianbian*, 542.

119. Mao Zedong, "Greet the New High Tide of the Chinese Revolution," in *Selected Works of Mao Tse-tung*, 4:119–24.

120. Odd Arne Westad, *Decisive Encounters: The Chinese Civil War, 1946–1950* (Stanford, CA: Stanford University Press, 2003), 107.

121. Ibid., 279.

122. Mao Zedong, "Present Situation and Our Tasks," report to the Central Committee, December 25–28, 1947, in *Selected Works of Mao Tse-tung*, 4:164.

123. CAMS Military History Research Division, *Zhongguo renmin jiefangjun quanguo jiefang zhanzhengshi*, 4:14–16, 649–51.

124. NDU War History Division, *Zhongguo renmin jiefangjun zhanshi jianbian*, 566.

125. Mao Zedong, "Manifesto of the Chinese People's Liberation Army," October 10, 1947, in *Selected Works of Mao Tse-tung*, 4:150. This political manifesto, drafted by Mao at Shenchuanpao, northern Shaanxi, and issued to the PLA general headquarters, is known as the October 10 manifesto.

126. CAMS Military History Research Division, *Zhongguo renmin jiefangjun quanguo jiefang zhanzhengshi*, 3:1–3.

127. Ibid., 3:2.

128. Ibid., 4:4–5.

129. For the Liao-Shen campaign, see ibid., 4:132–96; for the Ping-Jin campaign, see ibid., 4:407–80, and for the Huai-Hai campaign, see ibid., 4:272–357.

130. Qian, *Jundui zuzhi bianzhixue jiaocheng*, 40.

131. After Jiang proposed a cease-fire, Mao delivered several speeches and wrote several articles to explain why he and the CCP could not have peace talks with Jiang. See Mao Zedong, "On the War Criminal's Suing for Peace," "Statement on the Present Situation by Mao Tse-tung, Chairman of the Central Committee of the CCP," and "Comment by the Spokesman for the CCP on the Resolution of the Nanking Executive Yuan," in *Selected Works of Mao Tse-tung*, 4:309–24.

132. Mao Zedong, "Order to the Army for the Country-wide Advance," in *Selected Works of Mao Tse-tung*, 4:387–97.

133. CAMS Military History Research Division, *Zhongguo renmin jiefangjun quanguo jiefang zhanzhengshi*, 5:146–211; CAMS Military History Research Division, *Zhongguo renmin jiefangjun de qishinian*, 357.

134. Joseph W. Esherick, "Revolution in a Feudal Fortress," *Modern China* 24, no. 4 (October 1998): 370.

135. Suzanne Pepper, *Civil War in China: The Political Struggle, 1945–1949* (Berkeley: University of California Press, 1978), 75.

136. Dreyer, *China at War*, 7.

137. Meisner, *Mao's China*, 55–56.

138. David M. Finkelstein, *Washington's Taiwan Dilemma, 1949–1950: From Abandonment to Salvation* (Fairfax, VA: George Mason University Press, 1993), 208.

3. Transformation in Korea

1. Among the recent Chinese publications on the Korean War, see especially Chu Yun, *Chaoxian zhanzheng neimu quangongkai* (Declassifying the Inside Story of the Korean War) (Beijing: Shishi chubanshe, 2005); Shen Zhihua, *Mao Zedong, Stalin he chaoxian zhanzheng* (Mao Zedong, Stalin, and the Korean War) (Guangzhou: Guangdong renmin chubanshe, 2004); Wang Shuzeng, *Yuandong chaoxian zhanzheng* (The Korean War in the Far East) (Beijing: Jiefangjun wenyi chubanshe, 2000); NDU War History Division, *Zhongguo renmin zhiyuanjun zhanshi jianbian* (A Brief War-Fighting History of the CPVF) (Beijing: Jiefangjun chubanshe, 1992); Tan Jingjiao, *Kangmei yuanchao zhanzheng* (The War to Resist America and Aid Korea) (Beijing: Zhongguo shehui kexue chubanshe, 1990); Xu Yan, *Diyici jiaoliang: Kangmei yuanchao zhanzheng de lishi huigu yu fansi* (The First Encounter: A Historical Retrospective of the War to Resist America and Aid Korea) (Beijing: Zhongguo guangbo dianshi chubanshe, 1990); and CAMS Military History Research Division, *Zhongguo renmin zhiyuanjun kangmei yuanchao zhanshi* (War Experience of the CPVF in the War to Resist America and Aid Korea), 2nd ed. (Beijing: Junshi kexue chubanshe, 1990).

Among the recent Western publications on the Korean War, see especially Allan R. Millett, *The War for Korea, 1945–1950: A House Burning* (Lawrence: University Press of Kansas, 2005); William W. Stueck Jr., ed., *The Korean War in World History* (Lexington: University Press of Kentucky, 2004); Mark F. Wilkinson, ed., *The Korean War at Fifty: International Perspectives* (Lexington: Virginia Military Institute, 2004); Stanley Weintraub, *MacArthur's War: Korea and the Undoing of an American Hero* (New York: Free Press, 2000); Stanley Sandler, *The Korean War: No Victors, No Vanquished* (Lexington: University Press of Kentucky, 1999); Shuguang Zhang, *Mao's Military Romanticism: China and the Korean War, 1950–1953* (Lawrence: University Press of Kansas, 1995); Chen Jian, *China's Road to the Korean War: The Making of the Sino-American Confrontation* (New York: Columbia University Press, 1994); and Bruce Cummings, *The Origins of the Korean War*, 2 vols. (Lawrence: University Press of Kansas, 1981–90).

2. Chu Yun, *Chaoxian zhanzheng neimu quangongkai*, 161; Shen Zhihua, "China Sends Troops to Korea: Beijing's Policy-making Process," in *China and the United States: A New Cold War History*, ed. Xiaobing Li and Hongshan Li (Lanham, MD: University Press of America, 1998), 13.

3. MacArthur quoted in William W. Stueck Jr., *The Road to Confrontation: American Policy toward China and Korea, 1947–1950* (Chapel Hill: University of North Carolina Press, 1981), 3.

4. Ellis Joffe, *Party and Army: Professionalism and Political Control in the Chinese Officer Corps, 1948–1964* (Cambridge, MA: Harvard University Press, 1967), ix.

5. Mao Zedong, "Kangmei yuanchao de weida shengli he jinhou de renwu" (The Great Victory of the War to Resist America and Aid Korea and Our Task), in *Mao Zedong xuanji* (Selected Works of Mao Zedong) (Beijing: Renmin chubanshe, 1977), 5:101–6; Mao Zedong, "Guanyu kangmei yuanchao zhanzheng de baogao tigong" (Outline of the Speech on the War to Resist America and Aid Korea), speech at the twenty-fourth committee meeting of the central government, September 1953, in *Jianguo yilai Mao Zedong wengao*, 4:330.

6. Peng Dehuai, "Si'nianlai de junshi gongzuo zongjie he jinhou junshi jiansheshang de jige jiben wenti" (China's Military Experience in the Past Four Years and the Fundamental Issues for Our Future Military Development), speech at an expanded CMC meeting, December 1953, in *Peng Dehuai junshi wenxuan*, 468–69.

7. Liu Shaoqi, CMC telegram to Lin Biao and others, "Junwei tongyi siye chaoxian guanbing hui chaoxian" (Agree to Return the Korean Officers and Soldiers of the Fourth Field Army to Korea), January 11, 1950, in *Jianguo yilai Liu Shaoqi wengao*, 1:319.

8. Col. Lee Jong Kan, interview by the author, Harbin, Heilongjiang, July 2002. Also see Lee Jong Kan, "A North Korean Officer's Story," in Peters and Li, *Voices from the Korean War*, 76–84, and Nie Rongzhen, "Beijing's Decision to Intervene," in Li, Millett, and Yu, *Mao's Generals Remember Korea*, 47–48.

9. The Korean PLA soldiers returned to North Korea with 12,000 rifles, 620 machine guns, and 240 artillery pieces. Liu Shaoqi, telegram to Mao Zedong, "Junwei tongyi siye chaoxian guanbing hui chaoxian" (Agree to Return the Korean Officers and Soldiers of the Fourth Field Army to Korea), January 22, 1950, in *Jianguo yilai Liu Shaoqi wengao*, 1:320–21.

10. Mao Zedong, "Guanyu tongyi baowei guofeng wenti huiyi jueyi shixiang gei Nie Rongzhen de xin" (Memorandum to Nie Rongzhen: Agree on the Resolutions by the National Defense Conference), July 7, 1950, in *Jianguo yilai Mao Zedong wengao*, 1:428; Shuguang Zhang and Chen Jian, eds., *Chinese Communist Foreign Policy and the Cold War in Asia: New Documentary Evidence, 1944–1950* (Chicago: Imprint Publications, 1996), 156; Nie, "Beijing's Decision to Intervene," 39–40.

11. Lei Yingfu, "The Establishment of the Northeast Border Defense

Army, July 1950," in Xiaobing Li, Don Duffy, and Zujian Zhang, "Chinese Generals Recall the Korean War," *Chinese Historians* 7, nos. 1–2 (Spring–Fall 1994): 127–29; Xu, *Diyici jiaoliang*, 16–18; Feng Xianzhi and Li Jie, *Mao Zedong yu kangmei yuanchao* (Mao Zedong and the War to Resist America and Aid Korea) (Beijing: Zhongyang wenxian chubanshe, 2000), 4.

12. Chai Junwu (Chai Chengwen), "Zhu chaoxian shiguan linshi daiban Chai Junwu de gongzuo baogao" (Task Report by Chai Junwu, Charge of Chinese Embassy to North Korea), July 17, 1950, file 106-00001-04 (1), Archives of the PRC Ministry of Foreign Affairs, Beijing (hereafter cited as Foreign Ministry Archives).

13. Zhou Enlai, memorandum to North Korean ambassador Lee, "Guanyu jiaqiang zhongguo yu chaoxian youxian dianlu lianxi shi" (To Strengthen the Wired Communication Lines between China and [North] Korea), July 29, 1950, file 106-00023-02 (1), Foreign Ministry Archives.

14. Mao Zedong, CMC telegram to Gao Gang, August 5, 1950, in Xiaobing Li, Xi Wang, and Chen Jian, "Mao's Dispatch of Chinese Troops to Korea: Forty-six Telegrams, July–October 1950," *Chinese Historians* 5, no. 1 (Spring 1992): 64; Zhang and Chen, *Chinese Communist Foreign Policy*, 157.

15. Du Ping, "Political Mobilization and Control," in Li, Millett, and Yu, *Mao's Generals Remember Korea*, 62; Zhang, *Mao's Military Romanticism*, 81.

16. CAMS Military Research History Division, *Zhongguo renmin zhiyuanjun kangmei yuanchao zhanshi*, 6.

17. Chen Jiakang, "Guanyu chaoxian yaoqiu song jieke dengguo yuanchao wuzi ji tigong miaozhunqi shi" (Korea's Request for Aiming Equipment and Transporting Czechoslovakia's War Materials to North Korea), report to Zhou Enlai, September 3, 1950, file 106-00022-04 (1), 1, Foreign Ministry Archives.

18. Stalin quoted in Shen, "China Sends Troops to Korea," 28. Also see Shen, *Mao Zedong, Stalin he chaoxian zhanzheng*, 221.

19. Wang Shuzeng, *Zhongguo renmin zhiyuanjun zhengzhan jishi* (The True Story of the CPVF's War Experience) (Beijing: Jiefangjun wenyi chubanshe, 2000), 85; Shen, *Mao Zedong, Stalin he chaoxian zhanzheng*, 228–29; Nie, "Beijing's Decision to Intervene," 41.

20. Lin quoted in Shen, "China Sends Troops to Korea," 29; Chen, *China's Road to the Korean War*, 281n78.

21. For more detailed discussions of the Soviet factors, see Tao Wenzhao, *Zhongmei guanxishi, 1949–72* (PRC-U.S. Relations, 1949–72) (Shanghai: Shanghai renmin chubanshe, 1999), 24–25; Qi Dexue, "Youguan kangmei yuanchao zhanzheng de jige wenti" (Several Issues on Resisting the United States and Aiding the Korean War), *Zhonggong dangshi yanjiu* 1 (1998): 75–76; and Scobell, *China's Use of Military Force*, 82–89.

22. The Sino-Soviet Treaty of Friendship, Alliance, and Mutual Assistance stated that if one side was attacked by a third country, the other side "must go all out to provide military and other assistance." Mao Zedong, telegram to Liu Shaoqi, "Guanyu zhongsu huitan he wenjian qicao qingkuang" (On Sino-Soviet Negotiations and Document Drafting), January 25, 1950, in *Jianguo yilai Mao Zedong wengao*, 1:251–22; Zhang and Chen, *Chinese Communist Foreign Policy*, 140–41.

23. Peng Dehuai, "My Story of the Korean War," in Li, Millett, and Yu, *Mao's Generals Remember Korea*, 32.

24. Wang Yan, *Peng Dehuai zhuan* (Biography of Peng Dehuai) (Beijing: Dangdai zhongguo chubanshe, 1993), 372, 388; Xinghuo Liaoyuan Composition Department, *Zhongguo renmin jiefangjun jiangshuai minglu*, 1:20; Peng, "My Story," 30.

25. Peng Dehuai Biography Compilation Team, *Yige zhanzheng de ren* (A Real Man) (Beijing: Renmin chubanshe, 1994), 166–67; Peng, "My Story," 33.

26. Nie, "Beijing's Decision to Intervene," 42; Wang, *Peng Dehuai zhuan*, 401–3; Elleman, *Modern Chinese Warfare*, 246–47.

27. Mao Zedong, "Wojun yingdang he bixu ruchao canzhan" (CMC Order to Establish the CPVF), in *Mao Zedong junshi wenji*, 6:117; *Mao Zedong wenji* (A Collection of Mao Zedong's Works) (Beijing: Renmin chubanshe, 1999), 6:100–101; Zhang and Chen, *Chinese Communist Foreign Policy*, 164–65.

28. Peng quoted in Xu, "Chinese Forces," 48.

29. Peng concentrated a superior force so as to outnumber the enemy wherever the situation permitted. His goal was to eliminate entire enemy battalions, regiments, or divisions, rather than to simply repel the enemy from the peninsula. Peng Dehuai Biography Compilation Team, *Yige zhanzheng de ren*, 178; Peng, "My Story," 32–33; CAMS Military Research History Division, *Zhongguo renmin zhiyuanjun kangmei yuanchao zhanshi*, 11; Feng and Li, *Mao Zedong yu kangmei yuanchao*, 30.

30. Peng Dehuai, "Zai zhiyuanjun shiyishang ganbu dongyuan dahui shang de jianghua" (Speech at the CPVF Army and Division Commanders Meeting), October 14, 1950, in *Peng Dehuai junshi wenxuan*, 324.

31. For a more detailed discussion of the 1950 PLA demobilization, see Han and Tan, *Dangdai zhongguo jundui de junshi gongzuo*, vol. 1, chaps. 1–2.

32. Tan, *Kangmei yuanchao zhanzheng*, 24–25; Wang, *Yuandong chaoxian zhanzheng*, 1:79–80.

33. Col. Yang Shaojun, interview by the author, Beijing, July 1994. Yang served as a PLA recruiting officer during the early 1950s.

34. Among the recent Chinese books that credit the Korean War mobili-

zation to the victory of the civil war are Wang, *Yuandong chaoxian zhanzheng*, 1:138–39; Tan, *Kangmei yuanchao zhanzheng*, 24–25; and Xu, *Diyici jiaoliang*, 28–89.

35. Col. Yang, interview. Also see Li Hongjie, *Zhenyi de zhanzheng, weida de jingshen* (The Just War and Great Spirit) (Guangzhou: Guangdong renmin chubanshe, 2001), 20–22, and Zhao Shaoquan, *Xinbian zhongguo xiandaishi* (New History of Modern China) (Nanchang: Jiangxi renmin chubanshe, 1987), 3:41–42, 46–47.

36. Shen, *Mao Zedong, Stalin he chaoxian zhanzheng*, 229–30.

37. Ibid., 254nn51–52; Sulamith H. Potter and Jack M. Potter, *China's Peasants: The Anthropology of a Revolution* (Cambridge: Cambridge University Press, 1990), 35.

38. CAMS Military Research History Division, *Zhongguo renmin zhiyuanjun kangmei yuanchao zhanshi*, 8–9; provincial government files (1949–66), Heilongjiang Provincial Government Archives, Harbin.

39. Col. Yang, interview; CAMS Military History Research Division, *Zhongguo renmin zhiyuanjun kangmei yuanchao zhanshi*, 8.

40. Col. Yang, interview; Deng Lifeng, "Yuanshuai zuozhen: Gongheguo zhichu de junshi guanzhi" (Marshals Commanding the Cities: Municipal Military Administration during the PRC Early Years," in CAMS Military History Research Division, *Junqi piaopiao: Xinzhongguo 50 nian junshi dashi shushi* (PLA Flag Fluttering: Facts of China's Major Military Events in the Past 50 Years) (Beijing: Jiefangjun chubanshe, 1999), 1:42.

41. Bo Yibo, *Ruogan zhongda juece yu shijian de huigu* (Recollections of Certain Important Decisions and Events) (Beijing: Zhonggong zhongyang dangxiao chubanshe, 1991), 1:8; CCP Liaoning Provincial Revolutionary Military Committee, "Guanyu Shenyang chengshi huifu gongzuo de baogao" (Report on the City Recovery of Shenyang), December 1949, provincial government files (1948–68), Liaoning Provincial Government Archives, Shenyang.

42. CCP Central Committee, "Zhonggong zhongyang guanyu junshi guanzhi wenti de zhishi" (Central Committee's Instruction on the Military Administration), in Central Archives, *Zhonggong zhongyang wenjian xuanji*, 17:487–88.

43. Deng, "Yuanshuai zuozhen," 1:47–48.

44. CAMS Military Research History Division, *Zhongguo renmin zhiyuanjun kangmei yuanchao zhanshi*, 236–37; Zhang, *Mao's Military Romanticism*, 255, 258.

45. Xiaobing Li, "The Korean War," in *Encyclopedia of Contemporary Chinese Civilization: 1949–Present*, ed. Jing Luo (Westport, CT: Greenwood Press, 2005), 1:324–27.

46. Mao Zedong, "Wei zhengqu guojia caizhen jingji zhuangkuang de jiben haozhuan er douzheng" (Strive for Complete Recovery of Our Country's Financial and Economic Conditions), in *Mao Zedong xuanji*, 5:15–20.

47. PRC State Council and People's Supreme Court, "Youguan zhenfan gongzuo de zhishi" (Directive concerning the Suppressing of Counterrevolutionaries), in CCP Central Institute of Historical Documents, comp., *Jianguo yilai zhongyao wenxian xuanbian* (Selected Important Documents since the Founding of the PRC) (Beijing: Zhongyang wenxian chubanshe, 1992), 1:358–59.

48. CAMS Military History Research Division, *Zhongguo renmin jiefangjun quanguo jiefang zhanzhengshi*, 4:485–86, 488–90; Joseph K. S. Yick, *Making Urban Revolution in China: The CCP-GMD Struggle for Beiping-Tianjin, 1945–1949* (Armonk, NY: M. E. Sharpe, 1995), 176–77.

49. Du, "Political Mobilization and Control," 66.

50. Ibid., 67.

51. Capt. Zhou Baoshan, interview by the author, Harbin, Heilongjiang, April 2000. Also see Zhou Baoshan, "China's Crouching Dragon," in Peters and Li, *Voices from the Korean War*, 86.

52. Capt. Zhou, interview.

53. Zhou, "China's Crouching Dragon," 87.

54. Capt. Zhou, intervew; Zhou, "China's Crouching Dragon," 88.

55. CCP Heilongjiang Provincial Committee, "Guanyu dongbei bianfangjun houqin gongying yu zuozhan zhunbei de baogao" (Report on the Logistics Supplies and War Preparation for the NBDA Troops), September 30, 1950, provincial government files (1949–66), Heilongjiang Provincial Government Archives, Harbin; Zhou Zhong, *Kangmei yuanchao zhanzheng huoqinshi jianbianben* (A Concise History of the Logistics in the War to Resist America and Aid Korea) (Beijing: Jindun chubanshe, 1993), 18–19.

56. Xu, *Diyici jiaoliang*, 340–43; Zhang, *Mao's Military Romanticism*, 255; Shuguang Zhang, "China's Strategic Culture and the Cold War Confrontations," in *Reviewing the Cold War: Approaches, Interpretations, Theory*, ed. Odd Arne Westad (London: Frank Cass, 2000), 262.

57. There are a couple of explanations for this last-minute switch of leading commanders. First, Deng Hua was one of the best commanders in the Fourth Field Army and had just commanded a successful landing campaign at Hainan Island. Second, Huang Yongsheng, known as a playboy among the commanders, had just made a secret trip to Hong Kong for a good time. See Yang Di, *Zai zhiyuanjun silingbu de suiyueli* (My Years at the CPVF Headquarters) (Beijing: Jiefangjun chubanshe, 1998), 7–8.

58. Hong Xuezhi, "The CPVF's Combat and Logistics," in Li, Millett, and Yu, *Mao's Generals Remember Korea*, 107–9.

59. Yang, *Zai zhiyuanjun silingbu de suiyueli*, 47.

60. Hong Xuezhi, *Kangmei yuanchao zhanzheng huiyi* (Recollections of the War to Resist America and Aid Korea) (Beijing: Jiefangjun wenyi chubanshe, 1990), 37–38; Wang, *Yuandong chaoxian zhanzheng*, 1:152–55.

61. Yang, *Zai zhiyuanjun silingbu de suiyueli*, 51; Du, "Political Mobilization and Control," 73–74.

62. Hong, *Kangmei yuanchao zhanzheng huiyi*, 48–49.

63. Mao Zedong, "The Central Military Commission's Circular on the Combat Characteristics of South Korean Troops," October 30, 1950, in Xiaobing Li and Glenn Tracy, "Mao's Telegrams during the Korean War, October–December 1950," *Chinese Historians* 5, no. 2 (Fall 1992): 66–67.

64. The CPVF claimed to have eliminated fifteen thousand enemy troops during the first campaign. For more details, see CAMS Military Research History Division, *Zhongguo renmin zhiyuanjun kangmei yuanchao zhanshi*, 27, and Xu, *Diyici jiaoliang*, 47.

65. The American units Peng mentioned were three battalions of the U.S. First Cavalry Division. See Li, Millett, and Yu, *Mao's Generals Remember Korea*, 252n7.

66. Peng, "My Story," 33; CAMS Military Research History Division, *Zhongguo renmin zhiyuanjun kangmei yuanchao zhanshi*, 27.

67. Zhang, *Mao's Military Romanticism*, 106.

68. This statement explains the CPVF commanders' perception of the U.S. forces. The Chinese believed, for example, that the U.S. mechanized units had tremendous firepower and mobility but depended considerably on roads, bridges, air cover, and uninterrupted fuel supplies. Therefore, the U.S. troops tended to stay near roads and had no flexibility to occupy more advantageous terrain, thus providing the CPVF opportunities to separate them from each other. See CAMS Military Research History Division, *Zhongguo renmin zhiyuanjun kangmei yuanchao zhanshi*, 28.

69. Xiaobing Li, "Kim Il Sung," in *Magill's Guide to Military History*, ed. John Powell (Pasadena, CA: Salem Press, 2001), 952.

70. Hong, *Kangmei yuanchao zhanzheng huiyi*, 90–91.

71. Capt. Wang Xuedong, interview by the author, Harbin, Heilongjiang, April 2000. For more details, see Wang Xuedong, "The Chosin Reservoir: A Chinese Captain's Story," in Peters and Li, *Voices from the Korean War*, 119.

72. Cui Xianghua and Chen Dapeng, *Tao Yong jiangjun zhuan* (Biography of General Tao Yong) (Beijing: Jiefangjun chubanshe, 1989), 393.

73. Xu, *Diyici jiaoliang*, 58–59.

74. Capt. Wang Xuedong, interview.

75. Ibid.; Wang, "Chosin Reservoir," 121–22.

76. Capt. Wang Xuedong, interview.

77. Mao Zedong, telegram to Peng Dehuai, Gao Gang, Song Shilun, and Tao Yong, December 17, 1950, in *Mao Zedong junshi wenxuan*, 2:682–83.

78. Among the CPVF casualties in the second offensive campaign were fifty thousand noncombat dead. See CAMS Military Research History Division, *Zhongguo renmin zhiyuanjun kangmei yuanchao zhanshi*, 48, and Xu, *Diyici jiaoliang*, 60.

79. The CPVF claimed that the UNF had thirty-six thousand total casualties (including twenty-four thousand American troops). U.S. Army statistics show only seventeen thousand casualties. See CAMS Military Research History Division, *Zhongguo renmin zhiyuanjun kangmei yuanchao zhanshi*, 48, and Xu, *Diyici jiaoliang*, 59.

80. Bin Yu, "What China Learned from Its 'Forgotten War' in Korea," in Li, Millett, and Yu, *Mao's Generals Remember Korea*, 17.

81. In "What China Learned from Its 'Forgotten War' in Korea," Yu discusses some of the PLA's tactics, such as outnumbering the enemy when the situation permitted in order to wipe out entire enemy units; engaging the enemy in mobile operations; and achieving surprise whenever possible in order to avoid the usually superior enemy firepower. Ibid., 14.

82. Xiaobing Li, "China's Intervention and the CPVF Experience in the Korean War," in Wilkinson, *Korean War at Fifty*, 144–45.

83. Of these 8,500 casualties, 5,800 were CPVF casualties and 2,700 were NKPA casualties. The Communist forces claimed annihilation of 19,000 enemy troops during the campaign, most of whom were ROC troops. For detailed Chinese figures, see CAMS Military Research History Division, *Zhongguo renmin zhiyuanjun kangmei yuanchao zhanshi*, 48, and Xu, *Diyici jiaoliang*, 67.

84. Xiaobing Li, "Chinese Army in the Korean War, 1950–1953," *New England Journal of History* 60, nos. 1–3 (Fall 2003–Spring 2004): 282.

85. The CPVF announced their annihilation of seventy-eight thousand UNF troops in the fourth campaign. See CAMS Military Research History Division, *Zhongguo renmin zhiyuanjun kangmei yuanchao zhanshi*, 85, and Xu, *Diyici jiaoliang*, 80.

86. Liaoning provincial government, work reports and meeting minutes, January–May 1951, provincial government files (1948–68), Liaoning Provincial Government Archives, Shenyang; Xu, "Chinese Forces," 49, 51.

87. Xiaoming Zhang, *Red Wings over the Yalu: China, the Soviet Union, and the Air War in Korea* (College Station: Texas A&M University Press, 2002), 145–46.

88. Col. Zhao Zuorui, interview by the author, Shenyang, Liaoning, July 2002. Col. Zhao served as the political commissar of the 538th Regiment, 180th Division, Sixtieth Army of the CPVF. During the fifth campaign, his

regiment was assigned the mission of breaking through the UNF lines and leading the division's retreat to the north. When the regiment failed its mission, during the night of May 24, Col. Zhao lost contact with regimental headquarters. He was captured by the UNF on May 25 and became one of the 132,000 Chinese and North Korean POWs in the UNF camps. He and 7,094 other Chinese prisoners were repatriated to China in September 1953. For more details, see Zhao Zuorui, "Organizing the Riots on Koje," in Peters and Li, *Voices from the Korean War*, 243–58.

89. The Chinese still claimed to have annihilated eighty-two thousand UNF troops during the fifth campaign. See CAMS Military Research History Division, *Zhongguo renmin zhiyuanjun kangmei yuanchao zhanshi*, 109, and Xu, *Diyici jiaoliang*, 95–96.

90. Mao Zedong, "Guanyu zhunbei hetan huiyi youguan wenti gei Peng Dehuai de dianbao" (Telegram to Peng Dehuai: Issues on Truce Negotiations Preparation), July 2, 1951, in *Jianguo yilai Mao Zedong wengao*, 2:379–80.

91. Ministry of Foreign Affairs to Chinese charge d'affairs in P'yŏngyang (Gan Yetao), "Li Xiangchao lajing zhibing" (Lee Xiangchao's Visit to Beijing), February 17, 1953, 15; Ministry of Foreign Affairs to Northeastern Executive Committee, "Tongyi chaoxian pairen dao Andong dengdi gongzuo" (Arrange North Korean Representatives Working in Andong and Other Areas), April 3, 1953, 1; and Zhou Enlai, "6.25 jianghuagao (caogao)" (Speech [Draft] at the Third Anniversary of the Korean War), June 24, 1953, 24–25, in "Zhou Enlai zongli dui 1953 nian youguan chaoxian shiwuxing wendian de pifa yuanjian" (Premier Zhou Enlai's Approvals and Instructions on North Korean Telegrams and Documents, 1953), file 106-00034-01 (1), Foreign Ministry Archives.

92. Ministry of Foreign Affairs to Chinese charge d'affairs in P'yŏngyang, "Li Xiangchao lajing zhibing," 25.

93. Chai Chengwen and Zhao Yongtian, *Banmendian tanpan* (The P'anmunjŏm Negotiations), 2nd ed. (Beijing: Jiefangjun chubanshe, 1992), 200–203, 210; Clay Blair, *The Forgotten War: America in Korea, 1950–1953* (New York: Times Books, 1987), 961–64.

94. For more on trench warfare and underground tunnels, see CAMS Military Research History Division, *Zhongguo renmin zhiyuanjun kangmei yuanchao zhanshi*, 154–57, and Xu, *Diyici jiaoliang*, 122–25.

95. Capt. Zheng Yanman, interview by the author, Harbin, Heilongjiang, August 2002. Also see Zheng Yanman, "The Chinese Go Underground," in Peters and Li, *Voices from the Korean War*, 177–78.

96. Capt. Zheng, interview.

97. In 1952–53, the Chinese army had a total of 6.5 million troops, including 5.1 million PLA troops in China and 1.4 million CPVF troops in Korea. Xu, "Chinese Forces," 52–53.

98. I borrow the term "useful adversary" from Thomas J. Christensen's research on grand strategy and Sino-American relations. Thomas J. Christensen, *Useful Adversaries: Grand Strategy, Domestic Mobilization, and Sino-American Conflict, 1947–1958* (Princeton, NJ: Princeton University Press, 1996), 1–2.

99. Li, "Chinese Army in the Korean War," 286.

100. *Nie Rongzhen huiyilu* (Memoir of Nie Rongzhen) (Beijing: Jiefangjun chubanshe, 1984), 2:745–46; Xu, "Chinese Forces," 54; Li, "China's Intervention," 136–37.

101. The Soviet Union delivered weapons to China for sixteen infantry divisions in 1951 and for forty-four divisions in 1952–54. Xu Xiangqian, "The Purchase of Arms from Moscow," in Li, Millett, and Yu, *Mao's Generals Remember Korea*, 53.

102. Ministry of Foreign Affairs, "Guanyu woguo xiezhu polan yuanchao diyi di'erpi wuzi guojing de youguan wenjian" (Documents of Transporting Poland's First and Second Shipments of North Korea Aid Materials through China), April 20–October 25, 1951, file 109-00161-02 (1), Foreign Ministry Archives; "Guanyu woguo xiezhu luomaniya he jieke zhengfu jiesong chaoxian ertong ji zhuanyun yuanchao wuzi de youguan wenjian" (Documents of the Chinese Government Assisting the Governments of Romania and Czechoslovakia to Transport Korean Children [to Europe] and Korea Aid Materials), April 1–30, 1952, file 109-00232-01 (1), Foreign Ministry Archives.

103. Ministry of Railroad Transportation, "Guanyu woguo xiezhu luomaniya zhuanyun yuanchao wuzi de wanglai wenshu" (Reports and Documents on Assisting Romania to Transport North Korea Aid Materials), April 9–May 4, 1951, file 109-00144-02 (1), Foreign Ministry Archives.

104. Zhou, *Kangmei yuanchao zhanzheng huoqinshi jianbianben*, 87–88; Hong, "CPVF's Combat and Logistics," 135.

105. Hong, "CPVF's Combat and Logistics," 106.

106. Nie, "Beijing's Decision to Intervene," 53.

107. Col. Wang Po, interview by the author, Beijing, July 1994; Zhou, *Kangmei yuanchao zhanzheng huoqinshi jianbianben*, 25–29.

108. Ministry of Foreign Affairs to Foreign Affairs Office, Northeast China Executive Committee, "Guanyu xiezhu chaoxian jiejue yiyao canku shiyi" (Helping North Korea Construct More Medicine Warehouses), April 8, 1953, in "Zhou Enlai zongli dui 1953 nian youguan chaoxian shiwuxing wendian de pifa yuanjian"; Teng Daiyuan to Li Kenong, "Dongbei diqu chaoxian renminjun jiya chepi shi de zhihan" (About the Rail Cars in Northeast China Halted by the North Korean People's Army), June 29, 1951, file 106-00026-02 (1), Foreign Ministry Archives; Col. Wang Po, interview.

109. Shu Guang Zhang, "Command, Control, and the PLA's Offensive

Campaigns in Korea, 1950–1951," in Ryan, Finkelstein, and McDevitt, *Chinese Warfighting*, 110–11, 113.

110. Zhang, *Red Wings over the Yalu*, 146–48.

111. Xiaoming Zhang, "Air Combat for the People's Republic," in Ryan, Finkelstein, and McDevitt, *Chinese Warfighting*, 278.

112. Wang Hai, *Wode zhandou shengya* (My Military Career) (Beijing: Zhongyang wenxian chubanshe, 2000), 11–18, 34–38.

113. Wang Dinglie, *Dongdai zhongguo kongjun* (The PLAAF in Contemporary China) (Beijing: Zhongguo shehui kexue chubanshe, 1989), 17–25.

114. Zhang, *Red Wings over the Yalu*, 224–26; Wang, *Dongdai zhongguo kongjun*, 33–71.

115. Wang, *Wode zhandou shengya*, 112–13.

116. Ibid., 132, 144.

117. Shen, *Mao Zedong, Stalin he chaoxian zhanzheng*, 330.

118. Ibid., 334–35.

119. Zhang, *Red Wings over the Yalu*, 202–23; Shen, *Mao Zedong, Stalin he chaoxian zhanzheng*, 338.

120. Shen Zhihua, "Kangmei yuanchao zhanzheng zhongde sulian kongjun" (The Soviet Air Force in the Korean War), *Zhonggong dangshi yanjiu*, no. 2 (2000): 27–29; Zhang, *Red Wings over the Yalu*, 219–21.

121. Xu, "Chinese Forces," 49, 51.

122. Xiaobing Li, "Chinese Intervention in the Korean War," in *East Asia and the United States: An Encyclopedia of Relations since 1784*, ed. James I. Matray (Westport, CT: Greenwood Press, 2002), 94–96.

123. The Chinese official number was twenty-six thousand POWs held by the UNF. See Ministry of Foreign Affairs to Chinese charge d'affairs in P'yŏngyang, "Li Xiangchao lajing zhibing," and Zhou, "6.25 jianghuagao (caogao)," 24–25.

124. Xu, *Diyici jiaoliang*, 308–10.

125. CAMS Military Research History Division, *Zhongguo renmin zhiyuanjun kangmei yuanchao zhanshi*, 233–34.

126. Peter Hays Gries, *China's New Nationalism: Pride, Politics, and Diplomacy* (Berkeley: University of California Press, 2004), 56.

127. Chen Jian and Xiaobing Li, "China and the End of the Global Cold War," in *From Détente to the Soviet Collapse*, ed. Malcolm Muir Jr. (Lexington: Virginia Military Institute, 2006), 120.

4. Russianizing the PLA

1. Chen and Li, "China and the End of the Global Cold War," 121.

2. For the importance of the Sino-Soviet alliance, see Odd Arne Westad,

ed., *Brothers in Arms: The Rise and Fall of the Sino-Soviet Alliance, 1945–1963* (Washington, DC: Woodrow Wilson Center Press, 1998); Michael M. Sheng, *Battling Western Imperialism: Mao, Stalin, and the United States* (Princeton, NJ: Princeton University Press, 1997); Vladislav Zubok and Constantine Pleshakov, *Inside the Kremlin's Cold War: From Stalin to Khrushchev* (Cambridge, MA: Harvard University Press, 1996); and Gordon H. Chang, *Friends and Enemies: The United States, China, and the Soviet Union* (Stanford, CA: Stanford University Press, 1990).

3. Joffe, *Chinese Army after Mao*, 1.

4. Ibid., 2.

5. Frederick C. Teiwes, "Establishment and Consolidation of the New Regime," in *Cambridge History of China* (Cambridge: University of Cambridge Press, 1967), 14:89.

6. Fairbank and Goldman, *China*, 348–49.

7. Teiwes, "Establishment and Consolidation," 14:89–90.

8. The report of the CCP South Central Bureau was submitted by Deng Zihui to the Central Committee on November 26, 1950. Its main points are included in Liu Shaoqi, "Zhongyang zhuanfa zhongnanjiu zhenya fangeming jihua de tongzhi" (CCP Central Committee Announcement on the South Central Plan to Suppress Counterrevolutionaries), December 7, 1950, in *Jianguo yilai Liu Shaoqi wengao*, 2:591–92.

9. Ibid., 2:591.

10. PRC State Council and People's Supreme Court, "Youguan zhenfan gongzuo de zhishi," 1:358–59.

11. Mao Zedong, "Zhenya fangeming bixu shixing dang de qunzhong luxian" (Implement the Party's Mass Line in Suppressing Counterrevolutionaries), in *Mao Zedong xuanji*, 5:39–41.

12. Zhou Enlai, "Political Report at the First National Meeting of the Chinese People's Political Consultative Conference," October 23, 1951, in Harold C. Hinton, ed., *The People's Republic of China, 1949–1979: A Documentary Survey* (Wilmington, DE: Scholarly Resources, 1980), 82–84.

13. Peng Deng, "The Impact of the Korean War on the Chinese Society: The Mass Campaigns in 1951–52" (paper presented at the annual meeting of the Association of Asian Society, Chicago, IL, March 22–25, 2003).

14. Kenneth Lieberthal, *Revolution and Tradition in Tientsin, 1949–1952* (Stanford, CA: Stanford University Press, 1980), 168, table 8.

15. Li Yuming, Xu Fang, and Meng Jianhua, eds., *Zhonghua renmin gongheguo shi cidian* (Dictionary of PRC History) (Beijing: Zhongguo guoji guangbo chubanshe, 1989), 78.

16. Chow Ching-wen, *Ten Years of Storm: The True Story of the Communist Regime in China* (Westport, CT: Greenwood Press, 1960), 115, 133.

17. Bai Xi, *Kaiguo da zhenya* (The Great Suppression) (Beijing: Zhonggong dangshi chubanshe, 2006), 494.

18. Teiwes, "Establishment and Consolidation," 14:88.

19. Zhou Xiaohong, "Chinese Peasants' Participation in Politics and Government during Deng's Reform" (unpublished paper).

20. CCP Party History Research Division, *Zhongguo gongchandang lishi dashiji*, 226; Fairbank and Goldman, *China*, 350.

21. Li, *Zhongwai junshi zhidu bijiao*, 312; Shambaugh, *Modernizing China's Military*, 123.

22. Chen, *Mao's China*, 7.

23. Hu, *Zhongwai junshi zuzhi tizhi bijiao jiaocheng*, 94.

24. See, for example, Joffe, *Chinese Army after Mao*, 7, and Shambaugh, *Modernizing China's Military*, 96.

25. The compulsory service act became a law after it passed at the second plenary session of the First People's Congress on July 30, 1955. See Li, *Zhongwai junshi zhidu bijiao*, 232.

26. Chen, *Mao's China*, 60.

27. Mao Zedong, speech at the fourth plenary session of the First Chinese People's Political Consultative Conference, February 7, 1953, in *Jianguo yilai Mao Zedong wengao*, 4:45–46.

28. Mao quoted in *Jianguo yilai Mao Zedong wengao*, 4:1–2.

29. Mao, "Greeting the Fifth Anniversary of the Signing of the Sino-Soviet Treaty of Friendship, Alliance, and Mutual Assistance," February 12, 1955, in *Mao Zedong on Diplomacy* (Beijing: Foreign Languages Press, 1998), 151.

30. Deng Xiaoping, "In Memory of Liu Bocheng," October 21, 1986, in *Selected Works of Deng Xiaoping*, 2:185.

31. Xinghuo Liaoyuan Composition Department, *Zhongguo renmin jiefangjun jiangshuai minglu*, 1:6.

32. Deng, "In Memory of Liu Bocheng," 2:186.

33. Marshal Liu Bocheng's lecture is cited in Tao Hanzhang, *Sun Zi bingfa gailun* (Analysis of Sun Zi's *The Art of War*) (Beijing: Jiefangjun chubanshe, 1991).

34. Deng, "In Memory of Liu Bocheng," 2:187.

35. Peng, "Si'nianlai de junshi gongzuo zongjie he jinhou junshi jiansheshang de jige jiben wenti," 463–96.

36. Yao Lianrui, "Yige buying you de cuowu" (An Unnecessary Mistake), in CAMS Military History Research Division, *Junqi piaopiao*, 1:227–28.

37. Deng Lifeng, "Jianjunshi shang yici huashidai de huiyi" (A Historic Meeting of the PLA), in CAMS Military History Research Division, *Junqi piaopiao*, 1:163.

38. Ibid., 1:176–77.

39. Yao, "Yige buying you de cuowu," 1:226–27.

40. Deng, "In Memory of Liu Bocheng," 2:188.

41. Peng said many times at the CMC and other high command meetings, "We must learn from the Soviet Union." Peng and meeting minutes of June 5, 1953; January 26, 1954; and August 16, 1955, quoted in Wang, *Peng Dehuai zhuan*, 523, 541nn1–3, 552n1.

42. CAMS Military History Research Division, *Zhongguo renmin jiefangjun de qishinian*, 466–67.

43. Shen, *Mao Zedong, Stalin he chaoxian zhanzheng*, 371. Shen found the information in the archives of the Second Division, ROC Defense Ministry, Taiwan.

44. Yang Guoyu, *Dangdai zhongguo haijun* (Contemporary Chinese Navy) (Beijing: Zhongguo shehui kexue chubanshe, 1987), 48–49.

45. Shen, *Mao Zedong, Stalin he chaoxian zhanzheng*, 372.

46. Peng, "Si'nianlai de junshi gongzuo zongjie he jinhou junshi jiansheshang de jige jiben wenti," 474–76.

47. CAMS Military History Research Division, *Zhongguo renmin jiefangjun de qishinian*, 455, 461.

48. Jeanne L. Wilson, *Strategic Partners: Russian-Chinese Relations in the Post-Soviet Era* (Armonk, NY: M. E. Sharpe, 2004), 70.

49. Ming-Yen Tsai, *From Adversaries to Partners: Chinese and Russian Military Cooperation after the Cold War* (Westport, CT: Praeger, 2003), 25–27.

50. Peng Dehuai, "Guanyu fangwen Warsaw guo gei zhongyang de dianbo" (Telegrams to the Central Committee: Report on Visiting Warsaw Pact Countries), May 22, 1955, file 109-00555-01 (1), 13, Foreign Ministry Archives.

51. Wang Bingnan, Chinese ambassador to Poland, "Guanyu Peng Dehuai fangwen Poland gei waijiaobu de baogao" (Report to the Ministry of Foreign Affairs on Peng Dehuai's Visit to Poland), file 109-00555-01 (1), 2–3, Foreign Ministry Archives.

52. See, for example, Peng Dehuai, speech at the Eight Countries' Conference of the Warsaw Pact, May 13, 1955, and conversations with Polish and Soviet leaders, May 16–22, 1955. Peng, "Guanyu fangwen Warsaw guo gei zhongyang de dianbao," May 14, 16, and 22, 1955, files 109-00555-01 and 109-00556-01 (1), 6–7, 13–14, 15–19.

53. Deng, "Jianjunshi shang yici huashidai de huiyi," 1:180.

54. CAMS Military History Research Division, *Zhongguo renmin jiefangjun de qishinian*, 461.

55. Deng, "Jianjunshi shang yici huashidai de huiyi," 1:180.

56. CAMS Military History Research Division, *Zhongguo renmin jiefangjun de qishinian*, 462.

57. Ibid., 453–54.

58. Zhou, *Kangmei yuanchao zhanzheng huoqinshi jianbianben*, 12–14.

59. For example, the Third Field Army became the East China Command (ECC) and its four army groups, comprising fifteen armies stationed in six provincial and metropolitan commands, including Zhejiang, Fujian, Jiangsu, Shanghai, and coastal areas along the Taiwan Strait. See CAMS Military History Research Division, *Zhongguo renmin jiefangjun de qishinian*, 454–55, and Zhu, *Gun Barrel Politics*, 47–52.

60. CAMS Military History Research Division, *Zhongguo renmin jiefangjun de qishinian*, 457–58.

61. Ibid., 459–60; Xinghuo Liaoyuan Composition Department, *Zhongguo renmin jiefangjun jiangshuai minglu*, 1:1–10; Xiaobing Li, "Chinese Military Ranking and Promotion," in *China Today: An Encyclopedia of Life in the People's Republic*, ed. Jing Luo (Westport, CT: Greenwood Press, 2005), 2:402–5.

62. CAMS Military History Research Division, *Zhongguo renmin jiefangjun de qishinian*, 395–96.

63. Han and Tan, *Dangdai Zhongguo jundui de junshi gongzuo*, 2:86; CAMS Military History Research Division, *Zhongguo renmin jiefangjun de qishinian*, 458.

64. Li Dongye, "Yi dalian diyi haijun xuexiao de chuangjian" (The Founding of the First Naval Academy in Dalian), in PLAN History Compilation Committee, *Haijun: Huiyi shiliao* (The Navy: Memoirs and Historical Records) (Beijing: Haichao chubanshe, 1994), 2:634–37.

65. CCP Archival and Manuscript Research Division, *Zhou Enlai nianpu*, 1:138; Fu Jize and Li Keming, "Zai sulian de sannian qianting xunlian" (Three Years of Submarine Training in the Soviet Union), in PLAN History Compilation Committee, *Haijun*, 1:99–101.

66. Liu Bocheng, "Zai qingbao yu zhihuixi di'erqi biye dianli shang de jianghua" (Speech to the Second Graduating Class of the Departments of Operation and Intelligence), in *Liu Bocheng junshi wenxuan*, 518.

67. Ibid., 517–19.

68. Lt. Gen. Qin Chaoying (PLA, ret.; secretary general, China Society for Strategy and Management Research), interview by the author, Beijing, July 2002.

69. Ibid.

70. Deng, "Jianjunshi shang yici huashidai de huiyi," 1:179.

71. Spence, *Search for Modern China*, 533.

72. Chief Gen. Hao Bocun (Nationalist Army, ret.), interview by the author, Taipei, Taiwan, May 1994. Hao served as the GMD army commander on the offshore islands during the PLA attack on Jinmen in 1949.

73. Compilation Committee of ROC History, *Pictorial History*, 2:297. The GMD army officially claimed about 20,000 PLA casualties, including 7,200 prisoners. According to the author's interviews in both Taiwan and China, about 10,000 PLA casualties seems more accurate.

74. CMC [drafted by Mao Zedong], "Junwei guanyu gongji Jinmen dao shili de jiaoxun de tongbao" (CMC Circular on the Setback of the Jinmen Battle), October 29, 1949, in *Jianguo yilai Mao Zedong wengao*, 1:100–101. This document was sealed and issued by the CMC. In 1987, the Central Archival and Research Division of the CCP Central Committee found that the original document was drafted by Mao.

75. Mao Zedong, "Guanyu bingli bushu de yijian gei Lin Biao de dianbao" (Telegram to Lin Biao: My Suggestions on Your Troops' Disposition and Battle Array), October 31, 1949, in *Jianguo yilai Mao Zedong wengao*, 1:107. In this telegram, Mao alerted Lin, "Do not attack the Leizhou Peninsula, much less a chance to attack the Hainan Island."

76. Mao Zedong, "Junwei guanyu tongyi Dinghai zuozhan fang'an gei Su Yu deng de dianbao" (Telegram to Su Yu: For the Operation Plan of the Dinghai Campaign), November 4, 1949, and "Guanyu Dinghai zuozhan bushu gei Su Yu de dianbao" (Telegram to Su Yu: The Disposition of the Dinghai Campaign), November 14, 1949, in *Jianguo yilai Mao Zedong wengao*, 1:118, 120, 137. The latter reads, "In view of the military failure on Jinmen, you must check out closely and seriously all problems, such as boat transportation, troop reinforcement, and attack opportunity on the Dinghai Landing. If it is not well prepared, we could rather postpone the attack than feel sorry about it later."

77. He Di, "The Last Campaign to Unify China: The CCP's Unrealized Plan to Liberate Taiwan, 1949–1950," in Ryan, Finkelstein, and McDevitt, *Chinese Warfighting*, 88.

78. ROC Defense Department, *Guojun houqin shi* (Logistics History of the GMD Armed Forces) (Taipei, Taiwan: Guofangbu shizheng bianyiju, 1992), 6:199–200.

79. CMC [drafted by Mao], "Junwei guanyu gongji Jinmen dao shili de jiaoxun de tongbao," 1:101.

80. Yang, *Dangdai Zhongguo haijun*, 17.

81. CAMS Military History Research Division, *Zhongguo renmin jiefangjun zhanshi* (Warfighting History of the PLA) (Beijing: Junshi kexue chubanshe, 1987), 3:359.

82. Yang, *Dangdai Zhongguo haijun*, 48, 52.

83. Mao Zedong, "Guanyu tongyi Su Yu diao sigeshi yanxi haizhan deng wenti gei Liu Shaoqi de dianbao" (Telegram to Liu Shaoqi: Approve Su Yu's Disposing Four Divisions for Landing Campaign), February 10, 1950; "Mao

guanyu qiuding xianda Dinghai zaida Jinmen de fangzhen de piyu" (Mao's Comments on the Proposal of Attacking Dinghai First, Jinmen Second), March 28, 1950; and Mao Zedong, "Jiaqiang sanbing xunlian wenti gei Su Yu de dianbao" (Telegram to Su Yu: Instructions on Paratroops Training), in *Jianguo yilai Mao Zedong wengao*, 1:256–57, 282.

84. *Xiao Jinguang huiyilu* (Memoirs of Xiao Jinguang) (Beijing: Jiefangjun chubanshe, 1988), 2:8, 26.

85. He, "Last Campaign to Unify China," 82–83.

86. ROC Defense Department, *Guojun houqin shi*, 6:262, 277.

87. Finkelstein, *Washington's Taiwan Dilemma*, 332–33.

88. *Xiao Jinguang huiyilu*, 2:26.

89. Maj. Gen. William C. Chase (U.S. Army) arrived in Taiwan on May 1, 1951, to establish the Joint U.S. Military Assistance and Advisory Group, China. For more details, see Finkelstein, *Washington's Taiwan Dilemma*, 336.

90. *Ye Fei huiyilu* (Memoirs of Ye Fei) (Beijing: Jiefangjun chubanshe, 1988), 613–14.

91. Liu Xiao, *Chushi Sulian banian, 1955–1963* (My Eight-Year Mission to the Soviet Union, 1955–1963) (Beijing: Zhonggong dangshi ziliao chubanshe, 1986), 9–13.

92. Mao changed his mind about Chen's plan after initially approving it in October 1953. Mao worried that any large-scale landing campaign in the Taiwan Strait might cause an international crisis or a direct confrontation with the United States, which China wished to avoid so soon after the Korean armistice. See Hu Shihong, "Hengshuo donghai" (Couching the Lance in the East China Sea), in Nie Fengzhi et al., *Sanjun huige zhan donghai* (Three Services Wield Weapons in East China Sea Combat) (Beijing: Jiefangjun chubanshe, 1985), 38.

93. Hu, "Hengshuo donghai," 38; Xu Yan, *Jinmen zhizhan* (The Battle of Jinmen) (Beijing: Zhongguo guangbo dianshi chubanshe, 1992), 168.

94. Gen. Jiang Weiguo, interview.

95. Xu, *Jinmen zhizhan*, 171.

96. Dong Fanghe, *Zhang Aiping zhuan* (Biography of Zhang Aiping) (Beijing: Renmin chubanshe, 2000), 2:655; Xiaobing Li, "New War of Nerves: Mao's Legacy in Beijing's Policy toward Taiwan Strait," in *Journal of Chinese Political Science* 3, no. 1 (Summer 1997): 70.

97. Gen. Zhang Aiping had only one field army, the Twenty-fourth Army, available for his amphibious operations along the Zhejiang coast. The number of ECC troops had been dramatically reduced during the Korean War. The Ninth Army Corps, the main strength of the ECC, numbering about one hundred thousand men, including the Twentieth, Twenty-sixth, and Twenty-

seventh armies, left the Zhejiang-Jiangsu region for the Korean War in 1950 and did not return to east China after the war ended in 1953. The Twenty-fifth Army left Zhejiang Province and moved to Fujian Province in 1951. Mao Zedong, "Gei jiubingtuan Song Shilun de dianbao" (Telegram to Song Shilun, Commander of the Ninth Army Group), in *Mao Zedong junshi wenxuan*, 2:667; Xu, *Jinmen zhizhan*, 171.

98. Maj. Gen. Xu Changyou (vice commissar, PLAN East China Sea Fleet), interview by the author, Shanghai, April 2000. Xu served as Gen. Zhang Aiping's aide and then the deputy secretary-general of the CMC.

99. Xu, *Jinmen zhizhan*, 171.

100. Dong, *Zhang Aiping zhuan*, 2:663–64; Xiaobing Li, "PLA Attacks and Amphibious Operations during the Taiwan Straits Crises of 1954–55 and 1958," in Ryan, Finkelstein, and McDevitt, *Chinese Warfighting*, 146.

101. The air force bases in east coast cities, including Shanghai, Hangzhou, and Ningbo, were used by Zhang's jets in the air campaigns.

102. Gen. Jiang Weiguo, interview. Jiang Jieshi made his trip to the Dachen Islands without informing any GMD officials or American representatives in Taiwan other than his naval commanders. Gen. Jiang pointed out that his father recognized the strategic importance of these islands after the Korean War.

103. Dong, *Zhang Aiping zhuan*, 2:664–65; Li, "PLA Attacks," 148.

104. After 1955, Gen. Nie became the commander of the air forces of the Nanjing and Fuzhou regional commands, vice commander of both regional commands, and chief of the Nanjing Regional Command.

105. GMD and CIA officers on the scene were surprised by the timing of the artillery shelling. See CIA, "Report on the Chinese Offshore Islands Situation," September 9, 1954, CIA official file, 50318-Formosa (1), box 9, international series, Dwight D. Eisenhower Papers, Dwight D. Eisenhower Library, Abilene, KS.

106. He Di, "Taihai weiji he zhongguo dui Jinmen, Mazu zhengce de xingcheng" (Taiwan Strait Crises and the Chinese Policy toward Jinmen and Mazu), *Meiguo yanjui* 3, no. 1 (Fall 1988): 40.

107. Maj. Gen. Xu Changyou, interview, April 2000.

108. Ma Guansan, "Aozhan donghai yi dangnian" (Remember the Combat Years in the East China Sea), in Nie et al., *Sanjun huige zhan donghai*, 29.

109. Nie Fengzhi, "Yunji yingxiang zhen haikong" (Soaring Eagles Strike from the Clouds and Shake the Sea and Sky), in Nie et al., *Sanjun huige zhan donghai*, 16.

110. Dong, *Zhang Aiping zhuan*, 2:674–75; Han and Tan, *Dangdai Zhongguo jundui de junshi gongzuo*, 1:216–17; Li, "PLA Attacks," 152.

111. Jin Zigu, "Su Yu tongzhi zai zongcaimobu" (Comrade Su Yu at the Headquarters of the General Staff), in *Yidai mingjiang: Huiyi Su Yu Tongzhi* (A Well-Known General: Remembering Comrade Su Yu) (Shanghai: Shanghai renmin chubanshe, 1986), 478.

112. Christensen, *Useful Adversaries*, 60, 194.

113. *Nie Rongzhen huiyilu*, 2:721.

114. For more on the demobilization, see Liu Shaoqi, "Duiyu pingyuan junqu budui shengchan fasheng pianxiang wenti tongbao de piyu" (Instruction on the CMC Circular about the Regional Commands' Problem in Farming and Manufacturing), in *Jianguo yilai Liu Shaoqi wengao*, 2:11–12.

115. Hu, "Hengshuo donghai," 50–52.

116. Maj. Gen. Xu Changyou, interview, April 2000.

117. Han and Tan, *Dangdai zhongguo jundui de junshi gongzuo*, 1:215–16.

118. ECC telegram quoted in Lie Jianhua and Wang Jicheng, *Xinzhongguo haizhan neimu* (The Inside Story of New China's Naval Warfare) (Beijing: Zhongguo weiguo wenxue chubanshe, 1993), 93.

119. Peng's telegram quoted in ibid., 94.

120. Hu, "Hengshuo donghai," 50.

121. Di Jiu and Ke Feng, *Chaozhang chaoluo: Guogong jiaozhu Taiwan haixia jishi* (Record of the CCP-GMD Confrontation in the Taiwan Straits) (Beijing: Zhongguo gongshang chubanshe, 1996), 210–12.

122. Han and Tan, *Dangdai zhongguo jundui de junshi gongzuo*, 1:220–21.

123. In February 1955, the Seventh Fleet deployed aircraft carriers, cruisers, and up to forty destroyers to cover the evacuation of the Dachen Islands. *New York Times*, January 25 and February 7, 1955.

124. Han and Tan, *Dangdai zhongguo jundui de junshi gongzuo*, 1:222–23.

125. The "New Period Military Strategic Guideline," issued under Jiang Zemin's name in 1995, ordered the PLA to start the Two Transformations.

126. Memorandum of discussion at the 232nd meeting of the National Security Council, January 20, 1955, in *Foreign Relations of the United States, 1955–57* (Washington, DC: GPO, 1986), 2:70–71.

127. For Dulles's concerns about the Communist invasion of the offshore islands, see Dulles to the Department of State, February 25, 1955, in *Foreign Relations of the United States*, 2:307–10.

128. Gordon H. Chang, "To the Nuclear Brink: Eisenhower, Dulles, and the Quemoy-Matsu Crisis," *International Security* 12 (Spring 1988): 106.

129. John Foster Dulles, memorandum: meeting with Eisenhower, March 6, 1955, White House memoranda, box 3: meetings with the presi-

dent, 1955 (4), John Foster Dulles Papers, Dwight D. Eisenhower Library, Abilene, KS.

130. National Security Council, memorandum of discussion at the 245th NSC meeting, March 10, 1955, in *Foreign Relations of the United States*, 2:346–52; Gordon H. Chang and He Di, "The Absence of War in the U.S.-China Confrontation over Quemoy and Matsu in 1954–1955: Contingency, Luck, Deterrence?" *American Historical Review* 98, no. 5 (December 1993): 1511–14.

131. Dwight D. Eisenhower, president's news conference, March 16, 1955, in *Foreign Relations of the United States*, 2:332–33.

132. Nixon quoted in *Chicago Tribune*, March 18, 1955.

133. Xinhua News Agency, *China's Foreign Relations: A Chronology of Events, 1949–88* (Beijing: Foreign Languages Press, 1989), 525.

5. Building Missiles and the Bomb

1. Nie Rongzhen, "Jianxin qibu de woguo liangdan shiye" (A Rough Start to China's Nuclear and Missile Programs), in GAD Political Department, *Liangdan yixing: Zhongguo hewuqi daodan weixing yu feichuan quanjishi* (The Bomb, Missile, and Satellite: A Complete Record of China's Nuclear Bombs, Missiles, Satellites, and Space Programs) (Beijing: Jiuzhou chubanshe, 2001), 5.

2. Deng Xiaoping, "China Must Take Its Place in the Field of High Technology," in *Selected Works of Deng Xiaoping*, 3:273.

3. Burton Kaufman, *The Korean War: Challenges in Crisis, Credibility, and Command*, 2nd ed. (New York: McGraw-Hill, 1997), 177; John Foster Dulles, "A Policy of Boldness," *Life*, May 26, 1952, 146.

4. Kaufman, *Korean War*, 178.

5. Stephen Ambrose, *Eisenhower: Soldier, General of the Army, President-Elect, 1890–1952* (New York: Simon & Schuster, 1983), 547–48; Stephen Ambrose, *Eisenhower: The President* (New York: Simon & Schuster, 1984), 51–52.

6. The conversation between Mao and Khrushchev is quoted in Shi Zhe, *Zai lishi juren shenbian* (Reminiscences of Mao's Russian Interpreter) (Beijing: Zhongyang wenxian chubanshe, 1991), 572–73.

7. CIA, "Report on the Chinese Offshore Islands Situation."

8. Mao Zedong, "The Atom Bomb Cannot Scare the Chinese People," in *The Writings of Mao Zedong, 1949–1976*, ed. Michael Y. M. Kau and John K. Leung (Armonk, NY: M. E. Sharpe, 1986), 1:517.

9. John Wilson Lewis and Xue Litai, *China Builds the Bomb* (Stanford, CA: Stanford University Press, 1988), 35.

10. Ibid., 37–38.

11. Qian Sanqiang, "Laoyibei gemingjia guanxin zhongguo yuanzihe kexue fazan" (The Revolutionary Leaders Care about China's Nuclear Science), in GAD Political Department, *Liangdan yixing*, 78.

12. Li, "PLA Attacks," 157.

13. Mao, "Atom Bomb Cannot Scare," 1:516–17.

14. Mao Zedong, closing speech at the CCP National Conference, March 31, 1955, in *Mao Zedong wenji*, 6:394–96.

15. He Di, "Paper Tiger or Real Tiger: America's Nuclear Deterrence and Mao Zedong's Response" (paper delivered at the International Conference: Evidence on the Cold War in Asia, University of Hong Kong, January 8–10, 1996).

16. Lewis and Xue, *China Builds the Bomb*, 47–48.

17. Huang Liqun (senior fellow, Center for Research and Information, Space and Navigation Ministry), interview by the author, Beijing, July 2004; Lewis and Xue, *China Builds the Bomb*, 42.

18. Shambaugh, *Modernizing China's Military*, 235.

19. Mao Zedong, "Zhuhe zhongsu youhao tiaoyue wuzhounian gei Voroshilov, Bulganin, Molotov de dianbao" (Telegram to Voroshilov, Bulganin, and Molotov: Celebrating the Fifth Anniversary of the Sino-Soviet Friendship Treaty), February 12, 1955, in *Jianguo yilai Mao Zedong wengao*, 5:35–37.

20. Mao Zedong, "Zhuhe sujun jianjun sanshiqi zhounian gei Voroshilov, Bulganin, Molotov de dianbao" (Telegram to Voroshilov, Bulganin, and Molotov: Celebrating the Thirty-seventh Anniversary of the Founding of the Soviet Army), February 21, 1955, in *Jianguo yilai Mao Zedong wengao*, 5:41–42.

21. Lewis and Xue, *China Builds the Bomb*, 40.

22. *Nie Rongzhen huiyilu*, 2:800–801.

23. Contemporary China Compilation Committee, *Dangdai zhongguo de hegongye* (The Nuclear Industry in Contemporary China) (Beijing: Zhongguo shehui kexue chubanshe, 1987), 19–22.

24. *Nie Rongzhen huiyilu*, 2:803–4.

25. Yang, *Zouxiang polie*, 389–91.

26. *Nie Rongzhen huiyilu*, 2:775.

27. Huang, interview; CAMS Military History Research Division, *Zhongguo renmin jiefangjun de qishinian*, 523.

28. Han and Tan, *Dangdai zhongguo jundui de junshi gongzuo*, 2:76; Shambaugh, *Modernizing China's Military*, 166.

29. Zhang Jinfu, "Zhongguo kexueyuan yu liangdan yixing" (The Chinese Academy of Sciences and Nuclear, Missile, and Satellite Programs), in GAD Political Department, *Liangdan yixing*, 47.

30. Han and Tan, *Dangdai Zhongguo jundui de junshi gongzuo*, 2:99–100.

31. Chen and Li, "China and the End of the Global Cold War."

32. For a chronological development of the Sino-Soviet split, see Song Enfan and Li Jiasong, eds., *Zhonghua renmin gongheguo waijiao dashiji, 1957–64* (Chronicle of the People's Republic of China's Diplomacy, 1957–64) (Beijing: Shijie zhishi chubanshe, 2001), vol. 2, and Yang, *Zouxiang polie*, chaps. 13, 14.

33. Mao Zedong, "Zai Moscow gongchandang he gongrendang daibiao huiyi shang de jianghua" (Speech at the Moscow Conference of Communist and Workers' Parties), November 16, 1957, in *Jianguo yilai Mao Zedong wengao*, 6:625–44.

34. Chen, *Mao's China*, 71.

35. Yang, *Zouxiang polie*, 514–15.

36. Yang Kuisong, "Meisu lengzhan de qiyuan dui zhongguo geming de yingxiang" (Origins of the U.S.-Soviet Cold War and Its Impact on China's Revolution), in *Lengzhan yu zhongguo* (The Cold War and China), ed. Zhang Baijia and Niu Jun (Beijing: Shijie zhishi chubanshe, 2002), 51–88; Chen and Li, "China and the End of the Global Cold War."

37. Xu Yan, "1969 nian de zhongsu bianjing chongtu" (The Sino-Soviet Border Clashes of 1969), *Dangshi yanjiu ziliao*, no. 6 (1994): 6–10. Also see chap. 7 in this volume.

38. *Nie Rongzhen huiyilu*, 2:804; Yang, *Zouxiang polie*, 454.

39. *Nie Rongzhen huiyilu*, 2:806; Tang Xiuying, "Eci changtian" (A Sword Thrusting into the Sky), in GAD Political Department, *Liangdan yixing*, 366; World Military High-Tech Book Series Compilation Team, *Daguo yizhi: Dakai heheixiang* (The Powers' Will: Opening the Nuclear Black Box) (Beijing: Haichao chubanshe, 2000), 245.

40. Zhang Aiping, "Huigu yu jiyu" (Retrospect and Great Hopes), in GAD Political Department, *Liangdan yixing*, 23.

41. *Nie Rongzhen huiyilu*, 2:807–8.

42. Beidaihe is a beach area, located at the border of Hebei and Liaoning provinces, where Chinese leaders regularly take vacations and hold meetings during the summer.

43. Qian, "Laoyibei gemingjia guanxin zhongguo yuanzihe kexue fazan," 81.

44. Lewis and Xue, *China Builds the Bomb*, 46–7, 219, 236.

45. *Nie Rongzhen huiyilu*, 1:38–39.

46. On April 11, 1948, Mao, the CCP Central Committee, and the high command removed from Yan'an, the remote Communist capital in the northwest, to Chengnanzhuang, Fuping, Hebei, in north China. In late April, two GMD spies inside the PLA regional command headquarters discovered Mao's

residence. They passed the information to the GMD army. In early May, the GMD air force sent two B-25 bombers to Chengnanzhuang and raided Mao's residence. When Mao refused to leave his bedroom, Nie ordered his guards to carry Mao into the shelter. The B-25s dropped five bombs, one of which exploded in Mao's yard. Several days later, Nie moved Mao from Chengnanzhuang to Xibaipo. *Nie Rongzhen huiyilu*, 2:676–80.

47. Xinghuo Liaoyuan Composition Department, *Zhongguo renmin jiefangjun jiangshuai minglu*, 1:18.

48. Nie, "Beijing's Decision to Intervene," 48.

49. *Nie Rongzhen huiyilu*, 2:765.

50. Lewis and Xue, *China Builds the Bomb*, 47.

51. *Nie Rongzhen huiyilu*, 2:765, 785.

52. Ibid., 2:766.

53. Xu, *Junshijia Mao Zedong*, 198–99.

54. Ministry of Foreign Affairs, "Zhongguo canjia Geneva huiyi daibiaotuan zhunbei de wenti tigang" (Outline of the Proposals and List of the Chinese Delegation to the Geneva Conference), April 20, 1954, file 206-00055-18 (1), Foreign Ministry Archives.

55. Wang Bingnan, *Zhongmei huitan jiunian huigu* (My Nine Years of Sino-American Ambassadorial Talks in Retrospect) (Beijing: Shijie zhishi chubanshe, 1985), 16–18.

56. Ministry of Foreign Affairs, "Guanyu zhongmei dashiji daibiao zai Geneva huiyi de zhishi" (Instructions for the Chinese Delegation at the Geneva Conference), 1954–55, file 111-00009-01 (1), Foreign Ministry Archives.

57. Zhang Baijia and Jia Qingguo, "Steering Wheel, Shock Absorber, and Diplomatic Probe in Confrontation: Sino-American Ambassadorial Talks Seen from the Chinese Perspective," in *Re-examining the Cold War: U.S.-China Diplomacy, 1954–1973*, ed. Robert S. Ross and Jiang Changbin (Cambridge, MA: Harvard University Press, 2001), 178.

58. Ministry of Foreign Affairs Division of North American Region, "1954 nian Geneva huiyi hou woguo liuxuesheng huiguo qingkuang" (Report on the Returning Students after the 1954 Geneva Conference), July 31, 1955, file 111-00123-17 (1), Foreign Ministry Archives.

59. Ibid.

60. Huang, interview; Su Kuoshan, "Kouqi tiangong" (Opening the Door of the Universe), in GAD Political Department, *Liangdan yixing*, 335, 341.

61. Tang, "Eci changtian," 366.

62. Zheng Peiming, "Jianji changkong" (Rocket Soaring into the Sky), in GAD Political Department, *Liangdan yixing*, 319–20.

63. World Military High-Tech Book Series Compilation Team, *Daguo yizhi*, 273.

64. Peng Jichao, *Dongfang juxiang: Zhongguo hewuqi shiyan jishi* (The Big Bang in the East: Experiment Records of China's Nuclear Weapon) (Beijing: Zhongyang dangxiao chubanshe, 2005), 34–35.

65. U.S. House of Representatives, Select Committee on U.S. National Security and Military/Commercial Concerns with the People's Republic of China, *U.S. National Security and Military/Commercial Concerns with the People's Republic of China* (Washington, DC: Regnery, 1999), 12–13.

66. *Renmin ribao*, "Zhuming kexuejia Qian Xuesen tan 'sange daibiao'" (Renowned Scientist Qian Xuesen Views "Three Represents"), June 24, 2002.

67. World Military High-Tech Book Series Compilation Team, *Daguo yizhi*, 273.

68. Tu Yuanji, "Hangtian juxing" (Shining Star of Aerospace), in GAD Political Department, *Liangdan yixing*, 344–45; Shambaugh, *Modernizing China's Military*, 63.

69. Peng, *Dongfang juxiang*, 36.

70. *Nie Rongzhen huiyilu*, 2:795–96.

71. Nie Rongzhen, "Guanyu daodan, yuanzidan ying jianchi gongguan de baogao" (Report on Nuclear Bomb and Missile Research and Development), August 20, 1961, in *Nie Rongzhen junshi wenxuan*, 488.

72. Lewis and Xue, *China Builds the Bomb*, 40.

73. *Nie Rongzhen huiyilu*, 2:785, 792–93.

74. Qian, "Laoyibei gemingjia guanxin zhongguo yuanzihe kexue fazan," 74–75.

75. Ibid., 76.

76. Ibid., 77.

77. Ibid., 80–81.

78. Li Peicai, "Liangdan yuanxun" (The Founder of the Bomb and Missile), in GAD Political Department, *Liangdan yixing*, 432–33.

79. Ibid., 449–50.

80. Huang, interview.

81. *Nie Rongzhen huiyilu*, 2:777–78, 827–33.

82. *Renmin ribao*, "Zhuming kexuejia Qian Xuesen tan 'sange daibiao.'"

83. Zhang, "Zhongguo kexueyuan yu liangdan yixing," 39.

84. Li Fuze, "Woguo diyike renzao weixing fasheji" (Launching China's First Satellite), in GAD Political Department, *Liangdan yixing*, 236.

85. For more on the 1959–61 "natural disaster," see Fairbank and Goldman, *China*, 372–82, and Spence, *Search for Modern China*, 552–53.

86. Nie, "Jianxin qibu de woguo liangdan shiye," 11.

87. Mao quoted in Contemporary China Compilation Committee,

Dangdai zhongguo de guofang keji shiye (Defense Technology and Science in Contemporary China) (Beijing: Dangdai zhongguo chubanshe, 1992), 1:45.

88. Chen quoted in *Nie Rongzhen huiyilu*, 2:812; You, *Armed Forces of China*, 85.

89. *Nie Rongzhen huiyilu*, 2:812–13.

90. Ibid., 2:813.

91. Zhang Jinfu, "Tamen chuangzao le lishi" (They Made History), *Renmin ribao*, May 6, 1999.

92. CAMS Military History Research Division, *Zhongguo renmin jiefangjun de qishinian*, 525, 528.

93. *Nie Rongzhen huiyilu*, 2:819; Liu Bailuo, "Zhongyang zhuanman weiyuanhui yu liangdan yixing" (The Special Commission of the Central Committee and Nuclear Bombs), in GAD Political Department, *Liangdan yixing*, 96–97.

94. CAMS Military History Research Division, *Zhongguo renmin jiefangjun de qishinian*, 524.

95. Liu Xiyao, "Woguo liangdan yanzhi juece guocheng zhuiji" (Historical Decisions on Our Nuclear Research and Development), in GAD Political Department, *Liangdan yixing*, 60.

96. Ibid., 61.

97. Ibid., 61–62; Zhu Shaojun, "Pili yisheng chun, fengliu tianxia wen" (A Spring Thunder Shocks the World), in CAMS Military History Research Division, *Junqi piaopiao*, 1:376.

98. Zhu, "Pili yisheng chun, fengliu tianxia wen," 1:377.

99. According to Defense Minister Peng Dehuai, the total defense budget of China in 1956 was 6.1 billion yuan ($2.1 billion), about 20 percent of Chinese governmental expenses. Peng Dehuai, "Junshi jianshe gaikuang" (An Overview of China's Military Development), July 16, 1957, in *Peng Dehuai junshi wenxuan*, 584–601. Also see Shen Zhihua, "Youxian yuanzhu: Sulian yu zhongguo de heshiyan" (Supply on Restriction: Nuclear Research and Development of the Soviet Union and China, 1949–60), 2005, http://www3 .bbsland.com/cgi-bin/military.cgi.

100. Shen, "Youxian yuanzhu."

101. Liu, "Zhongyang zhuanman weiyuanhui yu liangdan yixing," 114.

102. Ibid., 100.

103. Hu Shihong, "Hangtian zuomingqu" (Space Sonata), *Renwu* 5 (1994): 65–67.

104. Nie Rongzhen, "Guanyu daodan hewuqi shiyan wenti" (About the Nuclear and Missile Tests), November 11, 1966, in *Nie Rongzhen junshi wenxuan*, 530–33; CAMS Military History Research Division, *Zhongguo renmin jiefangjun de qishinian*, 526.

105. *Nie Rongzhen huiyilu*, 2:821, 839; Yang Guihua, "Zhunbei zaoda, dada, da hezhanzheng de lishi huigu" (National Preparation for Total War and Nuclear War), in CAMS Military History Research Division, *Junqi piaopiao*, 2:567.

106. Maj. Gen. Xu Changyou, interview, April 2000.

107. Chen Chuangang, "Duanzao zhengyi zhi jian; lianzhu heping zhi dun" (Sharpen the Just Sword and Forge a Defense Shield), in CAMS Military History Research Division, *Junqi piaopiao*, 2:685.

108. *Nie Rongzhen huiyilu*, 2:766–67; Nie, "Jianxin qibu de woguo liangdan shiye," 21; Zhang, "Huigu yu jiyu," 23.

109. "From the first day it possessed nuclear weapons, China has solemnly declared its determination not to be the first to use such weapons at any time and in any circumstances, and later undertook unconditionally not to use or threaten to use nuclear weapons against non-nuclear-weapons states or nuclear-weapon-free zones." PRC State Council Bureau of Information, *White Papers of the Chinese Government*, 2:412.

110. PRC State Council Bureau of Information, *White Papers of China's National Defense in 2004* (Beijing: Foreign Languages Press, 2005), 4:703.

111. Shambaugh, *Modernizing China's Military*, 102.

112. Alastair I. Johnston, "Prospects for Chinese Nuclear Force Modernization: Limited Deterrence versus Multilateral Arms Control," in *China's Military in Transition*, ed. David Shambaugh and Richard H. Yang (New York: Oxford University Press, 1997), 162–65.

6. Crises and Politics

1. Ellis Joffe uses the term "professional generation" to distinguish the Chinese officers of the 1950s from the "guerrilla generation" of the 1930s. Joffe, *Party and Army*, x–xi.

2. Li, "PLA Attacks," 144, 167.

3. Ryan, Finkelstein, and McDevitt, "Patterns of PLA Warfighting," 15.

4. CAMS Military History Research Division, *Junqi piaopiao*, 1:293.

5. For recent accounts in English of the 1958 Taiwan Strait crisis, see Robert Accinelli, *Crisis and Commitment: United States Policy toward Taiwan, 1950-1955* (Chapel Hill: University of North Carolina Press, 1999); Xiaobing Li, Chen Jian, and David L. Wilson, trans. and eds., "Mao Zedong's Handling of the Taiwan Strait Crisis of 1958: Chinese Recollections and Documents," *Cold War International History Project Bulletin* 6–7 (Winter 1995–96): 208–19; Tun-jen Cheng, Chi Huang, and Samuel S. G. Wu, eds., *Inherited Rivalry: Conflict across the Taiwan Straits* (Boulder, CO: Lynne

Rienner Publishers, 1995); Nancy Bernkopf Tucker, *Taiwan, Hong Kong, and the U.S., 1945–1992: Uncertain Friendships* (New York: Twayne Publishers, 1994); Qiang Zhai, *The Dragon, the Lion, and the Eagle: Chinese-British-American Relations, 1949–1958* (Kent, OH: Kent State University Press, 1994); and Shuguang Zhang, *Deterrence and Strategic Culture: Chinese-American Confrontations, 1949–1958* (Ithaca, NY: Cornell University Press, 1992).

6. Among the recent books published in China on PLA amphibious operations are Luo Xuanyou, *Zhongyue taihai zhanzheng zhengzhan jishi* (Historical Records of the Sino-Vietnam and Taiwan Strait Wars) (Urumqi: Xinjiang renmin chubanshe, 2004); Shen Weiping, *8-23 paoji Jinmen* (8-23 Bombardment of Jinmen), 2 vols. (Beijing: Huayi chubanshe, 1999); Di and Ke, *Guogong jiaozhu Taiwan haixia jishi*; Li Jian, *Taihai liang'an zhanshi huigu* (History of the Military Conflicts over the Taiwan Strait) (Beijing: Huawen chubanshe, 1996); Xu, *Jinmen zhizhan*; Wang, *Dongdai zhongguo kongjun*; and Yang, *Dangdai zhongguo haijun*.

7. Xinhua News Agency, *China's Foreign Relations*, 197.

8. Mao Zedong, speech at a CMC meeting, July 18, 1958, in *Mao Zedong junshi wenji*, 6:442–43.

9. Han and Tan, *Dangdai zhongguo jundui de junshi gongzuo*, 2:387; Xu, *Jinmen zhizhan*, 205–6; Xiaobing Li, "New War of Nerves," 79.

10. Wang, *Dongdai zhongguo kongjun*, 334–36.

11. Gen. Jiang Weiguo, interview.

12. Wang, *Dongdai zhongguo kongjun*, 338–43; Xu, *Jinmen zhizhan*, 212–14; Shen, *8-23 paoji Jinmen*, 1:128–45.

13. Chief Gen. Hao, interview. Hao served as the garrison commander on Jinmen Island from 1957 to 1960.

14. FFC headquarters staff officer (PLA colonel, ret.), interview by the author, Hangzhou, Zhejiang, April 2000.

15. *Ye Fei huiyilu*, 653–54; Li, "PLA Attacks," 159.

16. CMC telegram to the FFC, July 25, 1958, quoted in Shen, *8-23 paoji Jinmen*, 1:76.

17. Mao Zedong to Peng Dehuai and Huang Kecheng, July 27, 1958, in *Jianguo yilai Mao Zedong wengao*, 7:326, 327.

18. *Ye Fei huiyilu*, 651–52.

19. Mao Zedong to Peng Dehuai, August 18, 1958, in *Jianguo yilai Mao Zedong wengao*, 7:348.

20. Mao quoted in Shen, *8-23 paoji Jinmen*, 1:188.

21. Ye had deployed a large shelling force, including artillery units from the Twentieth, Twenty-eighth, and Thirty-first armies, the Third Artillery Division, and the naval coastal artillery units. *Ye Fei huiyilu*, 655–56.

22. FFC headquarters staff officer, interview; Shen, 8-23 *paoji Jinmen*, 1:196.

23. Xu, *Jinmen zhizhan*, 224–28.

24. Ye told his staff members at the FFC headquarters about his confusion about Mao's policy during the 1958 crisis. FFC headquarters staff officer, interview.

25. The Jinmen GMD garrison received the intelligence before the PLA bombardment. President Jiang Jieshi inspected the GMD troops on Jinmen on August 20, 1958, three days before the PLA bombardment. Gen. Jiang Weiguo, interview; Chief Gen. Hao, interview; ROC Defense Ministry History Compilation and Translation Bureau, 8-23 *paozhan shengli 30 zhounian jinian wenji* (Recollection for the 30th Anniversary of the Victorious 8-23 Artillery Battle) (Taipei, Taiwan: Guofangbu yinzhichang, 1989), 1, 55.

26. Xu, *Jinmen zhizhan*, 228–30; Shen, 8-23 *paoji Jinmen*, 1:229–30; Li, Chen, and Wilson, "Mao Zedong's Handling of the Taiwan Strait Crisis," 208–9.

27. Chief Gen. Hao, interview.

28. ROC Defense Ministry History Compilation and Translation Bureau, 8-23 *paozhan shengli*, 25–26, 181.

29. Chief Gen. Hao, interview.

30. *Ye Fei huiyilu*, 666.

31. Ye quoted in Shen, 8-23 *paoji Jinmen*, 1:199–200; FFC headquarters staff officer, interview.

32. Mao Zedong, "Zai junwei guanyu dui Taiwan he yanhai Jiangzhan daoyu junshi douzheng de zhishigao shang de piyu" (Instruction on the CMC Orders for the Military Operations in the Taiwan Strait and against the GMD-Occupied Offshore Islands), September 3, 1958, in *Jianguo yilai Mao Zedong wengao*, 7:376–77; Xu, *Jinmen zhizhan*, 250–51; Shen, 8-23 *paoji Jinmen*, 1:359–60.

33. *Ye Fei huiyilu*, 659–61.

34. Shen, 8-23 *paoji Jinmen*, 1:398–400.

35. Xu, *Jinmen zhizhan*, 250–51.

36. Shen, 8-23 *paoji Jinmen*, 2:500.

37. Li, "PLA Attacks," 163.

38. Chief Gen. Hao, interview.

39. Xu, *Jinmen zhizhan*, 256–57.

40. Wang, *Dongdai zhongguo kongjun*, 345; ROC Defense Ministry History Compilation and Translation Bureau, 8-23 *paozhan shengli*, 33–34.

41. Han and Tan, *Dangdai zhongguo jundui de junshi gongzuo*, 1:395, 405.

42. Mao Zedong to Peng Dehuai and Huang Kecheng, October 5, 1958, in *Jianguo yilai Mao Zedong wengao*, 7:437.

43. Xu, *Jinmen zhizhan*, 268–69.

44. Mao Zedong, "Guancha guoji xingshi de ruogan guandian" (Some Viewpoints about the International Situation), speech at the fifteenth meeting of the Supreme State Council, September 8, 1958, in *Mao Zedong waijiao wenxuan* (Selected Diplomatic Papers of Mao Zedong) (Beijing: Zhongyang wenxian chubanshe and Shijie zhishi chubanshe, 1994), 348–52.

45. Ryan, Finkelstein, and McDevitt, "Patterns of PLA Warfighting," 15.

46. Xu, *Jinmen zhizhan*, 268–69.

47. Mao, "Guancha guoji xingshi de ruogan guandian," 348–52.

48. Peng Dehuai [drafted by Mao Zedong], "Gao Taiwan tongpao shu" (Message to Compatriots in Taiwan), in *Mao Zedong junshi wenxuan*, 1:365–66.

49. Peng Dehuai [drafted by Mao Zedong], "Zhonghua renmin gongheguo guofangbu mingling" (The Order of the PRC Defense Ministry), in *Mao Zedong junshi wenxuan*, 1:368–69.

50. Peng Dehuai [drafted by Mao Zedong], "Zaigao Taiwan tongpao shu" (Second Message to Compatriots in Taiwan), in *Jianguo yilai Mao Zedong wengao*, 7:468–70; also see Wu Lengxi, "Inside Story of the Decision Making during the Shelling of Jinmen," in Li, Chen, and Wilson, "Mao Zedong's Handling of the Taiwan Straits Crisis," 215.

51. Shen, 8-23 *paoji Jinmen*, 2:842; ROC Defense Ministry History Compilation and Translation Bureau, 8-23 *paozhan shengli*, 30, 34.

52. Joffe, *Chinese Army after Mao*, 16.

53. Jürgen Domes, *Peng Te-huai: The Man and the Image* (London: C. Hurst, 1985), 71.

54. Guo Zhigang, "Dui jundui tongshuai tizhi de tansuo" (Experimental Changes in the Commanding System), in CAMS Military History Research Division, *Junqi piaopiao*, 1:76, 77.

55. Han and Tan, *Dangdai zhongguo jundui de junshi gongzuo*, 1:42; Hu, *Zhongwai junshi zuzhi tizhi bijiao jiaocheng*, 33–35; Joffe, *Party and Army*, 44–45.

56. Maj. Gen. Xu Changyou, interviews by the author, Beijing, July 2004, April 2000.

57. Yang, *Zouxiang polie*, 423–44; Han and Tan, *Dangdai zhongguo jundui de junshi gongzuo*, 1:50–51; Joffe, *Party and Army*, 42–43.

58. Wang, *Peng Dehuai zhuan*, 578–81; Spence, *Search for Modern China*, 544–52.

59. Peng Dehuai Biography Compilation Team, *Yige zhanzheng de ren*, 243–46; Joffe, *Party and Army*, 102–5.

60. Mao quoted in Wang, *Peng Dehuai zhuan*, 624–26.

61. Zhu, *Gun Barrel Politics*, 103.

62. After his fall, in 1965, Peng had a chance to prove his innocence and loyalty by serving as the deputy director of the remote regional reconstruction in Sichuan, but he did not survive the Cultural Revolution of 1966–76. He was arrested again in 1966 and sent back to Beijing, where he was criticized, denounced, and tortured through the rest of the 1960s and early 1970s. Peng died in jail on November 29, 1974. After Mao's death in 1976, the Central Committee announced Peng's rehabilitation in 1978, and his funeral was held in Beijing later that year.

63. Westad, *Decisive Encounters*, 6.

64. CAMS Political Tasks Research Division, *Zhongguo gongchandang zhengzhi gongzuo qishinian* (Seventy Years of CCP Political Tasks in the Chinese Military) (Beijing: Jiefangjun chubanshe, 1992), 5:238.

65. Liu Han, *Luo Ronghuan yuanshuai* (Marshal Luo Ronghuan) (Beijing: Jiefangjun chubanshe, 1987), 911–13.

66. Zhu, *Gun Barrel Politics*, 128.

67. Li, "Chinese Military Ranking," 2:402–5.

68. CAMS Military History Research Division, *Zhongguo renmin jiefangjun de qishinian*, 491–92, 548–50.

69. Wang, *Peng Dehuai zhuan*, 579–82; Spence, *Search for Modern China*, 546–53.

70. Bo, *Ruogan zhongda juece yu shijian de huigu*, 2:1070–104.

71. Huang Zhongzhi, *Wenge zhong de nongcun jieji douzheng* (Village Class Struggle during the Cultural Revolution) (Beijing: Shehui kexue chubanshe, 1998), 49.

72. Zhou Xiaohong, "Rural Political Participation in the Maoist and Post-Maoist Periods" (unpublished manuscript).

73. Ibid.; Li Ruojian, "An Examination of Cadre Behavior during the Great Leap Forward," *Social Sciences Academic Report* 13 (1998): 6–7.

74. CAMS Military History Research Division, *Zhongguo renmin jiefangjun de qishinian*, 554–55.

75. Zhu, *Gun Barrel Politics*, 132.

76. CAMS Military History Research Division, *Zhongguo renmin jiefangjun de qishinian*, 491–92, 560–64.

77. Contemporary China Compilation Committee, *Dangdai zhongguo minbing* (Militias in Contemporary China) (Beijing: Zhongguo shehui kexue chubanshe, 1988), 43.

78. CAMS Military History Research Division, *Zhongguo renmin jiefangjun de qishinian*, 510.

79. Deng Lifeng, "Wending daju de xingdong" (PLA Action and National Stabilization), in CAMS Military History Research Division, *Junqi piaopiao*, 2:518–19.

80. John Lewis Gaddis, *The Cold War: A New History* (New York: Penguin, 2005), 75–78, 80–82.

81. Thomas B. Allen, "Twilight Zone in the Pentagon," in *The Cold War: A Military History*, ed. Robert Cowley (New York: Random House, 2005), 239.

82. Among the publications on the Sino-Indian War are Jiang Siyi and Li Hui, eds., *Zhong-yin bianjing ziwei fanji zhuozhan shi* (History of the Self-Defensive Counterattack Operations on the Sino-Indian Borders) (Beijing: Junshi kexue chubanshe, 1994); Xu Yan, *Zhong-yin bianjie zhizhan lishi zhenxiang* (The Historical Truth of the Sino-Indian Border War) (Hong Kong: Tiandi tushu, 1993); Melvyn C. Goldstein, Dawei Sherap, and William R. Siebenschuh, *A Tibetan Revolutionary* (Berkeley: University of California Press, 2004); Kenneth Conboy and James Morrison, *The CIA's Secret War in Tibet* (Lawrence: University Press of Kansas, 2002); Allen S. Whiting, *The Chinese Calculus of Deterrence: India and Indochina* (Ann Arbor: University of Michigan Press, 1975); Whitson, *Chinese High Command*; and Neville Maxwell, *India's China War* (New York: Pantheon Books, 1970).

83. Elleman, *Modern Chinese Warfare*, 260.

84. Xinhua News Agency, *China's Foreign Relations*, 259.

85. Cheng Feng and Larry M. Wortzel, "PLA Operational Principles and Limited War: The Sino-Indian War of 1962," in Ryan, Finkelstein, and McDevitt, *Chinese Warfighting*, 178.

86. Deng Lifeng, "Xin zhongguo diyici fanqinlue zhanzheng" (The First Anti-Aggression War of the New Republic), in CAMS Military History Research Division, *Junqi piaopiao*, 1:348.

87. Feng and Wortzel, "PLA Operational Principles," 177.

88. Deng, "Xin zhongguo diyici fanqinlue zhanzheng," 1:356. Indian records differ from the Chinese, listing total casualties of only seven thousand. See "The Sino-Indian War" in *The Oxford Companion to Military History*, ed. Richard Holmes (Oxford: Oxford University Press, 2001), 840.

89. Feng and Wortzel, "PLA Operational Principles," 193–94.

90. *Guofang* Editorial Department, ed., *Weile daying mingtian de zhanzheng* (To Win the Future War) (Beijing: Guofand daxue chubanshe, 1999), 29, 178.

91. Sgt. Li Weiheng, interviews by the author, Archeng, Heilongjiang, and Beijing, early 1990s. (Sgt. Li is the author's uncle.)

92. Ibid.

93. Ibid.

94. Joffe, *Chinese Army after Mao*, 2.

7. Border Conflicts and the Cultural Revolution

1. Among the Chinese publications on the French Indochina War are CCP Party History Compilation Team, *Zhongguo junshi guwentuan yuanyue kangfa shilu: Dangshiren de huiyi* (True Stories of the CMAG in the War to Aid Vietnam and Resist France: Personal Memoirs) (Beijing: Zhonggong dangshi chubanshe, 2002); He Shaobang, *Wei Guoqing shangjiang* (General Wei Guoqing) (Beijing: Zhongyang wenxian chubanshe, 2000); Xie Lifu, *Yuenan zhanzheng shilu* (Historical Narrative of the Vietnam War) (Beijing: Shijie zhishi chubanshe, 1993); and CMAG History Compilation Team, *Zhongguo junshi guwentuan yuanyue kangfa douzheng shishi* (Historical Records of the CMAG in the War to Aid Vietnam and Resist France) (Beijing: Jiefangjun chubanshe, 1990).

2. Among the Chinese publications on the Vietnam War are Guo Jinliang, *Qinli Yuezhan* (The Vietnam War in My Eyes) (Beijing: Jiefangjun wenyi chubanshe, 2005); CAMS Military History Research Division, *Meiguo qinyue zhanzhengshi* (War History of the U.S. Invasion of Vietnam) (Beijing: Junshi kexue chubanshe, 2004); Luo, *Zhongyue taihai zhanzheng zhengzhan jishi*; Chen Pai, *Yuezhan qinliji* (My Personal Experience in the Vietnam War) (Zhengzhou: Henan renmin chubanshe, 1997); and Wang Xiangen, *Yuanyue kangmei shilu* (True Stories of Aiding Vietnam and Resisting America) (Beijing: Guoji wenhua chubangongsi, 1990).

3. Roger C. Thompson, *The Pacific Basin since 1945* (New York: Longman, 1994), 87.

4. Among the recent publications in English on this topic are Cowley, *Cold War*; Malcolm Muir Jr. and Mark F. Wilkinson, eds., *The Most Dangerous Years: The Cold War, 1953–1975* (Lexington: Virginia Military Institute, 2005); Christian G. Appy, *Patriots: The Vietnam War Remembered from All Sides* (New York: Viking, 2003); George Donelson Moss, *Vietnam, An American Ordeal*, 4th ed. (Upper Saddle River, NJ: Prentice Hall, 2002); David Kaiser, *American Tragedy: Kennedy, Johnson, and the Origins of the Vietnam War* (Cambridge, MA: Harvard University Press, 2000); Qiang Zhai, *China and the Vietnam Wars, 1950–1975* (Chapel Hill: University of North Carolina Press, 2000); and Spencer C. Tucker, *Vietnam* (Lexington: University Press of Kentucky, 1999).

5. John L. Gaddis, foreword to Zhai, *China and the Vietnam Wars*, x.

6. Chen and Li, "China and the End of the Global Cold War."

7. CAMS Military History Research Division, *Zhongguo renmin jiefangjun de qishinian*, 566–68.

8. George C. Herring, *America's Longest War: The United States and Vietnam, 1950–1975*, 3rd ed. (New York: McGraw-Hill, 1996), 6.

9. William J. Duiker, *Sacred War: Nationalism and Revolution in a Divided Vietnam* (New York: McGraw-Hill, 1995), 56.

10. Moss, *Vietnam*, 40–41; Tucker, *Vietnam*, 47–48.

11. Among other things on the Vietnamese list were weapons and equipment to arm three infantry divisions and $10 million in cash. Liu Shaoqi, "Guanyu Yunnan junqing he yuanzhu yuenan wenti gei Mao Zedong de dianbao" (Telegram to Mao Zedong about the Aid to Vietnam and Military Situation in Yunnan), December 24, 1949, in *Jianguo yilai Liu Shaoqi wengao*, 1:226–27.

12. Luo Guibo served as the commander and political commissar of the Central Shanxi Military District in the Chinese civil war. In a telegram to the ICP Central Committee, drafted by Liu Shaoqi, the CCP Central Committee introduced Luo as the CCP "liaison representative" with a background of "provincial governor" and "political commissar." Luo became Chinese ambassador to North Vietnam on August 11, 1954. CCP Central Committee [drafted by Liu Shaoqi], telegram to ICP Central Committee, January 17, 1950, in *Jianguo yilai Liu Shaoqi wengao*, 1:356–57. Also see Liu Shaoqi, "Guanyu tong yuenan fangmian shangtan shixiang gei Mao Zedong deng de xin" (Letter to Mao Zedong and Other Leaders about Vietnam Issues), July 4, 1950, in *Jianguo yilai Liu Shaoqi wengao*, 2:266–68.

13. CCP Central Committee [drafted by Liu Shaoqi], "Zhongyang guanyu yuenan yaoqiu junyuan wenti gei zhongnanju deng de dianbao" (Telegram to CCP South Central and Southwest Bureaus), April 7, 1950, in *Jianguo yilai Liu Shaoqi wengao*, 2:16–17; Luo Guibo, "Wuchan jieji guoji zhuyi de guanghui dianfan: Yi Mao Zedong he Yuanyue kangfa" (An Exceptional Model of Proletarian Internationalism: Mao Zedong and the War to Aid Vietnam and Resist France), in CCP Party History Compilation Team, *Zhongguo junshi guwentuan yuanyue kangfa shilu*, 4.

14. CMAG History Compilation Team, *Zhongguo junshi guwentuan yuanyue kangfa douzheng shishi*, 14.

15. Liu quoted in Yu Huachen, "Yuanyue kangfa douzheng zhong de Wei Guoqing tongzhi" (Wei Guoqing in the War to Aid Vietnam and Resist France), in CCP Party History Compilation Team, *Zhongguo junshi guwentuan yuanyue kangfa shilu*, 32–33.

16. CCP Central Committee [drafted by Liu Shaoqi], "Gei Ho Chi Minh he Luo Guibo de dianbao" (Telegram to Luo Guibo and Comrade Ho Chi Minh), April 14, 1950, in *Jianguo yilai Liu Shaoqi wengao*, 2:43–44.

17. Mao told Wei Guoqing later, on June 27, that the Central Committee first had a job for him to head the Chinese mission to the UN. The UN, however, refused to accept the PRC as a member. Then the committee planned to establish an embassy in Great Britain with Wei as China's first ambassador.

But the two governments could not reach agreement on many things, so the Chinese mission was downgraded to consulate level. Thus Wei became the head of the CMAG to Vietnam. Yu, "Yuanyue kangfa douzheng zhong de Wei Guoqing tongzhi," 39.

18. Mao quoted in ibid., 38.

19. CMAG History Compilation Team, *Zhongguo junshi guwentuan yuanyue kangfa douzheng shishi*, 3–4.

20. CCP Central Committee [drafted by Liu Shaoqi], "Zhongyang guanyu Chen Geng fu yuenan zhuyao renwu de dianbo" (Telegrams to Chen Geng on His Mission in Vietnam), June 18 and 30, 1950, in *Jianguo yilai Liu Shaoqi wengao*, 2:256–57.

21. Zhai, *China and the Vietnam Wars*, 5.

22. Duiker, *Sacred War*, 76–77.

23. For example, Chen telegraphed his plan for the border campaign to Mao in Beijing on October 4, 1950. Mao had to talk to Ho, who finally accepted Chen's plan. Yu, "Yuanyue kangfa douzheng zhong de Wei Guoqing tongzhi," 46–48.

24. CMAG History Compilation Team, *Zhongguo junshi guwentuan yuanyue kangfa douzheng shishi*, 34.

25. CCP Central Committee, "Guanyu yuanzhu yuenan jianli junxiao wenti de piyu he dianbao" (Telegram to Luo Guibo and the ICP Central Committee on Establishing Military Academies in Vietnam), April 21, 1950, in *Jianguo yilai Liu Shaoqi wengao*, 2:73–75.

26. Guo Zhigang, "Xin zhongguo chengli chuqi de yici yuanwai junshi xingdong" (Foreign Military Assistance after the Founding of the New Republic), in CAMS Military History Research Division, *Junqi piaopiao*, 1:161.

27. CMAG, "Yuenan qingqiu zhongguo yuanzhu dami gei zhongyang de baogao" (Report to the Central Committee Requesting 1,500–2,000 Tons of Rice), May 15, 1951, file 106-00073-01 (1), Foreign Ministry Archives; CCP Central Committee [drafted by Liu Shaoqi], "Guanyu zhiyuan yuenan gei Guangxi, Yunnan he yuegong zhongyang de dianbao" (Telegrams to the CCP Provincial Committees of Guangxi and Yunnan and the ICP Central Committee), June 17, 18, 22, and July 2, 1950, in *Jianguo yilai Liu Shaoqi wengao*, 2:249–53.

28. Duiker, *Sacred War*, 86.

29. Guo, "Xin zhongguo chengli chuqi de yici yuanwai junshi xingdong," 1:162.

30. Ministry of Foreign Trade, "Zhongguo he yuenan 1953 nian maoyi xiedingshu" (Agreement of China's Trade with Vietnam in 1953), file 106-00078-02 (1), 3, Foreign Ministry Archives.

31. Han and Tan, *Dangdai zhongguo jundui de junshi gongzuo*, 1:520;

CAMS Military History Research Division, *Zhongguo renmin jiefangjun de qishinian*, 403.

32. Ministry of Postal Services, "Guanyu zhongguo he yuenan jiaohuan youjian de huiyi jiyao" (Minutes of Exchange Mails and Packages between China and Vietnam), October 29–November 6, 1952, file 106-00074-01 (1), 2–6, Foreign Ministry Archives.

33. Herring, *America's Longest War*, 32–34.

34. For Mao's quote and details on the Chinese diplomacy at the Geneva Conference in May–July 1954, see Zhou Enlai, "Gei Mao Zedong, Liu Shaoqi, he qita lingdaoren de dianbao" (Telegrams to Mao Zedong, Liu Shaoqi, and Other Leaders), June 10, 18, and July 20, 1954, files 206-Y0050 (2) and 206-Y0051 (3), Foreign Ministry Archives.

35. "Final Declaration of the Geneva Conference on Indochina, 1954," in *Major Problems in the History of the Vietnam War: Documents and Essays*, 2nd ed., ed. Robert J. McMahon (Lexington, MA: D. C. Heath, 1995), 124–26.

36. Duiker, *Sacred War*, 106–8, 120.

37. Mao Zedong, "Guanyu yuenan junshi bushu de piyu" (Instruction on the Military Arrangement in Vietnam), in *Jianguo yilai Mao Zedong wengao*, 4:480.

38. Zhai, *China and the Vietnam Wars*, 115–16.

39. Moss, *Vietnam*, 106.

40. Kaiser, *American Tragedy*, 311.

41. Liu quoted in Luo, "Wuchan jieji guoji zhuyi de guanghui dianfan," 6.

42. Li Ke and Hao Shengzhang, *Wenhua dageming zhong de renmin jiefangjun* (The PLA during the Cultural Revolution) (Beijing: Zhonggong dangshi ziliao chubanshe, 1989), 423.

43. Han and Tan, *Dangdai zhongguo jundui de junshi gongzuo*, 1:550.

44. Wang, *Dongdai zhongguo kongjun*, 397; Han and Tan, *Dangdai zhongguo jundui de junshi gongzuo*, 1:551.

45. Han and Tan, *Dangdai zhongguo jundui de junshi gongzuo*, 1:550.

46. Lt. Wang Xiangcai, interview by the author, Harbin, Heilongjiang, August 2003.

47. Ibid.

48. Wang recalled that he wrote three application essays before he was accepted into the party. Ibid.

49. Ibid.

50. Ibid.

51. Ibid.

52. Ibid. From 1965 through 1969, the PLA troops in Vietnam had several Chinese field hospitals near each division headquarters, clinics at the

regimental level, medical teams at the battalion level, and medics at the company level. See Han and Tan, *Dangdai zhongguo jundui de junshi gongzuo*, 1:554–55.

53. Wang did not sign up for another term of service after three years (1965–68). Lt. Wang Xiangcai, interview.

54. Chen, *Yuezhan qinliji*, 66–67.

55. Ibid., 69.

56. Ibid., 45–46, 21.

57. Ibid., 22.

58. According to Chinese records, between August 1965 and May 1969, PLA antiaircraft troops in Vietnam shot down 1,707 American planes, damaged 1,608 others, and captured forty-two American pilots. See Han and Tan, *Dangdai zhongguo jundui de junshi gongzuo*, 1:552.

59. Tucker, *Vietnam*, 178–97; Duiker, *Sacred War*, 230; David Halberstam, *Ho* (New York: Knopf, 1987), 116–17.

60. Marilyn B. Young, *The Vietnam Wars, 1945–1990* (New York: HarperCollins, 1991), 222.

61. Appy, *Patriots*, 461–69; Herring, *America's Longest War*, 276–78.

62. "After the opening of the Paris peace talks and the Johnson administration's suspension of the American bombing of the DRV in November 1968, China began to pull back its support troops from the DRV." Zhai, *China and the Vietnam Wars*, 179.

63. For example, Premier Zhou said on April 29, 1968, that the Soviet Union (like the United States) was apparently circling and containing China. Li Danhui, "Zhongsu zai yuanyue kangmei wenti shang de maodun yu chongtu" (Conflicts between China and the Soviet Union in Their Efforts to Aid Vietnam and Resist America), in *Lengzhan yu zhongguo* (The Cold War and China), ed. Zhang Baijia and Niu Jun (Beijing: Shijie zhishi chubanshe, 2002), 373n1.

64. Xinhua News Agency, *China's Foreign Relations*, 461–67.

65. Xiaobing Li, "Sino-Soviet Border Disputes," in Powell, *Magill's Guide*, 4:1423. Among the recent publications in English on the rise and demise of the Sino-Soviet alliance are Westad, *Brothers in Arms*, and Chang, *Friends and Enemies*.

66. Li, "Sino-Soviet Border Disputes," 4:1424.

67. Han and Tan, *Dangdai zhongguo jundui de junshi gongzuo*, 1:639–42; CAMS Military History Research Division, *Zhongguo renmin jiefangjun de qishinian*, 580–81.

68. Han and Tan, *Dangdai zhongguo jundui de junshi gongzuo*, 1:643–64; CAMS Military History Research Division, *Zhongguo renmin jiefangjun de qishinian*, 582.

69. Yang Kuisong, "Cong Zhenbao dao shijian dao zhongmei huanhe" (From the Zhenbao Island Incident to Sino-American Rapprochement), *Dangshi yanjiu ziliao*, no. 12 (1997): 7–8; Thomas Robinson, "The Sino-Soviet Border Conflicts of 1969: New Evidence Three Decades Later," in Ryan, Finkelstein, and McDevitt, *Chinese Warfighting*, 198–216.

70. Chen and Li, "China and the End of the Global Cold War."

71. Fairbank, Reischauer, and Craig, *East Asia*, 967.

72. May 16 circular quoted in Zhu, *Gun Barrel Politics*, 116.

73. Ibid., 117.

74. CCP Party History Research Division, *Zhongguo gongchandang lishi dashiji*, 283.

75. Mao quoted in Deng, *Deng Xiaoping and the Cultural Revolution*, 17.

76. Mao quoted in ibid., 20.

77. For more on the Great Proletarian Cultural Revolution, see Gao Meng and Yan Jiaqi, *Wenhua dageming shi nian shi* (Ten Years of the Cultural Revolution) (Tianjin: Tianjin renmin chubanshe, 1986); Li and Hao, *Wenhua dageming zhong de renmin jiefangjun*; and Meisner, *Mao's China*, chaps. 18–20.

78. Gao and Yan, *Wenhua dageming shi nian shi*, chap. 5; Meisner, *Mao's China*, 318.

79. Mao approved most of Lin's requests. See Mao's instructions and approvals in *Jianguo yilai Mao Zedong wengao*, 12:201, 209, 218, 226–68, 380, and 383.

80. CAMS Military History Research Division, *Zhongguo renmin jiefangjun de qishinian*, 559.

81. Lüshun Naval Command, "Lin Biao-Li Zuopeng fandang panjun zuixing wenjian huibian" (Document Collection on Lin Biao and Li Zuopeng's Criminal Activities of Attacking the Party and Betraying the PLA), October 1971, political files against the Lin-Li group (1971–72), 24–25, Lüshun Naval Base Archives, PLAN, Lüshun, Liaoning.

82. Ibid., 56.

83. CAMS Military History Research Division, *Zhongguo renmin jiefangjun de qishinian*, 559.

84. Lüshun Naval Command, "Lin Biao-Li Zuopeng fandang panjun zuixing wenjian huibian," 30.

85. Shi quoted in Guo Yongzhi, critique of Lin and Li, in ibid., 5.

86. Ibid., 7.

87. Deng Hongkui, critique of Lin and Li, in ibid., 36.

88. Zhou, "China's Crouching Dragon," 93.

89. Han and Tan, *Dangdai zhongguo jundui de junshi gongzuo*, 1:62; CAMS Military History Research Division, *Zhongguo renmin jiefangjun de qishinian*, 563–64.

90. Li Zhisui, *Private Life of Chairman Mao*, 512.

91. Fairbank, Reischauer, and Craig, *East Asia*, 969–71.

92. Among the publications on Marshal Lin Biao are Huang Yao and Yan Jingtang, *Lin Biao yisheng* (Lin Biao's Life) (Beijing: Jiefangjun wenyi chubanshe, 2004); Wang Zhaojun, *Shui shale Lin Biao* (Who Killed Lin Biao) (Taipei, Taiwan: Shijie tushu, 1994); Michael Y. M. Kau, ed., *The Lin Biao Affair: Power Politics and Military Coup* (White Plains, NY: International Arts and Science Press, 1975); and Martin Ebon, *Lin Piao: The Life and Writings of China's New Ruler* (New York: Stein and Day, 1970).

93. CCP Party History Research Division, *Zhongguo gongchandang lishi dashiji*, 305–8; CAMS Military History Research Division, *Zhongguo renmin jiefangjun de qishinian*, 564–65.

94. Mao quoted in Kau, *Lin Biao Affair*, 59–60.

95. Zhu, *Gun Barrel Politics*, 181.

96. CAMS Military History Research Division, *Zhongguo renmin jiefangjun de qishinian*, 565.

97. There has been much speculation about Lin's plane crash, including that it was the result of a Chinese missile attack, that the plane ran out of fuel, and that it was simply an accident. See Gao Wenqian, *Wannian Zhou Enlai* (Zhou Enlai's Later Years) (Hong Kong: Mingjing chubanshe, 2003), 350–55; Huang and Yan, *Lin Biao yisheng*, 490–507; and Ye Yonglie, *Gaoceng jiaoliang* (Struggle at the Top) (Urmuqi: Xinjiang renmin chubanshe, 2004), 369–76.

98. CAMS Military History Research Division, *Zhongguo renmin jiefangjun de qishinian*, 566.

99. CCP Party History Research Division, *Zhongguo gongchandang lishi dashiji*, 309.

100. Grasso, Corrin, and Kort, *Modernization and Revolution in China*, 234.

101. Deng, *Deng Xiaoping and the Cultural Revolution*, 189.

102. For the last phase of the Cultural Revolution, see Gao and Yan, *Wenhua dageming shi nian shi*, chaps. 6–7; Li and Hao, *Wenhua dageming zhong de renmin jiefangjun*; and Meisner, *Mao's China*, chap. 20.

103. Richard M. Nixon, *The Memoirs of Richard Nixon* (New York: Grosset & Dunlap, 1978), 390; Charles Freeman Jr., "The Process of Rapprochement: Achievements and Problems," in *Sino-American Normalization and Its Policy Implications*, ed. Gene T. Hsiao and Michael Witunsky (New York: Praeger, 1983), 2–3, 10–14.

8. Survivor and Reformer

1. For discussions from Chinese perspectives, see Gong Li, *Kuayue honggou: 1969–79 nian zhongmei guanxi de yanbian* (Bridging the Chasm: The Evolution of Sino-American Relations, 1969–79) (Zhengzhou: Henan

renmin chubanshe, 1992), 106–8, and Wang Taiping, ed., *Zhonghua renmin gongheguo waijiaoshi, 1970–78* (Diplomatic History of the PRC, 1970–78) (Beijing: Shijie zhishi chubanshe, 1999), 345–48.

2. Thomas A. Bailey, *A Diplomatic History of the American People*, 10th ed. (Englewood Cliffs, NJ: Prentice-Hall, 1980), 928.

3. Chen and Li, "China and the End of the Global Cold War."

4. The strategic-geopolitical interpretation has prevailed among scholars and policy practitioners both in China and in the United States. See, for example, Gong Li, *Mao Zedong waijiao fengyunlu* (A Historical Record of Mao Zedong's Diplomacy) (Zhengzhou, Henan: Zhongyuan nongmin chubanshe, 1996), 195–206; Qian Jiang, *Ping pong waijiao muhou* (Behind the Ping-Pong Diplomacy) (Beijing: Dongfang chubanshe, 1997), chap. 8; Robert S. Ross, *Negotiating Cooperation: The United States and China, 1969–1989* (Stanford, CA: Stanford University Press, 1995), chap. 1; and John W. Garver, *Foreign Relations of the People's Republic of China* (Englewood Cliffs, NJ: Prentice-Hall, 1993), 74–81.

5. Joffe, *Chinese Army after Mao*, 22.

6. For more on Deng Xiaoping's life during the Cultural Revolution, see Deng, *Deng Xiaoping and the Cultural Revolution*, chaps. 17–18.

7. Ding Wei, "1975 nian junwei kuoda huiyi" (The 1975 CMC Expanded Meeting), in CAMS Military History Research Division, *Junqi piaopiao*, 2:591; Merle Goldman and Roderick MacFarquhar, "Dynamic Economy, Declining Party-State," in *The Paradox of China's Post-Mao Reforms*, ed. Merle Goldman and Roderick MacFarquhar (Cambridge, MA: Harvard University Press, 1999), 4.

8. Deng Xiaoping, "The Army Needs to Be Consolidated," speech at a meeting of officers at the GSD, January 25, 1975, in *Selected Works of Deng Xiaoping*, 2:13–15.

9. Deng Xiaping, "The Task of Consolidating the Army," speech at an expanded meeting of the CMC, July 14, 1975, in *Selected Works of Deng Xiaoping*, 2:32.

10. Deng, "Army Needs to Be Consolidated," 2:13–15. According to Deng, the people's war in the PLA tradition was an irregular, guerrilla warfare with an emphasis on mass participation. The people's war under modern conditions emphasized military professionalism and up-to-date technology.

11. Ding, "1975 nian junwei kuoda huiyi," 2:604.

12. For details of the arrest of the Gang of Four, see Deng, *Deng Xiaoping and the Cultural Revolution*, 436–43.

13. See Li, *China's Leaders*, 7–9.

14. Deng Xiaoping, "Emancipate the Mind, Seek Truth from Facts, and Unite as One in Looking to the Future," keynote address at the third plenary

session of the Eleventh CCP Central Committee, December 13, 1978, in *Selected Works of Deng Xiaoping*, 2:150–63; CCP Central Committee, "Communiqué of the Third Plenary Session of the Eleventh CCP Central Committee," adopted December 22, 1978, in CCP Central Committee Research Department of Party Literature, ed., *Major Documents of the People's Republic of China—Seclected Important Documents since the Third Plenary Session of the Eleventh CCP Central Committee* (Beijing: Foreign Languages Press, 1991), 20–22.

15. Deng Xiaoping, "Carry out the Policy of Opening to the Outside World and Learn Advanced Science and Technology from Other Countries," October 10, 1978, in *Selected Works of Deng Xiaoping*, 2:143.

16. Jing Luo argues that "Deng's challenge to what had been the sacred principles opened up people's views, instilled confidence, and gave rise to a broad-based economic recovery." Jing Luo, "Reforms of Deng Xiaoping," in Luo, *China Today*, 1:119.

17. Deng Xiaoping, "The Present Situation and the Tasks before Us," speech at a meeting of cadres called by the CCP Central Committee, January 16, 1980, in *Selected Works of Deng Xiaoping*, 2:251.

18. Deng Xiaoping, "We Shall Speed Up Reform," conversation with Stefan Korosec, member of the Presidium of the Central Committee of the League of Communists of Yugoslavia, in *Selected Works of Deng Xiaoping*, 3:235.

19. Deng Xiaoping, "Opening Speech at the Twelfth National Congress of the CCP," September 1, 1982, in *Selected Works of Deng Xiaoping*, 3:14. Also see Hu Yaobang, "Create a New Situation in All Fields of Socialist Modernization," September 1, 1982, in CCP Central Committee Research Department of Party Literature, *Major Documents*, 267–328.

20. Deng Xiaoping, "China's Goal Is to Achieve Comparative Prosperity by the End of the Century," conversation with Masayoshi Ohira, prime minister of Japan, December 6, 1979, in *Selected Works of Deng Xiaoping*, 2:240.

21. Deng Xiaoping, "Planning and the Market Are Both Means of Developing the Productive Forces," excerpt from a conversation with leading members of the CCP Central Committee, February 6, 1987, in *Selected Works of Deng Xiaoping*, 3:203–4.

22. For more on Deng's reform movement, see Goldman and MacFarquhar, *Paradox of China's Post-Mao Reforms*; Orville Schell and David Shambaugh, eds., *The China Reader: The Reform Era* (New York: Vintage Books, 1999); and Willem Van Kemenade, *China, Hong Kong, Taiwan, Inc.* (New York: Vintage Books, 1997).

23. Li, "New War of Nerves," 65.

24. Among the recent publications in English on the Sino-American

rapprochement are William Burr, ed., *The Kissinger Transcripts: The Top-Secret Talks with Beijing and Moscow* (New York: New Press, 1999); Jim Mann, *About Face: A History of America's Curious Relationship with China, from Nixon to Clinton* (New York: Knopf, 1999); Rosemary Foot, *The Practice of Power: U.S. Relations with China since 1949* (Oxford: Oxford University Press, 1997); and Robert S. Ross, *Negotiating Cooperation: The United States and China, 1969–1989* (Stanford, CA: Stanford University Press, 1995).

25. Warren I. Cohen, *America's Response to China: A History of Sino-American Relations*, 4th ed. (New York: Columbia University Press, 2000), 206–7.

26. You Ji, "Meeting the Challenge of Multi-polarity: China's Foreign Policy toward Post–Cold War Asia and the Pacific," in *Asian-Pacific Collective Security in the Post–Cold War Era*, ed. Hung-mao Tien (Taipei, Taiwan: National Policy Institute, 1996), 233–73.

27. Qu Xing, "Dong'ou jubian he sulian jieti hou de zhongguo waijiao" (China's Foreign Policy since the Radical Changes in Eastern Europe and the Disintegration of the USSR), *Waijiao xueyuan xuebao* 4 (1994): 19–22.

28. "Promoting RMA with Chinese characteristics purports that we need to study and draw on the experience as well as lessons of RMA in other countries and of each hi-tech local war. Yet we cannot copy the entire mode of RMA of other countries." Xiong Guangkai, "Lun junshi geming" (On Revolution in Military Affairs) (paper presented at the Chinese Scientists' Forum on Humanities, April 16, 2003), in Xiong Guangkai, *Guoji zhanlue yu xin junshi biange* (International Strategy and Revolution in Military Affairs) (Beijing: Qinghua daxue chubanshe, 2003), 183.

29. Ibid., 180.

30. Chai Zhongguo, "Zhenhen shijie de zhanlie xingdong" (A Strategic Move Shocked the World), in CAMS Military History Research Division, *Junqi piaopiao*, 2:669.

31. Deng Xiaoping, "Speech at an Enlarged Meeting of the CMC," June 4, 1985, in *Selected Works of Deng Xiaoping*, 3:131–33.

32. Deng Xiaoping, "Streamline the Army and Raise Its Combat Effectiveness," speech at an expanded meeting of the CMC Standing Committee, March 12, 1980, in *Selected Works of Deng Xiaoping*, 2:284–87.

33. Deng, "Speech at an Enlarged Meeting of the CMC," 3:131.

34. Ibid., 3:133.

35. You Ji, "Changing Leadership Consensus: The Domestic Context of War Games," in *Across the Taiwan Strait: Mainland China, Taiwan, and the 1995–1996 Crisis*, ed. Suisheng Zhao (New York: Routledge, 1999), 87.

36. Goldman and MacFarquhar, "Dynamic Economy," 8.

37. Col. Wang Lilin, interview by the author, Beijing, July 2004.

38. Anita Chan, "The Social Origins and Consequences of the Tiananmen Crisis," in *China in the Nineties: Crisis Management and Beyond*, ed. David S. G. Goodman and Gerald Segal (Oxford: Oxford University Press, 1991), 113–14.

39. Zhou, "Rural Political Participation."

40. Dorothy J. Solinger, "China's Floating Population," in Goldman and MacFarquhar, *Paradox of China's Post-Mao Reforms*, 223–24.

41. Ibid., 228–29.

42. Col. Wang Lilin, interview.

43. Gerald Segal, "Foreign Policy," in Goodman and Segal, *China in the Nineties*, 173.

44. Zhai, *China and the Vietnam Wars*, 152–53.

45. CAMS Military History Research Division, *Zhongguo renmin jiefangjun de qishinian*, 586–87.

46. Haong Sun (member, Vietnamese Workers' Party Central Committee, and editor of the party newspaper), interview by Eric Pier, 1976, in Tian Fuzi, *Zhongyeu zhanzheng jishilu* (Factual Records of the Sino-Vietnam War) (Beijing: Jiefangjun wenyi chubanshe, 2004), 9–10.

47. Han and Tan, *Dangdai zhongguo jundui de junshi gongzuo*, 1:659–60.

48. Xie Guojun, "Zhongyue bianjing ziwei huanji zuozhan" (The Sino-Vietnamese Border War of Self-Defense and Counteroffense), in CAMS Military History Research Division, *Junqi piaopiao*, 2:624–25.

49. CAMS Military History Research Division, *Zhongguo renmin jiefangjun de qishinian*, 609–10.

50. Deng quoted in Tian, *Zhongyeu zhanzheng jishilu*, 16–18.

51. Deng quoted in ibid., 18.

52. Chen, *Mao's China*, 14.

53. Tian, *Zhongyeu zhanzheng jishilu*, 42–43.

54. Ibid., 43.

55. Xie, "Zhongyue bianjing ziwei huanji zuozhan," 2:629–30.

56. Tian, *Zhongyeu zhanzheng jishilu*, 327–28.

57. Col. Zhi Zhanpeng (PLA, ret.), interview by the author, Haikou, Hainan, August 2002.

58. Ibid. The combat report and statistics are also in Tian, *Zhongyeu zhanzheng jishilu*, 80.

59. Col. Zhi, interview.

60. Ibid.

61. Ibid.; Tian, *Zhongyeu zhanzheng jishilu*, 92, 107.

62. Col. Zhi, interview.

63. Tian, *Zhongyeu zhanzheng jishilu*, 92, 328.

64. Segal, "Foreign Policy," 173.

65. Tian, *Zhongyeu zhanzheng jishilu*, 92, 26–27.

66. Deng quoted in ibid., 25.

67. Vietnamese general, interview by Henry J. Kenny, "Vietnamese Perceptions of the 1979 War with China," in Ryan, Finkelstein, and McDevitt, *Chinese Warfighting*, 232.

68. Ibid.

69. For details of the battles between 1979 and 1984, see Han and Tan, *Dangdai zhongguo jundui de junshi gongzuo*, 1:679–82; Xie, "Zhongyue bianjing ziwei huanji zuozhan," 2:629–32; and CAMS Military History Research Division, *Zhongguo renmin jiefangjun de qishinian*, 613–14.

70. Tian, *Zhongyeu zhanzheng jishilu*, 72–73, 403.

71. For details of the battles between 1984 and 1987, see Han and Tan, *Dangdai zhongguo jundui de junshi gongzuo*, 1:684–86, and Xie, "Zhongyue bianjing ziwei huanji zuozhan," 2:634–35.

72. Pvt. Xu Xiangyao, interview by the author, Oklahoma City, OK, February 2005.

73. Ibid.

74. Ibid. According to Xu, the glory bomb was not just for infantry troops. All of the men and women who entered Vietnam in the 1980s, including nurses, doctors, and officers, carried this suicide device.

75. Ibid.

76. Deng Xiaoping, speech at a CMC meeting, 1986, in Tian, *Zhongyeu zhanzheng jishilu*, 55.

77. CMC, "Investigative Report on the Phenomenon of 'Localization' in the Officer Corps," March 18, 1989, in *The Tiananmen Papers: The Chinese Leadership's Decision to Use Force against Their Own People—in Their Own Words*, ed. Zhang Liang (New York: Public Affairs, 2001), 9.

78. Luo, "Reforms of Deng Xiaoping," 1:121.

79. David S. G. Goodman, "The Authoritarian Outlook," introduction to Goodman and Segal, *China in the Nineties*, 3–5.

80. See Charles Tilly, "Does Modernization Breed Revolution?" *Comparative Politics* 5, no. 3 (1973): 425–47.

81. Xiaosi Yang, "Politics of Deng Xiaoping," in Luo, *China Today*, 1:115.

82. Chan, "Social Origins and Consequences," 105.

83. Xiaobing Li, "Social-Economic Transition and Cultural Reconstruction in China," introduction to *Social Transition in China*, ed. Jie Zhang and Xiaobing Li (Lanham, MD: University Press of America, 1998), 1–18.

84. *Renmin ribao*, "The Necessity for a Clear Stand against Turmoil," April 26, 1989, reprinted in Zhang, *Tiananmen Papers*, 71–75.

85. Zhang, *Tiananmen Papers*, 121–22.

86. Ibid., 265.

87. In Zhang's *Tiananmen Papers*, eight generals are listed, but other sources have different numbers. For example, seven generals are mentioned in Suzanne Ogden, Kathleen Hartford, Lawrence Sullivan, and David Zweig, eds., *China's Search for Democracy: The Student and the Mass Movement of 1989* (Armonk, NY: M. E. Sharpe, 1992), 292.

88. Zhang, *Tiananmen Papers*, 265.

89. Martial Law Force Command, "Martial Law Situation Report, no. 3," May 19, 1989, in ibid., 227.

90. Zhang, *Tiananmen Papers*, 287–88, 302–3.

91. For more on the Tiananmen Square incident, see ibid. and Goodman and Segal, *China in the Nineties*.

92. Party Central Office Secretariat, "Minutes of the Politburo Standing Committee Meeting," June 3, 1989, in Zhang, *Tiananmen Papers*, 368–70.

93. The official records list 264 deaths, including 23 college students and 20 PLA soldiers and officers. The Beijing Red Cross estimated 2,600 deaths, and China Radio International reported in Beijing on June 4, 1989, that "several thousand people, mostly innocent citizens," had been killed by "heavily armed soldiers." See Zhang, *Tiananmen Papers*, 385, 389, 436.

94. Harlan Jencks, "Civil-Military Relations in China: Tiananmen and After," *Problems of Communism* 40 (May–June 1991): 22.

95. Shambaugh, *Modernizing China's Military*, 24.

96. Deng Xiaoping, "Build Socialism with Chinese Characteristics," conversations with the Japanese delegation to the second session of the Council of Sino-Japanese Non-governmental Figures, June 30, 1984, in CCP Central Committee Research Department of Party Literature, *Major Documents*, 1–5.

97. Xiaobing Li, "Reforming the People's Army: Military Modernization in China," *Journal of the Southwest Conference on Asian Studies* 5 (2005): 17.

98. Luo, "Reform of Deng Xiaoping," 1:121.

9. Technocrats and the New Generation

1. Jiang quoted in PRC State Council Bureau of Information, *White Papers of China's National Defense in 1998* (Beijing: Foreign Languages Press, 2000), 2:645.

2. Kenneth W. Allen, Dean B. Cheng, David M. Finkelstein, and Maryanne Kevlehan, *Institutional Reforms of the Chinese People's Liberation Army: Overview and Challenges* (Alexandria, VA: CNA Corporation, 2002), iii.

3. Wang Wenrong, "Xuexi guanche Jiang Zemin zhongda zhanlue sixiang" (Studying and Carrying out President Jiang's Important Strategic Thoughts), introduction to *Zhongguo tese de junshi biange* (Revolution of Military Affairs with Chinese Characteristics) by Sun Kejia (Beijing: Changzheng chubanshe, 2003), 1.

4. Col. Yang, interview.

5. R. Keith Schoppa argues that "for many in China, the actions cost the army a huge amount of respect." Schoppa, *Revolution and Its Past*, 422.

6. Theoretically, collective leadership was always in place in the CCP. But Mao Zedong and Deng Xiaoping, the first and second generations of CCP leadership, had dominated party politics and policymaking. Jiang Zemin actually put collective leadership into practice at the party center during his tenure. See Jiang Zemin, "On Improving the Party's Style of Work," speech at the fifth plenary session of the Fifteenth CCP Central Committee, October 11, 2000, in Jiang Zemin, *On the "Three Represents"* (Beijing: Foreign Languages Press, 2002), 92–95.

7. Jiang Zemin, "How Our Party Is to Attain the 'Three Represents' under the New Historical Condition," speech delivered during a tour of Guangdong Province, February 25, 2000, in Jiang, *On the "Three Represents,"* 8.

8. Li, *China's Leaders*, 25–26.

9. Jiang Shufeng, interview.

10. *Selected Documents of the Fifteenth CCP National Congress* (Beijing: New Star Publishers, 1997), 104–6.

11. Bin Yu, "China's Gun-Control Problem: Jiang vs. Hu?" *PacNet*, no. 40 (2004): 2.

12. You, "Changing Leadership Consensus," 88, 87.

13. Jiang Zemin, "Hold High the Great Banner of Deng Xiaoping Theory for an All-Round Advancement of the Cause of Building Socialism with Chinese Characteristics into the 21st Century," speech at the Fifteenth CCP National Congress, September 12, 1997, in *Documents of the Fifteenth CCP National Congress*, 31.

14. Yu, "China's Gun-Control Problem," 2.

15. Chai Zhongguo, "Zhengzhi hege, junshi guoying, zuofeng youliang, jilu yanming, baozhang youli" (Political Quality, Well-Trained Skill, Excellent Character, Strict Discipline, and Guaranteed Logistics Support), in CAMS Military History Research Division, *Junqi piaopiao*, 2:741.

16. Ibid., 2:746–47.

17. Jiang, "Hold High the Great Banner," 42–46.

18. PRC State Council Bureau of Information, *White Papers of China's National Defense in 1998*, 2:397.

19. Jane's Information Group, "Chinese Army: Professionalism, 1.10.6,"

China and Northeast Asia, Jane's Sentinel Security Assessments, http://sentinel.janes.com.

20. Wang, "Xuexi guanche Jiang Zemin zhongda zhanlue sixiang," 2.

21. Patricia Buckley Ebrey, Anne Walthall, and James B. Palais, *East Asia: A Cultural, Social, and Political History* (Boston: Houghton Mifflin, 2006), 581–82.

22. *Zhongguo chengshi jingji shehui nianjian, 1985* (Almanac of Chinese Urban Economy and Society, 1985) (Beijing: Zhongguo tongji chubanshe, 1988), 39; *Zhongguo chengshi tongji nianjian, 2000* (China's Urban Statistical Yearbook, 2000) (Beijing: Zhongguo tongji chubanshe, 2001), 3.

23. "Zhongguo shehui jiegou xianzhuang" (Contemporary China's Social Strata), in PRC Bureau of Statistics, *Zhongguo tongji nianjian, 2000*, 718.

24. *Military Service Law of the PRC* (Beijing: Law Press China, 2002), 5–7.

25. Xiong, "Lun junshi geming," 44.

26. Xiong Guangkai, "Jinru xinshiji de guoji zhanlue xingshi" (The International Strategic Situation at the Dawn of the New Century), interview, *Xuexi shibao*, December 30, 2000, 10–13.

27. Xiaobing Li, "Social Changes in China and Implications for the PLA," in *Civil-Military Relations in Today's China: Swimming in a New Sea*, ed. David M. Finkelstein and Kristen Gunness (Armonk, NY: M. E. Sharpe, 2006), 41–42.

28. Tianjin Garrison Command Headquarters, "Xinxi baozhang shi guofang jianshe de zhongxin" (Information System: The Key for National Defense), in *Guofang* Editorial Department, *Weile daying mingtian de zhanzheng*, 47.

29. Solinger, "China's Floating Population," 223–25, 228.

30. Li, "Social Changes in China," 46–48.

31. Sijin Cheng, "Conscription: From the Masses," in Finkelstein and Gunness, *Civil-Military Relations*, 241.

32. Amendment to article 11 of the constitution of the PRC, adopted at the first session of the Seventh National People's Congress, April 12, 1988.

33. Amendment to article 8 of the constitution of the PRC, adopted at the first session of the Eighth National People's Congress, March 29, 1993.

34. Amendment to article 11 of the constitution of the PRC, adopted at the second session of the Ninth National People's Congress, March 15, 1999.

35. Amendment to article 13 of the constitution of the PRC, adopted at the second session of the Tenth National People's Congress, March 14, 2004.

36. Li Heng, "Tigao renwu ganbu de zonghe suzhi" (Improve the Quality of the Officers in the People's Armed Forces Department), in *Guofang* Editorial Department, *Weile daying mingtian de zhanzheng*, 79.

37. The five autonomous regions, with large ethnic minorities, contain a

large proportion of agricultural workers and other lower-income groups. To-day, within each autonomous region, counties with ethnic minority concentrations are at greater disadvantage. For instance, according to a 2003 report, out of 104 poverty-stricken villages in Yili prefecture in Xinjiang Uygur Autonomous Region, 102 were national minority villages. Li Xiaoxiao and Zhou Mei, "A Comparative Study on Minority Women in Taiwan and Xinjiang," in *Taiwan in the Twenty-first Century*, ed. Xiaobing Li and Zuohong Pan (Lanham, MD: University Press of America, 2003), 83–96.

38. Many of these workers received only a fraction of their salaries, and some have protested to demand better conditions and new jobs. Continued state reforms will result in many more workers' losing their jobs in the coming years and will inevitably lead to growing labor unrest. Li, "Social Changes in China," 49.

39. Yang Jieshi (Chinese ambassador to the United States), interview by the author, Oklahoma City, OK, January 2004.

40. "Guanyu dangqian zhongguo shehui xingtai de yanjiu baogao" (Report on a Study of Contemporary China's Social Strata), in PRC Bureau of Statistics, *Zhongguo tongji nianjian, 2002*, 1047, 1044, 1047–48.

41. Jiang, "Hold High the Great Banner," 8–9; Song Ruilai, "Zhongguo shengyu zhuanxing de tedian yu yuanying" (Characteristics and Causes of the Fertility Transition in China), *Zhongguo renkou kexue* 5, no. 20 (1993): 149; Zhong Fenggan, "Cong fazhanzhong guojia de jiaodu kan zhongguo renkou jiegou de zhuanxing" (China's Demographic Transition Viewed from the Perspective of Developing Countries), *Renkou yanjiu* 1 (January 1990): 1–6; Lin Fuda, "Zhongguo shengyu bianhua de tedian" (Characteristics of the Fertility Transition in China), *Renkou yanjiu* 2 (February 1987): 1–9.

42. PRC State Council Bureau of Information, *Zhongguo renkou* (China's Population) (Beijing: Zhongguo jinrong jingji chubanshe, 2002), tables 31, 32, 41; PRC State Council Bureau of Information, *Zhongguo de jihua shengyu* (Family Planning in China) (Beijing: Zhongguo guowuyuan, 1995), 3–4, 14.

43. Ji Jianjun, *Henan renkou yanjiu* (A Study of the Henan Population) (Zhengzhou: Henan renmin chubanshe, 1999), 46–48; Fan Jian, "The Fertility Decline and the Demographic Transition in the PRC" (master's thesis, University of Wisconsin–Milwaukee, 2000), 5–7.

44. David Popenoe, "Family Decline in America," in *Morals, Marriage, and Parenthood: An Introduction to Family Ethics*, ed. Laurence D. Houlgate (Seattle: Washington Publishing, 1999), 141, 161.

45. *Zhongguo renkou shouce* (China Population Information Handbook) (Beijing: Jingji xueyuan chubanshe, 2003), 121–24.

46. Ibid., table 29.

47. Lt. Gen. Qin Chaoying, interview by the author, Beijing, December 2003.

48. Hebei Provincial Command officer, interview by the author, Langfang, Hebei, July 2002.

49. Lt. Gen. Qin, interview, December 2003.

50. Zhang Zhaozhong, *Shui neng daying xiayichang zhanzheng* (Who Will Win the Next War?) (Beijing: Zhongguo qingnian chubanshe, 1999), 395.

51. Li Changzhu, "Jiedu dusheng zinu bing" (Understanding the Only-Child Soldiers), *Zhongguo Wujing*, no. 31 (February 2001): 28–29.

52. Group army commanding officers, interviews by the author, Shenyang, Liaoning, July 2002, and Beijing, August 2002.

53. Hebei Provincial Command officer, interview.

54. Ji, *Henan renkou yanjiu*, 122; Fan, "Fertility Decline," 13.

55. Deborah Davis-Freedmann, "Old Age Security and the One-Child Campaign," in *China's One-Child Policy*, ed. Elizabeth Croll, Deborah Davis, and Penny Kane (London: Macmillan, 1985), 149–61.

56. Hebei Provincial Command officer, interview.

57. PRC State Council Family Planning Commission, *Zhongguo renkou yu jihua shengyu fa* (Population and Family Planning Law) (Beijing: Zhongguo guowuyuan, 2002), 2–4.

58. GPD planning officer, interview by the author, Beijing, December 2003.

59. Lt. Gen. Qin, interview, December 2003; You, "Changing Leadership Consensus," 87.

60. "Profiles of the Standing Committee Members of the Politburo of the Fifteenth CCP Central Committee: Zhang Wannian," in *Selected Documents of the Fifteenth CCP National Congress*, 135–37.

61. "Profiles of the Standing Committee Members of the Politburo of the Fifteenth CCP Central Committee: Chi Haotian," in *Selected Documents of the Fifteenth CCP National Congress*, 133–34.

62. Second Artillery Corps Headquarters Operation Department, "Zhuoyan gaojishu jubu zhanzheng tedian, jiaqiang erpao yubeiyi budui zhiliang jianshe" (Focus on Characteristics of Local, High-Tech War; Strengthen Quality Building of Second Artillery Corps Reserves), in *Guofang* Editorial Department, *Weile daying mingtian de zhanzheng*, 196.

63. Jiang quoted in Wang Baocun, "Information Warfare and RMA" (unpublished manuscript).

64. For more on Chi's hardline position, see John F. Copper, "The Origins of Conflict across the Taiwan Strait: The Problem of Differences in Percep-

tions," in Zhao, *Across the Taiwan Strait*, 43, and You, "Changing Leadership Consensus," 91–93.

65. For a detailed overview of the 1995–96 Taiwan Strait crisis, see Qi-mao Chen, "The Taiwan Strait Crisis," in Zhao, *Across the Taiwan Strait*, 127–62.

66. William Perry and Ashton Carter, *Preventive Defense: A New Security for America* (Washington, DC: Brookings Institute, 1999), 92–93.

67. Patric Tyler, *A Great Wall: Six Presidents and China* (New York: Public Affairs, 1999), 33, 195.

68. William Perry, public statements, March 11, 1996, in U.S. Department of Defense, *News Briefings*, March 12, 14, and 16, 1996.

69. Robert Ross, "The 1995–96 Taiwan Strait Confrontation: Coercion, Credibility, and the Use of Force," *International Security* 25 (Fall 2000): 120–23.

70. Ibid., 122.

71. Jiang, speech to the PLA delegation to the Tenth National People's Congress.

72. Li, *China's Leaders*, 8, 9–10.

73. Lu Hao (governor, Gansu Province), interview by the author, Oklahoma City, OK, April 2002. Hu Jintao worked in Gansu for twelve years, starting as a construction worker in 1968 and ending as the secretary of the Gansu Provincial Committee of the CYL in 1980. Also see "Profiles of the Standing Committee Members of the Politburo of the Fifteenth CCP Central Committee: Hu Jintao," in *Selected Documents of the Fifteenth CCP National Congress*, 116–18.

74. Cheng, "Conscription," 240, 247.

75. Xiong, "Lun junshi geming," 182–83.

76. Hu Jintao, speech at a Four Headquarters (Sizongbu) meeting, August 2000, quoted in *Taiyangbao*, September 5, 2000.

77. Gen. Zhang Zhen, speech at the Joint Warfare Seminar, NDU, 1997, in *Lun lianhe zhanyi* (On Joint Warfare), ed. Yu Shusheng (Beijing: Guofang daxue chubanshe, 1998), 2.

78. PRC State Council Bureau of Information, *White Papers of China's National Defense in 2004*, 645.

79. Ibid., 654.

80. Ibid., 644.

81. Li, *China's Leaders*, figure 1.1, table 3.3.

82. China's Economic Growth and Sustainability Development conference, Guangzhou, December 2003.

Conclusion

1. For example, Maj. Gen. Zhu Chenghu, dean of the NDU, told a group of foreign journalists in July 2005 that China would attack more than one hundred American cities with nuclear weapons if the United States interfered in a war between China and Taiwan. The U.S. Congress called for the Chinese general to be fired. The Chinese government, however, did not reject Zhu's speech, although a spokesperson from the Ministry of Foreign Affairs said that Zhu's speech was his own personal opinion. This spokesperson declined to comment on whether the speech represented the Chinese government's view. Jonathan D. Pollack pointed out that, although China is becoming more involved in "sub- and pan-regional security affairs," it is "acquiring military capabilities that it believes will ultimately enable a short-warning, high-intensity attack against Taiwan. These include a growing inventory of short-range ballistic missiles, advanced conventionally powered submarines and other naval platforms, longer-range aircraft, and a host of related capabilities." Wang Zheng, "U.S. Congress Calls for Sacking of Chinese General," *Epoch Times*, July 25, 2005; David Shambaugh, "The Rise of China and Asia's New Dynamics," in *Power Shift: China and Asia's New Dynamics*, ed. David Shambaugh (Berkeley: University of California Press, 2005), 11; Jonathan D. Pollack, "The Transformation of the Asian Security Order: Assessing China's Impact," in Shambaugh, *Power Shift*, 339.

Selected Bibliography

Chinese-Language Sources

Archival Collections

CCP provincial party committee files (1966–69). Liaoning Provincial Government Archives, Shenyang.

Korean War files. Archives of the PRC Ministry of Foreign Affairs, Beijing.

Political files against the Lin-Li group (1971–72). Lüshun Naval Base Archives, PLAN, Lüshun, Liaoning.

Provincial government files (1996–2000). Hainan Provincial Government Archives, Haikou.

Provincial government files (1949–66). Heilongjiang Provincial Government Archives, Harbin.

Provincial government files (1948–68). Liaoning Provincial Government Archives, Shenyang.

Sino-Soviet relations files. Archives of the PRC Ministry of Foreign Affairs, Beijing.

Sino-U.S. relations files. Archives of the PRC Ministry of Foreign Affairs, Beijing.

Books and Articles

Bai Gang. *Zhongguo nongmin wenti yanjiu* (Study of Chinese Peasants). Beijing: Renmin chubanshe (People's Press), 1993.

Bai Xi. *Kaiguo da zhenya* (The Great Suppression). Beijing: Zhonggong dangshi chubanshe (CCP Party History Press), 2006.

Bo Yibo. *Ruogan zhongda juece yu shijian de huigu* (Recollections of Certain Important Decisions and Events). 2 vols. Beijing: Zhonggong zhongyang dangxiao chubanshe (CCP Central Party Academy Press), 1991.

Cai Hesen. "Dangnei jihui zhuyi de lishi huigu" (History of the Party's Opportunists). *Dangshi yanjiu ziliao* (Party History Research Materials) 4, no. 2 (2001): 508–21.

CAMS Military History Research Division. *Junqi piaopiao: Xinzhongguo 50 nian junshi dashi shushi* (PLA Flag Fluttering: Facts of China's Major Military Events in the Past 50 Years). 2 vols. Beijing: Jiefangjun chubanshe (PLA Press), 1999.

———. *Meiguo qinyue zhanzhengshi* (War History of the U.S. Invasion of Vietnam). Beijing: Junshi kexue chubanshe (Military Science Press), 2004.

———. *Shanhaiguan zhizhan* (The Battle of Shanhaiguan). Beijing: Jiefangjun chubanshe (PLA Press), 1990.

———. *Zhongguo renmin jiefangjun de qishinian, 1927–97* (Seventy Years of the PLA, 1927–97). Beijing: Junshi kexue chubanshe (Military Science Press), 1997.

———. *Zhongguo renmin jiefangjun quanguo jiefang zhanzhengshi* (History of the PLA in the Chinese Civil War). 5 vols. Beijing: Junshi kexue chubanshe (Military Science Press), 1997.

———. *Zhongguo renmin jiefangjun zhanshi* (Warfighting History of the PLA). 8 vols. Beijing: Junshi kexue chubanshe (Military Science Press), 1987.

———. *Zhongguo renmin zhiyuanjun kangmei yuanchao zhanshi* (War Experience of the CPVF in the War to Resist America and Aid Korea). 2nd ed. Beijing: Junshi kexue chubanshe, 1990.

CAMS Political Tasks Research Division. *Zhongguo gongchandang zhengzhi gongzuo qishinian* (Seventy Years of CCP Political Tasks in the Chinese Military). 6 vols. Beijing: Jiefangjun chubanshe (PLA Press), 1992.

CCP Central Archival and Manuscript Research Division. *He Long nianpu* (A Chronological Record of He Long). Beijing: Zhongyang dangxiao chubanshe (CCP Party Academy Press), 1988.

———. *Mao Zedong nianpu, 1893–1949* (A Chronological Record of Mao Zedong, 1893–1949). 3 vols. Beijing: Zhongyang wenxian chubanshe (CCP Central Archival and Manuscript Press), 1993.

———. *Mao Zedong zhuan, 1893–1949* (Biography of Mao Zedong, 1893–1949). 2 vols. Beijing: Zhongyang wenxian chubanshe (CCP Central Archival and Manuscript Press), 1996.

———. *Zhou Enlai nianpu, 1898–1949* (A Chronological Record of Zhou Enlai, 1898–1949). Beijing: Zhongyang wenxian chubanshe (CCP Central Archival and Manuscript Press), 1990.

———. *Zhu De nianpu, 1886–1976* (A Chronological Record of Zhu De, 1886–1976). Beijing: Renmin chubanshe, 1986.

CCP Central Archives, comp. *Zhonggong zhongyang jiefang zhanzheng shiqi tongyi zhanxian wenjian xuanbian* (Selected Documents of the CCP Central Committee on the United Front during the War of Liberation,

1946–49). Beijing: Zhongyang dang'an chubanshe (CCP Central Archives Press), 1988.

———, comp. *Zhonggong zhongyang kangri zhanzheng shiqi tongyi zhanxian wenjian xuanbian* (Selected Documents of the CCP Central Committee on the United Front during the War of Resistance against Japan, 1937–45). Beijing: Zhongyang dang'an chubanshe (CCP Central Archives Press), 1985.

———, comp. *Zhonggong zhongyang wenjian xuanji, 1921–49* (Selected Documents of the CCP Central Committee, 1921–49). 18 vols. Beijing: Zhonggong zhongyang dangxiao chubanshe (CCP Central Party Academy Press), 1989–92.

CCP Central Archives, CCP Central Archival and Manuscript Research Division, and CCP Organization Department, comps. *Zhongguo gongchandang zuzhishi ziliao, 1921–97* (Documents of the CCP Organization's History, 1921–1997). 14 vols. Beijing: Zhonggong dangshi chubanshe (CCP Central Committee's Party History Press), 2000.

CCP Central Institute of Historical Documents, comp. *Jianguo yilai zhongyao wenxian xuanbian* (Selected Important Documents since the Founding of the PRC). 20 vols. Beijing: Zhongyang wenxian chubanshe (CCP Central Archival and Manuscript Press), 1992–98.

CCP Party History Compilation Team. *Zhongguo junshi guwentuan yuanyue kangfa shilu: Dangshiren de huiyi* (True Stories of the CMAG in the War to Aid Vietnam and Resist France: Personal Memoirs). Beijing: Zhonggong dangshi chubanshe (CCP Central Party History Press), 2002.

CCP Party History Research Division. *Zhongguo gongchandang lishi dashiji, 1919–87* (Major Historical Events of the CCP, 1919–87). Beijing: Renmin chubanshe (People's Press), 1989.

Chai Chengwen and Zhao Yongtian. *Banmendian tanpan* (The P'anmunjŏm Negotiations). 2nd ed. Beijing: Jiefangjun chubanshe (PLA Press), 1992.

Chen Pai. *Yuezhan qinliji* (My Personal Experience in the Vietnam War). Zhengzhou: Henan renmin chubanshe (Henan People's Press), 1997.

Chen Qingli. *Zhongguo nongmin suzhilun* (Quality of the Chinese Peasants). Beijing: Dangdai shijie chubanshe (Contemporary World Publishers), 2002.

Chen Yi. *Chen Yi junshi wenxuan* (Selected Military Papers of Chen Yi). Beijing: Jiefangjun chubanshe (PLA Press), 1996.

Chu Yun. *Chaoxian zhanzheng neimu quangongkai* (Declassifying the Inside Story of the Korean War). Beijing: Shishi chubanshe (Current Affairs Press), 2005.

CMAG History Compilation Team. *Zhongguo junshi guwentuan yuanyue kangfa douzheng shishi* (Historical Records of the CMAG in the War to

Aid Vietnam and Resist France). Beijing: Jiefangjun chubanshe (PLA Press), 1990.

Contemporary China Compilation Committee. *Dangdai zhongguo de guofang keji shiye* (Defense Technology and Science in Contemporary China). 2 vols. Beijing: Dangdai zhongguo chubanshe (Contemporary China Press), 1992.

———. *Dangdai zhongguo de hegongye* (The Nuclear Industry in Contemporary China). Beijing: Zhongguo shehui kexue chubanshe (China's Social Science Press), 1987.

———. *Dangdai zhongguo minbing* (Militias in Contemporary China). Beijing: Zhongguo shehui kexue chubanshe (China's Social Science Press), 1988.

———. *Wang Zhen zhuan* (Biography of Wang Zhen). 2 vols. Beijing: Dangdai zhongguo chubanshe (Contemporary China Press), 1999.

Cui Xianghua and Chen Dapeng. *Tao Yong jiangjun zhuan* (Biography of General Tao Yong). Beijing: Jiefangjun chubanshe (PLA Press), 1989.

Dai Yi. *Jianming qingshi* (Concise History of the Qing). 4 vols. Beijing: Renmin chubanshe (People's Press), 1980.

Di Jiu and Ke Feng. *Chaozhang chaoluo: Guogong jiaozhu Taiwan haixia jishi* (Record of the CCP-GMD Confrontation in the Taiwan Straits). Beijing: Zhongguo gongshang chubanshe (China Industrial and Commercial Press), 1996.

Dong Fanghe. *Zhang Aiping zhuan* (Biography of Zhang Aiping). 2 vols. Beijing: Renmin chubanshe (People's Press), 2000.

Dong Hanhe. *Xilujun nuzhanshi mengnanji* (Tragic Death of Female Soldiers of the Western Red Army). Beijing: Jiefangjun wenyi chubanshe (PLA Literature Press), 1990.

Dong Shigui. *Henan laonian renkou diaocha* (Aged Population in Henan). Zhengzhou: Henan renmin chubanshe (Henan People's Press), 1989.

Fan Jianghui. *Dajiang Wang Shusheng* (General Wang Shusheng). Beijing: Jiefangjun wenyi chubanshe (PLA Literature Press), 1998.

Fan Shuo. *Ye Jianying zhuan* (Biography of Ye Jianying). Beijing: Dangdai zhongguo chubanshe), 1995.

Feng Xianzhi and Li Jie. *Mao Zedong yu kangmei yuanchao* (Mao Zedong and the War to Resist America and Aid Korea). Beijing: Zhongyang wenxian chubanshe (CCP Central Archival and Manuscript Press), 2000.

GAD Political Department. *Liangdan yixing: Zhongguo hewuqi daodan weixing yu feichuan quanjishi* (The Bomb, Missile, and Satellite: A Complete Record of China's Nuclear Bombs, Missiles, Satellites, and Space Programs). Beijing: Jiuzhou chubanshe (Jiuzhou Press), 2001.

Gao Wenqian. *Wannian Zhou Enlai* (Zhou Enlai's Later Years). Hong Kong: Mingjing chubanshe (Mirror Books), 2003.

Ge Chumin, ed. *Laozhanshi yishi* (Personal Stories of Veterans). Beijing: Zhongguo duiwai fanyi chuban gongsi (China's Outreach and Translation Publishing Company), 2000.

Gu Yongzhong. *He Long zhuan* (Biography of He Long). Beijing: Dangdai zhongguo chubanshe (Contemporary China Press), 1993.

Guo Jinliang. *Qinli Yuezhan* (The Vietnam War in My Eyes). Beijing: Jiefangjun wenyi chubanshe (PLA Literature Press), 2005.

Guofang Editorial Department, ed. *Weile daying mingtian de zhanzheng* (To Win the Future War). Beijing: Guofand daxue chubanshe (National Defense University Press), 1999.

Han Huaizhi and Tan Jingqiao. *Dangdai zhongguo jundui de junshi gongzuo* (Contemporary Chinese Military Affairs). 2 vols. Beijing: Zhongguo shehui kexue chubanshe (China's Social Science Press), 1989.

Hao Bocun. *Ba'nian canmo zongzhang riji* (Diary of General Chief Staff for Eight Years). 2 vols. Taipei, Taiwan: Tianxia yuanjian chubanshe (Tianxia Publishing House), 2000.

———. *Buju* (No Fear). Taipei, Taiwan: Wusi shudian (May Fourth Books), 1995.

He Di. "Taihai weiji he zhongguo dui Jinmen, Mazu zhengce de xingcheng" (Taiwan Strait Crises and the Chinese Policy toward Jinmen and Mazu). *Meiguo yanjui* (American Studies) 3, no. 1 (Fall 1988): 26–49.

He Long. *He Long junshi wenxuan* (Selected Military Papers of He Long). Beijing: Jiefangjun chubanshe (PLA Press), 1989.

He Ming. *Jianzheng: Chaoxian zhanzheng zhafu qianfan Jieshi daibiao de riji* (Witness: Diary of a Representative for the Explanatory Task to Repatriate Chinese POWs). Beijing: Zhongguo wenshi chubanshe (China's History Literature Press), 2001.

He Shaobang. *Wei Guoqing shangjiang* (General Wei Guoqing). Beijing: Zhongyang wenxian chubanshe (CCP Central Archival and Manuscript Press), 2000.

Hong Xuezhi. *Kangmei yuanchao zhanzheng huiyi* (Recollections of the War to Resist America and Aid Korea). Beijing: Jiefangjun wenyi chubanshe (PLA Literature Press), 1990.

Hu Guangzheng. *Zhongwai junshi zuzhi tizhi bijiao jiaocheng* (Teaching Text for Comparative Study on Chinese and Foreign Military Organizations). Beijing: Junshi kexue chubanshe (Military Science Press), 1999.

Hu Qinghe. *Chaoxian zhanzheng zhong de nuren* (Women in the Korean War). Jinan, Shandong: Huanghe chubanshe (Yellow River Press), 1992.

Hu Shihong. "Hangtian zuomingqu" (Space Sonata). *Renwu* (Biographies) 5 (1994): 51–74.

Hu Wenyan, Zang Rong, Wang Zhihong, Xing Kebin, and Li Longgeng.

Zhongguo lishi (Chinese History). Beijing: Renmin jiaoyu chubanshe (People's Education Press), 1986.

Hu Yanlin, ed. *Renmin haijun zhengzhan jishi* (Historical Records of the People's Navy's Warfare). Beijing: Guofang daxue chubanshe (NDU Press), 1996.

Huang Yao and Yan Jingtang. *Lin Biao yisheng* (Lin Biao's Life). Beijing: Jiefangjun wenyi chubanshe (PLA Literature Press), 2004.

Huang Zhongzhi. *Wenge zhong de nongcun jieji douzheng* (Village Class Struggle during the Cultural Revolution). Beijing: Shehui kexue chubanshe (Social Science Press), 1998.

Ji Jianjun. *Henan renkou yanjiu* (A Study of the Henan Population). Zhengzhou: Henan renmin chubanshe (Henan People's Press), 1999.

Jiang Huaxuan, ed. *Zhongguo gongchandang zhongyao huiyi jiyao* (Minutes of the CCP's Important Meetings). Beijing: Zhongyang wenxian chubanshe (CCP Central Archival and Manuscript Press), 2001.

Jiang Siyi and Li Hui, eds. *Zhong-yin Bianjing ziwei fanji zhuozhan shi* (History of the Self-Defensive Counterattack Operations on the Sino-Indian Borders). Beijing: Junshi kexue chubanshe (Military Science Press), 1994.

Jiangsu Party History Research Committee, comp. *Zhonggong zhongyang Nanjingjiu: Zhonggong lishi ziliao* (The Nanjing Bureau of the CCP Central Committee: CCP Historical Documents). Beijing: Zhonggong zhongyang dangshi chubanshe (CCP Central Committee's Party History Press), 1990.

Jin Chongji. *Zhu De zhuan* (Biography of Zhu De). Beijing: Renmin chubanshe and Zhongyang wenxian chubanshe (People's Press and CCP Central Archival and Manuscript Press), 1993.

Jin Yuguo. *Zhongguo zhanshushi* (History of Chinese Tactics). Beijing: Jiefangjun chubanshe (PLA Press), 2003.

Li Baozhong. *Zhongwei junshi zhidu bijiao* (Comparative Study of Chinese Military System). Beijing: Shangwu yinshuguan (Shangwu Press), 2003.

Li Bingyan. *Da moulue yu Xin junshi biange* (Military Stratagem and the New Revolution in Military Affairs). Beijing: Jiefangjun chubanshe (PLA Press), 2004.

Li Hongjie. *Zhenyi de zhanzheng, weida de jingshen* (The Just War and Great Spirit). Guangzhou: Guangdong renmin chubanshe (Guangdong People's Press), 2001.

Li Jian. *Taihai liang'an zhanshi huigu* (History of the Military Conflicts over the Taiwan Straits). Beijing: Huawen chubanshe (Huawen Publishers), 1996.

Li Ke and Hao Shengzhang. *Wenhua dageming zhong de renmin jiefangjun* (The PLA during the Cultural Revolution). Beijing: Zhonggong dangshi ziliao chubanshe (CCP Central Committee's Party Historical Document Press), 1989.

Li Yuming, Xu Fang, and Meng Jianhua, eds. *Zhonghua renmin gongheguo shi cidian* (Dictionary of PRC History). Beijing: Zhongguo guoji guangbo chubanshe (China International Broadcasting Press), 1989.

Lie Jianhua and Wang Jicheng. *Xinzhongguo haizhan neimu* (The Inside Story of New China's Naval Warfare). Beijing: Zhongguo weiguo wenxue chubanshe (China's Foreign Literature Press), 1993.

Lin Fuda. "Zhongguo shengyu bianhua de tedian" (Characteristics of the Fertility Transition in China). *Renkou yanjiu* (Population Research) 2 (February 1987): 1–19.

Lin Hongzhan. *Zhongguo renmin jiefangjun X dang'an* (The PLA's X File). Taipei, Tawian: Bentu wenhua gongsi (Native Culture Publishing), 1996.

Liu Bocheng. *Liu Bocheng junshi wenxuan* (Selected Military Papers of Liu Bocheng). Beijing: Jiefangjun chubanshe (PLA Press), 1992.

Liu Han. *Luo Ronghuan yuanshuai* (Marshal Luo Ronghuan). Beijing: Jiefangjun chubanshe (PLA Press), 1987.

Liu Shaoqi. *Jianguo yilai Liu Shaoqi wengao, 1949–52* (Liu Shaoqi's Manuscripts since the Founding of the State, 1949–52). 4 vols. Beijing: Zhongyang wenxian chubanshe (CCP Central Archival and Manuscript Press), 2005.

Liu Xiao. *Chushi sulian banian, 1955–1963* (My Eight-Year Mission to the Soviet Union, 1955–1963). Beijing: Zhonggong dangshi ziliao chubanshe (CCP Central Party History Records Press), 1986.

Liu Zhan. *Zhongguo gudai junzhishi* (History of the Military System in Ancient China). Beijing: Junshi kexue chubanshe (Military Science Press), 1992.

Liu Zhaoxiang. *Zhongguo junshi zhidu shi* (History of the Chinese Military Institution). Zhengzhou, Henan: Dazhong chubanshe (Popular Press), 1997.

Lu Di. *Wang Shusheng dajiang* (General Wang Shusheng). Zhengzhou, Henan: Haiyan chubanshe (Haiyan Press), 1987.

Luo Xuanyou. *Zhongyue taihai zhanzheng zhengzhan jishi* (Historical Records of the Sino-Vietnam and Taiwan Strait Wars). 2 vols. Urumqi: Xinjiang renmin chubanshe (Xinjiang People's Press), 2004.

Mao Zedong. *Jianguo yilai Mao Zedong wengao, 1949–76* (Mao Zedong's Manuscripts since the Founding of the State, 1949–76). 13 vols. Beijing: Zhongyang wenxian chubanshe (CCP Central Archival and Manuscript Press), 1989–93.

———. *Mao Zedong junshi wenji* (Collected Military Papers of Mao

Zedong). 6 vols. Beijing: Junshi kexue chubanshe (Military Science Press), 1993.

———. *Mao Zedong junshi wenxuan: Neibuben* (Selected Military Papers of Mao Zedong: Internal Edition). 2 vols. Beijing: Jiefangjun zhanshi chubanshe (PLA Soldiers' Press), 1981.

———. *Mao Zedong waijiao wenxuan* (Selected Diplomatic Papers of Mao Zedong). Beijing: Zhongyang wenxian chubanshe (CCP Central Archival and Manuscript Press) and Shijie zhishi chubanshe (World Knowledge Press), 1994.

———. *Mao Zedong wenji* (A Collection of Mao Zedong's Works). 8 vols. Beijing: Renmin chubanshe (People's Press), 1993–99.

———. *Mao Zedong xuanji* (Selected Works of Mao Zedong). 5 vols. Beijing: Renmin chubanshe (People's Press), 1971–78.

National Military Museum of the Chinese People's Revolution, comp. *Zhongguo zhanzheng fazhanshi* (History of Chinese Warfare). 2 vols. Beijing: Renmin chubanshe (People's Press), 2001.

National Women Association Organization Department, comp. *Zhongguo nujiangjun* (Chinese Women Generals). Shenyang: Liaoning renmin chubanshe (Liaoning People's Press), 1995.

NDU. *Zhonggong dangshi jiaoxue cankao ziliao* (Reference Materials on Teaching and Studying CCP History). 27 vols. Beijing: Guofang daxue chubanshe (NDU Press), n.d.

NDU War History Division. *Zhongguo renmin jiefangjun zhanshi jianbian* (A Brief History of the PLA Revolutionary War). Beijing: Jiefangjun chubanshe (PLA Press), 2001.

———. *Zhongguo renmin zhiyuanjun zhanshi jianbian* (A Brief War-Fighting History of the CPVF). Beijing: Jiefangjun chubanshe (PLA Press), 1992.

Nie Fengzhi, Wang De, Wu Zaowen, and Hu Shihong. *Sanjun huige zhan donghai* (Three Services Wield Weapons in East China Sea Combat). Beijing: Jiefangjun chubanshe (PLA Press), 1985.

Nie Rongzhen. *Nie Rongzhen huiyilu* (Memoirs of Nie Rongzhen). 2 vols. Beijing: Jiefangjun chubanshe (PLA Press), 1984.

———. *Nie Rongzhen junshi wenxuan* (Selected Military Papers of Nie Rongzhen). Beijing: Jiefangjun chubanshe (PLA Press), 1992.

Peng Dehuai. *Peng Dehuai junshi wenxuan* (Selected Military Papers of Peng Dehuai). Beijing: Zhongyang wenxian chubanshe (CCP Central Archival and Manuscript Press), 1988.

———. *Peng Dehuai zisu* (Autobiography of Peng Dehuai). Beijing: Renmin chubanshe (People's Press), 1981.

Peng Dehuai Biography Compilation Team. *Yige zhanzheng de ren* (A Real Man). Beijing: Renmin chubanshe, 1994.

PLAN History Compilation Committee. *Haijun: Huiyi shiliao* (The Navy: Memoirs and Historical Records). 2 vols. Beijing: Haichao chubanshe, 1994.

PRC Bureau of Statistics. *Zhongguo tongji nianjian, 1989–2002* (China's Statistical Yearbooks, 1989–2002). Beijing: Zhongguo tongji chubanshe (China's Statistics Press), 1990–2003.

PRC State Council Bureau of Information. *Zhongguo de jihua shengyu* (Family Planning in China). Beijing: Zhongguo guowuyuan (PRC State Council), 1995.

———. *Zhongguo renkou* (China's Population). Beijing: Zhongguo jinrong jingji chubanshe (China Finance and Economy Publishing House), 2002.

PRC State Council Family Planning Commission. *Zhongguo renkou yu jihua shengyu fa* (Population and Family Planning Law). Beijing: Zhongguo guowuyuan (PRC State Council), 2002.

Qi Dexue. "Youguan kangmei yuanchao zhanzheng de jige wenti" (Several Issues on Resisting the United States and Aiding the Korean War). *Zhonggong dangshi yanjiu* (CCP History Research) 1 (1998): 65–82.

Qian Haihao. *Jundui zuzhi bianzhixue jiaocheng* (CAMS Graduate School Curriculum: Military Organization and Formation). Beijing: Junshi kexue chubanshe (Military Science Press), 2001.

ROC Defense Department. *Guojun houqin shi* (Logistics History of the GMD Armed Forces). 8 vols. Taipei, Taiwan: Guofangbu shizheng bianyiju (History and Political Publication Bureau of the Defense Department), 1992.

ROC Defense Department Bureau of Historical and Political Compilations. *Gu Zhutong jiangjun jinianji* (Recollection of General Gu Zhutong's Works). Taipei, Taiwan: Guofangbu shizheng bianyiju (Bureau of Historical and Political Compilations, ROC Defense Department), 1988.

ROC Defense Ministry History Compilation and Translation Bureau. *8-23 paozhan shengli 30 zhounian jinian wenji* (Recollection for the 30th Anniversary of the Victorious 8-23 Artillery Battle). Taipei, Taiwan: Guofangbu yinzhichang (Defense Ministry Printing Office), 1989.

Shen Weiping. *8-23 paoji Jinmen* (8-23 Bombardment of Jinmen). 2 vols. Beijing: Huayi chubanshe (Huayi Publishers), 1999.

Shen Zhihua, trans. and ed. *Chaoxian zhanzheng: Eguo dang'anguan de jiemi wenjian* (The Korean War: Declassified Documents from Russian Archives). 3 vols. Taipei, Taiwan: Zhongyang yanjiuyuan (Sini Academy Printing Office), 2003.

———. "Kangmei yuanchao zhanzheng zhongde sulian kongjun" (The Soviet Air Force in the Korean War). *Zhonggong dangshi yanjiu* (Studies on CCP History), no. 2 (2000): 19–32.

———— . *Mao Zedong, Stalin he chaoxian zhanzheng* (Mao Zedong, Stalin, and the Korean War). Guangzhou: Guangdong renmin chubanshe (Guangdong People's Press), 2004.

Shi Duqiao. *Zhongguo jindai junshi sixiangshi* (History of Military Thought in Modern China). Beijing: Guofang daxue chubanshe (National Defense University Press), 2000.

Shi Zhe. *Zai lishi juren shenbian* (Reminiscences of Mao's Russian Interpreter). Beijing: Zhongyang wenxian chubanshe (CCP Central Archival and Manuscript Press), 1991.

Sichuan Party History Research Committee, comp. *Nanfangjiu dangshi ziliao* (Party History Records of the CCP Southern Bureau). Chongqing, Sichuan: Chongqing renmin chubanshe (Chongqing People's Press), 1986.

Song Ruilai. "Zhongguo shengyu zhuanxing de tedian yu yuanying" (Characteristics and Causes of the Fertility Transition in China). *Zhongguo renkou kexue* (China's Journal of Population Science) 5, no. 20 (1993): 139–58.

Song Shaoming. *Wang Zhen chuanqi* (Legacy of Wang Zhen). 2 vols. Beijing: Changzheng chubanshe (Long March Press), 2001.

Sun Kejia. *Zhongguo tese de junshi biange* (Revolution of Military Affairs with Chinese Characteristics). Beijing: Changzheng chubanshe (Long March Press), 2003.

Tan Jingjiao. *Kangmei yuanchao zhanzheng* (The War to Resist America and Aid Korea). Beijing: Zhongguo shehui kexue chubanshe (China Social Science Press), 1990.

Tan Zheng. *Zhongguo renmin zhiyuanjun renwulu* (Veterans Profile of the CPVF). Beijing: Zhonggong dangshi chubanshe (CCP Party History Press), 1992.

Tao Hanzhang. *Sun Zi bingfa gailun* (Analysis of Sun Zi's *The Art of War*). Beijing: Jiefangjun chubanshe (PLA Press), 1991.

Tao Wenzhao. *Zhongmei guanxishi, 1949–72* (PRC-U.S. Relations, 1949–72). Shanghai: Shanghai renmin chubanshe (Shanghai People's Press), 1999.

Tian Fuzi. *Zhongyeu zhanzheng jishilu* (Factual Records of the Sino-Vietnam War). Beijing: Jiefangjun wenyi chubanshe (PLA Literature Press), 2004.

Tianjin Normal College Department of History, comp. *Zhongguo jianshi* (A Concise History of China). Beijing: Renmin jiaoyu chubanshe (People's Education Press), 1980.

Wang Bingnan. *Zhongmei huitan jiunian huigu* (My Nine Years of Sino-American Ambassadorial Talks in Retrospect). Beijing: Shijie zhishi chubanshe (World Knowledge Press), 1985.

Wang Dinglie. *Dongdai Zhongguo kongjun* (Contemporary Chinese Air Force). Beijing: Zhongguo shehui kexue chubanshe (China's Social Sciences Press), 1989.

Wang Hai. *Wode zhandou shengya* (My Military Career). Beijing: Zhongyang wenxian chubanshe (CCP Central Archives and Manuscript Press), 2000.

Wang Shuzeng. *Yuandong chaoxian zhanzheng* (The Korean War in the Far East). 2 vols. Beijing: Jiefangjun wenyi chubanshe (PLA Literature Press), 2000.

Wang Xiangen. *Yuanyue kangmei shilu* (True Stories of Aiding Vietnam and Resisting America). Beijing: Guoji wenhua chubangongsi (International Culture Publishing), 1990.

Wang Yan. *Peng Dehuai zhuan* (Biography of Peng Dehuai). Beijing: Dangdai zhongguo chubanshe (Contemporary China Press), 1993.

Wang Zhaojun. *Shui shale Lin Biao* (Who Killed Lin Biao). Taipei, Taiwan: Shijie tushu (World Books), 1994.

World Military High-Tech Book Series Compilation Team. *Daguo yizhi: Dakai heheixiang* (The Powers' Will: Opening the Nuclear Black Box). Beijing: Haichao chubanshe (Ocean Wave Publishing), 2000.

Wu Dianrao. *Zhu De.* Beijing: Kunlun chubanshe, 1999.

Wu Jiezhang. *Zhongguo jindai haijun shi* (Modern History of the Chinese Navy). Beijing: Jiefangjun chubanshe (PLA Press), 1989.

Wu Yan, Liao Shufang, and Qin Xingyi. *Zhongguo nongmin de bianqian* (Transition of the Chinese Peasants). Guangzhou: Guangdong renmin chubanshe (Guangdong People's Press), 1999.

Wu Ziyong. *Zhanzheng dongyuanxue jiaocheng* (Teaching Text for War Mobilization). Beijing: Junshi kexue chubanshe (Military Science Press), 2001.

Xiao Jinguang. *Xiao Jinguang huiyilu* (Memoirs of Xiao Jinguang). 2 vols. Beijing: Jiefangjun chubanshe (PLA Press), 1988.

Xie Lifu. *Yuenan zhanzheng shilu* (Historical Narrative of the Vietnam War). 2 vols. Beijing: Shijie zhishi chubanshe (World Knowledge Press), 1993.

Xinghuo Liaoyuan Composition Department. *Zhongguo renmin jiefangjun jiangshuai minglu* (Marshals and Generals of the PLA). 3 vols. Beijing: Jiefangjun chubanshe (PLA Press), 1987–92.

Xinhua News Agency. *Xinhuashe wenjian ziliao huibian* (A Collection of Documentary Materials of the New China News Agency). Beijing: Xinhuashe (New China News Agency), n.d.

Xiong Guangkai. *Guoji zhanlue yu xin junshi biange* (International Strategy and Revolution in Military Affairs). Beijing: Qinghua daxue chubanshe (Tsinghua University Press), 2003.

Xu Xiangqian. *Xu Xiangqian junshi wenxuan* (Selected Military Papers of Xu Xiangqian). Beijing: Jiefangjun chubanshe (PLA Press), 1992.

Xu Yan. *Diyici jiaoliang: Kangmei yuanchao zhanzheng de lishi huigu yu fansi* (The First Encounter: A Historical Retrospective of the War to Resist America and Aid Korea). Beijing: Zhongguo guangbo dianshi chubanshe (China's Radio and Television Press), 1990.

———. *Jinmen zhizhan* (The Battle of Jinmen). Beijing: Zhongguo guangbo dianshi chubanshe (China's Radio and Television Press), 1992.

———. *Junshijia Mao Zedong* (Mao Zedong as a Military Leader). Beijing: Zhongyang wenxian chubanshe (CCP Central Archival and Manuscript Press), 1995.

———. *Zhong-yin bianjie zhizhan lishi zhenxiang* (The Historical Truth of the Sino-Indian Border War). Hong Kong: Tiandi tushu (Tiandi Books), 1993.

Yang Di. *Zai zhiyuanjun silingbu de suiyueli* (My Years at the CPVF Headquarters). Beijing: Jiefangjun chubanshe (PLA Press), 1998.

Yang Guoyu. *Dangdai Zhongguo haijun* (Contemporary Chinese Navy). Beijing: Zhongguo shehui kexue chubanshe (China's Social Science Press), 1987.

Yang Kuisong. *Zouxiang polie: Mao Zedong yu Moscow de enen yuanyuan* (Toward the Split: Interests and Conflicts between Mao Zedong and Moscow). Hong Kong: Sanlian shudian (Joint Publishing), 1999.

Yang Shangkun. *Yang Shangkun huiyilu* (Memoirs of Yang Shangkun). Beijing: Zhongyang wenxian chubanshe (CCP Central Archival and Manuscript Press), 2001.

———. *Yang Shangkun riji* (Diary of Yang Shangkun). 2 vols. Beijing: Zhongyang wenxian chubanshe (CCP Central Archival and Manuscript Press), 2001.

Ye Fei. *Ye Fei huiyilu* (Memoirs of Ye Fei). Beijing: Jiefangjun chubanshe (PLA Press), 1988.

Ye Jianying. *Ye Jianying xuanji* (Selected Works of Ye Jianying). Beijing: Renmin chubanshe (People's Press), 1996.

Ye Yonglie. *Gaoceng jiaoliang* (Struggle at the Top). Urumqi: Xinjiang renmin chubanshe (Xinjiang People's Press), 2004.

Yidai mingjiang: Huiyi Su Yu Tongzhi (A Well-Known General: Remembering Comrade Su Yu). Shanghai: Shanghai renmin chubanshe (Shanghai People's Press), 1986.

Yu Shusheng, ed. *Lun lianhe zhanyi* (On Joint Warfare). Beijing: Guofang daxue chubanshe (National Defense University Press), 1998.

Zhang Baijia and Niu Jun, eds. *Lengzhan yu zhongguo* (The Cold War and China). Beijing: Shijie zhishi chubanshe (World Knowledge Press), 2002.

Zhang Guotao. *Wo de huiyi* (My Recollections). 2 vols. Beijing: Dongfang chubanshe (East Press), 2004.

Zhang Lin. *Dajiang Xu Haidong* (General Xu Haidong). Beijing: Jiefangjun wenyi chubanshe (PLA Literature Press), 1998.

Zhang Mingqing. *Junshi shehuixue* (Military Sociology). Beijing: Zhongguo shehui kexue chubanshe (China's Social Science Press), 2002.

Zhang Xiuping, Mao Yuanyou, and Huang Pumin. *Yingxiang zhongguo de yibaici zhanzheng* (The One Hundred Battles That Shaped China). Nanning: Guangxi renmin chubanshe (Guangxi People's Press), 2003.

Zhang Yutian. *Zhongguo jindai junshishi* (Military History of Modern China). Shenyang: Liaoning renmin chubanshe (Liaoning People's Press), 1983.

Zhang Zhaozhong. *Shui neng daying xiayichang zhanzheng* (Who Will Win the Next War?). Beijing: Zhongguo qingnian chubanshe (China Youth Press), 1999.

Zhao Shaoquan. *Xinbian zhongguo xiandaishi* (New History of Modern China). 3 vols. Nanchang: Jiangxi renmin chubanshe (Jiangxi People's Press), 1987.

Zhong Fenggan. "Cong fazhanzhong guojia de jiaodu kan zhongguo renkou jiegou de zhuanxing" (China's Demographic Transition Viewed from the Perspective of Developing Countries). *Renkou yanjiu* (Population Research) 1 (January 1990): 1–22.

Zhongguo chengshi jingji shehui nianjian, 1985 (Almanac of Chinese Urban Economy and Society, 1985). Beijing: Zhongguo tongji chubanshe (China Statistics Press), 1988.

Zhongguo chengshi tongji nianjian, 2000 (China's Urban Statistical Yearbook, 2000). Beijing: Zhongguo tongji chubanshe (China's Statistics Press), 2001.

Zhongguo renkou shouce (China Population Information Handbook). Beijing: Jingji xueyuan chubanshe (Economics Institute Press), 2003.

Zhou Enlai. *Zhou Enlai waijiao wenxuan* (Selected Diplomatic Papers of Zhou Enlai). Beijing: Zhongyang wenxian chubanshe (CCP Central Archival and Manuscript Press), 1990.

Zhou Zhong. *Kangmei yuanchao zhanzheng huoqinshi jianbianben* (A Concise History of the Logistics in the War to Resist America and Aid Korea). Beijing: Jindun chubanshe (Golden Shield Press), 1993.

Zhu De. *Zhu De junshi wenxuan* (Selected Military Papers of Zhu De). Beijing: Jiefangjun chubanshe (PLA Press), 1986.

Zhu Yuxiang. *Zhongguo jindai nongmin wenti yu nongcun shehui* (Peasant Issues and Rural Society in Modern China). Ji'nan: Shandong daxue chubanshe (Shandong University Press), 1997.

English-Language Sources

Archival Collections

Dulles, John Foster, Papers. Dwight D. Eisenhower Library, Abilene, KS.
Eisenhower, Dwight D., Papers. Dwight D. Eisenhower Library, Abilene, KS.
Hurley, Patrick, Papers. University of Oklahoma Library, Norman.
U.S. State Department files. RG 59. National Archives, College Park, MD.

Books and Articles

Accinelli, Robert. *Crisis and Commitment: United States Policy toward Taiwan, 1950-1955*. Chapel Hill: University of North Carolina Press, 1999.
Allen, Kenneth W., Dean B. Cheng, David M. Finkelstein, and Maryanne Kevlehan. *Institutional Reforms of the Chinese People's Liberation Army: Overview and Challenges*. Alexandria, VA: CNA Corporation, 2002.
Ambrose, Stephen. *Eisenhower: The President*. New York: Simon & Schuster, 1984.
———. *Eisenhower: Soldier, General of the Army, President-Elect, 1890–1952*. New York: Simon & Schuster, 1983.
Appy, Christian G. *Patriots: The Vietnam War Remembered from All Sides*. New York: Viking, 2003.
Babbin, Jed, and Edward Timperlake. *Showdown: Why China Wants War with the United States*. Washington, DC: Regnery, 2006.
Bailey, Paul J. *China in the Twentieth Century*. 2nd ed. Malden, MA: Blackwell, 2001.
Benton, Gregor. *New Fourth Army*. Berkeley: University of California Press, 1999.
Bernstein, Richard, and Ross H. Munro. *The Coming Conflict with China*. New York: Knopf, 1997.
Bianco, Lucien. *Origins of the Chinese Revolution, 1915–1949*. Stanford, CA: Stanford University Press, 1971.
Black, Jeremy, ed. *War in the Modern World*. London: Routledge, 2003.
Blair, Clay. *The Forgotten War: America in Korea, 1950–1953*. New York: Times Books, 1987.
Breslin, Shaun. *Mao: Profiles in Power*. New York: Longman, 1998.
Burr, William, ed. *The Kissinger Transcripts: The Top-Secret Talks with Beijing and Moscow*. New York: New Press, 1999.
Cambridge History of China. Vol. 14, *The People's Republic*. Cambridge: University of Cambridge Press, 1967.
CCP Central Committee Research Department of Party Literature, ed. *Major Documents of the People's Republic of China—Selected Important Docu-*

ments since the Third Plenary Session of the Eleventh CCP Central Committee. Beijing: Foreign Languages Press, 1991.

Chang, Gordon G. *The Coming Collapse of China*. New York: Random House, 2001.

Chang, Gordon H. *Friends and Enemies: The United States, China, and the Soviet Union*. Stanford, CA: Stanford University Press, 1990.

———. "To the Nuclear Brink: Eisenhower, Dulles, and the Quemoy-Matsu Crisis." *International Security* 12 (Spring 1988): 92–117.

Chang, Gordon H., and He Di. "The Absence of War in the U.S.-China Confrontation over Quemoy and Matsu in 1954–1955: Contingency, Luck, Deterrence?" *American Historical Review* 98, no. 5 (December 1993): 1500–1524.

Chang, Iris. *The Rape of Nanking: The Forgotten Holocaust of World War II*. New York: Basic Books, 1997.

———. *Thread of the Silkworm*. New York: Basic Books, 1995.

Chang, Jung, and Jon Halliday. *Mao: The Unknown Story*. New York: Knopf, 2005.

Cheek, Timothy. *Mao Zedong and China's Revolution: A Brief History with Documents*. Boston: Bedford/St. Martin's, 2002.

Chen Jian. *China's Road to the Korean War: The Making of the Sino-American Confrontation*. New York: Columbia University Press, 1994.

———. *Mao's China and the Cold War*. Chapel Hill: University of North Carolina Press, 2001.

Chen Jian and Xiaobing Li, "China and the End of the Global Cold War." In *From Détente to the Soviet Collapse*, edited by Malcolm Muir Jr. Lexington: Virginia Military Institute, 2006.

Chen Jian and David L. Wilson, eds. "All under the Heaven Is Great Chaos: Beijing, the Sino-Soviet Border Clashes, and the Turn toward Sino-American Rapprochement, 1968–1969." *Cold War International History Project Bulletin* 11 (Winter 1998–99): 155–75.

Cheng, Tun-jen, Chi Huang, and Samuel S. G. Wu, eds. *Inherited Rivalry: Conflict across the Taiwan Straits*. Boulder, CO: Lynne Rienner Publishers, 1995.

Chow Ching-wen. *Ten Years of Storm: The True Story of the Communist Regime in China*. Westport, CT: Greenwood Press, 1960.

Christensen, Thomas J. *Useful Adversaries: Grand Strategy, Domestic Mobilization, and Sino-American Conflict, 1947–1958*. Princeton, NJ: Princeton University Press, 1996.

Cohen, Warren I. *America's Response to China: A History of Sino-American Relations*. 4th ed. New York: Columbia University Press, 2000.

Compilation Committee of ROC History. *A Pictorial History of the Republic of China*. 2 vols. Taipei, Taiwan: Modern China Press, 1981.

Conboy, Kenneth, and James Morrison. *The CIA's Secret War in Tibet.* Lawrence: University Press of Kansas, 2002.

Cowley, Robert, ed. *The Cold War: A Military History.* New York: Random House, 2005.

Croll, Elizabeth, Deborah Davis, and Penny Kane, eds. *China's One-Child Policy.* London: Macmillan, 1985.

Cummings, Bruce. *The Origins of the Korean War.* 2 vols. Lawrence: University Press of Kansas, 1981–90.

Deng, Peng. "The Impact of the Korean War on the Chinese Society: The Mass Campaigns in 1951–52." Paper presented at the annual meeting of the Association of Asian Society, Chicago, IL, March 22–25, 2003.

Deng Rong. *Deng Xiaoping and the Cultural Revolution: A Daughter Recalls the Critical Years.* Trans. Sidney Shapiro. Beijing: Foreign Languages Press, 2002.

Deng Xiaoping. *Selected Works of Deng Xiaoping.* 3 vols. Beijing: Foreign Languages Press, 1994.

Domes, Jürgen. *Peng Te-huai: The Man and the Image.* London: C. Hurst, 1985.

Dreyer, Edward L. *China at War, 1901–1949.* New York: Longman, 1995.

Ebon, Martin. *Lin Piao: The Life and Writings of China's New Ruler.* New York: Stein and Day Publishers, 1970.

Elleman, Bruce A. *Modern Chinese Warfare, 1795–1989.* London: Routledge, 2001.

Esherick, Joseph W. *Reform and Revolution in China: The 1911 Revolution in Hunan and Hubei.* Berkeley: University of California Press, 1976.

———. "Revolution in a Feudal Fortress." *Modern China* 24, no. 4 (October 1998): 354–76.

Evans, Grant, ed. *Asia's Cultural Mosaic: An Anthropological Introduction.* New York: Prentice Hall, 1993.

Fairbank, John K., and Merle Goldman. *China: A New History.* Enl. ed. Cambridge, MA: Harvard University Press, 1998.

Fairbank, John K., Edwin O. Reischauer, and Albert M. Craig. *East Asia: Tradition and Transformation.* Revised edition. Boston: Houghton Mifflin, 1989.

Fan Jian. "The Fertility Decline and the Demographic Transition in the PRC." Master's thesis, University of Wisconsin–Milwaukee, 2000.

Fei Hsiao Tung. *China's Gentry.* Chicago: University of Chicago Press, 1953.

———. *Chinese Village Close-up.* Beijing: New World Press, 1983.

Feng, Chih. *Behind Enemy Lines.* Beijing: Foreign Languages Press, 1979.

Finkelstein, David M. *Washington's Taiwan Dilemma, 1949–1950: From Abandonment to Salvation.* Fairfax, VA: George Mason University Press, 1993.

Finkelstein, David M., and Kristen Gunness, eds. *Civil-Military Relations in To-day's China: Swimming in a New Sea.* Armonk, NY: M. E. Sharpe, 2006.

Foot, Rosemary. *The Practice of Power: U.S. Relations with China since 1949.* Oxford: Oxford University Press, 1997.

Foot, Rosemary, and Frank A. Kierman Jr., eds. *Chinese Ways in Warfare.* Cambridge, MA: Harvard University Press, 1974.

Gaddis, John Lewis. *The Cold War: A New History.* New York: Penguin, 2005.

Garver, John W. *Chinese-Soviet Relations, 1937–1945: The Diplomacy of Chinese Nationalism.* New York: Oxford University Press, 1988.

———. *Foreign Relations of the People's Republic of China.* Englewood Cliffs, NJ: Prentice-Hall, 1993.

Getz, Bill. *The China Threat: How the People's Republic Targets America.* Washington, DC: Regnery, 2000.

Goldman, Merle, and Roderick MacFarquhar, eds. *The Paradox of China's Post-Mao Reforms.* Cambridge, MA: Harvard University Press, 1999.

Goldstein, Melvyn C., Dawei Sherap, and William R. Siebenschuh. *A Tibetan Revolutionary.* Berkeley: University of California Press, 2004.

Goodman, David S. G., and Gerald Segal, eds. *China in the Nineties: Crisis Management and Beyond.* Oxford: Oxford University Press, 1991.

Graff, David A., and Robin Higham, eds. *A Military History of China.* Boulder, CO: Westview Press, 2002.

Grasso, June, Jay Corrin, and Michael Kort. *Modernization and Revolution in China: From the Opium Wars to World Power.* 3rd ed. Armonk, NY: M. E. Sharpe, 2004.

Gries, Peter Hays. *China's New Nationalism: Pride, Politics, and Diplomacy.* Berkeley: University of California Press, 2004.

Handel, Michael L. *Sun Tzu and Clausewitz Compared.* Carlisle, PA: Strategic Studies Institute, 1991.

Hinton, Harold C., ed. *The People's Republic of China, 1949–1979: A Documentary Survey.* Wilmington, DE: Scholarly Resources, 1980.

Hsiao, Ch'i-ch'ing. *The Military Establishment of the Yuan Dynasty.* Cambridge, MA: Harvard University Press, 1978.

Hsu, Immanuel C. Y. *The Rise of Modern China.* 6th ed. Oxford: Oxford University Press, 2000.

Isaacs, Harold R. *The Tragedy of the Chinese Revolution.* 2nd ed. Stanford, CA: Stanford University Press, 1961.

Jencks, Harlan W. *From Muskets to Missiles: Politics and Professionalism in the Chinese Army, 1945–1981.* Boulder, CO: Westview Press, 1982.

Ji, Jianjun. "The Unfinished Demographic Transition in China." *American Review of China Studies* 4, no. 1 (2003): 65–83.

Jiang Zemin. *On the "Three Represents."* Beijing: Foreign Languages Press, 2002.

Joffe, Ellis. *The Chinese Army after Mao.* Cambridge, MA: Harvard University Press, 1987.

———. *Party and Army: Professionalism and Political Control in the Chinese Officer Corps, 1948–1964.* Cambridge, MA: Harvard University Press, 1967.

Kaiser, David. *American Tragedy; Kennedy, Johnson, and the Origins of the Vietnam War.* Cambridge, MA: Harvard University Press, 2000.

Karmel, Solomon. *China and the People's Liberation Army.* New York: St. Martin's, 2000.

Kau, Michael Y. M., ed. *The Lin Biao Affair: Power Politics and Military Coup.* White Plains, NY: International Arts and Science Press, 1975.

Kau, Michael Y. M., and John K. Leung, eds. *The Writings of Mao Zedong, 1949–1976.* 3 vols. Armonk, NY: M. E. Sharpe, 1986–92.

Kaufman, Burton. *The Korean War: Challenges in Crisis, Credibility, and Command.* 2nd ed. New York: McGraw-Hill, 1997.

Keith, Ronald C. *The Diplomacy of Zhou Enlai.* New York: St. Martin's, 1989.

Kemenade, Willem Van. *China, Hong Kong, Taiwan, Inc.* New York: Vintage Books, 1997.

Kierman, Frank A., and John K. Fairbank, eds. *Chinese Ways in Warfare.* Cambridge, MA: Harvard University Press, 1974.

Kristof, Nicholas, and Sheryl Wudunn. *China Wakes: The Struggle for the Soul of a Rising Power.* New York: Vintage Books, 1994.

Kuhn, Philip A. *Rebellion and Its Enemies in Late Imperial China: Militarization and the Social Structure, 1796–1864.* Cambridge, MA: Harvard University Press, 1970.

Lary, Diana. *Warlord Soldiers: Chinese Common Soldiers, 1911–1937.* New York: Cambridge University Press, 1985.

Lewis, John Wilson, and Xue Litai. *China Builds the Bomb.* Stanford, CA: Stanford University Press, 1988.

Li, Cheng. *China's Leaders: The New Generation.* Lanham, MD: Rowman & Littlefield, 2001.

Li, He. *From Revolution to Reform: A Comparative Study of China and Mexico.* Lanham, MD: University Press of America, 2004.

Li, Xiaobing. "Chinese Army in the Korean War, 1950–1953." *New England Journal of History* 60, nos. 1–3 (Fall 2003–Spring 2004): 276–92.

———. "Social Changes in China and Implications for the PLA." In *Civil-Military Relations in Today's China: Swimming in a New Sea,* edited by David M. Finkelstein and Kristen Gunness, 26–47. Armonk, NY: M. E. Sharpe, 2006.

Li, Xiaobing, Chen Jian, and David L. Wilson, trans. and eds. "Mao Zedong's Handling of the Taiwan Strait Crisis of 1958: Chinese Recollections and Documents." *Cold War International History Project Bulletin* 6–7 (Winter 1995–96): 208–19.

Li, Xiaobing, and Hongshan Li, eds. *China and the United States: A New Cold War History.* Lanham, MD: University Press of America, 1998.

Li, Xiaobing, Allan Millett, and Bin Yu, trans. and eds. *Mao's Generals Remember Korea.* Lawrence: University Press of Kansas, 2000.

Li, Xiaobing, and Zuohong Pan, eds. *Taiwan in the Twenty-first Century.* Lanham, MD: University Press of America, 2003.

Li, Xiaolin. "Women in the Chinese Military." Ph.D. diss., University of Maryland, 1995.

Li Zhisui. *The Private Life of Chairman Mao: The Memoirs of Mao's Personal Physician.* New York: Random House, 1994.

Lieberthal, Kenneth. *Revolution and Tradition in Tientsin, 1949–1952.* Stanford, CA: Stanford University Press, 1980.

Lilley, James R., with Jeffrey Lilley. *China Hands: Nine Decades of Adventure, Espionage, and Diplomacy in Asia.* New York: Public Affairs, 2004.

Lilley, James R., and David Shambaugh, eds. *China's Military Faces the Future.* New York: M. E. Sharpe, 1999.

Liu Xiaoyuan. *A Partnership for Disorder: China, the United States, and Their Policies for the Postwar Disposition of the Japanese Empire, 1941–1945.* Cambridge: Cambridge University Press, 1996.

Loewe, Michael. *Everyday Life in Early Imperial China.* Indianapolis, IN: Hackett, 1968.

Lorge, Peter, ed. *Warfare in China to 1600.* Burlington, VT: Ashgate, 2005.

Lovejoy, Charles, and Bruce Watson, eds. *China's Military Reforms.* Boulder, CO: Westview Press, 1986.

Luo, Jing, ed. *China Today: An Encyclopedia of Life in the People's Republic.* 2 vols. Westport, CT: Greenwood Press, 2005.

Mann, Jim. *About Face: A History of America's Curious Relationship with China, from Nixon to Clinton.* New York: Knopf, 1999.

Mao Zedong. *Mao Zedong on Diplomacy.* Beijing: Foreign Languages Press, 1998.

———. *Selected Works of Mao Tse-tung.* 4 vols. Beijing: Foreign Languages Press, 1977.

Maxwell, Neville. *India's China War.* New York: Pantheon Books, 1970.

Meisner, Maurice. *Mao's China: A History of the People's Republic.* New York: Free Press, 1977.

Military Service Law of the PRC. Beijing: Law Press China, 2002.

Millett, Allan R. *Their War for Korea: American, Asian, and European Combatants and Civilians, 1945–1953.* Washington, DC: Brassey's, 2002.

———. *The War for Korea, 1945–1950: A House Burning.* Lawrence: University Press of Kansas, 2005.

Moss, George Donelson. *Vietnam, An American Ordeal.* 4th ed. Upper Saddle River, NJ: Prentice Hall, 2002.

Muir, Malcolm, Jr., and Mark F. Wilkinson, eds. *The Most Dangerous Years: The Cold War, 1953–1975.* Lexington: Virginia Military Institute, 2005.

Mulvenon, James C., and Andrew N. D. Yang, eds. *The People's Liberation Army as Organization.* Santa Monica, CA: Rand, 2002.

Murphey, Rhoads. *East Asia: A New History.* 4th ed. New York: Longman, 2007.

Needham, Joseph, and Robin D. S. Yates. *Science and Civilization in China.* Vol. 5, *Military Technology.* Cambridge: Cambridge University Press, 1994.

Neiberg, Michael S. *Warfare in World History.* London: Routledge, 2001.

Nelsen, Harvey W. *The Chinese Military System.* Boulder, CO: Westview Press, 1977.

Pepper, Suzanne. *Civil War in China: The Political Struggle, 1945–1949.* Berkeley: University of California Press, 1978.

Peters, Richard, and Xiaobing Li. *Voices from the Korean War: Personal Stories of American, Korean, and Chinese Soldiers.* Lexington: University Press of Kentucky, 2004.

Potter, Sulamith H., and Jack M. Potter. *China's Peasants: The Anthropology of a Revolution.* Cambridge: Cambridge University Press, 1990.

Powell, John, ed. *Magill's Guide to Military History.* Pasadena, CA: Salem Press, 2001.

PRC State Council Bureau of Information. *White Papers of the Chinese Government, 1996–2004.* 4 vols. Beijing: Foreign Languages Press, 1998–2005.

Ross, Robert S. *Negotiating Cooperation: The United States and China, 1969–1989.* Stanford, CA: Stanford University Press, 1995.

Ross, Robert S., and Jiang Changbin, eds. *Re-examining the Cold War: U.S.-China Diplomacy, 1954–1973.* Cambridge, MA: Harvard University Press, 2001.

Ryan, Mark A., David M. Finkelstein, and Michael A. McDevitt, eds. *Chinese Warfighting: The PLA Experience since 1949.* New York: M. E. Sharpe, 2003.

Saich, Tony, ed. *The Rise to Power of the Chinese Communist Party: Documents and Analysis.* Armonk, NY: M. E. Sharpe, 1996.

Saith, Ashwani, ed. *The Re-emergence of the Chinese Peasantry: Aspects of Rural Decollectivisation.* London: Croom Helm, 1987.

Sandler, Stanley. *The Korean War: No Victors, No Vanquished.* Lexington: University Press of Kentucky, 1999.

Sawyer, Ralph D. *Fire and Water: The Art of Incendiary and Aquatic Warfare in China.* Boulder, CO: Westview Press, 2004.

————. trans. *One Hundred Unorthodox Strategies.* Boulder, CO: Westview Press, 1996.

————, trans. *The Seven Military Classics of Ancient China.* Boulder, CO: Westview Press, 1993.

————. *The Tao of Spycraft: Intelligence Theory and Practice in Traditional China.* Boulder, CO: Westview Press, 2004.

Schell, Orville, and David Shambaugh, eds. *The China Reader: The Reform Era.* New York: Vintage Books, 1999.

Schoppa, R. Keith. *Revolution and Its Past: Identities and Change in Modern Chinese History.* 2nd ed. Upper Saddle River, NJ: Prentice Hall, 2006.

Schwartz, Benjamin I. *The World of Thought in Ancient China.* Cambridge, MA: Harvard University Press, 1985.

Scobell, Andrew. *China's Use of Military Force: Beyond the Great Wall and the Long March.* Cambridge: Cambridge University Press, 2003.

Selected Documents of the Fifteenth CCP National Congress. Beijing: New Star Publishers, 1997.

Shambaugh, David. *Modernizing China's Military: Progress, Problems, and Prospects.* Berkeley: University of California Press, 2002.

————, ed. *Power Shift: China and Asia's New Dynamics.* Berkeley: University of California Press, 2005.

Shambaugh, David, and Richard H. Yang, eds. *China's Military in Transition.* New York: Oxford University Press, 1997.

Shao, Kuo-kang. *Zhou Enlai and the Foundations of Chinese Foreign Policy.* New York: St. Martin's, 1996.

Sheng, Michael M. *Battling Western Imperialism: Mao, Stalin, and the United States.* Princeton, NJ: Princeton University Press, 1997.

Short, Philip. *Mao: A Life.* New York: Henry Holt, 1999.

Shum Kui-kwong. *Zhu De.* St. Lucia: University of Queensland Press, 1982.

Snow, Edgar. *Red Star over China.* New York: Grove Press, 1944.

Spence, Jonathan D. *Mao Zedong.* New York: Viking, 1999.

————. *The Search for Modern China.* 2nd ed. New York: Norton, 1999.

Stueck, William W., Jr., ed. *The Korean War in World History.* Lexington: University Press of Kentucky, 2004.

————. *The Road to Confrontation: American Policy toward China and Korea, 1947–1950.* Chapel Hill: University of North Carolina Press, 1981.

Sun-tzu. *The Art of War.* Translated by John Minford. New York: Viking, 2002.

————. *The Art of Warfare.* Translated by Roger T. Ames. New York: Ballantine Books, 1993.

Swope, Kenneth, ed. *Warfare in China since 1600.* Burlington, VT: Ashgate, 2005.

Teiwes, Frederick C. "Establishment and Consolidation of the New Regime." In *Cambridge History of China,* vol. 14, *The People's Republic.* Cambridge: University of Cambridge Press, 1967.

Tien, Hung-Mao, and Yun-han Chu, eds. *China under Jiang Zemin.* Boulder, CO: Lynne Rienner, 2000.

Tilly, Charles. "Does Modernization Breed Revolution?" *Comparative Politics* 5, no. 3 (1973): 425–47.

Tsai, Ming-Yen. *From Adversaries to Partners: Chinese and Russian Military Cooperation after the Cold War.* Westport, CT: Praeger, 2003.

Tsai, Wen-Hui. "Life after Retirement: Elderly Welfare in China." *Asian Survey* 27 (1987): 552–76.

Tucker, Nancy Bernkopf. *Taiwan, Hong Kong, and the U.S., 1945–1992: Uncertain Friendships.* New York: Twayne Publishers, 1994.

Tucker, Spencer C. *Vietnam.* Lexington: University Press of Kentucky, 1999.

U.S. Department of State. *Foreign Relations of the United States: China, Korea, Vietnam, and Indochina, 1945–1972.* 8 vols. Washington, DC: GPO, 1982–89.

U.S. House of Representatives, Select Committee on U.S. National Security and Military/Commercial Concerns with the People's Republic of China. *U.S. National Security and Military/Commercial Concerns with the People's Republic of China.* Washington, DC: Regnery, 1999.

Van de Ven, Hans. *Warfare in Chinese History.* Leiden, The Netherlands: Brill, 2000.

Waldron, Arthur. *From War to Nationalism: China's Turning Point.* Cambridge: Cambridge University Press, 1995.

————. *The Great Wall of China: From History to Myth.* New York: Cambridge University Press, 1990.

Weintraub, Stanley. *MacArthur's War: Korea and the Undoing of an American Hero.* New York: Free Press, 2000.

Westad, Odd Arne, ed. *Brothers in Arms: The Rise and Fall of the Sino-Soviet Alliance, 1945–1963.* Washington, DC: Woodrow Wilson Center Press, 1998.

————. *Decisive Encounters: The Chinese Civil War, 1946–1950.* Stanford, CA: Stanford University Press, 2003.

————, ed. *Reviewing the Cold War: Approaches, Interpretations, Theory.* London: Frank Cass, 2000.

Whiting, Allen S. *The Chinese Calculus of Deterrence: India and Indochina.* Ann Arbor: University of Michigan Press, 1975.

Whitson, William W. *The Military and Political Power in China in the 1970s.* New York: Praeger, 1972.

Whitson, William W., with Chen-hsia Huang. *The Chinese High Command: A History of Communist Military Politics, 1927–71.* New York: Praeger, 1973.

Wilkinson, Mark F., ed. *The Korean War at Fifty: International Perspectives.* Lexington: Virginia Military Institute, 2004.

Wilson, Jeanne L. *Strategic Partners: Russian-Chinese Relations in the Post-Soviet Era.* Armonk, NY: M. E. Sharpe, 2004.

Wortzel, Larry M. *Dictionary of Contemporary Chinese Military History.* Westport, CT: Greenwood Press, 1999.

Xiang, Lanxin. *Recasting the Imperial Far East: Britain and America in China, 1945–1950.* Armonk, NY: M. E. Sharpe, 1995.

Xinhua News Agency. *China's Foreign Relations: A Chronology of Events, 1949–88.* Beijing: Foreign Languages Press, 1989.

Xu Yan. "Chinese Forces and Their Casualties in the Korean War." Trans. Xiaobing Li. *Chinese Historians* 6, no. 2 (Fall 1993): 45–64.

Yick, Joseph K. S. *Making Urban Revolution in China; The CCP-GMD Struggle for Beiping-Tianjin, 1945–1949.* Armonk, NY: M. E. Sharpe, 1995.

You Ji. *The Armed Forces of China.* New York: I. B. Tauris, 1999.

Young, Marilyn B. *The Vietnam Wars, 1945–1990.* New York: HarperCollins, 1991.

Zarrow, Peter. *China in War and Revolution, 1895–1949.* New York: Routledge, 2005.

Zhai, Qiang. *China and the Vietnam Wars, 1950–1975.* Chapel Hill: University of North Carolina Press, 2000.

———. *The Dragon, the Lion, and the Eagle: Chinese-British-American Relations, 1949–1958.* Kent, OH: Kent State University Press, 1994.

Zhang, Jie, and Xiaobing Li, eds. *Social Transition in China.* Lanham, MD: University Press of America, 1998.

Zhang Liang, ed. *The Tiananmen Papers: The Chinese Leadership's Decision to Use Force against Their Own People—in Their Own Words.* New York: Public Affairs, 2001.

Zhang, Shuguang. *Deterrence and Strategic Culture: Chinese-American Confrontations, 1949–1958.* Ithaca, NY: Cornell University Press, 1992.

———. *Mao's Military Romanticism: China and the Korean War, 1950–1953.* Lawrence: University Press of Kansas, 1995.

Zhang, Shuguang, and Chen Jian, eds. *Chinese Communist Foreign Policy and the Cold War in Asia: New Documentary Evidence, 1944–1950.* Chicago: Imprint Publications, 1996.

Zhang, Xiaoming. *Red Wings over the Yalu: China, the Soviet Union, and the Air War in Korea.* College Station: Texas A&M University Press, 2002.

Zhang Yunqiu. "Economic Globalization and China's Urbanization in the Post-Mao Era." *American Review of China Studies* 6, no. 2 (2005): 83–94.

Zhao, Suisheng, ed. *Across the Taiwan Strait: Mainland China, Taiwan, and the 1995–1996 Crisis.* New York: Routledge, 1999.

Zhou, Kate Xiao. *How the Farmers Changed China: Power of the People.* Boulder, CO: Westview Press, 1996.

Zhu, Fang. *Gun Barrel Politics; Party-Army Relations in Mao's China.* Boulder, CO: Westview Press, 1998.

Zubok, Vladislav, and Constantine Pleshakov. *Inside the Kremlin's Cold War: From Stalin to Khrushchev.* Cambridge, MA: Harvard University Press, 1996.

Index